The Ruler's House

The Ruler's House

Contesting Power and Privacy in Julio-Claudian Rome

HARRIET FERTIK

Johns Hopkins University Press
Baltimore

© 2019 Johns Hopkins University Press
All rights reserved. Published 2019
Printed in the United States of America on acid-free paper
2 4 6 8 9 7 5 3 1

Johns Hopkins University Press
2715 North Charles Street
Baltimore, Maryland 21218-4363
www.press.jhu.edu

Library of Congress Cataloging-in-Publication Data

Names: Fertik, Harriet, 1987– author.
Title: The ruler's house : contesting power and privacy in Julio-Claudian Rome / Harriet Fertik.
Description: Baltimore : Johns Hopkins University Press, [2019] | Includes bibliographical references and index. | Text in English, with some text in Latin.
Identifiers: LCCN 2019004931 | ISBN 9781421432892 (hardcover : alk. paper) | ISBN 9781421432908 (electronic) | ISBN 1421432897 (hardcover : alk. paper) | ISBN 1421432900 (electronic)
Subjects: LCSH: Rome—History—Julio-Claudians, 30 B.C.–68 A.D. | Rome—Politics and government—30 B.C.–284 A.D. | Emperors—Dwellings—Rome. | Privacy—Rome—History—To 1500. | Emperors—Rome—Social life and customs. | Politics and culture—Rome—History—To 1500.
Classification: LCC DG278.3 .F47 2019 | DDC 937/.07—dc23
LC record available at https://lccn.loc.gov/2019004931

A catalog record for this book is available from the British Library.

Special discounts are available for bulk purchases of this book. For more information, please contact Special Sales at 410-516-6936 or specialsales@press.jhu.edu.

Johns Hopkins University Press uses environmentally friendly book materials, including recycled text paper that is composed of at least 30 percent post-consumer waste, whenever possible.

For Isaac

CONTENTS

Acknowledgments ix

Introduction *1*

1 Playing House: *New Families and New Rulers in Lucan's* Bellum Civile *21*

2 Contest and Control in the Emperor's House *39*

3 Where to See the Emperor: *Augustus and Nero in Rome* *60*

4 Exposing the Ruler: *Seneca on Visibility and Complicity* *79*

5 Interdependence and Intimacy: *Power at Home in Roman Pompeii* *104*

6 Bathing, Dining, and Digesting with the Ruler *129*

Conclusion *153*

Notes *169*
Bibliography *207*
Index Locorum *231*
General Index *234*

ACKNOWLEDGMENTS

I owe thanks first and foremost to my teachers. This book began as a dissertation at the University of Michigan, where I was fortunate to have the guidance of David Potter, Celia Schultz, Basil Dufallo, Elaine Gazda, and Mira Seo. When I was an undergraduate at the University of Chicago, Shadi Bartsch, Emanuel Mayer, Antonia Syson, and Peter White introduced me to some of the material and questions that I consider in these pages.

I hope someday to repay my peerless colleagues in the Department of Classics, Humanities, and Italian Studies and elsewhere at the University of New Hampshire. I could not have finished this book without Scott Smith, who read much of it at least twice and offered careful comments on every part. For mentorship and support, I am especially grateful to Amy Boylan, Stephen Brunet, Susan Curry, and Stephen Trzaskoma. Nora Draper (who probably never expected to see her name in a book about ancient Rome) shared her ideas about privacy and gave me many useful references. Rachel Trubowitz helped me to develop the book proposal. Ivo van der Graaff told me how to get permission to visit sites in Pompeii.

Kristina Milnor read my dissertation and gave me comments and suggestions for what to do next. Clara Bosak-Schroeder read the manuscript at a crucial stage and helped me work through the thorny process of revision. I am grateful to them and to the many people who read parts of the manuscript and shared their thoughts and expertise: Alex Dressler, Elaine Gazda, Christopher Gregg (on astonishingly short notice, and in the nick of time), Daniel Kapust, Joanna Kenty, Michael Leese, Michèle Lowrie, Paul Robertson, Alessandro Schiesaro, Mira Seo, Christopher Star, and Sarah Levin-Richardson, who also gave me invaluable guidance on finding images and securing permissions. I received fruitful questions and comments from audiences and discussants at the University of Wisconsin–Madison, the

University of Illinois at Urbana-Champaign, the Humboldt-Universität zu Berlin, and the Feminism and Classics conference at the University of Washington. The anonymous reviewers for Johns Hopkins University Press made this a better book. I am solely responsible for the ways in which it could be made better still.

The Writing Academy at the University of New Hampshire provided support and encouragement in the early stages of this project. The UNH Graduate School, the UNH Center for the Humanities, and the Alexander von Humboldt Foundation gave me funding and other resources (especially time) that made it possible to complete this book.

I thank the staff at Johns Hopkins University Press: Matt McAdam, who first took an interest in this project, Catherine Goldstead, who guided me through its conclusion, and Juliana McCarthy and Hilary Jacqmin. I was lucky to work with Richard Smoley, who as copyeditor made many improvements to the final manuscript, and with Thomas Broughton-Willett, who made the index.

An earlier version of chapter 1 was published as "Obligation and Devotion: Creating a New Community in Lucan's *Bellum Civile*" in *Classical Philology* 113.4 (2018), 449–71, © 2018 by The University of Chicago, and an earlier version of sections of chapters 3 and 4 appeared as "Privacy and Power: The *De Clementia* and the Domus Aurea" in *Public and Private in the Roman House and Society*, edited by Kaius Tuori and Laura Nissin, *Journal of Roman Archaeology Supplementary Series* 102 (2015), 17–29, © 2015 Journal of Roman Archaeology, LLC. I thank these journals for their courtesies in connection with printing this material here.

For constancy and wise counsel of many kinds, I am grateful to Claire Barner, Clara Bosak-Schroeder (again), Kira Bennett Hamilton, Ellen Cole Lee, Sarah Nerboso, and Joanna Price. My parents dedicated hours to this project in their own ways: my father, Philip Fertik, helped me put my prose in order, and my mother, Elizabeth Fertik, helped me put things in perspective. My partner Isaac Epstein helped to draw the maps, but that is the very least of what he did and does to make my work and my life possible. Whether he reads it or not, this book is for him.

The Ruler's House

Introduction

The house is a space to live in. It is also a space that makes us think. In this book, I examine how Romans thought about the house and what houses made them think about. I use the house to understand Roman ideas of privacy because it was an environment in which Romans contested the scope of communal concerns and regulated their encounters with the public eye. A strict opposition between privacy at home, the intimate space for the conjugal family, and the public square, in which members of the community encounter one another, was foreign to Roman culture.[1] While the Roman house, or *domus*, was in part the world of women and slaves, who were excluded from formal participation in the institutions of the polity, for elite men the house was also a stage for self-display and self-promotion, for receiving dependents, courting supporters, and performing their dominance in the world beyond their doors.[2] Yet the house was also a space in which these same elites confronted the fragility and contingency of the claim to exert power over others, both in their own case and in the case of those who sought to dominate them.

From the perspective of elite Roman men, privacy meant (1) to avoid public scrutiny and (2) to act without consequence for the political community, but the advantages, risks, and viability of privacy varied for different people at different periods. This book focuses on Roman contestations over privacy and power in the age of the Julio-Claudians, Rome's first imperial dynasty. This period provoked ancient thinkers (both those who lived under the Julio-Claudian emperors and those who looked back at them later) to reflect on the place of the house in the community and on the relationship of private and public life. The emperor's invasions into other people's private spaces, together with his efforts to conceal himself from hostile viewers, produced new concerns for political life in Julio-Claudian Rome.[3] Faced with these circumstances, Roman aristocrats, who had once been dedicated to self-display and self-promotion, began to appreciate the benefits of seclusion, including the potential to escape the emperor's attention and the dangers of his court.[4] Yet if the emperor threatened the privacy of his fellow-elites, at the same time he was the ultimate public figure in Rome: by the late first century CE, everyone except the emperor could be deemed a *privatus*, a private individual.[5]

The rise of one-man rule posed challenges for Roman conceptions of private and public, and the house offered a space for negotiating those challenges and their consequences. I argue that the ruler's privacy, whether he could maintain a space apart from the life of the community or avoid the public eye, was a central problem in Roman thinking about one-man rule. The ruler's house, far from being the space where he exercised the most control and where he could regulate his exposure to public view, was instead where he was most vulnerable, and where the security of his position, the relationship between ruler and ruled, and the coherence of the community itself were most called into question.

Private and Public

> The full development of the life of hearth and family into an inner and private space we owe to the extraordinary political sense of the Roman people who, unlike the Greeks, never sacrificed the private to the public, but on the contrary understood that these two realms could exist only in the form of coexistence.[6]
>
> —Hannah Arendt, *The Human Condition*

Privacy is a tricky concept to apply to ancient Rome, in part because the spheres of public and private were always fluid and contested in antiquity.[7] As Amy Russell has emphasized, the Latin word *publicus* is derived from *populus*, which in the Roman context referred primarily to the male citizen body.⁸ In the language of Roman law, *res publicae*, the property of the Roman people, are contrasted not only with *res privatae*, the property of individual persons, but with *res communes omnium*, those things that "by natural law are the common property of all," such as air and the ocean (*D*.1.8.2. pr.1).⁹ *Publicus* and *privatus* thus mark out things in which the Roman political community does or does not have a special stake.¹⁰ Cult rites were public if they were performed on behalf of the people rather than particular families or individuals.¹¹ The *iudicia publica*, or public courts, dealt with criminal disputes, but for most of their history they handled only political crimes, such as a magistrate's abuse of the powers of his office, rather than crimes against individuals, like murder or theft.¹² The quintessential public space in the city of Rome, the Forum Romanum, was distinguished during the Republic by its close associations with political activity (e.g., hearing speeches and legislation); later, Augustus endeavored to limit access to the Forum Romanum to adult male citizens (or at least to those who could procure a toga, the citizen's costume).¹³ Public life in the Roman world, then, was ideally centered on, and restricted to, a specific group.

For those Romans who enjoyed the exclusive privilege of participating in the life of the political community, privacy could be unwelcome. The political theorist and philosopher Hannah Arendt, a creative reader of ancient political thought, observed that "in ancient feeling the privative trait of privacy . . . was all-important; it meant literally a state of being deprived of something, and even of the highest and most human of man's capacities."¹⁴ This "highest and most human" capacity was the opportunity to distinguish oneself from one's peers by taking part in public life.¹⁵ Arendt's definition of *public* evokes the contrast in Roman law between *res publicae* and *res communes omnium*: *public* does not refer to the natural environment but rather to "the fabrication of human hands . . . [and] affairs which go on among those who inhabit the man-made world together."¹⁶ When Arendt argues that "an entirely private life" is "deprived of things essential to a truly human life," she foregrounds the evaluation of public and private that she associates with Greek and Roman antiquity.¹⁷ The problem with privacy, as Arendt has it, is "the absence of others; as far as they are concerned, private man does not appear, and therefore it is as though he did not exist. Whatever he does remains without significance and consequence to others."¹⁸ Arendt thus emphasizes the association between being significant to others and being visible to others, and this pairing (as we will see below) appears repeatedly in Roman thought on privacy.

Arendt has been criticized, especially by feminist theorists, for making too strict a demarcation between the city-state and the house, a boundary that is grounded in and reproduces "the misogynistic practices of the Athenian democratic polis."[19] In Arendt's reading of antiquity, especially Greek antiquity, the house was a "pre-political" space: she asserts that "the *polis* was distinguished from the household in that it knew only 'equals,' whereas the household was the center of the strictest inequality."[20] Yet Arendt also recognizes that the household in the ancient world was foundational for public life. She suggests that "privacy was like the other, the dark and hidden side of the public realm . . . to have no private place of one's own (like a slave) meant to be no longer human."[21] Private property mattered because only a property owner, who was "master over one's own necessities of life," could be "free to transcend his own life and enter the world all have in common."[22] Even as Arendt valorizes the public realm over the private, she allows that "those excluded from the world could find a substitute in the warmth of the hearth and the limited reality of family life," and she attributes "the full development of the life of hearth and family into an inner and private space" to the Romans rather than to the Greeks.[23] Arendt's treatment of the public and private is useful because she lays out important tensions in ancient thinking about the house. The house is a space distinct from the political community but also essential to participating in it: a retreat that is both limiting (especially for elites) and potentially desirable (especially for subalterns); a space of self-protection as well as obscurity.

I turn now to four snapshots of Roman thought about the house, four texts from the end of the first century BCE to the beginning of the second century CE.[24] These passages are not meant to serve as a complete overview of the complex social and political developments of this period, but together they illuminate key questions in the contestations over privacy and power that I will follow in the rest of this book. What is specific to the space of the house? What is the relationship between the house and the political community? Whose houses are politically meaningful, and whose are not? Who has the power to look inside?

1. Dionysius of Halicarnassus, a Greek historian and rhetorician, lived in Rome in the late first century BCE, the period of Augustus' ascent and (although his contemporaries may not have known it) the last days of the Republic. One fragment of his *Roman Antiquities*, a history of Rome from its origins to the wars with Carthage, treats obsession with domestic life as

a distinctive feature of Roman culture.²⁵ As Dionysius reports, the Athenians disdained laziness among their citizens, and the Spartans punished those who were disorderly in public places, but

> they took no precautions and set no guard over the affairs of the household, since they considered the gate of the courtyard to be the boundary-marker of freedom in life. But the Romans, after opening up the house and extending the office of the censors as far as the bedroom, established an overseer and guard over what took place there, since they believed the master should not be cruel in the punishment of slaves, nor the father harsh or mild beyond the norm in the rearing of his children, nor the husband unjust in association with his wife, nor children heedless of their old fathers, nor legitimate brothers litigious for the greater share instead of an equal portion, nor should symposia and drunkenness last all night, nor should there be recklessness and ruin of youths, nor abandoning the ancestral rites of sacrifices and burials, nor anything done contrary to what was fitting and advantageous to the state. (Dion. Hal. *Ant. Rom.* 20.13.2–3)²⁶

In Dionysius' account, the Greeks respect a boundary between the space of the house and the space of the city, while the Romans regard the house as a kind of public space, in that domestic life is closely intertwined with the welfare of the community as a whole.²⁷ Yet Dionysius points toward a Roman conception of privacy in two ways. First, Romans associate certain persons, relationships, and activities specifically with the household: the interactions between master and slave, father and child, husband and wife, and brother and brother, and the practices of feasting and drinking, ancestor cult, and funeral rites take place within the space of the house. Second, the Romans set limits on the visibility and accessibility of the house. The Roman house is not a free-for-all, a space that is continuously open to all audiences: rather, houses are opened up to specific observers (the censors) who are appointed to mind the interests of the polity. For the Romans in this fragment, all houses are worthy of scrutiny, and all can contribute to or impede the wellbeing of the community.

2. Livy, a Roman historian and contemporary of Dionysius, offers an interesting inversion of this account. He reports that one of Rome's first consuls, Publius Valerius Publicola, built a house at the top of the Velian hill and was subsequently accused of plotting to become king: this location, because it was invulnerable to attack, would allow Publicola to defend and preserve his dominance in the *res publica* (Livy 2.7.6). Faced with public

criticism, Publicola changes his plans: he announces that "the house of Publius Valerius will not stand in the way of your liberty, Quirites; . . . I shall not only move my house to level ground but I will place it beneath the hill, so that you may dwell above me and keep me, your fellow-citizen, in your sights" (*non obstabunt Publi Valeri aedes libertati uestrae, Quirites; . . . deferam non in planum modo aedes sed colli etiam subiciam, ut uos supra suspectum me ciuem habitetis*, 2.7.11). For Publicola, the relationship between the people and their leaders is an agonistic one, and the leader's house is a key space in which their contests play out. Unlike Dionysius' Romans, who are interested in what goes on in everyone's house, Publicola claims that the leader's house is especially significant. Furthermore, rather than opening his doors to political officials (like censors), he invites all of Rome to keep watch over his house. While this story is doubtless invented or embellished, Publicola's offer demonstrates that the house is a space where a Roman leader can perform his authority and his humility before an audience of his fellow-citizens.

3. Velleius Paterculus, in his *Roman History*, composed during the reign of Tiberius, likewise emphasizes the particular importance of the houses of the powerful for the political community. He tells a story about Marcus Livius Drusus, a tribune of the first century BCE, and the house he built in the city of Rome:

> When [Drusus] was building a house on the Palatine in that place, where the house that was once Cicero's and then Censorinus' and now Statilius Sisenna's stands, and his architect proposed that he build it in such a way that [Drusus] would be free from scrutiny and safe from onlookers and that no one would be able to look down into it, [Drusus] said, "Truly, if you have any talent, build my house so that whatever I do, everyone can see it." (Vell. Pat. 2.14.3)[28]

By the time that Velleius wrote, the Palatine hill was the site of the house of Augustus, and Velleius' depiction of Drusus is probably meant to evoke Augustus' efforts to present himself as a model of upright living (discussed further in chapters 2 and 3). Drusus' demand to be seen is key to his performance of his own social importance: he claims that he has nothing to hide from onlookers, and that his fellow Romans will benefit from witnessing his unerring moral rectitude.[29] Roman politicians during the Republic had long used their houses for self-promotion and self-display, but the desire to see and to be seen was only a part of the story for the ancient elite: to be exposed to view was also to be vulnerable to criticism, danger, and disgrace.[30]

One answer to this conundrum was controlled performance, or careful regulation of where, when, and how one was viewed by others. When he presented himself to visitors inside his house, the Roman aristocrat had greater control over his environment than he did in the forum, the theater, or city baths.[31]

Drusus' architect is sensitive to the potential for conflict between the tribune and his audience: he offers Drusus maximum control over access to his house, and this kind of control is fundamental to the experience of privacy.[32] The philosopher and privacy theorist Beate Rössler makes a useful distinction between privacy and inaccessibility: she notes that "a crevasse into which I have fallen is clearly not 'private'" even if it is inaccessible, and argues that "something counts as private if one can oneself control the access to this 'something.'"[33] Drusus claims that the people of Rome should have unlimited access to his house: he wants to demonstrate that he remains oriented toward the life of the community even when he is at home, and to assert that the affairs of his household are always a matter of public interest. The logic of Drusus' instructions to the architect, however, depends on his capacity to withdraw from public life. Drusus' house is not seamlessly integrated into the community, but a space that he chooses to make part of the community. He has the ability to reserve his house for himself, to control access to this space, even if he ostentatiously invites public view.

4. Pliny the Younger picks up on themes from all of these episodes in the *Panegyricus*, a laudatory speech for the emperor Trajan that he delivered in the Senate in 100 CE.[34] Pliny aims to emphasize the contrast between Trajan and his predecessor Domitian, a ruler who was deeply unpopular with the Roman aristocracy and who had been assassinated in 96. One key axis of comparison between the two emperors, at least in Pliny's speech, is their different attitudes toward what happens in the houses of those they rule. He observes,

> We like to complain that only the rulers we hate pry into our hiding places. For if good ones took the same care as bad ones do, you would find admiration, joy, and exultation everywhere in everyone's conversations with their wives and children, at our altars and hearths at home! . . . And moreover, while hate and love are opposites, they nevertheless are similar in this way, that we love good rulers with even more abandon in the same place where we freely hate bad ones. (Plin. *Pan.* 68.6–7)[35]

Pliny's rhetorical objectives in this speech are complex: panegyric serves not only to flatter the recipient of praise but also to establish the parameters of good and bad behavior and to set expectations for the ruler in the future. In chapter 4, I will return to the problems that praising the ruler presents for Julio-Claudian political thought. My concern here is what Pliny thinks happens in the house, and how the house informs his notion of who an emperor ought to be. He associates the house with retreat from public view, with wives and children, and with sharing strong emotions (joy and love as well as hate). For Pliny, good emperors are less anxious than the Romans of old whom Dionysius described, who set the censors to keep watch over household life: Trajan is a good ruler in part because he does not intrude into other people's houses. Nevertheless, he assumes that any emperor, good or bad, is able to peer into the houses of his subjects, although the good ones refrain from doing so. And just as Publicola and Drusus chose to present themselves to public view, here Pliny welcomes the emperor into the houses of the Roman elite, where he can observe and receive their love.

As Pliny describes it, however, the emperor is not only the observer but also the observed. Later in his speech, he declares, "above all else, high rank means that nothing is allowed to be hidden, nothing can remain secret; for emperors not only their houses but their very bedrooms and most intimate hiding places are opened up, and all their secrets are exposed and revealed to rumor" (*habet hoc primum magna fortuna, quod nihil tectum, nihil occultum esse patitur; principum uero non domus modo sed cubicula ipsa intimosque secessus recludit, omniaque arcana noscenda famae proponit atque explicat,* 83.1).[36] In Dionysius' Rome, the censors stood at the doorways of citizens' bedrooms, but in Pliny's, the public eye follows the emperor into bed. Pliny surely knows that emperors could actually hide in their houses, that they were able to avoid public scrutiny of their doings. His declaration serves in part as a warning: whatever the emperor thinks he is hiding now, he should remember that it might be revealed in the future, and that rumors will spread regardless of what he chooses to share. Yet Pliny's emphasis on the exposure of the emperor's house, his insistence that the emperor is always visible, is also a way of expressing the emperor's lack of privacy in another sense. When Pliny claims that everyone can see the emperor's "most intimate hiding places," what he means is that everyone wants to know what happens there: the emperor and the emperor's house are uniquely central to the life of the community as a whole. If Dionysius weighted the public significance of all Roman houses equally, and Livy and Velleius knew that some were more important than others, for Pliny it is ultimately only the ruler's house that counts.

My aim in this book is not to present a historical narrative that would take us from the world of Dionysius to Pliny, but to investigate different Roman responses to the ruler's private life, and most importantly to explain why his privacy (or the absence of it) mattered. We might imagine that the emperor's supreme position allowed him to claim all the benefits of publicity and all the protections of privacy—that he was able to present himself to public view and to participate in public life only in the ways and at the times that he found most advantageous, or most desirable.[37] This characterization was probably roughly true in terms of actual social practice and experience, although the emperor also had to confront the expectations of his peers and the precedents set before him, and to weigh the risks of rejecting or violating them. Nevertheless, the emperor's power to intrude into other people's houses and to conceal himself from the public eye was not the only consideration for Roman thinkers as they responded to one-man rule. As I will show in the chapters that follow, the ruler's lack of privacy—his exposure to scrutiny and the entanglement of his house with the polity—provoked anxieties about the fragility of the new regime and the vulnerability of the community as a whole.

The Rise of One-Man Rule

Augustus, the founder of Rome's first imperial house, was a key figure in the transition to one-man rule, but he was also only one in a series of leaders who seized extraordinary powers in the late Republic.[38] Gaius Asinius Pollio, a historian in the early first century CE, began his narrative of contemporary Roman history with the "first triumvirate," an agreement in the mid–first century BCE between Pompey, Caesar, and Crassus—prominent military commanders and political officials—to support one another's pursuit of high office and long-term commands in the provinces.[39] The conflicting ambitions between these men eventually led to civil war between Caesar and Pompey in the 40s BCE. Caesar, the victor, was named dictator. The dictatorship was an established Republican magistracy, but it was an emergency position, limited to one year: Caesar was appointed dictator four times, and the last dictatorship, granted in early 44 BCE, was intended to be perpetual.[40] When a group of senators assassinated Caesar in 44, his great-nephew and adopted son, Octavian, rose to prominence. He defeated the last of his serious rivals at the battle of Actium in 31. In 27, along with a collection of other privileges, the Senate gave him the name Augustus ("revered").

Augustus' novel position combined and expanded a number of traditional Republican offices and powers.[41] The scope of Augustus' *imperium*, his power to command Roman citizens and to impose punishments on them, was unprecedented. While magistrates in the Republic were granted *imperium*, their actions were subject to veto by their colleagues. The sphere in which a magistrate could exercise *imperium*, moreover, was geographically limited: the *imperium* of the *proconsul* applied in his province, but not when he returned to the city of Rome. Augustus' *imperium* was unique. He enjoyed *imperium* as a proconsul in the provinces allotted to him by the Senate in 27 BCE, but he did not lose that *imperium* when in the city of Rome, although he could also not legally exercise it when in the capital. The legal basis of his authority in Rome was the *tribunicia potestas*, or the power of the tribune, an office that in the Republic could only be held by plebeians (Augustus received this power despite his patrician status). In 19 BCE, his *imperium* was expanded so that he could exercise it both in the provinces and in Rome.[42] Augustus sought to present himself as *princeps*, the "first" or "foremost," rather than as a new *rex*, or king, but he also sought unparalleled authority in Roman political life.[43]

Although many tensions in first-century politics can be traced back to the Republic, Augustus and his successors produced new pressures.[44] The emperor's influence transcended not only that of his fellow aristocrats but also that which the Republican ruling class had once enjoyed.[45] At this early period of the principate, from the rise of Augustus in the late first century BCE to the fall of Nero in 68 CE, expectations for how the emperor and his house should be understood and represented were in flux and subject to continuous experimentation.[46] The emperors themselves took part in crafting their own images, but they did not act alone. Multiple players, from the Senate in Rome to local elites in cities throughout the empire, produced portraits of the emperor and his family, and these representations express different attitudes toward who the emperor was and ought to be.[47] Ancient historians and biographers, who wrote their narratives of the Julio-Claudians decades after the dynasty met its grisly end, associate different emperors with different approaches to one-man rule, and with different kinds of ruling houses.

Augustus and Nero, discussed further in chapters 2 and 3, demonstrate the fluidity of imperial self-presentation and representation in this period.[48] I focus on these two emperors because they were the founder and final head (respectively) of the Julio-Claudian house and because they provide a valuable conceptual contrast. Augustus sought to present himself as *primus inter pares*, first among equals, and as the embodiment of traditional Roman virtues, especially those associated with the head of the household, the *paterfamilias*.[49] Augustus was only one participant in the construction of his image (as Nandini Pandey has recently emphasized), but while others offered their own representations of the first *princeps*, domestic austerity and paternal authority are recurrent concerns in the ancient debate over who Augustus was and over the standard he set for his successors.[50] Nero, who presented himself as an artist and a god, came to represent a very different model of the ruler: his legacy in ancient literature was ultimately defined by domestic extravagance and weakness, his dedication to luxury, and his failure to control the women of his household.

Comparisons of Augustus and Nero, furthermore, are a frequent motif in ancient texts.[51] Seneca, Nero's tutor and advisor, wrote a treatise on clemency to inaugurate Nero's reign, which begins with extravagant praise of the youthful emperor: he tells Nero, "Now no one talks about the divine Augustus or the early days of Tiberius Caesar, nor looks for a model outside yourself for you to imitate" (*nemo iam diuum Augustum nec Ti. Caesaris prima tempora loquitur nec quod te imitari uelit exemplar extra te quaerit, Clem.* 1.1.6). The biographer Suetonius, writing in the early second century CE, reports that Nero promised that he would "rule according to Augustus' guidelines" when he first came to power (*ex Augusti praescripto imperaturum*, Suet. *Ner.* 10.1), but his audience would recognize how false that promise turned out to be. The object of my study, however, is not ancient assessments of Augustus and Nero as "good" or "bad" emperors, but the different questions about one-man rule that these emperors and their houses prompted in ancient thinking. If the emperor failed to demonstrate his authority and austerity at home, what challenges did this pose to Roman ideas of who could or should participate in politics?

Political Thought and Julio-Claudian Rome

During his narrative of the reign of Tiberius, Tacitus explains his choice of subject in the *Annals*, his history of Rome that extends from the death of Augustus to the fall of Nero:

> I know that most of the things that I have reported and will report may seem small and trivial to recall: but no one can compare these chronicles with the writing of those who set down the ancient doings of the Roman people. They recorded, with frank digression, great wars, the sacking of cities, kings expelled and captured, . . . the quarrels of consuls against tribunes, agrarian and corn laws, the contests of the aristocracy and the plebs. Our work is narrow and less glorious . . . But now that the Roman polity is nothing other than the rule of one man, it may be advantageous to collect and report these matters, since . . . more people learn from the experiences of others. (*Ann.* 4.32–3)[52]

Tacitus wrote approximately half a century after Nero's death, but he suggests that the early principate offers his readers insight not simply into a particular historical period but into the political order of the world they live in. Roman thinkers who lived under the Julio-Claudians, as well as those who wrote about them afterward, attended to the basic political questions that dynastic monarchy brought to the forefront.[53] Some of the most important of these concerns involved the ruler's privacy: the interactions between the ruler's house and the life of the community as a whole, and the consequences of the ruler's encounters with the public eye.

The public significance of the emperor's private life was a central concern in the Julio-Claudian period. This book builds on Kristina Milnor's invaluable study of femininity and domesticity in Augustan culture. Milnor argues that the tension between the public prominence of women and the obsession with female virtue as it is displayed in the home was a key development of the Augustan age. Domestic life, the feminine sphere, became central to Augustan politics; at the same time, Augustan discourse asserted a strict boundary between house and state.[54] While Milnor shows how Roman ideas of gender unsettle the notions of "public" and "private," I investigate how Roman conceptions of one-man rule challenge this dichotomy. The women of the emperor's house were formally excluded from politics, but as I discuss in chapter 2, in Roman historiography imperial women become the most valuable interpreters of the new regime, uniquely able to recognize and demonstrate the fragility and contingency of the emperor's rule.

For ancient thinkers, the entrenchment of one-man rule in Rome was a provocation to reflect on and challenge longstanding ideas of power. Regardless of the institutional limits on the emperor's authority in the first century CE, Roman texts conjure and confront the specter of an absolute ruler.⁵⁵ In Seneca's treatise *On Clemency*, Nero appears as a character in the text, describing his position to himself: "What Fortune wants to grant each human being, she proclaims through my lips; peoples and cities find cause to rejoice at my pronouncement; . . . the thousand swords that my peace restrains are brandished when I give the nod" (*quid cuique mortalium Fortuna datum uelit, meo ore pronuntiat; ex nostro responso laetitiae causas populi urbesque concipiunt . . . haec tot milia gladiorum, quae pax mea comprimit, ad nutum meum stringentur*, Clem. 1.1.2). Seneca's account of the emperor's supreme power to command, and the acquiescence of those he rules, is a kind of domination, as Max Weber defined it: "the situation in which the manifested will (command) of the ruler or rulers is meant to influence the conduct of one or more others (the ruled) and actually does influence it in such a way that their conduct . . . occurs as if the ruled had made the content of the command the maxim of their conduct for its very own sake."⁵⁶ The ruler's command guides the actions of the ruled; the ruled, furthermore, must to some degree accept the ruler's command as a valid basis for action in itself, regardless of the fact that it emanates from the ruler.

Specific instances of command and obedience, however, are not the sole effect of power relationships: the dominance of the ruler also manifests itself in how all members of a community understand the choices available to them, and especially the limits and restrictions on those choices.⁵⁷ In one of his philosophical letters, when he describes the earliest governments of humankind, Seneca asserts that "the first mortals . . . considered the same man to be both leader and law, and they relied on the judgment of someone better. For it is natural for the lesser to submit to the more powerful" (*primi mortalium . . . eundem habebant et ducem et legem, commissi melioris arbitrio; natura est enim potioribus deteriora summittere*, 90.4).⁵⁸ This instinct to obey, in Seneca's view, was advantageous when rulers were virtuous, and "good obedience was given to the good ruler" (*cum bene imperanti bene pareretur*, 90.5) but it persisted even "after vices crept in and rule changed into tyranny" (*postquam subrepentibus uitiis in tyrannidem regna conuersa sunt*, 90.6). Human beings did not refuse to obey the authority of the new tyrants: only wise lawgivers limited their power.⁵⁹ Seneca evidently recognizes the significance of what Arendt calls the "instinct of submission." She observes, "if we should trust our own experiences in these matters, we should know that the instinct of submission, an ardent desire to obey and be ruled by some strong man, is at least as prominent in human psychology as the will to power, and, politically, perhaps more relevant."[60] One key problem for Roman political thought in the Julio-Claudian age is how the ruled acknowledges and thus confirms his own subordination. Yet the ruler's need for recognition, I will argue, also reveals that the positions of ruler and ruled are unstable, continuously subject to negotiation and vulnerable to challenge.[61]

The Julio-Claudian age provoked questions about how one man could dominate the rest, and it raised similar concerns about the extent to which the ruler's subjects could claim power over one another. The political community of imperial Rome was in one sense more inclusive than the citizen body of the Roman Republic: those who were formally excluded from political institutions (such as women) were necessarily included in the community, whether they liked it or not, insofar as they too were subject to the emperor and part of his audience.[62] In many of the texts I examine in this book, the ascendance of a sole ruler flattens or undermines the distinctions between those he rules, as elite men contend with the women of the imperial household (chapter 2) or imagine what they have in common with women and slaves (chapters 4 and 6). One of the problems that I will trace in Julio-Claudian political thought is the reluctant expression of solidarity from the traditional aristocracy (that is, the writers of Latin literature and philosophy) with subordinate groups in their society.[63] Of course, in actual practice, the Roman world was highly stratified, and these hierarchies were maintained through violent force. Yet the imperial regime inspired some of the Roman elite to ask how different they really were from everyone else, and thus to reflect on the tenuousness of their claims to dominance.

Classicist and political theorist Joy Connolly has advocated considering a range of literary genres to study Roman political thought.[64] My sources for one-man rule in the Julio-Claudian imagination include the mythological kings in Senecan tragedy (chapter 4), the military leaders in Lucan's epic *Bellum civile* (chapter 1), and the fabulously wealthy freedman Trimalchio in Petronius' novel *Satyricon* (chapter 6). These texts all make the house a space in which to interrogate the position of the ruler, and all were likely composed under the later Julio-Claudians, a moment when it was possible to draw contrasts both with the Republic and with the novelty of the principate under Augustus and his first successor Tiberius.[65] Many accounts of Julio-Claudian political culture focus on aristocratic anxieties in the face of one-man rule, when the emperor increasingly monopolized outlets for glory, and when imperial favor offered new paths to social advancement for those close to the emperor and the imperial house. The rise of one-man rule, in these analyses, provoked an inward turn among the Roman elite, who had lost access to political power and needed to assess the risks and benefits of public exposure and self-display. Matthew Roller has shown that Seneca devised a value system for his elite readers that was compatible with their new political reality: by practicing self-control and self-judgment, educated aristocrats could affirm their superiority both to social upstarts and to tyrants.[66] Shadi Bartsch locates the emergence of the concept of selfhood in early imperial philosophy.[67] Christopher Star traces the obsession with self-construction, self-command, and self-presentation across literary genres in Julio-Claudian Rome, from Seneca's philosophical treatises and tragedies to Petronius' novel.[68] In these studies, aristocratic vulnerability to the emperor and the intellectual strategies that Roman thinkers developed in self-defense are the key concerns of Julio-Claudian political culture.

While this work has focused on the responses of the Roman elite to the imperial gaze, in this book I examine the ruler's exposure to the gaze of his subjects, and the consequences of his exposure for Roman conceptions of the community. As Roman thinkers become attentive to the care of the self, they are, at the same time, anxious about the fragility of the political community under the emperor and their own responsibility towards it. In chapter 4, I show how Seneca makes the subordinate's gaze essential to establishing the ruler's dominance. Because the ruler depends on the recognition of those who are subordinate to him, the subordinate plays a key role in constructing and securing the order of the community. As we will see, the ruler reveals his reliance on those he is supposed to dominate even when he compels his subjects to acknowledge his power. The ruler's need to be seen by his subjects, to be visible to them, undermines his ability to avoid the public eye and compels them to reckon with their complicity in acknowledging and affirming his power.

Roman literature has received greater interest from political theorists in recent years, but few of these studies have included archaeological evidence as sources for Roman political thought.[69] This book puts literary texts, which were produced by and for a tiny minority of the inhabitants of the Empire, in conversation with a material world that was available to a much wider audience. In chapters 2 and 3, I treat ancient historiography, monuments to the imperial family, and houses where emperors lived as participants in a debate about what it meant to be emperor. Building on studies of the representation and self-representation of the Julio-Claudians, I focus on the ideas of one-man rule expressed by imperial images and architecture.[70] In chapter 5, I examine contestations over privacy and power in the houses of Pompeii, a modest town on the Bay of Naples that came under Roman rule in the early first century BCE and was buried by the eruption of Vesuvius in 79 CE. Art and architecture on the Bay of Naples allows us to imagine how a broader range of inhabitants of the Roman world understood the house as a space to establish and to challenge relations of power. Fergus Millar once described the age of Augustus as "a revolution of consciousness . . . that there was an individual ruler, whose name and image appeared everywhere . . . and to whom appeal could be made."[71] Although aristocrats at the emperor's court and householders in Pompeii had vastly different experiences of this "revolution of consciousness," and although they may never have had the opportunity to learn about one another's perspectives, I locate points of contact between political thought in Latin literature and everyday practices in the Roman world, and thus reconstruct a broader discourse on power and community in the early Empire. This discourse, I argue, emphasizes the interdependence and intimacy between the ruler and the ruled. These considerations were surely not exclusively Roman, but I will suggest that Roman political thinkers were especially sensitive to them, and that this sensitivity was driven by the face-to-face nature of politics in the *domus*.

In focusing on the ruler's privacy in Julio-Claudian Rome, I address a problem that Russell raised in her study of elite competition for control of public space during the Republic. Russell distinguishes public space in part by asking who can control access to and movement in that space.[72] The fall of the Republic marked the end of elite competition over public space and, in a sense, of public space itself, since Augustus claimed control over the whole city of Rome.[73] Nevertheless, emperors did not always successfully exercise control over public space or even their own houses, and their contemporaries did not always welcome their failures. As I will argue, the singular role of the emperor in the political order amplified the communal significance both of what he did and of what he endured. Threats to his safety and to his ability to exert control represented threats to the stability of the community, or (more precisely) threats to the emperor could always be redefined as public dangers. If one-man rule abolished public space, it also undermined the notion of private space, including and especially for the ruler himself: the ruler's unique position in the community necessarily compromised the distinction between his private world and the life of the community as a whole.

Overview

> In an ideal world, you have a political life, I think, and an intimate life and they don't have to be involved too much in each other. But when times are hard, there's no separation. Everything you do in your life is political and it has to be thought about in that way, this kind of moment we're in right now, for example.
> —*Zadie Smith,* Fresh Air, *November 21, 2016*

Political transformation, as author Zadie Smith notes, affects the way in which we make distinctions between our private worlds and the world of the community to which we belong. The Julio-Claudian period was such a transformative moment in Roman culture. The house was a space that Romans used to describe, define, and contest dynastic monarchy and its significance for the political community. Each of the following chapters focuses on different aspects of the world of Roman houses, from family bonds and elite self-display to everyday life and bodily functions. Roman houses, both literary representations and material environments, reveal the central role of intimacy and interdependence in Roman conceptions of power. For Romans in the early Empire, the ruler's house becomes a site for confronting the fragility of one-man rule and the contingency of claims to rule over others.

The first two chapters focus on contests about and in the world of the family. I begin in chapter 1 with Lucan's *Bellum civile*, an epic account of the civil wars that led to the end of the Republic and the birth of the principate. This poem was composed in the 60s CE, but I start with it because the events of the narrative are chronologically prior to Julio-Claudian rule. While civil war disrupts family ties in Lucan's poem, soldiers and commanders learn to play the role of kinsmen for one another. The three big men in Lucan's poem (Julius Caesar, Cato, and Pompey) claim an intimacy with their troops that mimics familial bonds of obligation and devotion. In Lucan's epic, commanders and soldiers learn to trade traditional family life for a new family that embraces all members of the community. Chapter 2 takes up ancient disputes about who belonged to the emperor's family, which was known in antiquity as the *domus Augusta*, and who had the authority to decide. Images of the imperial family in municipal monuments show that the membership and hierarchy of the emperor's family was subject to negotiation between multiple players. Different emperors (especially Augustus) sought to present themselves as the dominant figures in their households, but literary texts become increasingly attentive to the emperor's failure to control his family members. Most notably, in Tacitus' *Annals* the women of the imperial family become indicators of the fragility and contingency of one-man rule.

In chapter 3, I move from the imperial family to the space of the emperor's house, and to how he uses that house to make his unique position in the polity visible. Augustus' Palatine *domus*, which became associated in antiquity with his modesty and aversion to public attention, appears to represent a stark alternative to Nero's Domus Aurea, a luxury villa in the city that celebrated the emperor's inability to escape the public eye. Both houses, however, express a similar conception of the ruler as a person who is defined by his lack of privacy, although they embody divergent attitudes toward the public eye.

Chapter 4 focuses on the visibility of the ruler in Seneca's political thought. I begin with the *De clementia*, the only Roman philosophical treatment of one-man rule. In this text, Seneca is largely unconcerned with where the ruler lives: in his account, the ruler is always exposed to the public eye, and this exposure threatens both his own security and the stability and cohesion of the community. Next, I concentrate on dramatic moments in Seneca's *Agamemnon* and *Thyestes* in which the ruler's house is opened up and exposed to view. Seneca's tragic kings depend on the gaze of others, on being seen by those they rule, and their subjects must confront their own complicity in acknowledging and sustaining the dominance of the ruler.

In chapter 5, I leave the world of emperors and kings and turn to the everyday life of households in Roman Pompeii. The self-promotion of the elite householder was only one aspect of life in these houses. I argue that theatrical imagery in domestic frescoes encouraged householder and visitor to recognize their interdependence. Moreover, the multifunctional character of domestic spaces gave visitors intimate access to the life of the house, beyond the householder's performance of dominance.

In chapter 6, I continue with the daily life of the house, focusing on banquets and bodily functions in Petronius' *Satyricon* and Seneca's *De ira*. One distinctive feature of elite households in the Roman world was their ability to accommodate the basic bodily needs of their inhabitants. I show

how dining, bathing, and using the toilet at the ruler's house challenge the hierarchy of ruler and ruled in these texts. For the fabulously wealthy freedman Trimalchio in the *Satyricon* and for the kings, emperors, and grandees in *De ira*, the banquet compels the ruler to acknowledge the bodily needs he shares with those he rules, and thus to reveal the ways in which he is essentially equal to them.

While I treat the Julio-Claudian era as a provocative moment for Roman political thought, and I consider the ways in which my texts speak to the concerns of that moment, throughout this book I attend to (in Connolly's phrasing) "possible meanings that were not . . . expressed openly or given special emphasis" in the historical context of Julio-Claudian Rome.[74] When Roman thinkers emphasize the ruler's vulnerability, when they describe the interdependency of ruler and ruled or dwell on the exposure of the ruler to the public eye, they reveal their aversion to disrupting the status quo and their proclivity for stability: they assume that, even in the restrictive and dangerous world of Julio-Claudian Rome, they still have something left to lose. Tacitus' accounts of the prosecutions for insult to the emperor Tiberius, which I discuss in the conclusion, dramatize the obsession with security in Julio-Claudian political thought. The *delatores*, "accusers" or "informers," monitor speech and action in the households of the Roman elite: they present their findings as threats to the emperor and to the polity as a whole, and they produce a culture of fear, suspicion, and restriction. In responding to these charges, I argue, the senators reaffirm the association of the emperor's safety with communal security. Tacitus' stories of invasions into elite private life are, furthermore, valuable prompts for interrogating assumptions about the risks of privacy in the digital age.[75] Advocates of privacy rights in the twenty-first century admit that protecting the privacy of individuals comes with certain risks to public order or even public safety: the challenge is not to deny these dangers but to recognize that loss of privacy comes with its own disadvantages.[76] Similarly, Tacitus' narrative points to what we sacrifice, and to the dangerous limits we impose on our political imagination, when we make security our most important goal. When we think with the Romans, we must understand mutual vulnerability as an inevitable component of what it means and what it costs to live together.

CHAPTER ONE

Playing House
New Families and New Rulers in Lucan's *Bellum Civile*

Lucan wrote his epic *Bellum civile*, or *Civil War*, in the mid-60s CE, just before the end of the reign of the emperor Nero, the last ruler of the Julio-Claudian dynasty. This poem tells a story of the civil wars between Caesar and Pompey in the 40s BCE, a conflict that eventually led to the rule of Caesar's grandnephew Augustus and the house that he founded. Lucan's poem is in part a response to Vergil's *Aeneid*, the foundational epic for Augustan Rome, and to Caesar's *De bello civili*, his prose account of the wars with Pompey.[1] I focus on Lucan's treatment of the family, which is a key site in his account of the rise of one-man rule. While many studies have examined the devastating effects of the civil wars on family bonds in the poem, I argue that Lucan's narrative of the conflict is not simply destructive.[2] The mutual devotion between commanders and soldiers in the *Bellum civile* shows how one-man rule can create new relationships between members of the community. Soldiers and commanders form bonds that parallel those they know from their own households, and they come close to providing the recognition and devotion that family members perform in the epic. Lucan's poem presents a seductive new political order, in which ruler and ruled learn to play the role of family members for one another.

The disruption of family life is a recurring problem in the *Bellum civile*.³ Lucan explains the origins of the civil war between Caesar and Pompey in familial terms: Pompey's marriage to Julia, Caesar's daughter, had kept the peace between the two men, but "the trust was broken by [her] death and the leaders were allowed to start a war" (*morte tua discussa fides bellumque mouere/permissum ducibus*, 1.119–20).⁴ While Lucan criticizes Caesar for his single-minded pursuit of power, the dictator's disregard for his relationship with his former son-in-law is among his most serious outrages: "it's a shame, Caesar, and it always will be, that the height of your crimes aided you—that you fought with a dutiful son-in-law" (*dolet, heu, semperque dolebit/quod scelerum, Caesar, prodest tibi summa tuorum, / cum genero pugnasse pio*, 6.303–6). Caesar's crime against the polity arises as much from his failure to respect traditional family ties as from his failure to be a good Republican citizen.

Romans had no specific term for *nuclear family*: the most common Latin terms for family, *familia* and *domus*, could refer to enslaved members of the household as well as those joined by kinship. Yet the bonds between spouses and between parents and children had a privileged status in Roman conceptions of familial obligations, and *pietas*, duty to family, community, and gods, was a central value in Roman culture.⁵ In *On Duties*, Cicero calls the marital bond the "first fellowship" (*prima societas in ipso coniugio est*); the relationship between parents and children (*in liberis*) is second, followed by "one house, all things in common" (*una domus, communia omnia, Off.* 1.54).⁶ While the Roman father is often associated with total authority over the lives and deaths of his children, parents were also expected to attend to their children's welfare, especially by providing for them in their wills.⁷ In Roman ideals of family life, as Richard Saller has established, *pietas* involved care and devotion, not just obedience.⁸ The paradigmatic example of *pietas* is Vergil's hero Aeneas, who rescues both his young son and his aged father from Troy. The Temple of Pietas in Rome was supposedly erected on the site of a prison where a daughter nursed her starving mother as she waited to be executed (Val. Max. 5.4–7; Pliny *NH* 7.121).⁹ The *Ad Herennium*, a rhetorical manual from the first-century BCE, treats *pietas* as a natural law according to which parents and children care for one another (*parentes a liberis et a parentibus liberi coluntur*, 2.19).¹⁰

The soldiers in Lucan's poem repeatedly express their longing to go back to their families, from Caesar's soldiers, who beg leave to die in the arms of their wives (5.278–82), to Pompey's allies, who confess that they love their children more than the cause of the Republic (9.227–36). Yet while these men associate special recognition and devotion with the domestic sphere, commanders and soldiers in the poem also fulfill these obligations for one another. The intimacy between commanders and soldiers in Lucan's epic is in part a reflection of the conditions of war itself. The narrative takes place mostly on the battlefield, where the combatants are very far from home. The good *dux*, or commander, is a standard figure in Roman military narratives: he exhibits his dedication to his soldiers by tending to their needs and by rewarding them for their services, and he has the capacity to inspire their allegiance and to command their obedience.[11] The *Bellum civile*, however, is set in a moment when the power of the *dux*, and especially the loyalty of troops to their commander, became the basis for political authority: as military leaders in this poem interact with their troops, they foreshadow and audition for the political order of the principate.[12]

Lucan's account of war and political conflict is also an account of the transformation of the world of the family, for both the ruler and the ruled. The military leaders in the *Bellum civile* compete not only with each other but also with the families that their men have left behind and that they repeatedly invoke in contrast to their lives in warfare. Throughout the epic, however, Caesar, Cato, and Pompey perform and receive familial devotion. When Caesar cares for his soldiers and recognizes their service to him, he fulfills his role as their leader but also mimics the actions of wives and mothers in the epic. Even as Cato and Pompey fight against Caesar, their relationships with their men mirror both familial ties and Caesar's bond with his troops.[13] On both sides of the civil war, intimacy between leaders and soldiers takes the place of the intimacy between family members. In Lucan's vision of one-man rule, everyone becomes part of the ruler's house.

Longing for the Family

When Rome receives the news that Caesar has crossed the Rubicon and is making his way to the capital, Lucan compares the city to a mother preparing to mourn the death of her son. Her shock at her son's death keeps her from beginning to formally mourn: "the mother, with her hair torn, does not seek the arms of her slaves to cruelly beat her breast . . . she raves and broods over the body and marvels at the disaster" (*nec mater crine soluto/exigit ad saeuos famularum bracchia planctus . . . incubat amens/miraturque malum*, 2.23–28).[14] This metaphorical mother foreshadows the actions of the *matronae* in Rome, who assemble to mourn their community and to recognize the importance of the ties among kinsmen and fellow-citizens.

The women occupy the temples and overwhelm the gods with their lamentations and their prayers: in the city of Rome, "no altar lacked a parent to show her ill-will" (*nullis defuit aris/inuidiam factura parens*, 35–36). As Alison Keith observes, Lucan does not criticize these women for taking their mourning to the streets rather than remaining in their homes: their actions are commensurate with the desperation that civil war creates.[15] By exclaiming over their losses, the Roman women insist on the enduring value of family relations. Even as civil war has turned kinsmen against one another, the *matronae* use their bodies to display their sorrow and to assert that family bonds remain worthy of reverence.

As these women mourn, they play a role that is familiar for women in martial epic, a role the soldiers in the *Bellum civile* are mindful of.[16] When Caesar's troops revolt, they make women's mourning a signal distinction between the world of the family and the world of war. Claiming to be exhausted by their years of service to Caesar, the soldiers ask how long their current way of life is supposed to last.[17] A distinctive aspect of Lucan's epic is that it gives voice to the masses of people (especially although not exclusively soldiers) whose lives are absorbed into their leaders' civil war.[18] The men address their commander with one voice: "now look upon our white hair and our weak hands, and see our useless arms. Our life is wasted away, we have spent our life's span in wars: release us, as old men, to death" (*iam respice canos/ inualidasque manus et inanis cerne lacertos./usus abit uitae, bellis consumpsimus aeuum:/ad mortem dimitte senes*, 5.274–77).[19] Caesar's soldiers make complaints that are communal, but they ask for a death that is appropriate for an individual member of a family and community, rather than for a nameless soldier: "Not to set dying limbs on the hard earth, not to strike the helmet with our fleeing breath and not to search for a right hand to close our eyes for death; [but] to fall with a wife's tears, and to know the pyre built for one" (*non duro liceat morientia caespite membra/ponere, non anima galeam fugiente ferire/atque oculos morti clausuram quaerere dextram/ coniugis inlabi lacrimis, unique paratum/scire rogum*, 5.278–82). They want to receive appropriate honors when they die, and they associate the good death not with combat but with the domestic sphere. The soldiers emphasize the care that the man who dies at home can expect to receive: "the pyre built for one" and the sorrow of his wife, for whom mourning his death is a specific responsibility and not a matter of chance (as it would be for whomever the dying soldier might find to close his eyelids).[20] When the mutineers demand this kind of death, they affirm their respect for the relationship between husband and wife in that they acknowledge the value of the wife's duties toward her husband. The soldiers' concern is not simply the funeral rite in itself: rather, they want to be recognized and included in a family unit, and the moment of death is a key occasion for performing and receiving this recognition.

When the mutineers in Caesar's camp demand to leave Caesar's service, they are motivated not only by sentiment, but by a sense of their own need and dependence.[21] Fighting for Caesar has left them poor and vulnerable: the soldiers complain that, when they captured Rome, they respected their fellow citizens and the gods (*quos hominum uel quos licuit spoliare deorum*, 271) and so emerged "pious with poverty" (*paupertate pii*, 273). They have committed "every crime" (*omne nefas*, 272) on Caesar's behalf, with no spoils to show for it. Their interest in wealth, in profiting from civil war, aligns with Caesar's "mercenary approach toward his interactions with peers and subordinates."[22] Yet the mutineers' attention to economic gain also reveals the tangible significance of their desire to die at home. In offering Caesar their service, these men have cut themselves off from sources of support beyond Caesar himself. Caesar has a choice: he can either recognize the mutineers' years of dedication by providing substantive compensation, or he can send them back to the family members, who will recognize their merits by honoring their deaths.[23]

The Pompeian forces at Ilerda, whom Caesar defeats in 49 BCE, express similar desires to those of the mutineers. When Caesar pardons the Pompeians, the narrator exclaims at their good fortune:

> Happy is he who, while the whole world gives way from destruction, knows where he will go to rest.[24] No battles call them when they are wearied, no trumpets break their steady sleep. Now wife and tender children and humble homes and their own land receive them, since they return as natives. Fortune even lifts this burden from them, free from care—anxious partiality is absent from their minds: one [Caesar] is the creator of their salvation, the other [Pompey] was their commander. Thus happily they watch civil wars without prayers. (4.393–401)[25]

Pompey's men expect to return to their own families and houses, where they can live detached from the conflict and indifferent to the victory or defeat of either *dux*. They seem to imagine that their home lives have remained insulated from the upheavals of the civil wars, and that when they leave the battlefield, they can go back to the way things once were. Caesar's mutineers had a similar point of view: they believed that, should Caesar release them from their service in war, they could die in peace, mourned by their families as individuals, grieved for their absence as kinsmen rather than as subordinates.

The lamentations of the *matronae* in Rome, however, cast doubt on this possibility. One of the women, speaking to and for her companions, suggested that their world was about to be fundamentally transformed: she told them, "Now, wretched mothers, beat your breasts, now tear your hair, and don't delay your grief or save it for the worst of evils. Now you have the power to weep, while the fortune of the leaders hangs in the balance. When one of them has conquered, you will need to rejoice" (*nunc . . . o miserae, contundite pectora, matres, / nunc laniate comas neue hunc differte dolorem / et summis seruate malis. nunc flere potestas / dum pendet fortuna ducum: cum uicerit alter gaudendum est*, 2.38–42).

The *matronae* in Rome understand that they are facing a future in which the victorious commander will compel them to give up their grieving for what they have lost and instead to celebrate what they have gained. Yet the matron's pronouncement is not only a prediction that the victor will silence critique. In the new order of one-man rule, there will be no place for the grief that gives priority to the bonds between private citizens, or for the special role of wives and mothers in expressing that grief. After the civil war is over, the women of Rome will no longer represent an alternative to life on the battlefield, one that soldiers can long to return to: rather, they will become like all other followers of a victorious leader, rejoicing at his—and their—success.

Near the end of the poem, after Pompey's defeat, his allies from Cilicia (a region in Asia Minor) imagine the kind of domestic future that the Roman women bring into question.[26] They address Cato, who has taken command of Pompey's army, and tell him that they intend to abandon the Roman war and return home:

> Pardon us, Cato: love of Pompey brought us to arms, not love of civil war, and we joined in because of our partiality. He has fallen whom the world preferred to peace and our cause is dead: allow us to see our ancestral hearth-gods and our deserted home and our sweet children again. For what end will there be to battle if it is neither Pharsalia nor Pompey? The prime of our lives is spent, let us die in safety; let our old age see the fires we deserve: civil war can scarcely promise tombs to its leaders. (9.227–36)[27]

Pompey's allies suggest that for the duration of the civil war, Pompey took the place of their families and their homes. Now that Pompey has lost, they intend to return to their *penates*, *domus*, and *nati* (hearth gods, houses, and children), to which they owe their greatest devotion in normal circumstances.[28] The Cilicians abandon Pompey's cause and so give up the *amor* that took them away from their families. Their argument, however, shows that they have failed to understand the stakes of the conflict, that the victorious Caesar, and his descendants, achieve a dominance that is not limited to the field of battle. After Caesar wins, no one can simply abandon their leader and head for home: he will follow them there.

Lucan's epic draws attention to the ways that war undermines and competes with the world of the *domus*. On the battlefield, the commander's need for loyalty and service cuts his troops off from the family units to which they belong. The Roman matron suggests that the conclusion of the war will eliminate the traditional roles of wives and mothers as mourners of the dead.

The military leaders in Lucan's epic, and the system of one-man rule that they prefigure, offer a kind of solution to this problem. While the soldiers and the women of Rome draw attention to the privileged significance of family bonds, Caesar, Cato, and Pompey step in to fulfill the obligations that family members once performed for one another. Even as they disrupt and displace the special status of family ties, they put something else in its place. The breakdown of traditional family relationships opens up a space for a new conception of the family, one in which the mutual devotion that characterizes family ties can be fulfilled by the bond between ruler and ruled.

Caring for the Ruled

While Caesar sends Pompey's men back home, he does not do the same for the mutineers in his own army: he puts the leaders of the uprising to death, and the rest are evidently stunned back into loyalty (5.364–74). Yet this is not the end of the story, and though Caesar rejects his troops' demands, as the war continues he establishes new terms as to how they can be fulfilled. At the battle of Pharsalus, a devastating loss for the Pompeian side and the turning point in Lucan's account of the civil war, Caesar presents himself as the primary caretaker of the men that follow him. After Pompey's defeat, Cato emerges as one of Caesar's fiercest opponents, but he also claims a privileged intimacy with his soldiers that reflects Caesar's example of leadership.

Regardless of their divergent political aims, both Caesar and Cato enact the displacement and transformation of familial devotion that accompanies the rise of one-man rule.

Caesar's actions at Pharsalus correspond to his soldiers' demands for recognition and respect, and his attention to his troops recalls the devotion the *matronae* showed to their kinsmen. Before the fighting begins, Caesar claims that he can pick out specific soldiers in the crowd, and so suggests that he knows them not as a nameless mass but as individual actors. He asks his troops, "Which soldier's sword shall I not know? And when the quivering lance crosses the sky, I shall not fail to tell from whose arm it was thrown" (*cuius non militis ensem / agnoscam? caelumque tremens cum lancea transit / dicere non fallar quo sit uibrata lacerto*, 7.287–89). In warning his troops that they must dedicate themselves to victory, Caesar declares that he respects their efforts on his behalf. During the battle, Caesar notes each soldier's actions and responses:

> He even examines their swords, which are completely drenched in blood, which shine just with a bloody tip, which hand shakes with the grip of the sword, who holds his spear loosely, who tightly, who performs violence for his commander, who is pleased to fight, who changes his expression when he has killed a fellow citizen. (7.560–65)[29]

The repetition of singular verbs and pronouns in this passage, as Caesar identifies individual men and their particular actions during the battle, offers a striking contrast with the mutiny earlier in the poem, when the troops spoke with a single voice. During the revolt, the Caesarians complained, "*we* have captured our ancestral houses . . . *we* have spent our life in wars" (*cepimus . . . patriae . . . tecta . . . bellis consumpsimus aeuum*, 5.270, 276). The mutineers also feared that they would meet their fate alone on the battlefield, searching for "a hand to close our eyes" (*oculos morti clausuram quaerere dextram*, 5.280). While the soldiers at Placentia imagined that they would die in a homogeneous mass, in fact Caesar is present to recognize them and to care for their bodies. In a remarkable and gruesome moment, Caesar uses his own hands to stop the bleeding from his soldiers' wounds: "he himself presses and sets his hand against many men's wounds, which are about to spill out all their blood" (*uolnera multorum totum fusura cruorem / opposita premit ipse manu*, 7.566–67).[30] Caesar, as he touches the bodies (and bodily fluids) of his wounded men, imitates the physical contact associated with familial devotion in previous episodes in the epic. When the grieving mother, the metaphorical embodiment of all of Rome, sees her son's corpse, she "presses his limbs, stiff as life escapes them, and his lifeless face and his eyes bulging in death" (*cum membra premit fugiente rigentia uita / uoltusque exanimes oculosque in morte minaces*, 2.25–26); when the mutineers described their last moments, they imagined their wives shedding tears over their bodies (*coniugis inlabi lacrimis*, 5.281). Caesar's victory means that he is not literally a mourner: although he takes note of his fallen men when he "visits the corpses spread over the wide fields" (*obit latis proiecta cadauera campis*, 7.565), the Caesarians are not only triumphant but ever on the move, fighting and pushing forward while the Pompeians fall.[31] Yet in his encounters with his troops, through his attention to their movements and his contact with their bodies, he plays the role of a family member who must acknowledge and tend to those closest to him.

Caesar's performance of devotion on the battlefield serves his own ends and his need to defeat his opponents. Lucan describes Caesar in the midst of battle as a Fury, intent on slaughter: he is "a madness and spur to rage for the troops . . . like Bellona shaking her bloody whip" (*rabies populis stimulusque furorum . . . sanguineum ueluti quatiens Bellona flagellum*, 7.557–68), and he drives his troops into battle with the butt of his spear (*uerbere conuersae . . . hastae*, 7.577). At the same time, however, he takes on the role of the dutiful spouse and parent who provides the recognition and care that his dependents require: the question is not whether Caesar really is a devoted family member, but to what extent his men may regard him as such.[32] Even as Caesar is unrelenting in his dedication to the crime of civil war, he asserts his privileged relationship with his soldiers. He claims that the interests of his subordinates carry more weight than his own advancement:

> This business isn't about me, but I pray that your multitude will be free, that you will hold authority over all nations. I myself desire to return to private life and to play the modest citizen in a plebeian toga, but so long as you are allowed everything, there is nothing that I refuse to be.[33] Rule while I am in disfavor. (7.264–69)[34]

Caesar's humility here, and his insistence that he has put away his own desires to promote the welfare of his soldiers, is in part a rhetorical posture, although he does not hesitate to express the savagery of his intentions a few moments later, when he urges his men to rend the faces of their kinsmen (7.323). Even pretending that he supports the interests of his men over his own, however, allows him to claim the role of his followers' most important source of support.³⁵ Through his performance at Pharsalus, Caesar makes an argument for the self-sufficiency and completeness of his bond with his troops: there is no need for his soldiers to return to their families because he can provide them with everything they need.³⁶

The reciprocal devotion between Caesar and his soldiers represents a stark alternative to Caesar's treatment of his enemies in the civil war. At the close of his address to his troops before the battle, Caesar distinguishes between the enemies who fight back and those who (wisely) choose to flee: "I beg you, boys, that none of you wish to cut down an enemy from behind: let whoever flees be a fellow citizen. But while the spears gleam, do not let any vision of devotion nor your parents spied on the opposite side disturb you; rend the revered faces with your sword" (*uos tamen hoc oro, iuuenes, ne caedere quisquam/hostis terga uelit: ciuis qui fugerit esto. /sed, dum tela micant, non uos pietatis imago/ulla nec aduersa conspecti fronte parentes/commoueant; uoltus gladio turbate uerendos*, 7.318–22).³⁷ With this speech, as Matthew Roller observes, Caesar both acknowledges "the power of claims of kinship" and rejects them, proposing innovative rules for how to define "the community of moral obligation": the soldiers owe devotion not to their kinsmen but to those who fail to resist the Caesarian troops.³⁸ Roller also shows that Caesar's demands for loyalty in the *Bellum civile* anticipate the oaths that communities across the Roman world swore to Augustus and his successors when they promised to esteem the emperor's welfare beyond that of themselves or their families.³⁹ Caesar's chilling insistence that his men turn against their kinsmen, however, also makes palpable the contrast between his devotion to his followers and his hostility to his enemies. If Caesar requires total commitment from those under his command, he also insists that he will commit himself to their protection. During the battle itself, Caesar "forbids his troops to charge against the people, and points out the Senate. He knows what the blood of the empire is, what its guts are, where to attack Rome" (*in plebem uetat ire manus monstratque senatum:/scit cruor imperii qui sit, quae uiscera rerum,/unde petat Romam*, 7.578–80). Caesar's enthusiasm for spilling the blood of the Senate is directly opposed to his response to his wounded men, when he staunches the blood pouring out from their wounds (7.566–67): this inversion signals Caesar's commitment to those who obey him as well as his terrifying animosity against those who stand in his way.

The split between Caesar's recognition of his supporters and rejection of his opponents continues after his victory at Pharsalus, when Caesar refuses to build funeral pyres for the Pompeians and leaves their bodies to rot (7.796–99). The morning after the battle, he picks a picnic spot where he can see the putrefying corpses of his opponents: "he marks the rivers, displaced by flows of blood, and the bodies in heaps that equal the lofty hills, he watches the piles sinking into gore and he counts Magnus' multitudes, and a place is prepared for dining, where he can recognize the faces and forms of his enemies" (*cernit propulsa cruore/flumina et excelsos cumulis aequantia colles/corpora, sidentis in tabem spectat aceruos/et Magni numerat populos, epulisque paratur/ille locus, uoltus ex quo faciesque iacentum/agnoscat*, 7.789–94). This is a gruesome panorama, but the bloodied rivers are again most remarkable in light of Caesar's care of his men during the battle and his efforts to keep their blood from mingling with that of their enemies. Caesar's ability to play different roles in his encounters with different parties indicates that, in this epic, there is a way out of endless civil war.[40] Caesar's expression of commitment to those who dedicate themselves to him, and of hostility to those who do not, points to the potential for establishing a new order in which all members of the Roman community make themselves the objects of Caesar's devotion rather than of his enmity. The intensity of Caesar's loyalty to his followers will define and sustain the new community that arises when he is the unquestioned leader of the Roman people. This loyalty is most keenly felt when it can be contrasted with his relationship to outsiders.

Caesar defeats Pompey at Pharsalus, but he continues to face opposition, and Cato the Younger is one of his most resolute and prominent challengers. Cato loudly proclaims his opposition to Caesar and to the world order that Caesar represents. Cato hopes that his participation in the war will transform it from a conflict between two potential despots (Caesar and Pompey) to one between the Republic and those who threaten it. Early in the epic, he claims that he wants Pompey to win "with me among his troops . . . so that he does not think that he has conquered for himself" (*me milite . . . ne sibi se uicisse putet*, 2.322–23). Some scholars accept Cato's self-evaluation, reading him as the champion of the Republic and the hero of the poem; others are more skeptical, noting parallels between Cato's self-presentation as sole defender of Rome and Caesar's hunger to be Rome's sole ruler.[41] Cato's performance of familial devotion is one aspect of his role in the poem that recalls Caesar's own, and like Caesar he points to the difficulties of distinguishing between family relations and the bond between the ruler and the ruled.

At Cato's first appearance in the poem, he expresses the depth of his attachment to the Republic by describing himself as Rome's parent:

> Just as grief itself bids the parent, bereaved by the death of his sons, to lead the long funeral procession to the tomb, and he is pleased to have thrust his hands into the black flames and to have held the torches blackened from the heaped up mound of the funeral pyre, I shall not be torn away before I embrace you, Rome, when you are lifeless, and I shall pursue your name, Liberty, and your empty ghost.[42] (2.297–303)[43]

For Cato, as for the *matronae* and the Caesarian mutineers, mourning practices and funeral rites exemplify the devotion and recognition that family members owe to one another. When the narrator calls Cato the "true parent of the fatherland" (*parens uerus patriae*, 9.601), he affirms Cato's conception of himself.[44] Yet to be the parent of one's country is far from unproblematic in the context of civil war and the rise of one-man rule: when Cato acts as the parent of Rome, he mimics Caesar's actions as *dux*, however unintentionally, and thus steps into the role of autocrat rather than Republican hero. Caesar, the consummate commander at Pharsalus, showed his devotion to his men in order to elicit their loyalty and rouse their energy; he moved among the soldiers, encouraged them, and tended to their wounds. Cato performs similar actions when he consoles the people and urges them into battle. After the battle of Pharsalus, Cato leads the resistance to Caesar even though Pompeian defeat is all but assured. As commander of the Pompeian forces, Cato "received the fatherland when it was in need of a guardian, warmed the people's shaking limbs, [and] returned swords that were cast down to fearful hands" (*patriam tutore carentem/excepit, populi trepidantia membra refouit, /ignauis manibus proiectos reddidit enses*, 9.24–26). While the narrator insists that Cato took on these duties without desiring to rule (*nec regnum cupiens*, 9.27), Cato's behavior is nevertheless consistent with the exchange of devotion that Caesar modeled during the battle at Pharsalus and with the relationship expected between ruler and ruled.

Cato's actions also mirror Caesar's during his brutal march with his soldiers in the desert. Cato and his army are on the verge of dying of thirst, when one soldier manages to fill his helmet with water and offers it to his commander. Cato's response, however, is not what the soldier expected: "'Did I appear so soft to you that I am unequal to this trivial heat? You are much more worthy of this penalty, that you drink while the people are thirsty!' Thus driven by anger, he threw down the helmet, and the water sufficed for everyone" (*"usque adeo mollis primisque caloribus inpar/sum uisus? quanto poena tu dignior ista es,/qui populo sitiente bibas!" sic concitus ira/excussit galeam, suffecitque omnibus unda*, 9.507–10). Cato's harshness here accords with his exemplary austerity.⁴⁵ Yet this scene also serves as a parallel to Caesar's speech before the battle of Pharsalus. On the battlefield, Caesar insisted that his own desires meant nothing in comparison to the advantage of the troops (7.264–69). In the desert, when Cato declares that the people's suffering takes precedence over his own (9.509), he also suggests that the role of the leader is to give preference to the welfare of his subordinates. To be the father of his country means that Cato, whether or not he desires power for its own sake, must play the part of the ruler.

When Cato takes command of Pompey's forces, he acts as *pater patriae*, as *dux*, and as ruler, but he plays multiple and potentially conflicting roles even before he joins the fighting. When he is still in Rome, Cato marries Marcia, once his wife and now another man's widow, in a ceremony that is defined by its differences from traditional wedding rites. There is no decoration of the house (2.350–59), no fine clothes for the bride or groom (2.360–66), and no sex: "they do not try the compacts of their former bed: his strength resists even just love" (*nec foedera prisci/sunt temptata tori: iusto quoque robur amori/restitit*, 2.378–80).⁴⁶ Marcia draws attention to the strangeness of their union when she promises that she will be satisfied with the "empty name of marriage" (*nomen inane/conubii*, 2.342–43). Lucan claims that Cato rejects the customs of marriage because he is "the father of the city and the husband of the city" (*urbi pater est urbique maritus*, 2.388). As *maritus urbi*, however, Cato shows decidedly less physical restraint than he does in his marriage to Marcia. Cato does not touch his wife, but he "warms the people's shaking limbs" (*populi trepidantia membra refouit*, 9.25) on the battlefield; his actions here mirror Pompey's behavior toward his wife Cornelia, when Pompey "warms her limbs with his embrace" (*refouet conplexibus artus*, 8.67).⁴⁷ The strict boundaries that Cato observes in his marriage with Marcia do not constrain his relationship with the people, and he plays the part of father of the city and husband of the city at the same time. For Cato to be both the father and the husband of Rome gestures toward the changing political system, in which the ruler must be all things to all men, and in which the ties that join members of a family become indistinguishable from the ties between the ruler and the ruled.

Loving the Ruler

The familial devotion that informs the relationship between ruler and ruled in *Bellum civile* appears not only in the actions of the rulers, but in the responses of the ruled. While the mutineers in Caesar's army demanded to return to their families, the mass suicide of another Caesarian unit suggests that the ruled can learn to value their bond with the ruler above all else.

Vulteius is in command of three rafts in the Adriatic when Pompeian forces surround them: since he realizes that escape is impossible, Vulteius urges his men to kill each other rather than submit to the enemy. Vulteius seeks to be regarded as an *exemplum* of courage and self-sacrifice, and to transform himself into a spectacle of devotion to the Caesarian side.[48] There is one person, however, whose recognition he especially hopes to receive: "let's earn this with our great courage, that Caesar, when he has lost us few amid so many thousands, will call it a defeat and a disaster" (*magna uirtute merendum est, / Caesar ut amissis inter tot milia paucis / hoc damnum clademque uocet*, 4.512–14). The mutineers described two types of death, one on the battlefield in an anonymous heap, the other at home, in the presence of their grieving wives; Vulteius, however, insists that Caesar is capable of recognizing the sacrifice of his men, and that Caesar's acknowledgment is worth the most gruesome end. Vulteius proclaims not only his submission to Caesar but the exceptional intimacy of the bond he shares with his commander: he laments that "we know that it is worth little, Caesar, to fall on our own swords for you, but we are under siege and have no greater proof of how much we love" (*suis pro te gladiis incumbere, Caesar, / esse parum scimus; sed non maiora supersunt / obsessis tanti quae pignora demus amoris*, 4.500–502). The narrator roundly rejects Vulteius' claims to be an *exemplum* of *uirtus* (4.575–79), and when Pompey's officers discover the bodies of Vulteius and his men, they marvel "that any commander could be worth so much to anyone" (*ducibus mirantibus ulli / esse ducem tanti*, 4.572–73). Nevertheless, Vulteius believes that the *dux* does, in fact, merit such an astonishing performance, and Vulteius' expression of love for Caesar has its parallels on the Pompeian side.

Pompey is Caesar's main opponent, but at the beginning of the poem Lucan highlights the ways they resemble one another: the civil war broke out in part because "Caesar could not stand to have anyone ahead of him, and Pompey could stand no equal" (*nec quemquam iam ferre potest Caesarue priorem / Pompeiusue parem*, 1.125–26).[49] The desire to rule, however, is not the only thing that Pompey shares with Caesar: the devotion that Pompey's followers express for their fallen commander recalls the intimacy that joined Caesar and his troops. Pompey's men care for his body as they would care for their family members, and as they would expect their families to care for them. Cordus, the quaestor and companion who performs Pompey's funeral rites, appears at first to be an inconsequential figure.[50] The description of the funeral, however, transforms Cordus into a member of Pompey's family, as he plays the role of parent and spouse to his commander.

The funeral takes place under unusual circumstances for a Roman leader. Pompey is assassinated aboard a royal vessel by the agents of the young pharaoh; the Egyptians take his head as proof to show to Caesar, and they abandon Pompey's body.[51] After rescuing Pompey's corpse from the water and setting it on dry land, Cordus "clung to Magnus and poured his tears over every wound" (*incubuit Magno lacrimasque effudit in omne/uolnus*, 8.727–28).[52] Two words, *incubuit* and *lacrimas*, are particularly significant in this context. The verb *incubo* appears in a key funeral scene earlier in the poem, when the city of Rome on the brink of civil war is compared to a house in mourning, and the mother of the house clings to her son's body in her grief (*incubat*, 2.27). As Cordus weeps for Pompey, he enacts the death that Caesar's mutineers desire for themselves when they ask "to fall with a wife's tears" (*coniugis inlabi lacrimis*, 5.281). If Pompey had died at home, he could have expected the same treatment from his family that he receives from Cordus. Later, Cordus takes material to build a fire from a pyre constructed for another corpse: he asks pardon from the dead man, insisting that the body, because it is not under guard, must be unloved (*nec ulli/cara tuo*, 8.746–47).[53] Yet this corpse has received the funeral rites that the mutineers desired, namely "the pyre built for one" (*unique paratum . . . rogum*, 5.281–82), and Cordus provides the same honor for the fallen Pompey. As Cordus enacts Pompey's funeral, he becomes a substitute for Pompey's closest kin.

Lucan not only treats Cordus as Pompey's parent or spouse in a general sense, but casts him in the role of Pompey's wife Cornelia, who observes the burial from Pompey's boat. Cordus implies that he acts in Cornelia's place, as she will be responsible for Pompey's remains if they can return home: "if fortune allows us to return to Italy, these holy remains shall not remain in this place, but Cornelia, Magnus, will receive you and take you from my hand to an urn" (*Fortuna recursus/si det in Hesperiam, non hac in sede quiescent/tam sacri cineres, sed te Cornelia, Magne,/accipiet nostraque manu transfundet in urnam*, 8.767–70). Cordus does express his regret for Cornelia's absence: Cordus acknowledges women's traditional role as mourners, begging the gods to be satisfied that "Cornelia does not lie here with her hair undone . . . that his unhappy wife is absent from the duties of his pyre" (*Cornelia fuso/crine iacet . . . abest a munere busti/infelix coniunx*, 7.739–42). As Keith observes, both women and social subordinates can take on the responsibilities of mourning in Lucan's poem, although she sees Cornelia as the most important of Pompey's mourners, while Cordus fulfills these obligations "insofar as he can."[54] When Cordus tends to Pompey's body, however, his performance challenges the distinctiveness of the intimacy between husband and wife as opposed to the bond between the soldier and commander. Cordus' devotion to his leader raises this very question—whether he can fill the place of Pompey's wife at his side, whether family members are still needed to perform familial devotion, or whether other sources of respect and recognition can take their place.

Cornelia, in her turn, laments that she is unable to play her rightful role in Pompey's funeral, and thus that she cannot publicly recognize the significance of their bond.[55] She defines her role as wife in terms of her duties to her deceased husband:

> "Fortune, was I thus unworthy," she said, "to have ascended my husband's pyre and to cling to the man and cover his cold limbs, to burn up my torn hair and to arrange Magnus' body, scattered by the sea, to pour out floods of tears over all his wounds . . . will I never be allowed to do my duties for my husbands? Will I never beat my breast beside full funeral urns?" (9.55–59, 68–69)[56]

Cornelia's account of the appropriate funeral rites mirrors Cordus' activities: although she wants to weep and brood over the body, it is Cordus who fulfills these functions.[57] As she describes the funeral rite in detail, Cornelia emphasizes the physicality of mourning (clinging to the body, covering it with her hair and with her tears) and the contrast between her lament and the actions she wants to perform. Later, Cornelia performs a kind of substitute funeral for her husband (9.175–78). Cordus performed rites for Pompey's corpse, but Cornelia must settle for collecting Pompey's military costume and equipment: "that, for the wretched woman, was the ashes of Magnus" (*ille fuit miserae Magni cinis*, 9.179).[58] While Cornelia is excluded from the place that she regards on her own, it is less clear that Pompey requires her attention. Caesar's mutineers were afraid to end their lives unrecognized and forgotten, and begged to die in the presence of their wives, but

Cordus gives Pompey the kind of death the mutineers wanted (a weeping mourner, the single pyre), even though his wife cannot be with him. Pompey's troops even seem to rival Cornelia in their misery at the loss of Pompey: they experience "grief without precedent and never known" (*exemploque carens et nulli cognitus aeuo / luctus*, 9.169–70), and when they see Cornelia suffering, their mourning increases (*rursus geminato verbere plangunt*, 9.173). The intimacy between Pompey and his men threatens to set distinct social ties (commander and soldier, husband and wife) on an equal plane: the wife's care becomes one of the many expressions of devotion that the ruler can expect from those subordinate to him. The special importance of Cornelia's role as Pompey's wife is undermined if Cordus and Pompey's men (however reluctantly) are able to fulfill her obligations.

One reason that Pompey's men can compete with Cornelia is that they learn how to mourn from her, and not only for Pompey but also for their comrades. When they watch Cornelia beat her breast, tear her hair, and collect Pompey's possessions, they are inspired to tend to the corpses of those lost at Pharsalus: "all devotion follows her lead, and mounds arise throughout the shore and pyres are set for the ghosts of Thessaly" (*accipit omnis / exemplum pietas, et toto litore busta / surgunt Thessalicis reddentia manibus ignem*, 9.178–80).[59] These makeshift funeral rites, like Pompey's, are in part a reflection of the exigencies of war, but they also further challenge the distinction between family relationships and bonds created on the battlefield. While Cornelia raged that she was excluded from Pompey's pyre, and Caesar's soldiers associated proper funeral rites with the circle of the family, Pompey's troops play the part of devoted family members for one another. The intensity of their devotion to and mourning for Pompey makes those far-away relationships less necessary: in comparison to their attachment to the ruler, all bonds between the ruled are equivalent.

Conclusion

In the *Bellum civile*, the family and the battlefield are spaces that reveal the potential attractions of one-man rule for those who experience it. The kinds of devotion that family members perform in the epic, from recognition to bodily contact to mourning, also occur in the intimate relations between commanders and soldiers during the civil war. Military leaders in Lucan's poem become both objects of devotion and providers of care: they learn to take the place of family members for their followers, and they teach them to live with this new kind of intimacy. Lucan's epic is not just a contest over the fate of the Republic, but over the significance of family bonds in the new order that the civil wars create: if Caesar can learn to be their parent and their spouse, will his men still need or want to go back home? To whom will it matter, and how much, if Caesar is sincere or if he is "just" playing a role?

Lucan committed suicide in 65 CE, after he was implicated in a conspiracy to assassinate the emperor Nero, who was the last descendant of Julius Caesar to rule Rome.[60] Nevertheless, the idea of familial intimacy between ruler and ruled that Lucan evokes in the *Bellum civile* seems to have appealed to Nero. Tacitus reports a remarkable speech of Nero's to the people of Rome in 64 CE, shortly after the fire that devastated the city. The emperor chose to cancel a trip to the East and to stay home, explaining that

> He had seen the sorrowful expressions of the citizens, heard their secret complaints, because he was about to go on such a long journey, while they could not even endure his short departures, accustomed to be restored (*refoueri*) by the sight of the *princeps* in the face of chance events. Therefore just as in private relationships the closest bonds (*necessitudines*) were strongest, in this way the Roman people carried the most weight and he had to obey them when they held him back. (Tac. *Ann.* 15.36)[61]

For Nero, being emperor means that all relationships and all claims of obligation are necessarily secondary to his bond with the people.[62] If Nero's forefather Caesar won the contest for power in Rome, Nero claims that he has won the contest for love. He inscribes himself into the emotional world of the family: the people are his most intimate relations, his *necessitudines*, and they look to him to be restored revived (*refoueri*) in times of trouble—just as Pompey revived his wife (*refouet*, 8.67) and Cato revived his troops (*refouit*, 9.25). Lucan's epic points to the unnerving implications of Nero's profession of familial attachments with those he rules. The danger in the poem is not that the ruler may fail to devote himself to his subjects, but that the devotion he gives and receives may satisfy the needs that family members used to fulfill.

Lucan wrote about the formation of familial bonds between ruler and ruled during a period when the ruler's family were prominent figures in the Roman world. The questions of how to define the emperor's family, who belonged to it and what its place in politics should be, were key issues of debate in the Julio-Claudian period. In the next chapter, I focus on contests within and about the Julio-Claudian house, and the importance of those contests for defining the role of the emperor himself.

CHAPTER TWO

Contest and Control in the Emperor's House

The year 2 BCE was an interesting one for Augustus as *princeps* and as a father in his own household. This was the year when the Senate and the Roman people granted him the title of *pater patriae*, father of the fatherland, an honor that distinguished him as a benefactor and protector of Rome.[1] It was also the year that he condemned his daughter Julia to exile for the crime of adultery. These two events draw our attention to the importance of familial bonds, especially between fathers and children, in Roman efforts to conceptualize power, and to the ways that these relationships were fields of conflict and competition. The *Institutes of Gaius*, a legal commentary compiled in the late second century CE, point to the father's authority over his children as a "distinctive right of Roman citizens, for hardly any other peoples have the kind of power we hold over our children" (*ius proprium ciuium Romanorum . . . fere enim nulli alii sunt homines qui talem in filios suos habent potestatem qualem nos habemus*, Gai. *Inst.* 1.55).[2] At least in the case of Augustus, however, Gaius' suggestion that Roman fathers "held" power over their households is too glib: in ancient accounts, the first *princeps* is distinguished not only for his efforts to exercise his authority in his household, but also for the continuous resistance he faced in doing so.

In the last chapter, I focused on the contests for power in Lucan's epic account of the Roman civil wars, and on how those contests transformed the world of the family in the poem. I now examine the place of the emperor's family, the *domus Augusta*, in contests to define the role of the emperor in Julio-Claudian Rome. The phrase *domus Augusta* is first attested at the end of Augustus' reign, in a poem Ovid composed around 13 CE (*Pont.* 2.2.74), and near the beginning of Tiberius' rule, in three inscriptions from 19 CE.[3] Republican aristocratic families in the Republic had emphasized the *familia*, which referred to relations through the paternal line, rather than the *domus*, which typically included both paternal and maternal relations.[4] Under the principate, *domus* replaced *familia* as the preferred term for the aristocratic family unit. Augustus emphasized the *domus* rather than the *familia* in order to include relations through his sister Octavia and his daughter Julia in his family group, a valuable asset since he fathered no sons himself.[5] The membership and hierarchy of the *domus Augusta* was always in flux: by arranging marriages and adoptions, or by exiling family members who displeased him, the *princeps* could assert some control over who was in and who was out.[6] Other people's attitudes toward the emperor's family, however, did not necessarily correspond to the emperor's own point of view. Local elites were not passive recipients of instructions from the capital, but rather depicted the emperor and the imperial family to suit their own preconceptions and concerns.[7] In doing so, they presented their own visions of the *domus Augusta* and claimed the authority to define what it was. Ancient historians include episodes of conflict, often centered on the women in the emperor's family, that undermine the emperor's authority in and over the *domus Augusta*. Material and literary representations of the Julio-Claudian family reveal an ongoing debate over who belonged to the emperor's house, and, most crucially, who had the authority to decide.

I begin by examining images of the imperial family that offer divergent versions of the makeup of the *domus Augusta*. Drawing on Olivier Hekster's recent analysis of the importance of local traditions for dynastic imagery in the Empire, I show how local communities presented their own visions of the imperial *domus*, and thus raise the question of whose vision of the emperor's house should be trusted. These competing images of the Julio-Claudian family find an analogue in ancient literary texts, in the contests between the emperors and their family members. Some emperors, notably Augustus, sought to present themselves as the dominant figures in their households, but literary texts from the mid-first to early second century CE become increasingly attentive to the emperor's failure to establish his paternal authority. These contests for control in the emperor's house show elite Roman audiences that the emperor's power is always the result of conflict and negotiation, not an irrevocable truth. Most notably, imperial women in Tacitus' *Annals* become indicators of the contingency of the emperor's claims to power and of the fragility of one-man rule.

Defining the *Domus Augusta*

One of the most remarkable monuments from the age of Augustus is the Ara Pacis Augustae, the Altar of the Augustan Peace, which was dedicated by the Senate and constructed in Rome between 13 and 9 BCE. This was the first public monument in Rome to include sculptural reliefs with images of a family.[8] The dedicators of this monument situated Augustus and his family among their aristocratic peers in Rome. The north and south walls of the Ara Pacis show the *princeps* and his household (men, women, and children) taking part in a religious procession along with senators and priests. Livia, Augustus' wife, appears in the first group on the south frieze.[9] She is accompanied by Marcus Agrippa, son-in-law of the *princeps*, and a young boy, who is either Augustus' grandson or a foreign prince raised in his house.[10] Few other figures on the Ara Pacis, however, can be securely identified as portraits of specific individuals: what the figures share, as Beth Severy points out, is "an artificial family resemblance; even though many of them were not genetically related. . . . What is thus most stressed is the group entity of the family itself, and the role of Augustus as its *pater*."[11] Here on the Ara Pacis, the emperor's family members are publicly significant insofar as they can claim a connection to the *princeps* himself.

The Sebasteion, constructed in Aphrodisias in Asia Minor between 20 and 60 CE, offers a very different image of the emperor's family and the emperor's place within it. The city of Aphrodisias claimed a special relationship with the Julio-Claudians, dating back to their support for Julius Caesar and Octavian during the Roman civil wars of the first century BCE, and this monument reflects this bond and their attachment to the Julian house in particular.[12] The Sebasteion consisted of a temple and two portico buildings that bordered the path approaching the temple, one north and one south. These buildings are especially notable for sculptural reliefs that depict the Olympian gods together with members of the Julio-Claudian family, and in these images Agrippina the Younger plays a prominent role.[13] She was Augustus' great-granddaughter and two different emperors, Claudius

Figure 2.1. Claudius and Agrippina. Relief from the Sebasteion at Aphrodisias. New York University Excavations at Aphrodisias (G. Petruccioli)

(her husband) and Nero (her son), were linked through Agrippina to the founder of their dynasty. In one relief from the south building of the monument (dated to the late Claudian or early Neronian period), Claudius stands between a togate figure, a personification of the Senate or the *populus Romanus*, and Agrippina (she carries ears of wheat, a motif that assimilates her to the goddess Demeter).[14] The togate figure crowns Claudius with an oak wreath, and the emperor joins hands with Agrippina. The linked hands (*dextrarum iunctio*) suggest that they are harmonious partners, if not equals, and Claudius is the first emperor to be represented with his wife in this pose.[15]

This image is especially striking in comparison with other reliefs of Claudius from the same building of the Sebasteion, in which the emperor takes a decidedly dominant stance. In one, Claudius raises a weapon over a personification of Britannia, who lies at his feet, subject and conquered. Claudius stands in heroic nudity at the center of another relief, as two women (personifications of land and sea) kneel below him and offer gifts (a cornucopia and an oar).¹⁶ Claudius and Agrippina, by contrast, stand together, at the same level even if Agrippina remains in the background. A similar dynamic informs the representation of Agrippina and Nero on the north building. Here Agrippina is not only the emperor's partner but in fact his creator: outfitted with a crown and cornucopia in the guise of Tyche, she places a laurel wreath on Nero's head, indicating his ascent to imperial rule.¹⁷ For the sponsors of the Sebasteion, Agrippina's relationship to both Claudius and Nero, and her part in producing and sustaining their authority, is essential to the representation of the emperors themselves. In

Figure 2.2. Nero and Agrippina. Relief from the Sebasteion at Aphrodisias. New York University Excavations at Aphrodisias (G. Petruccioli)

contrast to the Ara Pacis, these reliefs draw attention to the exceptional status of members of the imperial house, and emphasize the interdependence between the emperor and his family.

The Ara Pacis and Sebasteion are just two examples of the vast body of images of the emperor's house, from municipal monuments and statue groups to small portraits on coins, scale weights, and scabbards.[18] These two monuments do not exactly conflict with one another: they were dedicated in different times (during Augustus' reign or under that of his successors), in different places (Rome, the imperial capital, and Aphrodisias, a town in the Greek East), and by different people (the Senate of Rome and municipal elites). Nevertheless, they represent distinct visions of the family that ruled Rome: the Ara Pacis and the Sebasteion show that different groups in the empire could present their own conceptions of the emperor's family, who belonged to it, and what status they held within it. These divergent ideas of the imperial house suggest that the *domus Augusta* had different meanings, and took different forms, in different settings.

When communities made dedications and decreed honors for the emperor and his family, they were guided not only by messages from the capital but by local traditions, values, and interests.[19] The funerary honors for Augustus' grandsons Lucius and Gaius in Pisae (modern Pisa), dedicated in 2 and 4 CE, illustrate these processes of communication and innovation.[20] The Pisan decree for Lucius follows a decree of the Senate at Rome, which detailed the honors that local governments should establish for Lucius. The decree for Gaius, however, as Greg Rowe has shown, contains inventions of the magistrates at Pisae.[21] While the decree for Lucius had simply listed his official titles (augur, consul designate, *princeps iuventutis*), the decree for Gaius is more colorful and effusive. The decree reports the circumstances of Gaius' death in an epic style, asserting that the young man died "waging a war beyond the farthest borders of the Roman people and . . . defeating or accepting the surrender of the most warlike and most powerful nations."[22] Notably, the Pisans assert a special connection with Gaius when they praise him as "most just and most like his father in his virtues and the sole defense of our colony." With these funeral honors, the Pisans present their own understanding of the emperor's house, according to which the emperor's family members reflect the emperor's greatness (Gaius is "most like his father in virtues") and also deserve esteem in their own right (he is the "sole defense" of Pisae).[23]

While the Pisan honors affirm the special distinction that Gaius and Lucius received from Augustus, local communities did not always adopt the *princeps'* accounting of the *domus Augusta*. Tiberius reportedly vetoed honors that the Senate had awarded his mother Livia, and she rarely appears in coins issued by the central mints during Tiberius' reign. Yet she was honored as a patron of building projects and as priestess of the deified Augustus in communities across the Empire, and provincial coins emphasize her role as mother and grandmother.[24] Furthermore, epigraphic evidence indicates that local authorities did not consistently respond to official sanctions against members of the imperial house.[25] Augustus exiled his daughter Julia in 2 BCE, but cities in the Greek East might have retained her image in dynastic monuments: no securely identified portraits of Julia survive, but her name appears in multiple inscriptions that accompanied dynastic statue groups, and there is no evidence for attempts to alter those inscriptions after Julia's disgrace.[26] Even after Caligula exiled his sisters Agrippina the Younger and Julia Livilla, they continued to be honored as benefactors in Mytilene, a city where their parents, Agrippina the Elder and Germanicus, had once resided.[27] Some discrepancies probably reflect practical obstacles to renovating dynastic monuments, and those responsible for their upkeep might well hesitate to follow the latest news, in case future emperors changed their minds (for example, Caligula restored the reputation of his mother Agrippina the Elder after Tiberius had condemned her to exile).[28] Even if these images did not reflect events in the capital, however, they are no less meaningful as representations of the *domus Augusta*. Hekster has emphasized the success of imperial programs of dynastic imagery when there was a "shared field of reference between the emperor and those he tried to reach."[29] Local residents, not the emperor, were the regular viewers of these municipal monuments: disgraced members of the *domus Augusta* could remain important for local audiences.[30]

Agrippina the Younger offers the most striking evidence for the persistent visual presence of a member of the *domus Augusta* despite the emperor's objections. As the sister of Caligula, wife of Claudius, and mother of Nero, Agrippina appears repeatedly in imperial portraiture.[31] When Nero first came to power, his mother was celebrated in coinage issued by the central mints: in order to highlight his descent from Augustus, Nero took the exceptional step of "including matrilineal descent in his full name" and was "the first Roman emperor to include both his parents' ancestry in his nomenclature."³² One extraordinary coin, dated to 55 CE, features jugate busts of Nero and Agrippina, and a coin from the previous year presents busts of mother and son facing one another.³³ These portraits, apparently modeled on Seleucid and Ptolemaic images, were unprecedented in Roman coinage, but they reflect Agrippina's singular status in the Julio-Claudian period. Nero eventually turned against his mother, finally orchestrating her murder in 59 CE. Already in 56, however, Agrippina had abruptly disappeared from central coinage, but she continued to be portrayed in provincial coins, identified as the mother of the emperor, and the numerous surviving portraits of Agrippina indicate that they were produced up to the time of her death.³⁴ In his study of Roman dynastic imagery, Hekster explains that "the sudden disappearance of Agrippina references in central coinage did not cohere with local expectations, and thus had little effect."³⁵ For some inhabitants of the Roman Empire, Agrippina remained a member of their vision of the *domus Augusta*, no matter the changes in Rome. Images of Agrippina need not be interpreted as an act of resistance to the emperor, but they do suggest that, in practice, the emperor was not the sole arbiter of who was recognized as a member of the ruling house.

An honorary monument from Amisus, situated on the coast of the Black Sea, offers further evidence of local favor for a member of the imperial family whom the emperor did not promote. The Amisus statue group included images of Nero, his late stepbrother Britannicus, and his wife Poppaea.³⁶ It was probably dedicated between 63 and 65 CE, the years of Poppaea's marriage to Nero and eight years after Britannicus' death. By including Nero, Poppaea, and Britannicus together, the citizens of Amisus expressed their vision of the *domus Augusta*, as an entity that included the emperor, his relation to previous rulers (Britannicus was the son of Claudius), and the prospect of dynastic continuity (Poppaea).³⁷ For the elites of Amisus who dedicated this monument, determining the emperor's attitude toward each figure they represented was not as important as asserting their ties to the ruling house in Rome in the past, present, and future.

The diverse images of the imperial house show that the emperor's idea of the *domus Augusta* did not automatically take priority over more local concerns and interests. Those who honored the Julio-Claudian family did not always acknowledge the emperor's authority to define his household, nor they did always trust that his vision of the *domus Augusta* should outweigh theirs. In the remainder of this chapter, I will look at more immediate challenges to the emperor's power over and in the *domus Augusta*. The problem of determining the membership and hierarchy of the emperor's family, and the efforts of different players to contest the emperor's determination, are persistent features of ancient accounts of Julio-Claudian rule.

Dominating the *Domus Augusta*

Years before Octavian became Augustus, his sometime rival, sometime partner Mark Antony "accused him (over and above his speedy marriage with Livia) of snatching the wife of a former consul away from the banquet room and off to a bedroom, right in front of her husband, and then bringing her back to the party with red ears and rather disheveled hair" (*super festinatas Liuiae nuptias obicit et feminam consularem e triclinio uiri coram in cubiculum abductam, rursus in conuiuium rubentibus auriculis incomptiore capillo reductam*, Suet. *Aug.* 69.1).[38] Octavian's violence against the woman at the banquet is a performance of his dominance over her and over her husband. Antony tells this story to undermine his rival, but it is in some ways consistent with Octavian's later conduct as first head of the family that ruled Rome. In ancient literature, the first *princeps* recognizes the opportunities that his household affords him for asserting his dominance: he becomes a model of masculine performance of power in the house, even in the face of continuous resistance.

In Roman law, the *paterfamilias*, or head of the household, was distinguished by his *patria potestas*, the capacity to control free as well as enslaved persons.[39] Ancient accounts of the first *princeps* play with his recurrent efforts to demonstrate his control over his household, and with the constant difficulties he faced in doing so. Augustus was infamous for his repeated, and repeatedly thwarted, attempts to secure a successor by arranging marriages and adoptions.[40] He married his only child, his daughter Julia, to his nephew Marcellus, but he died. Next, he married Julia to Agrippa, his closest associate, and after Agrippa's death, to Tiberius, who was required to divorce his first wife to marry Julia instead. Augustus adopted Agrippa as well as Julia's and Agrippa's children, Lucius and Gaius, but these two died as young men, and he eventually had to settle on Tiberius, the son of his wife Livia. Tiberius already had a son of his own, but he was required to adopt his nephew Germanicus (also a grandnephew of Augustus) as his heir.[41]

Ensuring a line of succession was only one of Augustus' troubles as *princeps* and as a *pater*. When Seneca describes the risks that Augustus faced, from military campaigns to competitors for political office, he includes the *princeps'* daughter Julia and her lovers, "noble young men bound to adultery as if to an oath of service," on the list of things that "terrified [Augustus] in his declining years" (*filia et tot nobiles iuuenes adulterio uelut sacramento adacti iam infractam aetatem territabant*, Sen. *De brev. vit.* 4.5). Augustus eventually exiled not only his daughter but also two of his grandchildren, Julia the Younger and Agrippa Postumus, the former for adultery and the latter for his "disgraceful and insolent nature" (*ob ingenium sordidum ac ferox*, Suet. *Aug.* 65.1). Suetonius reports that Augustus always called the three of them "his three boils and three tumors" (*tris uomicas ac tria carcinomata sua*, 65.4). His child and grandchildren must have embarrassed the *princeps* in part because they failed to conform to his program of rejuvenating Roman morals. Among the most distinctive developments of the Augustan age were the *lex Iulia de maritandis ordinibus* (18 BCE) and the *lex Pappia Poppaea* (9 CE), legislation that outlawed adultery and rewarded childbearing, among other provisions.[42]

Augustus' uncooperative descendants also represented a more fundamental challenge to his dominance over the *domus Augusta*.[43] Julia's popularity with the people of Rome conflicted with Augustus' performance of paternal power: at a public gathering, the people begged Augustus to recall her from exile, but "he could in no way be moved, and before the assembly he wished on them the same sort of wives and daughters" (*exorari nullo modo potuit . . . tales filias talesque coniuges pro contione imprecatus*, Suet. *Aug.* 65.3). This occasion might have presented an opportunity for Augustus to yield and win popular favor, but he resolutely resisted the people's demands: the question was not only whether or not Julia should be recognized as a member of the emperor's household, but who should be trusted to decide. Augustus aimed to demonstrate that his command over the *domus Augusta* ought to be paramount, but the people's sympathies for Julia indicated that the *princeps'* authority to make judgments about his household was not always secure.

Tiberius faced similar problems in his efforts to perform his control over the membership and hierarchy of the *domus Augusta*. When Germanicus, Tiberius' adopted heir, died in 19 CE, his widow Agrippina the Elder became one of Tiberius' rivals. She was Augustus' granddaughter, and Tacitus claims that "nothing got under Tiberius' skin more than people's passionate enthusiasm for Agrippina, since they called her the glory of the fatherland, the last of Augustus' blood, the sole example of a bygone age" (*nihil tamen Tiberium magis penetrauit quam studia hominum accensa in Agrippi-*

nam, cum decus patriae, solum Augusti sanguinem, unicum antiquitatis specimen appellarent, Ann. 3.4). Other ancient historians emphasize Tiberius' animosity toward his daughter-in-law; she was ultimately exiled in 29 CE and later committed suicide.[44] Tiberius conformed to the example set by Augustus, not because Augustus would have rejected Agrippina, but because the first *princeps* also sought to perform his authority regardless of popular sentiments. By removing Agrippina from his *domus*, Tiberius insisted on the primacy of his own accounting of the *domus Augusta* in contrast to anyone else's.

The Augustan performance of paternal authority promises a kind of stability in the political community: if everyone trusts the emperor's judgments about the membership and hierarchy of the *domus Augusta*, Rome can avoid the disruption that competition and conflict within his household might bring.[45] As we will see, aristocratic Romans criticized emperors who failed to control their households, but the emperor's assertion of dominance over the *domus Augusta* also posed certain risks to his elite male peers. Caligula, Tiberius' successor, married his sister Drusilla to a former consul, but then "took her away and kept her openly as his lawful wife; when he was ill, he also set her up as heir of his property and his power" (*abduxit et in modum iustae uxoris propalam habuit, heredem quoque bonorum atque imperii aeger instituit*, Suet. *Calig.* 24.1). Caligula's relations with and promotion of his sister were unorthodox, but he also followed the Augustan model of rule to its logical, if extreme, conclusion. The emperor claims total authority to order his household as he sees fit, whatever the constraints of prior relationships (such as Drusilla's marriage) or norms of behavior, and without concern for the objections of others.[46]

When Claudius, the next Julio-Claudian emperor, married Agrippina the Younger, his own niece and another of Caligula's sisters, he seemed conscious of the problems that the emperor's claims to control the *domus Augusta* might produce. Claudius finds himself in need of a new bride after his previous wife, Messalina, was executed for adultery. In contrast to Augustus and Tiberius, who exiled women of their household over the protests of the people, Claudius declares that he will marry Agrippina in order to comply with the will of Rome: "asked whether Caesar would yield to the people's demands and the Senate's authority, he responded that he was one of the citizens and could not overcome consensus" (*percontatusque Caesarem an iussis populi, an auctoritati senatus cederet, ubi ille unum se ciuium et consensui imparem respondet*, Tac. *Ann.* 12.5).[47] Lucius Vitellius, a censor and one of Agrippina's supporters, praises the emperor in the Senate, contrasting Claudius' modesty (*modestia*) with earlier days, when "wives were snatched away as the Caesars desired . . . another pattern was to be established, according to which the emperor would accept a wife" (*abripi coniuges ad libita Caesarum . . . statueretur immo documentum, quo uxorem imperator acciperet,* 12.6). Vitellius may be alluding to the behavior of both Caligula and young Octavian: Claudius' acquiescence to the Senate and the Roman people, Vitellius suggests, is to be preferred to the aggression of his predecessors. Yet Claudius' marriage is not a sign of the prestige of the Senate under his rule. The emperor chooses Agrippina on the advice of his freedmen, whom he invites to counsel him in selecting his next bride (*in consilium uocat ac promere sententiam et edicere rationes iubet,* 12.1).[48] As Tacitus describes him, the emperor is at the mercy of freedmen's arguments, Agrippina's charms (*Agrippinae inlecebris,* 12.3), and the "slavish tricks" (*seruilis fallacias,* 12.4) of Vitellius. When Claudius yields his authority over his household, he makes room for challengers who are at odds with the proclivities of the aristocracy and with their expectations for who can participate in Roman political life.

Claudius' marriage to Agrippina was far from the first example of this emperor's failure to dominate his *domus*. Messalina is notorious for eluding her imperial husband: she even stages a wedding to her lover Silius while Claudius is still alive (11.26–27).[49] It is the emperor's freedmen, anxious about their own prospects at the court, who take action (11.28). Narcissus, one of the most prominent members of Claudius' household staff, accuses Silius of usurping the emperor's place in his home and beyond it: if Claudius does not want to demand that Silius return the emperor's house, slaves, and the other trappings of his rank (*ne domum seruitia et ceteros fortunae paratus reposceret*), the emperor should at least remember that "the people, Senate, and army have seen the marriage, and if you do not act quickly, the husband will take Rome" (*matrimonium Silii uidit populus et senatus et miles; ac ni propere agis, tenet urbem maritus,* 11.30). Narcissus reminds Claudius of the role that others play in recognizing the emperor, and of Messalina's capacity to influence their acknowledgment of his authority. Claudius even begins to doubt himself, "overcome with fear . . . so that he repeatedly asked whether he himself ruled the empire, whether Silius was a private citizen" (*eo pauore offusum . . . ut identidem interrogaret an ipse imperii potens, an Silius priuatus esset,* 11.31). When Narcissus takes the emperor to Silius' house, he points out that Messalina's new husband has taken possession of household objects that once belonged to Claudius' family (*quidquid auitum Neronibus et Drusis*, 11.35). Messalina, too, is a piece of imperial property, and (like the emperor's family possessions) she informs how others decide who the emperor is. If the emperor's authority over his *domus* could be contested, as we will see, the contest extended to the emperor's position outside his *domus* too.

Agrippina's *Domus*: A Different Standpoint

In his first speech to the Senate (an address likely composed by his tutor, Seneca), the new emperor Nero sought to win the approval and allay the concerns of the Roman aristocracy. According to Tacitus' account, the seventeen-year old ruler promised that "nothing in his household would be up for sale or open for solicitation; house and state would be kept separate" (*nihil in penatibus suis uenale aut ambitioni peruium; discretam domum et rem publicam*, *Ann.* 13.4).[50] Here Nero articulates the stakes of competition and jostling for influence in the imperial *domus*: the possibility of currying favor with the members of the emperor's household, such as the women and freedmen, necessarily compromises the distinction between the emperor's house and the polity. By contrast, when the emperor asserts his dominance in his household, there are fewer opportunities for informal and indirect exercise of power by figures other than the *princeps*. The *Annals* were composed in the early second century CE, so Tacitus' audience was well aware that Nero's guarantee of *discreta domus et res publica* had failed, and that other members of his household, especially his mother, Agrippina the Younger, had repeatedly called the emperor's authority into question.

Ancient sources tend to relegate certain groups to the shadowy realm of influence rather than of political power. If women, slaves, and freedmen obtain power through means other than those available to the senatorial aristocracy, then their actions are by definition suspect, and potentially evidence of social breakdown.[51] In recent years, however, scholarship on the early Empire has offered a more complex picture of the emperor's household, of the roles and functions of its members in the management of the empire, and of the ways that different players in the world of the court could assert their authority over one another and even over the emperor himself.[52] My question is not whether the emperor's family members were legitimate or illegitimate political players, but what these figures reveal about ancient conceptions of the emperor's position.[53] Nero's family, especially the women, are central to Tacitus' narrative of his reign, a narrative that challenges not only Nero's fitness to rule but also the extent to which any emperor could hope to dominate the *domus Augusta*.

Nero is distinguished from other Julio-Claudian rulers by his youth, his mother's role in his accession and in his reign, and his self-indulgence; while all of these characteristics could describe other emperors, Nero is the climax of a pattern established by his predecessors.[54] In the *Annals*, Nero represents the problems all dynastic rulers encounter: his reign is a kind of unplanned experiment, in which all factors that might destabilize the political community under one-man rule simultaneously come into play. I argue that Tacitus' account of the women in Nero's house allows us to look beyond the emperor's own perspective and objectives: the imperial *domus* under Nero highlights the openings for disruption that threaten all monarchical regimes.

Ancient historians, including Tacitus, used emperors' wives, mothers, and daughters to level critiques against specific emperors, and against "an imperial system which by its very nature gave household life a presence on the public stage."[55] These accounts of tensions and disputes in the emperor's *domus* also draw attention to the ways in which emperors are dependent on and vulnerable to their family members. This vulnerability is cause for alarm in the world of the *Annals*, in which women are properly confined to the margins of politics. When it comes to analysis of power relations, however, marginal figures possess certain advantages: feminist standpoint theory argues that oppressed groups can develop a "standpoint," or "a source of critical insight about how the dominant society thinks and is structured."[56] "Others" within a society are uniquely positioned to critique the worldview that marks them as outsiders and subordinates. Tacitus' project does not align with the political objectives of standpoint theory, and we do not know how the historical Agrippina the Younger, to take one example, perceived the world in which she lived (although she wrote memoirs, they have not survived).[57] I use standpoint theory as a strategy of literary interpretation, to make sense of the meaning of women in Tacitus' narrative of the imperial court. The women of Nero's house serve as guides to power relations in Tacitus' *Annals*: because the emperor's family members operate outside the traditional framework of aristocratic political institutions, they are able to challenge the "naturalness" of a political system that officially excludes them.[58] Figures like Agrippina the Younger, Nero's wife Poppaea, and Claudius' daughter Octavia reveal that the order of the society they inhabit is always subject to change. Despite Tacitus' antagonism toward a regime that blurs *domus* and *res publica*, in the *Annals* these women are uniquely able to demonstrate the contingencies on which the emperor's power depends, to argue against the emperor's claims to dominance.[59] To equate the life of the polity with the world of the emperor's household, as Tacitus does, is both to challenge the emperor's power and to draw attention to the fragility of one-man rule.

From the beginning of her rise at Claudius' court, Agrippina presents complications for the emperor's control of his household. Following Agrippina's marriage to Claudius, Tacitus declares, "the state was transformed from that moment and all things were submitted to a woman," although her rule was "a strict and almost manly subjugation" (*uersa ex eo ciuitas et cuncta feminae oboediebant . . . adductum et quasi uirile seruitium*, 12.7).[60] Her dominance is especially apparent in Tacitus' account of the death of Claudius in 54 CE, which ancient historians claim that Agrippina engineered.[61] Tacitus reports that Agrippina recruits Halotus, the emperor's food taster, to sprinkle the poison in a dish of mushrooms for the emperor to eat. Much to Agrippina's chagrin, Claudius almost digests the poison and survives; it falls to his doctor Xenophon to thrust a feather down the emperor's throat (as if to help him vomit up the food that is troubling him) and thus to finish off the murder (12.66). Tacitus uses Claudius' death to emphasize the public significance of the emperor's house, in contrast to the institutions of the Roman state:

> Meanwhile the Senate was summoned and consuls and priests made vows for the health of the *princeps*, while he (although he was already dead) was protected with coverings and poultices, until matters were arranged to strengthen Nero's claim to rule. First of all, as if she were overwhelmed by grief and was seeking solace, Agrippina embraced Britannicus, calling him the spitting image of his father and using various tricks to keep him from leaving the room. She also detained his sisters Antonia and Octavia and shut off every entrance with guards, and frequently sent out announcements that the *princeps* was on the mend. (12.68)[62]

This account steers our attention to the city beyond the palace, then back to the upheaval within the household, and then again to the reception of these events in the outside world. When Tacitus shows Agrippina in command of the emperor's household, he takes his reader to a moment when the impulse to respect aristocratic men, and to overlook everyone else, is misguided and misleading. The magistrates and the priests, the traditional foci of public life, stand outside the world in which the key decisions are being made: Tacitus' audience needs to unlearn their preconceptions about who shapes the life of the community. Their best guide to this new way of thinking about politics, moreover, is Agrippina herself, who appreciates the power that those nearest the emperor can wield.[63] The murder of Claudius inverts the circumstances that attended his wedding to Agrippina: in that instance, Claudius waited inside the palace while the Senate discussed the suitability of the marriage (*opperiri intra palatium*, 12.5). Now Claudius is again trapped in his house, but the imperial house has become the only space for political action, and the men who hold public office are excluded from it. Agrippina has no formal position in traditional political institutions, but it is nevertheless her perspective on politics that is most reliable.

The Agrippina that Tacitus presents is not unique in the history of ruling women in Rome: she is a perceptive reader of the political world that she inhabits in part because she has learned from her predecessors. Tanaquil, wife of one of the early Roman kings, also took care to conceal her husband's death in order to prepare the way for the successor she had chosen (Livy 1.41). Much closer to Agrippina's own time, when Augustus died, Livia "surrounded the house and the roads with keen guards, and happy reports were spread abroad, until (when everything was provided for as the circumstances advised) the same report declared that Augustus had died and Tiberius had come to power" (*acribus namque custodiis domum et uias saepserat Liuia, laetique interdum nuntii uulgabantur, donec prouisis quae tempus monebat simul excessisse Augustum et rerum potiri Neronem fama eadem tulit, Ann.* 1.5). Both Livy and Tacitus are (to be sure) employing standard criticisms of conniving women in power, and it is no surprise that Tacitus' Agrippina might be modeled on her foremothers.[64] Agrippina's reprise of their roles, however, is precisely what makes her character a valuable guide to Roman thinking on one-man rule. The combination of the weak emperor (Claudius), his cunning wife (Agrippina), and his young heir (Nero) makes this episode an important test case for the kind of politics that is always a risk under one-man rule. While Claudius' death offers Agrippina, and figures like her, the opportunity to take power, it is not an exceptional event, but one that Rome has experienced before and must always expect to repeat.[65]

Sometimes Agrippina is successful in convincing her contemporaries to recognize the fact that she is not a private figure, that as part of the emperor's *domus* she is necessarily influential in the world of the *res publica*. Under

Claudius, a group of imprisoned Britons come to entreat Claudius for mercy, and the emperor and his wife receive them seated side-by-side, on separate daises (12.36–7). Tacitus declares that "it was surely something new and foreign to the old ways, for a woman to preside over Roman standards: she carried herself as a partner of the empire birthed by her ancestors" (*nouum sane et moribus ueterum insolitum, feminam signis Romanis praesidere: ipsa semet parti a maioribus suis imperii sociam ferebat*, 12.37).[66] On another occasion, when Claudius staged a naval battle as a spectacular entertainment, they presided together, the emperor in a military cloak, and Agrippina in a Greek soldier's mantle made of golden cloth (*chlamyde aurata*, 12.56).[67] These episodes of Agrippina's self-display are surely meant to symbolize Claudius' weakness, but they also point to a process of negotiation over how to understand and to represent the public role of the emperor's wife. Was it better to conceal her from public view, and thus to assert a distinction between the emperor's house and the political community, or to present her in style, and thus to acknowledge her privileged relationship with the emperor? During the early days of Nero's reign, the Senate seems to have grappled with this very question when they allowed Agrippina to attend a meeting of the Senate, when they discussed decrees that undermined acts of Claudius: "The senators, who were called to the Palatine for this reason, arranged it so that she [Agrippina] would stand by the doors added at the back of the room, concealed by a curtain, which kept her from seeing but not from hearing" (*obtinuere patres, qui in Palatium ob id uocabantur ut adstaret additis a tergo foribus uelo discreta, quod uisum arceret, auditus non adimeret*, *Ann.* 13.5). The curtain keeps Agrippina out of sight, and thus serves to deflect attention from her influence in the early years of Nero's reign.[68] Yet even as Agrippina remains concealed, she has made her way into a traditionally male space.[69] Her presence indicates that the Roman male aristocracy has had to grapple with, and respond to, the reality of this woman's power in the emperor's house.

While Agrippina endeavors to win recognition of her status, this is a contest that she can and does lose. In one episode, a delegation from Armenia comes to plead a case before Nero: Agrippina "would have ascended the emperor's platform and gone to sit together with him, but—while the others were transfixed by fear—Seneca advised him to go to meet his mother as she approached. Thus, shame was prevented under the pretext of filial devotion" (*escendere suggestum imperatoris et praesidere simul parabat, nisi ceteris pauore defixis Seneca admonuisset uenienti matri ocurreret. ita specie pietatis obuiam itum dedecori*, 13.5).⁷⁰ Tacitus claims that allowing Agrippina to join the emperor would have been a disgrace (*dedecori*); it is clear that he does not admire her gumption.⁷¹ Her move to sit beside her son, however, is not an impulsive act of female transgression, but a conscientious effort to adapt established modes of political display for her own purposes. Augustus used to sit between the consuls in their curule chairs during Senate meetings to indicate that he had the same authority as they did, even though he did not have their title.⁷² Agrippina uses the tactics of her male predecessors to assert a claim to power even though she has no official standing to do so: in a sense, she calls into question the authority of her male peers to exclude her from among them. Tacitus' assertion that those present were "transfixed with fear" at Agrippina's approach reflects elite male anxiety over the rise of imperial women in politics, but he makes it clear that this contest between the emperor's mother and the Senate could have ended in Agrippina's favor.

Agrippina's opportunities for asserting her dominance and demanding recognition are short-lived, as Nero soon turns against his mother: she is ultimately put to death on Nero's orders. Yet even though Agrippina becomes Nero's victim, she also serves as a kind of limitation on the emperor's ability to rule others: she identifies alternatives to Nero and thus calls his supremacy into question. When she loses Nero's favor, Agrippina actively seeks rivals to her son. Tacitus claims that she "welcomed tribunes and centurions as friends; she showed respect to the names and distinction of noble men who still remained, as though she were looking for a leader and a faction" (*tribunos et centuriones comiter excipere, nomina et uirtutes nobilium, qui etiam tum supererant, in honore habere, quasi quaereret ducem et partis*, 13.18).⁷³ The emperor's mother apparently enjoyed some success in her efforts to find supporters, as Nero took action to isolate her from her partisans: "so that she would not be visited with crowds of people participating in the morning *salutatio*, he divided the household and moved his mother to Antonia's [Claudius' mother's] former house" (*ne coetu salutantium frequentaretur, separat domum matremque transfert in eam quae Antoniae fuerat*, 13.18). Attention and endorsement from Agrippina, who was mother of the emperor and also great-granddaughter of Augustus, was a valuable commodity, and it was one that she could exploit to the detriment of her son's authority. When the emperor begins to contemplate murdering his mother, surely the easiest way to be rid of her influence and machinations, Burrus, the captain of his praetorian guard, objects: he reminds Nero that "the praetorians were bound to the whole house of the Caesars, and because they remembered Germanicus, they would not dare violence against his progeny" (*ille praetorianos toti Caesarum domui obstrictos memoresque Germanici nihil aduersus progeniem eius atrox ausuros respondit*, 14.7).[74] Whatever the preferences of the emperor, Agrippina has influence and standing that he has to contend with. Agrippina understands that the emperor wants the recognition of his family, who confirm that the emperor belongs to their group and has a particular place in it.[75]

Agrippina was later accused of supporting the imperial ambitions of Rubellius Plautus, who was (like Nero) a great-great-grandson of Augustus: the rumor was that Agrippina intended "to attack the Republic again, through marriage to him and on his authority" (*coniugioque eius et imperio rem publicam rursus inuadere*, 13.19).[76] Although Agrippina naturally denied the charges, the notion that she had the power to promote alternative emperors was not far-fetched. Octavia, who was the daughter of Claudius and Nero's wife, exercises a similar authority, albeit indirectly. When Nero wants to divorce Octavia and to marry his mistress Poppaea, he delays his plans, according to Tacitus, because of "[Octavia's] father's name and the people's favor" (*nomine patris et studiis populi*, 14.59). This concern seems to have been familiar to Nero's contemporaries: in the *Octavia*, a historical tragedy usually dated to the years following the wars of 69 CE, a chorus of the Roman people complains that "no new bride should enter the bedroom of our *princeps*, and his wife, Claudius' offspring, should keep her ancestral gods" (*nec noua coniunx nostri thalamos / principis intret teneatque suos / nupta penates Claudia proles*, Oct. 276–78). Nero ultimately goes through with his new marriage. Octavia's supporters pull down the statues of Poppaea, carry the images of Octavia on their shoulders, and restore them to public spaces in the city (*effigies Poppaeae proruunt, Octauiae imagines gestant umeris, spargunt floribus foroque ac templis statuunt*, 14.61). Like the local communities who retained honorary monuments for disgraced members of the imperial house, the people of Rome use images to express their own conception of the *domus Augusta*, countering the emperor's point of view. Poppaea advises the emperor to be wary of Octavia's partisans: she warns Nero, "if they lose hope that Octavia will be Nero's wife, they will give her a husband" (*si desperent uxorem Neronis fore Octauiam, illi maritum daturos*, 14.61). Poppaea worries that Octavia is supposed to belong to the emperor: Octavia, not Poppaea, indicates to others whom they ought to recognize as the ruler.[77] In a delightful accident of history, Poppaea's conversation with Nero is a kind of inversion of a story about Nadezhda Krupskaya, Lenin's widow, and Stalin: when Stalin objected to Krupskaya agitating against him, he warned her that she should keep quiet or he would find someone else to be Lenin's widow.[78] Poppaea warns Nero that when he replaces his wife, the people might find someone else to be emperor.

None of these women overthrow the emperor and install a new one. The popular favor that Octavia receives does not ultimately protect her from Nero's violence. When Nero signals his displeasure with his mother, Agrippina's supporters largely desert her (13.19). While Claudius was emperor, Messalina's marriage to Silius (discussed above) was primarily a threat to him because other parties (the Senate, people, and army) were aware of what she had done. Yet while they do not succeed in ousting the emperor, these women show that his authority is more tenuous than he would like to claim.[79] They offer Tacitus' elite male audience a valuable way to read the politics of one-man rule: they point to potential hiccups in the emperor's project to establish his singular dominance, and they remind those around them to look for moments when the emperor fails. In Tacitus' narrative, the emperor's house is the place where his authority is least secure, and where his position most clearly depends on contests that are not always under his control.

Conclusion

If we consider the emperor's house from the perspective of the emperor himself, it is a space that affords him valuable opportunities to perform his authority. Augustus and those of his successors who followed his approach aimed to assert their control over the makeup and hierarchy of their household, regardless of the resistance they encountered from within the *domus* or from outside it. Both visual and literary representations of the Julio-Claudian household, however, suggest that the validity and value of the emperor's conception of the *domus Augusta* was subject to debate in the Julio-Claudian period and in later narratives of it. Local communities could adhere to established practices for honoring members of the *domus Augusta* even when circumstances in Rome had changed. Tacitus' account of the *domus Augusta* under Claudius and Nero exposes not just the weakness of particular rulers but the volatility of one-man rule: the constant conflicts for dominance in the imperial household remind Tacitus' audience of the instability and contingency of any emperor's claims to power.

These contests in Nero's *domus* called into question some deeply held ideas about power, and about who could and could not claim it, among the

Roman elite. Augustus' performance of dominance, even when unsuccessful, at least reaffirmed traditional conceptions of who was most important in the life of the polity: the *princeps* who maintained his control over his household as *paterfamilias* promised Rome's ruling class some continuity between the old order and the new. Nero's house, by contrast, represents a more obvious rupture with the past: the overweening women in Tacitus' narrative are a problem for his aristocratic readers, who might object both to an excessively dominating *princeps* and to the women who emerged into the life of the polity when he failed to keep his household in line. In the next chapter, I turn to another aspect of rulers' houses, the architecture of imperial residences, and to how the emperor, his contemporary audience, and later ancient historians used these spaces to contest and define one-man rule.

CHAPTER THREE

Where to See the Emperor

Augustus and Nero in Rome

The "Consolation to Livia," an anonymous first-century poem once attributed to Ovid, offers comfort and advice to the wife of Augustus on the death of her son Drusus. The poet reminds Livia that her grief is not a private affair. While the people look to Livia for a model of strength and endurance, she lives subject to public observation:

> The same things don't suit both the common people and their leading lights: Fortune has set you on high and commanded you to protect your honored place: Livia, bear your burden. You draw eyes and ears to yourself, we observe your deeds, nor can the ruler's speech be concealed. Remain in your high place and rise above your sorrows, and keep your spirit unshaken as much as you can. (347–55)[1]

The poet's assertion that Livia is exposed to her subjects' gaze is in part intended to flatter: the fact that she attracts attention is proof of her "honored place" (*locum honoratum*) as well as of the special position of the emperor's *domus* in Rome. Yet Livia in the "Consolation" is also supposed to be wary of the eyes of others. She has to restrain her display of grief in order to defend (*tueri*) her place and stay (*mane*) in her high position. By claiming that the ruler's speech cannot be concealed (*nec uox missa potest principis ore tegi*), the poet emphasizes the association between ruling and being seen, regardless of the actual resources available to the emperor and his family to manage their encounters with the public eye. The visibility of the ruler and his house in Julio-Claudian political culture and thought is the focus of the following two chapters.

In this chapter, I examine houses built by Julio-Claudian emperors, which were sites for experimenting with imperial visibility. The emperors who built their palaces and the writers who discussed them participated in debates over where and how the emperor should be seen. Should the emperor present himself to public view? Who was his most important audience? What were the advantages and costs, for ruler and ruled, if he was invisible? I focus on Augustus' complex on the Palatine hill and Nero's Domus Aurea (figure 3.1), which were both spaces to stage encounters with the public eye. The architecture and locations of these houses show that they were designed to attract and impress observers in the city of Rome. Ancient historians, however, make Augustus and Nero representatives of competing visions of the emperor's relationship to the public eye, and thus of his place in the community.

Even if the emperor was not personally visible, seeing the emperor's house was one way to see the emperor himself. In Livy's account of the earliest days of the Republic, the consul Publius Valerius Publicola (discussed in the introduction) discomfited his fellow citizens when he began to build a house at the top of the Velian hill: they read the house as a sign of the man's excessively ambitious disposition (Livy 2.7.6). To quiet their fears, Publicola promised to build a house that would allow his neighbors to keep an eye on him (*uos supra suspectum me ciuem habitetis*, 2.7.11). To see Publicola's house was to see what place Publicola claimed in Rome—as aspiring king or as modest citizen-leader. One way of penalizing elite Romans was to destroy their houses, thus ensuring that no presence of the disgraced would be visible in the landscape.[2] After Cicero, the foremost orator and politician of his day, was sent into exile, his enemy Clodius demolished his house on the Palatine hill, building a shrine to the goddess Libertas, Liberty, in its place. When Augustus inherited the estates of his rival Vedius Pollio, he tore down the house and had a public portico built where Pollio once lived, so that he would have no monument (μνημόσυνον) in Rome (Dio Cass. 54.23.6).[3] For the ruling class in Rome, the house secured the place of its owner in the life of the community and in the public eye.

Augustus' constructions on the Palatine included grand public buildings and his own *domus*, a space that some ancient writers, notably Suetonius, associated with the humility and self-restraint of the first *princeps*.[4] Augustus' Palatine house embodies the tension between seeking public attention and performing ambivalence toward the public eye, a tension that was central to the self-presentation of Julio-Claudian emperors and ancient assessments of their efforts. Augustus' assertion of modesty suggests that he was wary of provoking his fellow aristocrats in Rome, but it was also an implicit acknowledgment that the emperor belonged at the center of public attention. In Nero's Domus Aurea, by contrast, the emperor flaunted and celebrated his own publicity: his palace recreates a country villa in the middle of the capital, and so suggests that the emperor's affairs always require an audience, even in a space associated with leisure and distance from the demands of urban life. While Augustus and Nero aimed to perform different attitudes toward their own visibility, both of their houses make lack of privacy and exposure to public view key aspects of what it means to rule in Rome. Tiberius' Villa Iovis on the island of Capri, with which I conclude this chapter, expresses a very different attitude toward the emperor's publicity. The archaeological evidence shows that this site was designed to accommodate and impress visitors, although it was also remote and difficult to reach: in a sense, the emperor's guests on Capri became an audience for his vanishing act. In the historical accounts, however, Tiberius is famous for moving to Capri in an effort (not always successful) to conceal himself from view. Tacitus and Suetonius, I argue, use Tiberius' house to show that the emperor is always impossible to ignore—even when those he rules would most like to look away.

The House of Augustus on the Palatine Hill

In his handbook on winning elections in Rome, Cicero's brother Quintus emphasized the importance of the house to successful political campaigns. He encouraged those who sought political office to maintain the goodwill of "intimates and members of the household . . . tribesmen, neighbors, freedmen, even slaves, for essentially all the talk that makes your reputation in the forum comes from sources from your house" (*quisque est intimus ac maxime domesticus . . . tum ut tribules, ut uicini, ut clientes, ut denique liberti, postremo etiam serui tui; nam fere omnis sermo ad forensem famam domesticis emanat auctoribus, Comment. pet.* 17). He reminds his readers of the value of a full house at the *salutatio*, the morning reception of clients (35), and notes that dinner parties promote the host's reputation for generosity (44). The *domus* is a tool for the self-promotion of the Roman ruling class as well as a symbol of the commitments and attitudes that Quintus expects from his readers. "Take care," Quintus urges candidates, "that approach to you is open day and night, not only by the gates of your house but even in your face and your brow . . . since if they indicate that you are secretive and withdrawn by disposition, an open door is of little help" (*curaque ut aditus ad te diurni nocturnique pateant, neque solum foribus aedium tuarum sed etiam uultu ac fronte, quae est animi ianua; quae si significat uoluntatem abditam esse ac retrusam, parui refert patere ostium*, 44). Quintus insists on the advantages of exposure for elites in the city of Rome: the *domus* is a space where they hope to attract the public eye, and where they expect to be seen.

The Palatine hill had long been a desirable neighborhood for the Roman ruling class.[5] Among the most famous of the Palatine houses of the first century BCE was Cicero's, which he described as being "in view of nearly the entire city" (*in conspectu prope totius urbis, Dom*. 100). Regardless of the truth of Cicero's claim, he associates the possession of a Palatine house with visibility, with the capacity to attract the kind of public attention that Republican aristocrats sought and competed to acquire. Beginning in the first century BCE, however, the Palatine became specifically associated with Augustus, his successors, and the emperors who followed them. Even before the conclusion of the civil wars that secured his unique position in Rome, Octavian acquired extensive properties on the Palatine, where he gradually built a complex that included his *domus*, temples, library, and porticos.[6] His first Palatine house, purchased sometime after the Battle of Philippi in 42 BCE, had belonged to Hortensius Hortalus, a celebrated orator in the late Republic (and a rival of Cicero's).[7] By the time of his victory at Naulochus in 36 BCE, Octavian had obtained other Palatine real estate: Velleius Paterculus reports that Octavian dedicated these new acquisitions to public use (*publicis se usibus destinare professus est*) and that he promised to build a portico and a temple for Apollo (2.81.3). According to Dio Cassius' much later account, the Roman people responded to these dedications by voting to honor Octavian with a house built at the public expense (49.15.5). Augustus made part of his house public when he became *pontifex maximus* in 12 BCE (54.27.3). After a fire in 3 CE devastated the *princeps*' house and the nearby temple of the Magna Mater, the people contributed money to have the house rebuilt (55.12.4). Augustus made the entire house public, either (Dio says) as a response to the public donations or because as *pontifex maximus* he was required to live in a place that was both private and public (ἐν τοῖς ἰδίοις ἅμα καὶ ἐν τοῖς κοινοῖς, 55.12.5).

The development and plan of Augustus' constructions on the Palatine remain controversial, and the *princeps*' house is among the most debated components of the complex.[8] The structure often identified as the House of Augustus, built on two terraces on the southwestern slope of the Palatine, is in many ways an unremarkable structure. Scholars have questioned whether this house could have served the needs of the *princeps* for reception and social life: it may have been only one of a network of houses for the *princeps* and his family on the Palatine.[9] The size of the peristyle courtyard and two largest rooms of the so-called House of Augustus are comparable to those found in the grander houses of Pompeii, and the building has no monumental entrance.[10] Rooms on the lower terrace are decorated with frescoes that evoke urban architecture, common motifs in contemporary houses on the Bay of Naples.[11] Recent excavations have shown that the lower terrace of the house was demolished during the development of the complex in the *princeps*' own day, and that his residence was moved further up the hill, to the same level as the Temple of Apollo.[12] He dedicated this temple in 28 BCE together with the Greek and Latin libraries, two collections that were housed within a single building.[13] Later, when he became *pontifex maximus* in 12 BCE, Augustus established a cult of Vesta on the Palatine, although it is unclear whether the dedication included a new temple: a base from Sorrento, usually dated to the Augustan or Tiberian period, may depict a round Ionic temple (emulating the Temple of Vesta in the Forum Romanum) near the house of the *princeps*, but this identification is disputed.[14] Another prominent element of the complex was the portico of the Danaids, the daughters of the mythical king Danaus, who ordered his daughters to murder their husbands (sons of Danaus' rival and brother, King Aegyptus) on their wedding night. Evidence for this structure is limited, but it seems to have stood before the temple and to have included a series of herms, images of the Danaids, perhaps portraying their eventual fate in the underworld: carrying leaking vessels of water for eternity.[15] The connotation of these figures in the space of the Augustan complex is much debated. While they are treacherous wives, they are also submissive daughters and conquered foreigners, at once effective agents of their father and doubly subject to Roman male power.[16]

Beyond presenting the images of the Danaids, the portico served a practical function, as a location for leisurely walks in the city of Rome.[17] Like

Augustus' other closest neighbors on the Palatine, the portico of the Danaids was a typical form of urban public architecture.[18] The association between the *princeps'* house and the Temple of Apollo is evident in Ovid's descriptions of the Palatine: in the *Fasti*, the poet divides the complex between Augustus, Apollo, and Vesta (*Fast.* 4.949–50), and in the *Metamorphoses*, he calls Apollo *Phoebe domestice* (*Met.* 15.865), casting the deity as Augustus' household god.[19] Roman temples served as museums as well as cult sites: the Temple of Apollo contained an image of Diana by the famed Greek sculptor Timotheus (although it would only have been accessible to visitors on feast days).[20] The book collection in the library was probably available only by invitation, but this space could also be used for public literary recitations and for displaying works of art, and Augustus convened meetings of the Senate there as well.[21] The house of the first *princeps* was embedded in the political, religious, and cultural life of the city.[22]

Augustus' buildings on the Palatine can be explained in part as a continuation of elite competition for control of space in the city of Rome.[23] The Augustan complex called attention to the standing of the builder and to the benefactions that he had granted to the city, and so it fulfilled the functions of self-display and self-aggrandizement traditionally associated with the elite Roman *domus*. Nevertheless, as Nandini Pandey has persuasively argued, Augustus was not the sole author or sole interpreter of the Palatine.[24] Others contributed to the integration of his house into public space. Augustus received honorary decorations from the Senate and the Roman people for the door of his house: laurel leaves and an oak wreath, the *corona civica*, symbols of Augustus' victory and service to the citizens of Rome.[25] In 2 BCE, following decrees of the Senate and the people, an inscription honoring Augustus as *pater patriae* was set up in Augustus' own vestibule, a sign not just of his prominence but also of the presence and participation of other members of the polity.[26]

My interest here is not Augustus' capacity to coerce others to accede to his authority, or the advantages that others might derive from expressing their commitment to the new regime, but in how Augustus' complex reflected and embodied debates about imperial publicity. One of the most influential ancient participants in these debates was Suetonius, who, writing in the early second century CE, emphasized the modesty and simplicity of Augustus' house, which he called "inconspicuous in extent and in elegance" (*neque laxitate neque cultu conspicuis*, Suet. *Aug.* 72.1). Suetonius' account, as Kristina Milnor has persuasively argued, reflects the efforts of the first *princeps* to present himself as "a man whose simple, unaffected private persona contrasts sharply with the grandeur of his role in public life."[27] As Suetonius has it, Augustus' "thriftiness was clear in his household goods and furnishings, and even now in his beds and tables that survive, most of which hardly meet the standards of private refinement" (*instrumenti eius et supellectilis parsimonia apparet etiam nunc residuis lectis atque mensis, quorum pleraque uix priuatae elegantiae sint*, 73).[28] Nothing about Augustus' daily life (setting aside the regal luxuries he enjoyed as a younger man) would draw the public eye: the porticos and rooms in his house were small and made from ordinary building materials (72.1), and his bed was "humble and modestly fitted out" (*humili et modice instrato*, 73). While Augustus' Palatine house was surrounded by structures and symbols that attested to his central role in the polity and his service to the city, Suetonius emphasizes the indifference of the first *princeps* to attracting an audience. He reports that Augustus usually wore "house" clothing (*ueste domestica*) woven by the women of his family, but that he kept his "public" dress (*forensia*) in his bedroom "at the ready for sudden and unexpected occasions" (*ad subitus repentinosque casus parata*, 73).[29] The *princeps*' typical attire suggests that he would rather avoid public attention, a posture out of sync with the traditional expectations for the ruling elite in Rome. He is always prepared to put on a different costume and thus to present himself to public view, but the simplicity of his dress, like the modesty of his furnishings, is meant to indicate that he prefers retreat to visibility most of the time.

The names of Augustus' properties on the Palatine also attest to his interest in regulating his exposure to the public eye.[30] The testimony of the ancient historians suggests that he acquired a number of properties on the Palatine that had once belonged to members of the Roman elite.[31] Suetonius' biographies, as T. P. Wiseman has shown, indicate that the Palatine residence of the *princeps* was not a single building but in fact "a complex of separate houses with streets and alleys between them," and that the different components of the residence continued to be known by the names of their former owners (e.g., the House of Hortensius, the House of Catulus).[32] Even as Augustus' house incorporated and surpassed the houses of the former leading lights of Rome, the names of these spaces also served to present the *princeps* as one figure in a larger ruling elite, who did not demand attention for himself alone.

Augustus' performance of modesty did not persuade all of his contemporaries. In one of Ovid's *Tristia*, a book of his own poetry visits Rome, where it marvels at Augustus' residence, deeming it "a house worthy of a god" (*tectaque digna deo*, *Tr.* 3.1.34).³³ Suetonius' attention to Augustus' aversion to the public eye represents one vision of appropriate imperial behavior, not a comprehensive account of what the house of the *princeps* was really like. Furthermore, the notion that the emperor should be ambivalent about his own visibility is most meaningful if he has trouble hiding himself from view. Despite his emphasis on the emperor's reserve, Suetonius describes the Palatine house as a site of constant activity, claiming that "if [Augustus] ever wanted to do anything in secret or without interruption, he had a particular place on the upper floor . . . he went there or to the suburban dwelling of one of his freedmen" (*si quando quid secreto aut sine interpellatione agere proposuisset, erat illi locus in edito singularis . . . huc transibat aut in alicuius libertorum suburbanum*, 72.2). As Suetonius has it, the *princeps* is usually visible and accessible: he must exert special effort to escape the demands of other people and to avoid being seen.³⁴ The goal for the Augustan ruler is to ostentatiously demur before the public eye.

Suetonius' admiration for the first *princeps*' modesty reflects the appeal of Augustus' stance for his fellow members of the elite. On the one hand, the Palatine complex makes Augustus' house part of the city and acknowledges that the *princeps* can never really get away from public life; on the other, he endeavors to express his aversion to special attention, to perform his ambivalence about being seen. This kind of performance must have been difficult to execute, and in ancient literary accounts, few of Augustus' successors even come close. For Suetonius, Augustus is the *princeps* who learns how to live with his peers in the city of Rome: Suetonius' portrait of Augustus produces a standard that his readers could use to assess later rulers and their houses. Nero, the last emperor of Augustus' dynasty, became associated in antiquity with a very different kind of *domus*, and with a very different attitude toward exposure and retreat.

Leisure in the Limelight: Nero's Villa in the City

Nero began building the Domus Aurea, his Golden House, in 64 CE, after a fire that destroyed numerous houses, apartment blocks, shops, porticos, shrines, and temples in the imperial capital: Tacitus reports that only four of the city's fourteen regions survived unscathed (*Ann.* 15.41). Whether or not Nero started the fire himself (ancient sources present different views on this question), he apparently seized the opportunity to experiment with his domestic space.³⁵ Among the most remarkable features of Nero's Domus

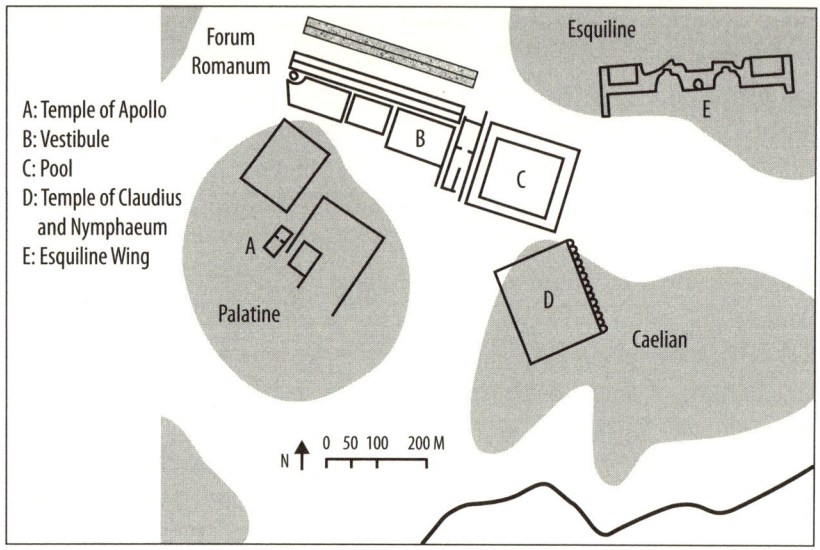

Figure 3.1. Palatine and Domus Aurea. After Champlin, 2003, 189, and https://commons.wikimedia.org/wiki/File:Seven_Hills_of_Rome-it.svg

Aurea was a huge rectangular pool bordered with porticos. Pools were familiar component in villas, the country estates that offered the Roman aristocracy some scope for privacy.[36] At least notionally, as I will discuss below, elite Romans came to associate the villa with *otium*, or leisure, and with retreat from the demands of the city.[37] With the Domus Aurea, however, Nero celebrated his lack of privacy: by building a coastal retreat in the middle of Rome, the emperor presented his private life to public view, and this visibility was both consequence and indicator of his absolute power.

In his biography of Nero, Suetonius reports a popular joke that Nero's house was taking over the capital and so the Romans should leave town (Suet. *Nero* 29). Excavations have shown that the Domus Aurea included land once occupied by residences, shops, and bathing facilities, all destroyed in 64 CE.[38] Much of the area dedicated to Nero's new palace, however, was already imperial property (such as the Gardens of Maecenas on the Esquiline), and the sources that criticize the Domus Aurea do not report popular outcry against the Domus Transitoria, the house Nero built in the valley prior to the fire.[39] The Domus Aurea included construction in the valley between the Palatine and the Esquiline hills, now occupied by the Colosseum, and on the Oppian spur of the Esquiline.[40] An east-west road between the Palatine and the valley intersected with a north-south road between the valley and the Circus Maximus: foundations of porticos where the roads met at the western edge of the valley suggest that this point was the monumental entrance to the complex.[41] Visitors to the complex followed the road that now joins the Temple of Venus and Roma to the Colosseum, passing through the multistoried vestibule that was to house a colossal statue of Nero (Suet. *Nero* 31.1).[42] The statue was probably finished after Nero's death, but the original design likely called for an image of the solar deity Sol/Helios with the attributes of the emperor.[43] Neronian foundations excavated in the Temple of Venus and Roma indicate that the foundation of the temple belonged to the Domus Aurea (as later accounts of Hadrian's life also suggest) and that the vestibule and atrium of the Domus Aurea had the same orientation as the temple podium today.[44] Excavations in the area of the Colosseum, east of the entrance to the complex, have uncovered a drainage system for an artificial lake. Remains of foundations discovered nearby suggest that the lake was rectangular in shape and surrounded by multistoried porticos.[45] The pool was supplied with water from a monumental *nymphaeum*, a fountain that Nero built abutting the Temple of the Deified Claudius on the Caelian hill.[46] The other main component of the Domus Aurea, on the Esquiline hill northeast of the valley, was a vast complex of rooms, as well as pools and fountains, built around a domed octagonal hall. The largest surviving spaces are a pentagonal courtyard and peristyle to the west of the octagonal hall, and these may have been copied, for symmetry, on the west side of the original complex.[47] The frescoes of the Esquiline palace resemble Fourth Style paintings from houses on the Bay of Naples, usually dated to the mid–first century CE, around the period of Nero's rule. Theatrical motifs, most notably the stage building or *scaenae frons*, are especially common in the Domus Aurea frescoes, a type of imagery (discussed further in chapter 5) that encourages viewers to be mindful of the act of viewing and the experience of being visible to an audience.[48]

Among the different buildings associated with the Domus Aurea, the Esquiline wing is by far the best preserved, and the most recent monograph dedicated to the Domus Aurea focuses almost exclusively on this part of the palace.[49] Ancient writers, however, also found the pool and park in the valley worthy of special attention. Tacitus claims that the most striking features of the Domus Aurea were not "gems and gold, already widespread and commonplace for luxury" (*gemmae et aurum . . . solita pridem et luxu uulgata*), but rather the "fields and pools and, like a wilderness, woods on one side and open spaces and vistas on the other" (*arua et stagna et in modum solitudinum hinc siluae inde aperta spatia et prospectus*, *Ann.* 15.42). Suetonius marvels at "the mile-long triple porticos" and "the pool that resembled the sea, surrounded by buildings that looked like cities, and the lands beyond picked out with fields and vineyards, pastures and woods" (*porticus triplices miliarias . . . stagnum maris instar, circumsaeptum aedificiis ad urbium speciem, rura insuper aruis atque uinetis et pascuis siluisque uaria*, Suet. *Nero* 31.1). Suetonius' description of the Domus Aurea recalls literary accounts of villas, which sometimes likened the villa to a city to emphasize the owner's dominance of the rural landscape, as well as images of coastal houses in Pompeian frescoes, in which colonnaded water features are a frequent motif.[50] The ancient historians' interest in the incorporation of water, beautiful views, colonnaded architecture and natural landscapes in the Domus Aurea evokes key aspects of aristocratic recreation on the Italian coast. Suetonius' comment on the "fields and vineyards" at the Domus Aurea is also reminiscent of the agricultural functions of the villa, of the production of wealth that made elite *otium* possible.

While the Domus Aurea dominated a central sector of the urban landscape, it recreated life at the coastal villa, or *villa maritima*, a world that notionally existed in tension with the capital.[51] In actual practice, as Annalisa Marzano has amply demonstrated, the *villa maritima* was a productive and profitable enterprise: fish breeding, cultivation of flowers, raising game and birds, agriculture, quarrying, and even glassmaking have been documented at these sites.[52] Villas were also important spaces for aristocratic display of wealth and power, just like elite houses in Rome.[53] Literary sources, however, tend to emphasize the opportunities for indulgence, cultured recreation, and luxurious retirement that the villa provided, in contrast to the urban *domus*.[54] The villa of Servilius Vatia, a praetor under Tiberius, is a case in point. Seneca describes it as a place where "that rich former magistrate, known for nothing so much as leisure, grew old" (*ille praetorius diues, nulla alia re quam otio notus, consenuit*, *Ep.* 55.3). The prime advantage of Vatia's villa was its proximity to Baiae, a resort town on the Bay of Naples: Seneca muses that "it was clever of Vatia to choose this place for his sluggish and senile recreation" (*non stulte uidetur elegisse hunc locum Vatia in quem otium suum pigrum iam et senile conferret*, 55.7).[55] Seneca wants to distinguish between the life of true *otium*, which only the philosopher attains, and the life of a Vatia, "who flees business and men" (*qui res et homines fugit*, 55.5), but he recognizes that, for most people, retreat and *otium* are one and the same: "people think that the man of leisure is retired and without care and satisfied in himself" regardless of his virtue (*otiosum enim hominem seductum existimat uulgus et securum et se contentum*, 55.4).

Vatia's contemporaries, Seneca explains, admired his villa in part because it allowed him to withdraw from the political intrigues and upheaval at the emperor's court (55.3). The villa and the Bay of Naples offer safety and protection for aristocrats in imperial Rome who, in comparison to elites like Cicero in the late Republic, had less to gain, and more to lose, from seeking public recognition and attention.[56] Even Roman elites who were less fearful of the emperor imagined the villa as a space apart from the exertions of urban life. Pliny the Younger is especially fond of his villa in Laurentum: it is not far from the city, "so you can stay there once you've done the things that need doing" (*ut peractis quae agenda . . . possis ibi manere*, 2.17.2). At Laurentum, he enjoys the beauty of the landscape (2.17.3), study (2.17.8), and pleasant walks (2.17.17–19). His favorite suite of rooms offers "profound and secret solitude" (*alti abditique secreti*, 2.17.22); this is a space so removed from the activity of his household that, when he stays there, "I even imagine that I am absent from my villa" (*abesse mihi etiam a uilla mea uideor*, 2.17.24).[57] Pliny is eager to describe the advantages of his villa to his correspondent, and he clearly expects that guests will want to stay with him (2.17.9), but he also takes pleasure in relaxation and in privacy, a pleasure that is rooted in, and made possible by, his villa outside Rome.

While Pliny, like Vatia and Seneca, left Rome to indulge in *otium*, Nero built his villa in the city itself.[58] Yet the site that Nero chose for his new palace, particularly the valley between the Palatine and the Esquiline, hardly suited retirement or repose: as Miriam Griffin and others have observed, the neighborhood must have experienced considerable traffic. Nero rebuilt the Temple of Fortuna as part of the Domus Aurea; markets, some built by Nero, stood in close proximity to the new palace; the Sacra Via, which Nero also rebuilt, "finished at his front door."[59] The position of Nero's estate in the midst of the city served to express and promote his power: he proclaimed the importance of his role in the community by making his house an unavoidable element of the urban environment. Nero's palace included two main roads that joined the Palatine hill to the valley, so that Romans on their way to the Forum Romanum, as Penelope Davies points out, "were forced to cross the new imperial estate . . . becoming part of [Nero's] crowd."[60] Nero's palace was located not to provide him with a retreat in the midst of the urban landscape, but to attract attention to his house and to himself. Even when the emperor was not in Rome, which was a frequent occurrence in the final years of Nero's reign, the presence of his palace made the emperor present to the inhabitants of the city. The colossus of the emperor would add to this effect.

Nero's vast colonnaded pool and gardens in the valley were better situated to be shared with the inhabitants of Rome than to serve as the emperor's exclusive pleasure palace. Some assessments of the Domus Aurea, most notably Edward Champlin's, emphasize that Nero's populism, as well as his love of publicity, are essential to making sense of the design of his palace: Champlin argues that the valley section of the Domus Aurea was intended to be a public park, like the Gardens of Agrippa, which also included an artificial pool.[61] Nero could also have made his grounds available to the public on specific occasions, rather than dedicating them to public use. During the Republic, aristocrats could court popular favor by opening their *horti*, their luxurious and quasi-rural estates in Rome, for public banquets.[62] Pompey received the people in his gardens in 61 BCE, where he distributed bribes during a consular election (Plut. *Pomp.* 44.3).[63] After the battle of Munda in 45 BCE, Caesar took the opportunity of his fifth triumph to throw a banquet for the *plebs Romana* at his gardens across the Tiber (the same gardens that he later willed to the people).[64] We have no accounts of Nero opening his pool for public use or even for occasional public entertainments: he died only a few years after he began to build his new house, and the construction in the valley appears to have been unfinished.[65] Receiving the people of Roman in his urban villa, however, would be consonant with the tradition of large-scale festivities and public works that powerful Romans undertook to secure popular support.[66] Nero's own penchant for grand displays of hospitality is well attested. To celebrate the birth of his daughter, he hosted games at his villa in Antium.[67] Before the Great Fire in Rome, Tacitus reports that Nero "threw parties in public places and used the whole city as his house" (*publicis locis struere conuiuia totaque urbe quasi domo uti,* 15.37). For one of these opulent festivities, the emperor had a fleet of ships built and put them out to sail in Agrippa's pool in the Campus Martius. On board the main ship, Nero staged a wedding with his slave, and the emperor himself played the bride (15.37). While Nero was accused of singing about the fall of Troy while the fire raged in 64 CE, he does not seem to have been indifferent to the plight of the populace: Tacitus, generally hostile to Nero, reports that he opened his own gardens for those displaced by the fire, built temporary housing, and had provisions brought in (*Ann.* 15.39).[68]

The Domus Aurea, furthermore, does not seem to have instigated popular resentment immediately after Nero's death. During his brief rule in 69 CE, Otho paid to complete Nero's palace, apparently in an effort to capitalize on the former emperor's popularity among the people: Suetonius reports that when Otho "was addressed as 'Nero' by the lowliest of the common people, he made no objection" but rather adopted Nero's name in his official correspondence, restored Nero's statues, and "in his first act as emperor, approved fifty thousand sesterces to complete the Domus Aurea" (*ab infima plebe appellatus Nero nullum indicium recusantis dedit . . . nec quicquam prius pro potestate subscripsit quam quingenties sestertium ad peragendam auream domum*, Suet. *Otho* 7).[69] Otho's activities accord with other indications in the ancient historians that the people of Rome were sorry to lose Nero, which suggests they did not associate his palace with despotic oppression.[70]

The site of Nero's parks and colonnaded pool in a congested area of the city, the precedents of powerful Romans hosting the people at their gardens, and Otho's deployment of Nero's legacy all argue in favor of the populist reading of the Domus Aurea promoted by Champlin and other scholars. If Augustus' performance of domestic modesty was directed at an elite audience, sensitive to excessive self-aggrandizement on the part of the *princeps*, Nero's extravagant hospitality to the people of Rome would be abrasive and objectionable to his fellow aristocrats. Visitors to the Domus Aurea, to be sure, would not think of themselves as the emperor's equals: the enormous statue of the emperor at the vestibule of the complex would remind anyone in doubt of who was master of the estate.[71] Most importantly, there must have been regulations and limitations on behavior for visitors to Nero's house. A four-line epigram from the poet Lucillius (*AP* 11.184), who was active during Nero's reign, may describe the fate of an ill-behaved visitor to the Domus Aurea: this poem tells the story of Meniskos, who was burned alive for stealing golden apples from the gardens of the Hesperides. Louis Robert argued that Meniskos was not a mythological character but a thief who stole from Nero's Golden House and subsequently suffered a gruesome punishment.[72] Robert's interpretation is disputed, but in any case it does not preclude the idea of public access to the palace: Meniskos' transgression is theft, not simply trespassing. Even when Pompey and Caesar welcomed the people to their *horti*, they used guards and physical barriers to regulate the movements of their guests.[73] Likewise, access to Nero's complex was probably permitted under certain conditions, but prohibited at others. The Domus Aurea was most likely an environment where the emperor could present himself to public view on special occasions, and where he could stage encounters between himself and the people of Rome.

The Domus Aurea was a villa that the emperor and his subjects could enjoy together, but it was also an expression of the lack of privacy that distinguished the emperor from everyone else. The pool and porticos of the Domus Aurea revealed the emperor as he was in his coastal retreats, a world typically far removed from downtown Rome: to visit the grounds of Nero's artificial lake was to gain some perspective on the life of the emperor when he was away from the urban venues of circus, theater, or Senate house. Pliny emphasized the special perspective he acquired on the emperor's character when he visited Trajan at his villa in Centum Cellae in Etruria: at Trajan's estate, Pliny notes, it was possible "to examine the emperor's justice, seriousness, and affability, in a secluded place, where these things are especially laid open" (*principis iustitiam grauitatem comitatem in secessu quoque ubi maxime recluduntur inspicere*, 6.31.2). Yet while Trajan and Pliny combine business with pleasure, dealing with judicial proceedings during the day and enjoying the leisure of country life in the evening (6.31.13), the Domus Aurea makes Nero's leisure a part of life in the capital city.[74] Insofar as Nero's palace evoked the world of the emperor in his coastal retreats, it also served to flaunt the relevance of the emperor's private life, of his *otium* outside the city, for all of his subjects. By recreating a coastal retreat in the heart of an urban environment, Nero asserted that even his *otium*, his recreation and leisure, was uniquely meaningful for the life of the community, and was thus uniquely compelling for the public gaze. While the Domus Aurea might allow the people to enjoy the emperor's pleasures, their access to them was in fact a reflection of the emperor's own importance. Only Nero's villa was worthy of such scrutiny, and the Domus Aurea brought it to Rome, where it could be seen.

The Domus Aurea was a suitable house for an emperor who aimed to capture the attention of those he ruled: Nero might have been pleased to receive a poem like the "Consolation to Livia," assuring him that he "drew eyes and ears" to himself. For Nero, the capacity to make himself visible is the ultimate expression of his singular position in the community. Dangers attended a Neronian obsession with self-display, as Augustus' reputation for domestic modesty, and his efforts to cultivate that reputation, make clear. Nevertheless, just like the extravagant residence of the last Julio-

Claudian ruler, the complex that the first *princeps* built on the Palatine also claimed a central place in the community. In the ancient accounts, Augustus and Nero represent different attitudes toward visibility, one cautious (Augustus) and the other celebratory (Nero), but both of their houses define the emperor as the most important object of the public eye, as a person who cannot really retreat from view. To conclude this chapter, I turn to another imperial house, Tiberius' villa on Capri, and to an emperor's performance of invisibility.

The Invisible Emperor: Tiberius on Capri

Tiberius left Rome for Campania in 26 CE and never returned. His purpose, according to Tacitus, was to get away from the city, although his declared aim was to dedicate temples in the region. Once that business was completed, Tiberius "issued an edict that his peace and quiet should not be disturbed . . . and concealed himself on the island of Capri" (*edicto monuisset ne quis quietem eius inrumperet . . . Capreas se in insulam abdidit*, *Ann.* 4.67). Tacitus' description of Capri indicates the lengths that emperor goes to in order to hide himself from view, an expenditure of imperial energy that matches the force of his illicit desires. Capri was remote: there was no harbor nearby, and no one could approach it without being noticed by Tiberius' guard (*neque adpulerit quisquam nisi gnaro custode*, 4.67). Tiberius took up residence at his twelve villas on the island where, Tacitus reports, "as much as he had once been intent on the public business, he unleashed himself on equally secret dissipation and injurious leisure" (*quanto intentus olim publicas ad curas tanto occultiores in luxus et malum otium resolutus*, 4.67). Suetonius describes Tiberius' retirement in similar terms: the emperor "obtained the freedom of seclusion, and with the eyes of the state more or less removed, he finally spilled out all the vices that he had concealed (although badly) for so long" (*secreti licentiam nanctus et quasi ciuitatis oculis remotis, cuncta simul uitia male diu dissimulata tandem profudit*, *Tib.* 42.1). In these texts, when Tiberius abandons the capital, he reveals the impossibility of imperial retreat, as the stories that spread about his doings continue to expose him to public view. The ancient historians emphasize Tiberius' secrecy (*occultiores*, Tac. *Ann.* 4.67; *secreti*, Suet. *Tib.* 42.1), but do not question their sources for his (supposedly) private life: the invisible Tiberius simply becomes the rumors that are told about him.[75]

The literary accounts distinguish Tiberius by the extent of his efforts to avoid being seen: hiding is Tiberius' "trademark," as Caroline Vout puts it, in ancient texts.[76] As in the case of Augustus' Palatine house, however, the archaeological evidence for Tiberius' life on Capri tells a different story, if not necessarily a contradictory one. The vast size of the imperial properties on the island indicates that they were not expected to house a single man in solitude. The Villa Iovis, which occupied an area of seven thousand square meters, was built around a rectangular courtyard surrounded by porticos that led to the four wings of the villa.[77] The entrance to the villa, on the southwest, was accessible by an ascending staircase that offered a dramatic view of the palace to those ascending it.[78] In addition to the entrance to the palace, the south wing housed a bathing complex, while the west side contained guest quarters as well as service spaces.[79] The imperial quarters were on north side of the complex, at its highest level of elevation.[80] The east wing of the palace was dominated by three grand spaces suitable for audiences or receptions: the central of the three offered an impressive view of the coast, from Naples to Paestum.[81] There was even a signaling tower on the south side of the Villa Iovis, which likely made for easier communications between Capri and Rome.[82]

The architecture of the Villa Iovis shows that it was intended to accommodate and impress visitors, just like the villas of subsequent emperors, who received privileged guests and large crowds, especially for games, at their country estates.[83] Even Tacitus and Suetonius admit that Tiberius did not live on his island palace in isolation. When Tiberius left Rome, he took some companions along: Tacitus describes it as a small entourage (*arto comitatu*, 4.58), but in addition to the prefect of his praetorian guard, Sejanus, the jurist Nerva, and another distinguished *eques*, the group included a number of learned literary men (4.58). Tacitus' list, of course, does not include the slaves and freedmen who must have been present to serve the emperor and manage his estates.[84] Tiberius also seems to have had a number of visitors from Rome: the children of Tiberius' late adopted son Germanicus, including the future emperor Caligula, were among his guests, as was Vitellius, another emperor-to-be.[85] Many fewer people would be able to visit the emperor on Capri than in Rome, but the difficulties of the journey must have been part of the effect of the villa: guests became witnesses to the emperor's extraordinary ability to retreat from view, but this performance only worked if he had an audience in the first place.

One of the most remarkable features of the literary accounts of Tiberius' retirement is what a bad job he does of keeping himself out of sight. Suetonius and Tacitus claim that Tiberius never again set foot in the capital, but even in their accounts he interrupts his retirement and seems on the verge of returning to the city. We meet Tiberius in the gardens of Caesar and at the seventh milestone along the Appian Way (Suet. *Tib.* 72.1), "near to Rome" (*urbem iuxta*, Tac. *Ann.* 6.39), and "up against the walls of the city" (*moenia urbis adsidens*, Tac. *Ann.* 4.58).[86] He exposes himself in other ways as well: when the Senate indicts Cotta Messalinus for making insulting remarks about the imperial family, Tiberius sends a letter to Rome to defend Cotta, in which he describes his personal distress (*perire me cotidie sentio*, *Ann.* 6.6). Tacitus observes that "neither rank nor solitude protected Tiberius from confessing the torment of his heart and his own punishments" (*Tiberium non fortuna, non solitudines protegebant quin tormenta pectoris suasque ipse poenas fateretur*, *Ann.* 6.6). Even while he is on Capri, Tiberius cannot avoid revealing himself to Rome. The trouble with Tiberius is not just that he retires from public life, but that he is unable to fully retreat. Instead, the emperor "sailed around Campania, wavering about entering Rome, or, since he had decided otherwise, pretending that he would come. And often, after landing nearby, at gardens near the Tiber, he sought again the rocks and solitude of the sea because of his shame at his crimes and his lusts, which inflamed him so uncontrollably that he raped and defiled—as kings do—freeborn youths" (*Ann.* 6.1).[87]

The emperor's proximity, the prospect of his return, is no less disturbing to Tacitus than his abandoning Rome to pursue his dangerous and secret desires. When Tiberius skulks around the city, he reminds his unfortunate subjects of his ongoing public significance, regardless of whether he can be seen.

Conclusion

The three emperors' houses that I have discussed in this chapter were sites for contesting the rules of imperial visibility and the relationship between emperor and audience in Julio-Claudian Rome. Augustus' Palatine complex and Nero's Domus Aurea made the public ascendance of these men visible in the landscape of the city. Even Tiberius' island retreat was built in anticipation of visitors, witnesses to the emperor's exceptional power and his splendid retirement. Suetonius' and Tacitus' later responses to these houses reflect the negotiations between emperors and their viewers over how visible the emperor should be, as well as the anxieties that seeing too much of the emperor could provoke in those he rules. For the elite readership of Tacitus and Suetonius, an emperor takes risks not only when he attempts to evade the public eye but also when he demands too much public attention, when he insists that his subjects watch him and thus confirm his dominance. In the next chapter, I turn to the consequences of the ruler's visibility in the work of Seneca the Younger, the philosopher, dramatist, and courtier who too often found himself in the emperor's audience.

CHAPTER FOUR

Exposing the Ruler
Seneca on Visibility and Complicity

In a diatribe against the dissipation and frivolousness of Roman society, Seneca counts domestic theatrical productions among the regrettable predilections of his contemporaries. He complains, "the private stage resounds throughout the city, men and women leap and dance on it, husbands and wives fight over who can dance more enticingly" (*priuatum urbe sonat tota pulpitum; in hoc uiri, in hoc feminae tripudiant; mares inter se uxoresque contendunt uter det latus mollius*, Sen. *Q. Nat.* 7.32.3).[1] Seneca is attuned both to the attractions of performing before an admiring audience and to the risks of exposure to the public eye: he suggests that those who turn their houses into theaters take too much pleasure in the limelight to worry about the negative attention they may receive for indecent behavior. He advises the stars of the household theater circuit to leave the stage and devote their time to the study of philosophy (*Q. Nat.* 7.32.4). Seneca's anxieties about self-display can be interpreted as part of the aristocratic turn from the pursuit of public glory to the cultivation of the self, a development which looms large in scholarship on Julio-Claudian Rome.[2] Under the Empire, the Roman aristocracy did not derive the same advantages from self-promotion as they did during the Republic, when they competed with their peers for recognition and for offices. The emperor, who surpassed all the rest as a recipient and distributor of honors, was the primary object of public attention.[3] And while the emperor's approval was crucial to elite advancement, it was also dangerous to attract his notice: it could be safer to retreat entirely from public life, and thus not to be seen at all.[4]

Seneca's treatments of rule in the *De clementia* and in his regal tragedies raise different problems for the power dynamics of viewing and visibility in Julio-Claudian Rome. Seneca was a philosopher and dramatist as well as a leading figure at Nero's court, where he served as tutor and speechwriter for the young emperor. In the *De clementia*, which Seneca composed around 56 CE and addressed to Nero himself, the ruler is an object of scrutiny at all times and in all places.[5] The rulers in Seneca's *Thyestes* and *Agamemnon* are not only exposed to the gaze of those they rule but dependent on it to confirm their power. These plays center on the pursuit of revenge (Atreus seeks retribution against his brother Thyestes, and Clytemnestra and Cassandra both want vengeance from Agamemnon), but these revenge stories are also dramas about getting and holding power over others.[6] In Seneca's tragedies, those who seek revenge and those who seek to rule need to be seen by those they dominate, and the king's house is a space where his subjects participate in acknowledging and confirming his rule.

While in the previous chapter I focused on emperors' attitudes toward being seen and on how their houses shaped their interactions with the public eye, I now turn to Seneca's assessment of the ruler's visibility from the perspective of those he rules. The ruler's house appears only fleetingly in the *De clementia*, but I discuss this text because of Seneca's attention to visibility in his treatment of power. The ruler in the *De clementia* has little opportunity to retreat behind closed doors or to regulate his exposure to public view, and his lack of privacy threatens both his own security and the cohesion of the polity. The royal house is the main location of the drama in both *Thyestes* and *Agamemnon*, in which kings demand witnesses to their dominance, and their witnesses confront their own complicity. In Seneca's philosophy and tragedy, the visibility of the ruler, his exposure to public view and dependence on the gaze of those he rules, undermines the hierarchy of ruler and ruled.

Visibility and Vulnerability in the *De Clementia*

Seneca's explicit goal in the *De clementia* is to counsel Nero to practice clemency.[7] He distinguishes between *clementia* (clemency), which he associates with appropriate moderation and restraint, and *misericordia* (pity), which is "the vice of a petty mind that gives way at the sight of the suffering of others" (*uitium pusilli animi ad speciem alienorum malorum succidentis*, 2.5.1).[8] He draws on a range of genres to support his case, from Hellenistic kingship treatises to panegyric to Stoic philosophy.[9] The *De clementia* also speaks directly to Seneca's immediate context at Nero's court, and to the demands of his responsibility to guide the teenage ruler.[10] In the course of advising Nero, however, Seneca offers a broader account of what it means to rule and what sets the ruler apart from the rest. He describes the ruler as someone "who has power over all things" (*qui omnia potest*, 1.8.5) and who also faces unique limitations: he warns Nero, "you cannot depart from your lot in life; it haunts you and follows you wherever you go, with great fanfare . . . you have no more success in hiding than the sun" (*aberrare a fortuna tua non potes; obsidet et te quocumque descendis magno apparatu sequitur . . . tibi non magis quam soli latere contingit*, *Clem.* 1.8.2–4). The *De clementia* thus offers an important supplement to the models of the emperor's publicity that I explored in the previous chapter. While Augustus crafted a performance of modesty and aversion to the public eye, and Nero touted his unique place in the spotlight, for Seneca the ruler's attitude toward self-display is irrelevant: publicity is simply proof and effect of the ruler's dominance. The key question in the *De clementia*, I will argue, is not how and where the ruler displays himself, or how and where he watches others, but the communal consequences of the ruler's inevitable visibility. The philosopher's assessment of this publicity, moreover, is decidedly pessimistic: the absolute ruler's exposure to those he rules makes the ruler vulnerable and thus threatens the stability of the community as a whole.

Seneca begins the *De clementia* by promising to make Nero visible to himself. He tells the young emperor, "I have decided to write about clemency . . . so that I can play the role of a mirror, so to speak, and show you to yourself as you reach the greatest pleasure of all" (*scribere de clementia . . . institui, ut quodam modo speculi uice fungerer et te tibi ostenderem peruenturum ad uoluptatem maximam omnium, Clem.* 1.1.1).[11] If Nero admires his own reflection, others can enjoy looking at him too: when a clement ruler passes by, his subjects do not "run away as if some dreadful or dangerous creature had leapt from its lair, but fly to him like a bright and beneficent star" (*non, tamquam malum aliquod aut noxium animal e cubili prosilierit, diffugiunt, sed tamquam ad clarum ac beneficum sidus certatim aduolant*, 1.3.3).

Seneca's effusive praise for Nero, then, is bound up with a warning that he is being watched. When he tells the emperor, "the lowly and the great alike marvel at your clemency . . . nor is anyone so assured of his own innocence that he is not happy to watch clemency granted to human foibles" (*aequalis ad maximos imosque peruenit clementiae tuae admiratio . . . nec est quisquam, cui tam ualde innocentia sua placeat, ut non stare in conspectu clementiam paratam humanis erroribus gaudeat*, 1.1.9), he reminds him that he renders his judgments in the presence of an audience.[12] In noting that "generosity of spirit . . . can be seen more clearly on the judge's bench than on the floor" (*magnanimitas . . . meliusque in tribunali quam in plano conspicitur*. 1.5.3), Seneca implies that the judge's cruelty would be equally visible.[13]

Seneca emphasizes Nero's exposure to the public eye and draws a sharp contrast between the ruler and the ruled when he observes that "few perceive our movements; we are allowed to go out and come back and change our clothes without the public noticing; you have no more success in hiding than the sun. There is much light facing you, all eyes are turned towards it; you think that you 'go out'? You rise" (*nostros motus pauci sentiunt, prodire nobis ac recedere et mutare habitum sine sensu publico licet; tibi non magis quam soli latere contingit. multa contra te lux est, omnium in istam conuersi oculi sunt; prodire te putas? oreris*, 1.8.4).[14] Comparisons between the ruler and the sun, or assimilation of the ruler to the sun or the sun god, were standard features of Greek and Roman ruler cult.[15] Yet while the grandeur of the solar metaphor in the *De clementia* does suggest the extent of the emperor's power, it primarily emphasizes his visibility. The ruler is like the sun not because of his beauty, brilliance, or crucial role in sustaining human life, but because none of his movements or changes in appearance pass without comment. The question of whether the emperor should show his distaste for this extraordinary publicity (according to the Augustan model) or embrace it (as in Nero's Domus Aurea) is, in the *De clementia*, beside the point. The main thrust of Seneca's sun metaphor is that being the object of attention, at all times and in all places, is an essential aspect of the ruler's position in the community.

The visibility of the sole ruler should motivate him, Seneca claims, to practice clemency. He warns that Nero cannot be compared to those "who are concealed in the crowd, whose virtues struggle for a long time to become visible and whose vices lurk in the darkness. Rumor takes hold of your deeds and words" (*qui in turba . . . latent, quorum et uirtutes ut appareant diu luctantur et uitia tenebras habent; uestra facta dictaque rumor ex-*

cipit, 1.8.1). He distinguishes the emperor from his fellow aristocrats precisely because of his unique experience of the public eye: when Seneca describes Augustus' anxieties about his reputation, he observes that "any of us ought to have had enough faith in good conscience against negative opinions; rulers have to pay a great deal of attention even to rumor" (*quilibet nostrum debuisset aduersus opiniones malignas satis fiduciae habere in bona conscientia, principes multa debent etiam famae dare, Clem.* 1.15.5). Seneca's valorization of conscience, as Matthew Roller has argued, was part of a larger project to reshape the ethical system of the elite in the early Empire: because opportunities for public glory were limited under the principate, Seneca aims to persuade his readers that "*conscientia* is the only authoritative moral judge and is superior to any external judges."[16] The ruler, however, is always in the public eye, and so he has no choice but to concern himself with public judgment.[17]

Other members of the ruling class might get a taste of the emperor's experience, but only in specific contexts. In one of his letters, Seneca warns Lucilius, a magistrate in Sicily, to be wary of gossip about his behavior, and he suggests that Lucilius' problem is that he is a big fish in a small pond: "anything that stands out among its neighbors is great in the place where it stands out . . . you are now great in your province, although you look down on yourself" (*quidquid inter uicina eminet magnum est illic ubi eminet . . . tu nunc in prouincia, licet contemnas ipse te, magnus es, Ep.* 43.2–3). While Lucilius attracts attention in a restricted environment, this kind of scrutiny is a constant concern for the absolute ruler; there can be no place where the emperor does not "stand out" in comparison with those near him. In his *Consolation to Polybius*, an earlier work addressed to a freedman of the emperor Claudius, Seneca describes the problems of publicity in similarly limited terms. Even as Seneca reminds Polybius that his exalted position makes it impossible for him to conceal his actions (*nihil horum quae facis posse subduci, Polyb.* 6.1), he also attributes Polybius' status to Caesar's favor (6.2). Polybius' prominence, and thus the attention he receives, is due to his close relationship to the emperor; if Polybius were to fall out of imperial favor, he would escape the public eye. His own efforts, particularly his intellectual accomplishments, also contribute to the scrutiny he faces (6.2), but Seneca describes Polybius' distinguished standing (*magnam personam*) as something that he must endeavor to protect and maintain (*haec tibi tuenda est*, 6.1). The absolute ruler, by contrast, need exert no effort to secure his place in the public eye, but he can also do nothing to escape it. Seneca tells Nero, "It is the highest degree of slavery to be unable to become less; but you share that very fate with the gods. For heaven also keeps them chained, and they are not permitted to come down any more than it is safe for you to do so: you are fixed to your pediment" (*est haec summae magnitudinis seruitus, non posse fieri minorem; sed cum dis tibi communis ista necessitas est. nam illos quoque caelum alligatos tenet, nec magis illis descendere datum est quam tibi tutum: fastigio tuo adfixus es*, 1.8.3). The ruler resembles the gods not only because of his dominance, but also because his high position is inescapable.

This attention to unavoidable visibility as a distinctive aspect of the ruler's position also appears in the *Apocolocyntosis*, a vicious satire on the deification of Claudius. Attacks on Claudius' appearance are a key component of this text, which is usually attributed to Seneca and dated to the same period as the *De clementia*.[18] We first encounter Claudius through the report of a senator who "says that he saw Claudius making his way [up to the heavens] 'with unequal steps'" (*Claudium uidisse se dicet iter facientem 'non passibus aequis,' Apocol.* 1.2). The emperor arrives on Mount Olympus, where he makes a questionable impression on his fellow gods: Hercules "was deeply disturbed. . . . When he noticed [Claudius'] figure, which was of an unfamiliar sort, his unusual gait, his voice that belonged not to an earthly animal but to sea monsters, hoarse and confused, he thought that his thirteenth labor had arrived" (*sane perturbatus est . . . ut uidit noui generis faciem, insolitum incessum, uocem nullius terrestris animalis sed qualis esse marinis beluis solet, raucam et implicatam, putauit sibi tertium decimum laborem uenisse*, 5.3). For Seneca, Claudius' body is unfit to be seen and thus unfit to occupy a position that always attracts public notice.[19] Describing Claudius' death, Seneca claims that the emperor's "deathbed speech rang out among all mankind, since he made a bigger sound from that orifice which he spoke through more easily: 'woe is me, I think I have shat myself'" (*ultima uox eius haec inter homines audita est, cum maiorem sonitum emisisset illa parte, qua facilius loquebatur: 'uae me, puto, concacaui me,'* 4.3). Seneca emphasizes not only the embarrassment of Claudius' final moments but the wide (even universal) audience that is forced to witness it. Nero emerges as a better ruler in large part because his subjects will prefer looking at him rather than at Claudius: as Christopher Star notes, "the focus of the political theory is squarely on bodily appearance. The good king . . . is attractive; the bad king is ugly."[20] Apollo enthusiastically introduces the new emperor, exclaiming "such a Caesar is here, such a Nero will Rome now gaze upon. Let his shining face glow with cheerful splendor and may his hair spill around his lovely neck" (*talis Caesar adest, talem iam Roma Neronem / aspiciet. flagrat nitidus fulgore remisso / uultus et adfuso ceruix formosa capillo*, 4.1.30–32).[21] The old emperor was not fit for public view and thus not really suitable to be emperor at all; the new emperor is superior because he will provide Rome with a more pleasing and more appropriate object of attention. The *Apocolocyntosis* establishes visibility as a fact of life for all rulers, good or bad, ugly or beautiful: to rule is to be exposed to the public eye.

The *De clementia* is hardly unique in its attention to the publicity of the ruler. Yet this text is concerned not only with the ruler's visibility but also with his vulnerability, and for rulers, whether human or animal, the two are closely related. Seneca pays special attention to the plight of the "king" of the bees, whom he calls "a prodigious model for great kings" (*exemplar . . . magnis regibus ingens*, 1.19.3) in the human community.[22] According to Seneca, the ruler of the hive "has extraordinary beauty and is unlike the rest both in size and splendor" (*insignis regi forma est dissimilisque ceteris cum magnitudine tum nitore*, 1.19.2), but he has no stinger (*sine aculeo*, 1.19.3). This is a trying situation in the bee world, since bees as a rule are quick to anger (*iracundissimae*) and given to fighting (*pugnacissimae*). The remarkable beauty and size of the bee king must attract attention, but he has no weapons against a hostile audience. The emperor has plenty of weapons of his own, but in Seneca's assessment he is worse off than his counterpart among the bees: the human ruler is likely to be tempted to act on his violent impulses. Nature "did not wish [the king bee] to be cruel or to seek costly revenge . . . and left him anger without arms" (*noluit illum natura nec saeuum esse nec ultionem magno constaturam petere . . . et iram eius inermem reliquit*, 1.19.3), but the human ruler will want to do harm, even though "it is necessary that he experience fear to the same degree that he wishes to provoke fear" (*tantum enim necesse est timeat quantum timeri uoluit*, 1.19.5). In Seneca's assessment, the king bee should teach the human ruler to be mindful of his own vulnerability, and to mistrust his capacity to defend himself.

If the human ruler is always the object of public attention, he is also always a possible target of attack. As Seneca describes it, the ruler lives surrounded by enemies: he claims, "I can go alone into any part of the city without fear, although no companion follows me, although I have no guard, no sword at my side; you must live armed in your own peace" (*possum in qualibet parte urbis solus incedere sine timore, quamuis nullus sequatur comes, nullus <custos> sit mihi, nullus ad latus gladius; tibi in tua pace armato uiuendum est,* 1.8.2).[23] There is no doubt that the ruler requires exceptional defenses; the only question is whether he will attempt to protect himself with citadels (*arces*), walls, and towers (*muris turribusque*), or choose clemency, which "will keep the king safe even out of doors" (*saluum regem clementia in aperto praestabit,* 1.19.6).[24] If the ruler foregoes clemency and penalizes those who cross him, his actions affect not only his victims but also the way that everyone perceives him: Seneca insists, "just as lightning strikes only endanger a few, but frighten everyone, the censures that the most powerful rulers issue terrify more people than they harm" (*ut fulmina paucorum periculo cadunt, omnium metu, sic animaduersiones magnarum potestatum terrent latius quam nocent,* 1.8.5). Whoever witnesses the ruler's cruelty winds up as one of his opponents, "since frequent vengeance restrains the hatred of a few, but provokes the hatred of all" (*regibus certior est ex mansuetudine securitas, quia frequens uindicta paucorum odium opprimit, omnium irritat,* 1.8.6). The approving audience that Nero enjoyed at the opening of the text might always become a more suspicious and threatening one.

From the beginning of the text, when Seneca held up a mirror to allow Nero to gaze at himself, the *De clementia* repeatedly distinguishes the ruler from the ruled by the claims he makes on public attention and by his exposure to the public eye. There is one striking moment, however, when the ruler seems to retreat from view. Seneca observes,

> There is a good reason why peoples and cities agree to love and protect their kings to such an extent and to throw down their bodies and their substance when the ruler's safety demands it. . . . Just as the whole body serves the mind and, since the body is larger and more attractive, the delicate mind remains in hiding and conceals itself in some unknown place, nevertheless hands, feet, and eyes do its business, this skin protects it . . . thus this immense multitude surrounds the soul of one man and is ruled by his breath and directed by his reason, since it would press upon itself and break apart through its own strength, if it were not supported by his counsel. (1.3.4–5)[25]

When he describes the relationship of the ruler to the political community as one between the mind and the body, Seneca draws on a longstanding trope of classical literature and political thought.[26] This metaphor sits uneasily with other images of the ruler in the *De clementia*, such as the ruler as the sun (1.8.4), as the king bee (1.19.3), as a shining star (1.3.3), as the admired judge (1.1.9; 1.5.3), as the favorite subject of rumor (1.8.1; 1.15.1), or as a god "fixed to his pediment" (1.8.3). Here the ruler is not the most striking member of the community, the one who is most worth paying attention to and who cannot escape public scrutiny. He rules and directs the whole, but he is also slight (*tenuis*) and in hiding (*in occulto*), protected by a skin made up the multitude of his subjects, surrounded by their fearsome strength. Yet if he has found a way to avoid being seen, in doing so he affirms his ongoing vulnerability and even his dependence on those he rules.

For the ruler, Seneca declares, "the one unconquerable fortress is the love of the citizens" (*unum est inexpugnabile munimentum amor ciuium*, 1.19.6). Seneca's advice to Nero, that he must be wary of provoking fear, that he should seek to be loved rather than hated, may strike us as disingenuous or (at best) misguided: surely the emperor of Rome can muddle through without the love of those he rules.[27] Seneca knows that rulers rarely follow the course of action he prescribes: he notes, "clemency will make any house it comes to happy and peaceful, but in a palace, insofar as it is rarer, it is even more marvelous" (*clementia, in quamcumque domum peruenerit, eam felicem tranquillamque praestabit, sed in regia, quo rarior, eo mirabilior*, 1.5.4). When Seneca works to persuade the ruler to protect himself from danger, he also argues that these dangers have consequences for the polity as a whole. When Seneca urges the ruler to deter potential enemies by restraining his anger, he insists that "if anyone supposes that the king is safe where nothing is safe from the king, he is in error; security must be bargained for with mutual security" (*errat enim si quis existimat tutum esse ibi regem ubi nihil a rege tutum sit; securitas securitate mutua paciscenda est*, 1.19.5).[28] In advising the emperor to "bargain" for his security, Seneca also addresses the emperor's potential bargaining partners: he suggests to his readers that the security of the ruler and the security of his subjects are interdependent. If the ruler defends himself by showing clemency to his subjects, his subjects must also see defending the king as a form of self-defense, and dangers to the ruler as dangers to the larger community.

In Seneca's view, protecting the ruler is how the ruled "love their own safety . . . for he is the bond that keeps the *res publica* together" (*suam itaque incolumitatem amant . . . ille est enim uinculum per quod res publica cohaeret*, 1.4.1). What happens if a ruler fails to serve as the "bond" that sustains the *res publica*? Seneca has only limited interest in this question in the *De clementia*: the Roman people (*populus*), he argues, ought to "bear the reins, and if it ever breaks away from them or does not permit them to be restored after they have come off ... the end of Roman submission will be the end of Roman rule" (*ferre frenos, quos si quando abruperit uel aliquo casu discussos reponi sibi passus non erit ... idemque huic urbi finis dominandi erit qui parendi fuerit*, 1.4.2). Seneca's priority is the consistency of the ruler's power and the stability that he offers. For better or for worse, ruler and ruled depend on one another: Seneca insists that "Caesar has so entangled himself with the state that one is unable to separate from the other without peril for both, for the former needs strength and the latter needs a head" (*ita se induit rei publicae Caesar ut seduci alterum non posset sine utriusque pernicie; nam et illi uiribus opus est et huic capite*, 1.4.3). As Julia Mebane notes, when Seneca frames the relationship of ruler and ruled "as a matter of necessity rather than choice, [he] is able to sidestep the question of whether the Principate is the best form of governance. What is ideal ... becomes irrelevant in light of what is necessary."[29] It is the fact that ruler and ruled are interdependent, that the ruler is inextricably bound up with those he rules, that makes it possible to the equate his well-being with the welfare of the community. "If public things have more pull with reasonable men than private things," Seneca argues, "it follows that the person on whom the *res publica* turns is more beloved too" (*si sanis hominibus publica priuatis potiora sunt, sequitur ut is quoque carior sit in quem se res publica conuertit*, 1.4.3). The ruler is the fulcrum of the political community, and so his vulnerability is a problem not just for himself, but for everyone else: threats he faces have a cascading effect on the political community as a whole.

In the conclusion to this book, I will return to the limitations that this conception of the ruler's public significance imposes on Roman political thought. For now, it is important to note how the interdependence of ruler and ruled informs Seneca's account of the ruler's visibility, of his life in the public eye. When Seneca warns that the ruler, like the sun, cannot conceal himself from view and is always under observation (1.8.4), he ignores the problem of whether Nero might carry out nefarious deeds in secret. In a sense, from Seneca's point of view, it matters little whether we can actually see the emperor: the problem is that the ruler can never really be said to retreat from public life, from the life of the community as a whole. By representing the ruler as visible and exposed, Seneca frames the polity under one-man rule as an inherently vulnerable one.

Power Play

Seneca's *De clementia* spells out the radical implications of the ruler's visibility and the communal consequences when the ruler (whatever his preferences) cannot escape from public view. Whether he likes it or not, the *De clementia* argues, the emperor is on display to those he rules, and they watch him because their fates are necessarily bound up with his. The visibility of the ruler and the gaze of the ruled are likewise recurrent motifs in Seneca's *Thyestes* and *Agamemnon*, in which the ruler cannot ensure his authority without making himself visible to an audience. As in the *De clementia*, the ruler in these tragedies is distinguished from other members of the community by his exposure to the public eye.[30]

The dramatic form has important consequences for Seneca's political thought. By presenting the voices of different characters and by bringing the space of the king's house to life, these plays allow us to consider the visibility of the ruler from multiple perspectives, and to enter into the fragility and interdependence of the relationship between ruler and ruled. As we will see, the ruler and his house are exposed to view at key moments in these plays. When the ruler is made visible, he reveals the complicity of those he rules in maintaining his power.

Two issues have dominated much of the scholarship on Seneca's tragedy. The first is which dramatic literature and theatrical traditions he drew on. Seneca was familiar with classical Athenian tragedy, and his dramas are clearly in dialogue with earlier texts, including plays that are no longer available for modern readers (Seneca's *Thyestes* is the only complete tragic treatment of the myth of Thyestes and Atreus to survive from antiquity). Postclassical developments in tragedy and dramatic techniques, including the tragedies of the Republican period, were another key source of influence for Seneca, but very little evidence for Roman tragedy other than Seneca's survives.[31] While it is sometimes difficult to determine the ways in which Seneca responded to and reworked earlier Greek and Roman dramas, the fact that his plays belong to the genre of tragedy is significant in itself. Tragedy, because of its associations with the myths of kings and ruling houses, offered a form uniquely suitable to exploring the relationship between ruler and community. To write a tragedy was to select a language in which the political questions of the early Empire—the meaning of power, the nature of the bond between ruler and ruled—could be most aptly discussed.[32]

The second persistent debate about Senecan drama concerns how and where these plays were performed. It was once widely accepted that they were intended exclusively for recitation in houses or small recital halls; more recently, however, scholars have recognized that Seneca's dramas could have been staged in a variety of ways in the ancient world, from full-scale productions to extracted scenes to small performances in elite households.[33] Furthermore, whether or not they are performed, dramatic texts evoke discussion, communication, and exchange between audience and actor, viewer and viewed. Regardless of how ancient audiences encountered Seneca's plays, the form of tragedy itself suggests that viewers are present to observe, and perhaps to participate in, the events of the drama.[34] The kings in *Thyestes* and *Agamemnon* secure their power through self-display, and they require acknowledgment and recognition from those subordinate to them. By emphasizing the ruler's need for an audience, Seneca reveals the ways in which the ruled cooperate in establishing and maintaining the position of the ruler.

In the *De clementia*, Seneca spoke as a counselor of the ruler, laying out the consequences of his visibility both for the ruler and for the community as a whole. In *Thyestes* and *Agamemnon* the rulers themselves reflect on their own visibility, and they offer varied assessments of what it means to live in the public eye. *Thyestes* centers on the House of Atreus in the generation before the Trojan War, and on the conflict between the two brother kings, Atreus and Thyestes.[35] Prior to the events of Seneca's narrative, Thyestes had driven Atreus out of the kingdom and taken his brother's wife for himself. Atreus managed to retake the throne and to expel his brother, but he remained dedicated to taking revenge against him. At the beginning of the play, Atreus invites his brother to return home to Argos and promises reconciliation and joint rule. Thyestes is duped, and the play concludes with one of the most repellent episodes in classical mythology: Atreus sacrifices Thyestes' sons, prepares a feast with their flesh, and serves the meal to their unwitting father. Atreus himself, however, is unperturbed by the prospect of committing this crime or of being recognized for it. Early in the drama, he steels himself for action: "Go on, my soul, do something which no age to come will approve, but none will be silent about" (*Age, anime, fac quod nulla posteritas probet, / sed nulla taceat, Thy.* 191–92).[36] Atreus' attitude toward his own reputation is utterly opposed to the concerns of his servant, who attempts to dissuade him from his scheme to ruin his brother.

Servant: Do you not fear the hostile gossip of the people?
Atreus: This is the greatest benefit of kingship, that the people are compelled both to endure and to praise their master's deeds.
Servant: Those who praise because of their fear also become hostile because of their fear. But whoever seeks the glory of true favor desires to be praised with feeling rather than with speech.
Atreus: Even a lowly man can get true praise; only a powerful man can get false praise. Let them wish for what they don't want. (204–13)[37]

For both Atreus and his servant, as this conversation suggests, the king's pursuit of revenge is not a private matter: the deeds he commits will be visible to those he rules, and they will confirm the distinction between the king and his subjects. So far from fearing what the people will say about him, or hoping to conceal his actions from their view, Atreus looks forward to being exposed: false praise, the response of those who see him for who he really is but remain subordinate to his power, is an attractive prospect for Atreus.

The servant ultimately offers a surprisingly positive response to the king: after Atreus warns him to keep the plot against Thyestes a secret, the servant insists, "I don't need to be warned. Fear and faithfulness keeps it closed up in my breast, but mostly faithfulness" (*haud sum monendus: ista nostro in pectore/fides timorque, sed magis claudet fides*, 334–35). Even if the servant's final profession of loyalty is disingenuous, he shows the truth of Atreus' assertion that "only a powerful man can get false praise," and thus confirms Atreus' position as ruler.[38] At an earlier moment in their exchange, the servant had tried to convince Atreus to attend to "shame, care for the law, integrity, devotion, and faithfulness" (*pudor/ . . . cura iuris sanctitas pietas fides*, 216–17) but Atreus dismissed them as "private goods" (*priuata bona*, 218). Atreus is no *privatus*: he accepts and delights in the scrutiny and judgment of those he rules. The servant's protestations, that power without those virtues is unstable (*instabile regnum*, 217), do not convince the king. Atreus reveals the limits of Seneca's arguments for the ruler's self-restraint in the *De clementia*: it is the king's subjects, not the king himself, who might be most concerned about stability, and who will have to decide what they are willing to do in order to preserve it.

Atreus is familiar with at least part of the argument of the *De clementia*—that the ruler is distinguished from the rest by his lack of privacy, his continuous exposure to the public eye. Other characters in Seneca's plays also accept this association between power and visibility. In *Agamemnon*, Clytemnestra acknowledges her exposure to the public eye as she contemplates murdering her husband: when her nurse suggests that she can keep her guilt a secret, Clytemnestra objects that "every crime of the royal house shines out" (*perlucet omne regiae uitium domus*, *Ag.* 148).[39] Unlike Atreus, Clytemnestra hesitates about whether to continue with her plan and seems to fear the revelation of her actions to her subjects, but she never believes that she can commit this crime and escape public scrutiny. After Thyestes accepts his brother's invitation to return to the palace at Argos, he emphasizes that his new position will put an end to the obscurity he enjoyed during his exile:

> I do not have a house that is set on the peak of a high mountain and looms over the lowly citizens to make them tremble, nor do I have brilliant ivory gleaming on my towering ceilings, nor woods that wave, planted on my rooftops . . . but I am not feared, my house is safe without arms, and for modest circumstances great peace is assured. (*Thy.* 455–69)[40]

In Thyestes' estimation, the ruler is always an object of attention, and is thus exposed to hostility as well as to reverence.[41] Whether the ruler desires attention (like Atreus) or fears it (like Clytemnestra and Thyestes), he cannot avoid the risks or pleasures that come with having an audience.

Thyestes' speech echoes the wish of the chorus when they exclaim, "Stand in power on the palace's slippery slope, if you want it; let me be satisfied with sweet peace, and may I rest gently in my humble place" (*stet quicumque uolet potens / aulae culmine lubrico: / me dulcis saturet quies; / obscuro positus loco / leni perfruar otio*, 391–95).[42] Here the chorus aims to emphasize the risks of falling for those who have risen too high, and Thyestes similarly claims to prefer a lowly position to an overly exalted one.[43] The picture he offers of the palace, however, also draws our attention to how the ruler appears to the rest of the city, and thus allows us to take up the perspective of the ruled. Thyestes describes the ruler's house as his subjects see it—the palace that stands above the city, shining with ivory and adorned with inviting gardens. Even as the house separates the ruler from the ruled and symbolizes their distinct positions in the community, it also links them together—the house of the ruler attracts the attention of the ruled and keeps their gaze fixed on him. It is to the perspective of the ruled that I turn in the next section, and to how and why they watch the king's house.

Seeing and Sustaining the Ruler's House

When Thyestes muses on the royal palace, his account is one of many descriptions of the house of the Atreid kings that appear throughout *Thyestes* and *Agamemnon*. *Ekphrasis*, or detailed description, is a distinctive feature of Senecan tragedy.[44] Descriptive passages in Seneca's plays dramatize the acts of revealing (that is, of exposing what used to be, or usually is, concealed) and of viewing; they also draw attention to the presence of an audience, both within the world of the drama (other characters in the play) and beyond it (the spectators at the theater). Just as Seneca's tragic rulers acknowledge that they are visible to those they rule, in these scenes subordinate figures gain privileged access to the ruler's house. Furthermore, Seneca's dramatic enactments of revelation and viewing point to the subordinates' complicity in maintaining both the established order and their own inferior position within it.

The most memorable descriptive passage in Senecan tragedy appears in the *Thyestes*, during an exchange between a messenger and the chorus, the people of Argos (623–788).[45] When the messenger announces that Atreus has killed his nephews and served them to Thyestes to eat, he lingers over his description of the grove where the boys met their deaths.[46] This grove is located deep within the palace of the Atreids, where the members of the ruling family take the auspices to begin their reigns, consult the oracle, and display the spoils of war (*Thy.* 651–664). The messenger leads his audience on a tour of the royal house, beginning with the face the palace presents to the outside world, and gradually revealing the interior that is supposed to be hidden from view:

> On the highest peak sits part of Pelops' house, facing south: its facade reaches up like a mountain and bears down on the city and keeps the people, unyielding to its kings, within range; here gleams the immense roof, large enough to hold a crowd, and its gilded beams are supported by lofty columns of wondrous marble. Behind these parts that are commonly known, which the people revere, the splendid house extends into many rooms. A secret place lies deep inside the palace, embracing an ancient grove in a deep valley, the innermost part of the kingdom. (641–652)[47]

First, the messenger describes the palace as it appears to most viewers: a massive and menacing structure that looms over the city, shining with marble and gold (646–47). Next, he contrasts these features of the house, the ones "known to the people" (*uulgo nota*, 648), with the secret grove that is concealed within the palace, "the innermost part of the kingdom" (*penetrale regni*, 652).[48] He then gives a detailed picture of the very grove that he claims is exclusive to the royal family, noting its density and darkness and identifying the types of trees it contains (652–54); he dwells especially on an oak tree where the Atreids hang their victory trophies and a dank swamp that he likens to the river Styx (655–67). The report ends with a description of the grove at night, when it is especially mysterious and unfamiliar: "it is said that in the unseeing night here the gods of the dead groan, the grove sounds with shaking chains and the ghosts wail" (*hinc nocte caeca gemere ferales deos / fama est, catenis lucus excussis sonat / ululantque manes*, 668–70). Yet even as the messenger insists on distinguishing between the facade and the interior of the palace, between the visible and the invisible, he undermines this division: when he shares information that (he claims) had only been known by a select few, he brings the palace down from its lofty position above the city so that the people can look inside it. His account of the palace serves to demolish the boundary between the palace and polity, ruler and ruled. The grove is intimately connected with the royal house and its history, and the messenger's account exposes the kings to their subjects and gives the subordinate members of the community special knowledge of those who dominate them.

In the messenger's description of the palace of the Atreids, there is ultimately no difference between *ista uulgo nota* (what is known to the people) and *penetrale regni* (the innermost part of the kingdom)—the pretense of secrecy is no more than a pretense. It is true that the community is also under observation: the messenger describes the people as *contumax* (644), resistant or unyielding, to the authority of the royal house, and he notes that the palace that sits above the city keeps the people "within range" (*sub ictu*, 645), presumably to control their behavior. Yet while the palace allows the ruler to observe the ruled, it is not meant to protect him from the gaze of his subjects. The mass and splendor of the palace suggest that it is the most prominent feature of the landscape, and that it has been constructed precisely to attract attention from those who live beneath it. When the messenger describes the interior of Atreus' house, he fulfills the purpose for which it was built: not to give the ruler a place to hide, but to compel the entire community to look up and acknowledge his presence. Watching the ruler and the ruler's house, and learning about what the ruler does inside of it, is not necessarily a desirable experience for the ruled, but the act of viewing is key to their experience of subjection just as visibility is key to the ruler's experience of power. The messenger follows his description of the king's palace with a story of the most recent events that took place there: he explains how Atreus butchered his nephews and how Thyestes unwittingly consumed them.[49] The chorus never explicitly acknowledges the messenger's account: in the ode that follows (789–884), they exclaim at the sudden darkness and strange movements of the stars, but they do not expressly associate these events with Atreus' crimes.[50] Refusing to reckon with the knowledge that the messenger has offered is a kind of self-defense on the part of the chorus. When the messenger describes Thyestes' predicament, he observes that his one advantage is his ignorance of what has taken place (*in malis unum hoc tuis / bonum est, Thyesta, quod mala ignoras tua*, 782–83). This good fortune, however, will not last: the messenger exclaims that "we have to look; all evils will be revealed" (*uidendum est. tota patefient mala*, 788). The messenger is most concerned with what Thyestes will be forced to see (namely, proof that he has eaten his children); his declaration, however, also evokes the predicament of the chorus and the audience, who have been forced to acquire special insight into the grim world of the House of Atreus.

The messenger's revelation of the events in the grove recalls the opening of the *Thyestes*, when the ghost of Tantalus, the grandfather of Atreus and Thyestes, discovers the new horrors that are about to overtake his house. Tantalus is at first unaware of how or why he has returned from the land of the dead: he asks, "Which god pulled me out from my hellish dwelling, where I grasp at food that flees my greedy mouth? . . . Have they found something worse than being parched with thirst in the midst of the waves, worse than always gasping from hunger?" (*Quis inferorum sede ab infausta extrahit / audio fugaces ore captantem cibos? . . . peius inuentum est siti / arente in undis aliquid et peius fame / hiante semper*, 1–2; 4–6). Shortly after Tantalus' arrival, however, a Fury arrives to reveal the new crimes about to consume Tantalus' descendants, and to enlist Tantalus in carrying out the destruction of his house. The Fury contrasts the beautiful facade of the palace with the activity going on inside it: "Adorn the high columns and make the joyous gates lush with laurel branches, kindle a fire worthy of your arrival . . . now make the cauldrons froth over the fires, tear up the limbs and toss them in, let blood pollute the ancestral hearths, set up the banquets" (*ornetur altum columen et lauro fores / laetae uirescant, dignus aduentu tuo / splendescat ignis . . . ignibus iam subditis / spument aena, membra per partes eant / discerpta, patrios polluat sanguis focos, / epulae instruantur,* 54–62). The decorated columns and laurel trimmings stand at odds with the action of the narrative to come: if the festive exterior proclaims a new order of familial reconciliation and harmony, the polluted hearths and sinister banquets correspond to Atreus' true intentions.[51] At the very beginning of the drama, then, the Fury provides Tantalus with insight into the royal house that surpasses what any other characters enjoy. The people of Argos rejoice that the brothers' dispute has been resolved (*fratrum composuit minas,* 338), and Thyestes and his sons, totally ignorant of Atreus' plot, choose to return to the palace (421–90); even Atreus himself remains unaware of Tantalus' return from the underworld and of the Fury's participation in his own pursuit of revenge. While Tantalus is only present in the opening scene of the play, he gains an almost singular perspective on the events that follow.

Tantalus' point of view is not quite unique, because he shares it with the spectators of the drama.[52] Regardless of whether Seneca's tragedies were ever presented on stage in antiquity, the dramatic form points to the possibility of a viewer who exists outside the world of the play, but who nonetheless bears witness to the events that take place within it. Another ghostly prologue in the Senecan tragic corpus also implies the presence of an audience for the drama: *Agamemnon* begins when the ghost of Thyestes, who is both Atreus' brother and Agamemnon's uncle, is recalled from the underworld to predict the latest iteration of bloodshed that his family is to endure. This play, too, takes place in the Atreid palace, a house that Thyestes knows all too well. He announces, "I see my father's—I mean, my brother's household gods. This is the old threshold of the house of Pelops . . . on this couch they sit on high, those who wave the scepter with a proud hand. This is the place for convening the Senate, this is the place for banquets" (*uideo paternos, immo fraternos lares. / hoc est uetustum Pelopiae limen domus / . . . hoc sedent alti toro / quibus superba sceptra gestantur manu, / locus hic habendae curiae—hic epulis locus, Ag.* 6–11).[53] When the ghost describes the royal house, he orients the audience to the theatrical setting and thus indicates that the tragedy will unfold before an audience. His repeated gestures to the stage (This! This!) summon the viewer to see the world that he sees, to recognize and acknowledge the space that he is creating. The ghost's speech, moreover, explicitly emphasizes the privileged perspective of the audience. In observing that Agamemnon "will bare his throat for his own wife" (*daturus coniugi iugulum suae,* 43), Thyestes' ghost points out the contrast between the characters in the drama and the audience of the play: the former are unaware of what awaits them or hesitate to follow the course of action that the myth prescribes, while the latter are well familiar with what has happened and what will happen to the House of Atreus.[54]

Yet the audiences of *Agamemnon* and *Thyestes*, like the ghost of Tantalus, do not come to the king's house just to look. In *Thyestes*, the Fury needs Tantalus to take part in cursing the house. She begins her speech by summoning him, the "detestable ghost," to "drive on these impious household gods with madness" (*detestabilis umbra . . . penates impios furiis age*, *Thy.* 23–24). She urges Tantalus to "stir up the *penates*, summon hatred, slaughter, funerals, and fill the whole house with Tantalus" (*misce penates, odia caedes funera / accerse et imple Tantalo totam domum*, 52–53); to "upset the house, bring the battles and the love of the sword, an evil thing for kings, with you" (*perturba domum / inferque tecum proelia et ferri malum / regibus amorem*, 83–85); and to "spread this madness in the whole house" (*hunc, hunc furorem diuide in totam domum*, 101). She identifies Tantalus as a key spectator of the horrors to come, proclaiming, "let them down blood mixed with wine while you observe" (*mixtus in Bacchum cruor / spectante te potetur*, 65–66). The ghost at first attempts to resist, announcing, "I will stand here and keep the crime from coming" (*stabo et arcebo scelus*, 95), but as soon as the Fury torments him with whips, snakes, and hunger and thirst (96–99), he assents to her commands: "I follow" (*sequor*, 100). Tantalus' participation, then, is not voluntary, but it is required for the Fury to bring down the House of Atreus.[55] When the Fury tells Tantalus that "the house feels your arrival and shudders all over from the unholy touch" (*sentit introitus tuos / domus et nefando tota contactu horruit*, 103–4), she suggests that he is the true agent of its ruin. She requires Tantalus to accomplish her work: as soon as she determines that it is complete, she orders him to leave (*actum est abunde. gradere ad infernos specus*, 105). Tantalus' ghost and the Fury, as Alessandro Schiesaro notes, represent "a creative conflict between passive forces . . . which try to resist the drama's violence, and active forces . . . which create and further the dramatic action," a conflict that persists throughout the narrative of the *Thyestes*.[56] Tantalus' submission, however, also reveals the challenge of distinguishing between active and passive players. The Fury decides how and where Tantalus' capacity for destruction will be put to use, but without his acknowledgment and participation she cannot perform her dominance.

The audience in *Thyestes* and *Agamemnon* fulfill an analogous role to Tantalus'. No characters in *Thyestes*, other than the ghost, know about the

Fury's part in the drama: after the first scene, only the audience remains to bear witness to the Fury's control, and thus to ensure her continuing authority. In *Agamemnon*, the ghost's speech serves not only to reveal but also to create the world of the palace, in that by describing the dramatic setting the ghost of Thyestes brought it into being. His act of creation, however, could not stand on its own: he required the participation of the audience to accept and follow his vision of the palace, and thus to set the drama in motion. The audience of each drama, whether they watch actors perform or read a text, must look where the narrative directs them, but their engagement also makes the illusion of the drama possible.[57] From the very opening of these tragedies, the audience that watches the play becomes a partner in constructing a world that others rule.

Part of the drama of these plays is seeing—and experiencing—the ways that dominant and subordinate both conflict and cooperate with one another. The messenger in *Thyestes* claims that the Atreid palace bears down on a recalcitrant people, but as he describes Atreus' crimes within the house, the people of Argos fulfill Atreus' desire for acknowledgement and recognition. The ghost of Tantalus initially resists the Fury's commands, and her persistence shows that she needs him to realize her plans. Although the audience cannot alter the narrative, the ghostly prologues of both plays point to the special role of the viewer in the creation of the drama. Even if they have little opportunity to change or to reject the rules, those who watch the ruler's house acquire special knowledge of how the dramatic world works and play a crucial role in sustaining that world. In Seneca's tragic universe, as I explore further below, spectatorship and self-exposure, seeing and being seen, serve to destabilize the hierarchy of ruler and ruled.

The Theater of the Complicit

In *Thyestes* and *Agamemnon*, the act of viewing is simultaneously an expression of power and of powerlessness. Atreus, of all Seneca's tragic kings, is probably the most successful at securing his power, and he certainly takes the most delight in performing his own dominance. He is also the ruler who best recognizes his dependence on his subordinates and actively seeks their participation in confirming his supremacy. Early in the play, in his conversation with his servant, Atreus revealed his enjoyment of the lack of privacy, the inability to escape the public eye, which came with his status as ruler. After tricking his brother into eating the flesh of his own sons, Atreus enters the stage in triumph, but he is not satisfied with having accomplished his schemes: he needs Thyestes to bear witness to them as well, and thus to confirm Atreus' authority.[58] He gives orders for the doors of the palace to be opened and describes the scene within:[59]

> You throng of slaves, release the temple gates, open the joyous house. . . . I do not wish to look at him when he is wretched, but while he is becoming wretched. The house is exposed, it gleams with torches! He reclines, resting on gold and purple, supporting his head, heavy with wine, on his left hand. He belches. O, I am the most eminent of the gods, and the king of kings! (*Thy.* 901–12)[60]

Atreus orders the palace to be opened because his vengeance has no consequence if no one is aware of it.[61] Beyond his devotion to revenge, Atreus' desire for exposure also demonstrates his understanding of the relationship between visibility and power, and thus of the essential role of the subordinate in the manifestation of Atreus' authority. Even as Atreus reveals the interior of the royal house to the audience and (within the world of the play) to his subjects, he argues with himself about what kind of audience will be sufficient to recognize his deeds: he proclaims, "would that I could detain the gods as they flee, and bring them down and urge them on so that they all would see the avenging feast; but it is enough that the father sees" (*utinam quidem tenere fugientes deos / possem, et coactos trahere, ut ultricem dapem / omnes uiderent—quod sat est, uideat pater*, 893–95). Atreus regrets that he cannot compel the gods to watch him and thus to affirm his power, but Thyestes is an adequate observer because he is the object of Atreus' desire for revenge. When Atreus presents the heads of Thyestes' children and asks if their father recognizes them (*natos ecquid agnoscis tuos*, 1005), Thyestes replies: "I recognize my brother" (*agnosco fratrem*, 1006). Thyestes becomes a witness to who Atreus truly is, in contrast with the sham performance of reconciliation and peace that he made earlier in the drama.[62] He is also a witness to the dominance that his brother achieved in his successful pursuit of vengeance.

Atreus only regrets that he did not get the right kind of recognition from his miserable brother, because Thyestes ate his dinner without knowing whom he was eating: "he shredded his children with his impious mouth, but he did it unknowing, but they were unknowing" (*scidit ore natos impio, sed nesciens, / sed nescientes*, 1067–68). Even as Atreus imagines the ways he could have caused greater grief, he recognizes his dependence on his miserable brother: what matters most to Atreus is Thyestes' perception of his suffering and who has caused it. Beyond simply compelling his brother to submit to his will, he needs Thyestes to acknowledge (*agnoscis*) that Atreus is dominant over him.

In the *Thyestes* it is Atreus, the king himself, who opens up the palace and demands an audience; in the *Agamemnon*, it is Cassandra, a female slave and prisoner of war, who exposes the royal house to view.[63] Seneca takes a very different approach to Cassandra's vision of the murder of Agamemnon than Aeschylus did. While Aeschylus' Cassandra foresees the murder of the king (Aesch. *Ag.* 1099–1129, 1223–38), and then enters the palace to be killed together with him (1333–71), Seneca's Cassandra has a vision of the murder in real time, as it happens: she reports the events inside the palace, and she survives until the end of the play.[64] The immediacy of Cassandra's vision makes her a participant in enacting the events she describes: they come to pass as she gives voice to them, and her account is the only one provided to the chorus and to the audience. She sees Agamemnon, reclining in a splendid Trojan garment; Clytemnestra, urging him to put on the clothes she wove for him; Agamemnon becoming entangled in his cloak; Aegisthus stabbing Agamemnon, and Clytemnestra attacking her husband with an ax (*Ag.* 881–900). If Cassandra begins her speech as a spectator, as C. J. Littlewood puts its, she ends it as "a prophet who delights in . . . controlled narration" and "makes the vengeance her own."[65] When Cassandra announces that Agamemnon has died, her speech would be as suitable for the murderess herself as it is for the observer: "He's finished; it is done. The head, cut off, barely hangs on by a small flap and blood flows from the body here, the face lies there with a groan" (*habet, peractum est. pendet exigua male / caput amputatum parte et hinc trunco cruor / exundat, illinc ora cum fremitu iacent*, 901–3).[66] Yet even as Cassandra takes pleasure in the murder, she remains conscious of her own subject status: "A great thing is happening inside, enough to make up for ten years. But what is this? My soul, rise up and take the reward of your madness: we Phrygians, once conquered, have conquered. Go on, Troy, rise up: while you lie low, you have made Mycenae your equal; your victor retreats!" (*Res agitur intus magna, par annis decem. / eheu quid hoc est? anime, consurge et cape / pretium furoris: uicimus uicti Phryges. / bene est, resurgis Troia; traxisti iacens / pares Mycenas, terga dat uictor tuus!*, *Ag.* 867–71). Cassandra alternates between claiming that Agamemnon and Mycenae have met their ruin and acknowledging that she and her city have been forced into submission: she orders herself and Troy to rise up (*consurge; resurgis*) because they had previously fallen down (the Trojans are *uicti;* their city is *iacens*). Cassandra, then, is deeply aware of her subordinate position, but she nevertheless claims ownership of the actions of her conquerors: it is for her and Troy, not for themselves, that Clytemnestra and Aegisthus carry out the murder.

In a sense, Clytemnestra and her consort come to power only because Cassandra sees and recognizes the significance of their crime: in reporting the death of Agamemnon, Cassandra proclaims the beginning of a new regime. Earlier in the play, Clytemnestra explained her grievances against Agamemnon in terms of familial betrayal: he killed their daughter (166) and violated his marriage with Clytemnestra to become "the husband of a captive and Priam's son-in-law" (*captae maritus . . . et Priami gener*, 191). The most compelling reason to kill Agamemnon, in Clytemnestra's estimation, is to protect her children from Cassandra, their "mad stepmother" (*furens nouerca*, 199). When Clytemnestra remembers Agamemnon's position as king, she even considers forgiving him for the wrongs he committed against her as her husband. She tells Aegisthus, "there is one law for the throne, another for the private bed" (*lex alia solio est, alia priuato in toro*, 264). For Clytemnestra, the murder is primarily an act of personal vengeance; when she interprets the situation as a political problem, she comes close to reconciling with the king. Cassandra, by contrast, focuses on the political consequences of Agamemnon's death—that is, the reversal of the Trojan War and the rise of new rulers in Mycenae. Nevertheless, when she celebrates the downfall of her captor Agamemnon and the dominance of his opponents, she necessarily reaffirms her own subjugation.[67] Cassandra cannot enact her own revenge or direct the course of events, but she bears witness to the authority of those who rule her and thus helps to create it.

To conclude, I turn to another Senecan tragedy in which a woman's gaze has a creative power. This woman is a subordinate figure in her world and a minor character in the drama. In one of the most unusual scenes from Seneca's *Oedipus*, the blind prophet Tiresias is summoned to perform an *extispicium* to identify the murderer of the late king Laius.[68] He is accompanied by his daughter, Manto, who describes the ritual, the unusual responses of the fire and of the sacrificial animals, and the features of the animal entrails (*Oed.* 303–99). Although the signs she finds are difficult for Tiresias to interpret (the rite is ultimately a failure), Manto's capacities for sight and for speech make the rite perceptible to her father, the king, and the audience.[69] She reports what she sees in great detail, expressing her horror at the odd behavior of the flames (*horresco intuens*, 323) and marveling at how the animals' organs make her hands shake (*agitata trepidant exta, sed totas manus/quatiunt*, 354–55) and jump from her grasp (*uiscera effugiunt manum*, 380). Manto performs the *extispicium* in the service of her father, and they both—as Tiresias makes clear—are following the order of higher powers: when the pair arrive onstage, he explains, "where my fatherland calls me, where Phoebus calls me, I follow: let the fates be drawn out ... you, daughter, guide your sightless father, and report the plain signs of the fateful ceremony" (*quo uocat me patria, quo Phoebus, sequar:/fata eruantur ... tu lucis inopem, gnata, genitorem regens/manifesta sacri signa fatidici refer*, 296–97; 301–2). While Tiresias is dependent on his daughter's powers of sight, the anxious king Oedipus is likewise dependent on the prophet and his daughter in order to see what is taking place. Midway through the ritual, Oedipus is temporarily blinded: Manto exclaims that "thick smoke surrounds the king's head, settles even more closely around his very eyes, and has hidden the foul light with its dense cloud" (*ambitque densus regium fumus caput/ipsosque circa spissior uultus sedet/et nube densa sordidam lucem abdidit*, 325–27). Oedipus' loss of vision foreshadows his fate at the end of the play, when he pulls his eyes from their sockets with his own hands, but it also draws attention to more immediate difficulties: the ruler is utterly reliant on those whom he is expected to command. In this scene, the interactions between the dominant players (the king commands the seer, the seer commands his daughter) and the subordinate (the seer obeys the king, the daughter obeys her father) call these very categories of power into question, as the rulers submit themselves, albeit briefly, to the authority of the ruled.

Conclusion

In Seneca's account of one-man rule, the ruled can be active and calculating participants in their own subjection. By emphasizing the exposure and vulnerability of the ruler in the *De clementia*, Seneca urges his readers to be more wary of the risk of upheaval than of the costs of submission. Subordinate figures in Seneca's tragic worlds are ultimately complicit in strengthening the hierarchy that confines them: Thyestes, Cassandra, the subjects of the Atreid kings, and the audience all acknowledge and validate the power of those who dominate them, and thus they become responsible for preserving the structure of the community of which they are a part. When Seneca invites us to look at the king and inside the king's house, he illustrates the ways in which the king is exposed to our gaze and relies on our recognition.

Seneca's political thought is not simply a reflection of the historical events that he experienced at the imperial court, but he seems to have been aware of his own role in recognizing and strengthening the Julio-Claudian rulers, and so of his own capacity to foment change: Seneca was one of the alleged participants in the Pisonian conspiracy to murder Nero in 65 CE.[70] The plot was ultimately a failure, and as I discuss further in the conclusion to this book, the Pisonian conspirators seemed to have aimed to replace Nero rather than to end monarchy in Rome. Nevertheless, the Pisonian conspiracy represented a moment of tenuousness during the rise of one-man rule at Rome: these events revealed the potential of the ruler's subjects to refuse to recognize him, even when the power of the ruler appears to be absolute.[71]

Seneca's writings accentuate the points of possible disruption in a system of domination that requires the engagement of both ruler and ruled to maintain the order of their community. His tragedies make drama from a conundrum that may have been especially relevant to aristocrats in Julio-Claudian Rome: audiences who were familiar with submitting to the emperor's will might encounter Seneca's plays and recognize the ways in which they made possible their own subordination. Yet the interdependence of ruler and ruled in Seneca's drama also evokes relations of power that were familiar outside the emperor's court and in far less rarefied parts of the Roman world. In the next chapter, I focus on negotiation and cooperation among the inhabitants of houses in Roman Pompeii.

CHAPTER FIVE

Interdependence and Intimacy
Power at Home in Roman Pompeii

To study the place of the house in Roman ideas of one-man rule, I have examined emperors' houses and literary texts produced in close proximity to emperors' courts. In this chapter, I turn to the houses of Roman Pompeii, a modest town on the Bay of Naples and a very different milieu from the capital city. Pompeian houses and Latin literature engage with shared political problems, and we can draw on their responses to those problems to tell a larger story. My goal is not to elide the distinctions between Pompeii and the city of Rome, or between local elites and the ruling class of the Empire, but to tease out the specific conceptions and experiences of power that these two worlds shared.

Julio-Claudian writers, as Matthew Roller has persuasively argued, frequently compare the emperor to the elite householder: they draw on the range of social roles of the *paterfamilias*, from father and host to slave owner, to define good and bad rulers.[1] The material world of Pompeian houses gives us access to how Romans beyond the imperial aristocracy thought about the householder, and thus to the imaginative resources available to them for making sense of rulers and what it meant to rule. The householder, like the emperor himself, existed within a hierarchy that was subject to negotiation.² While in legal terms the householder was the ultimate arbiter of the persons and activities that took place within his household, archaeological evidence offers a much more complex picture of power relations in the world of the house.³ The architecture and art of the Pompeian *domus*, I will argue, frame the relationship between householder and visitor not only as one of dominance (the control of the *paterfamilias* over all inhabitants of his household) but as one of interdependence and intimacy (mutual attachments and shared obligations) between the *paterfamilias* and the rest.

Pompeii was formally allied with Rome beginning in the fourth century BCE, when Rome's power in the Italian peninsula was steadily increasing. Pompeii's earliest fortifications, however, had already been constructed in the sixth century BCE. The city enjoyed close contact with the Greek communities in Southern Italy, and its street grid and first modest forum were developed under the Samnites in the third and second centuries. In 81 BCE, after the Social Wars (in which Pompeii fought against Rome, on the losing side), Sulla established a colony of Roman veterans in the city. By the first century CE, the urban landscape of Pompeii would have been unsurprising and navigable to inhabitants of urban communities throughout the Roman Empire: beginning with Sulla, but continuing in the Augustan age and through the early Empire, Pompeii saw significant transformations in its public architecture, especially the construction of new temples, monuments, commercial spaces, public baths, and an amphitheater.⁴ Elements of Italian and Greek culture in Pompeii, moreover, might well align with the preferences and expectations of the Roman arrivals to the city.⁵ Houses that were built around an atrium or a front hall, and which are frequently associated with Roman social and political practices, were constructed in Pompeii from the third century and appear to have been preserved after the Roman colonization of the city: as Shelley Hales observes, "the houses of Samnite Pompeii were considered Roman enough for their new roles, Roman enough to house the veterans, and, perhaps more importantly, Roman enough to allow Pompeian occupants to participate successfully in the life of the colony."⁶ Pompeii, while not originally a Roman town, took part in defining what was required and what it meant to belong to the Roman world.

Recent scholarship has argued for the emergence of an elite *koine* in the Mediterranean in the second and first centuries BCE: this *koine* consisted of shared visual and architectural forms, literary texts, and (eventually) efforts to cultivate and promote ties to Rome.⁷ At around this same time,

Campania became a favorite region for elites from the city of Rome to find leisure and luxury, and Pompeii could count aristocratic villas and resorts (like Baiae, one of Nero's favorites) among its neighbors.[8] More specific contacts between Pompeii and the Julio-Claudian aristocracy have also been documented. While the evidence is sparse, some inscriptions and graffiti suggest a connection between the evidently prosperous *gens Poppaea* in Pompeii, who were associated with a number of properties in the town, and the *gens Poppaea* in Rome, the senatorial family to which Nero's wife Poppaea belonged; the empress has even been proposed as an owner of Villa A in Oplontis, built near Pompeii.[9]

When Pompeii was buried by the eruption of Mount Vesuvius in 79 CE, the Julio-Claudians no longer ruled in Rome, but the emergence of the principate had left its mark on the landscape. The temple to Augustan Fortune and inscriptions commemorating imperial cult activity, as well as other dedications honoring emperors and their families, show that Pompeii was attentive to and engaged with the imperial house, as were other cities across the Empire.[10]

Both the archaeological remains of Pompeii and Latin literary accounts of household life point to the house as a space where social status and social bonds are performed, negotiated, and questioned. In this chapter, I first show how theatrical and mythological frescoes encouraged visitors to reflect on the act of viewing and the relation of viewer and viewed, and so communicated the interdependence of host and guest in the household. Next, I argue that the multifunctionality of domestic space blurred the line between insider and outsider in the *domus*, thus emphasizing the intimate bond between the *paterfamilias* and those who visited him. Archaeological evidence for the *domus* shows that the head of the household was not simply an exemplar of dominance, whether malignant or benign: instead, he was implicated in more fragile and contestable relations of power.

Scenes of Seeing in Domestic Art

The ideal of the elite Roman house as a space devoted to self-display, open to public view and subject to scrutiny, emerges in part from literary sources that suggest that householders kept (and were expected to keep) their front doors open during the day.[11] Pompeian atrium houses, like the House of the Tragic Poet (VI.8.3–5), seem to accord with the literary record: the axial plan (figure 5.1) allows the viewer to look from the door into the atrium (3) (the front hall of the house, with a pool, or *impluvium*, that collected rain-

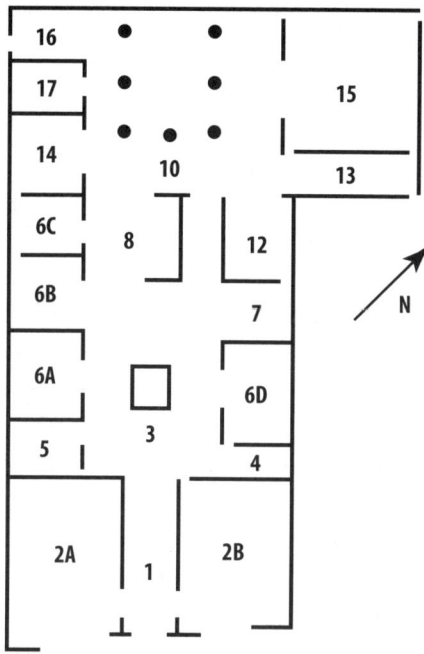

Figure 5.1. Plan of the House of the Tragic Poet, Pompeii VI.8.3–5. After Baldassare and Carratelli, 1990–2003, vol. 4, 527.

water), past the *tablinum* (8) (an intermediate room often identified as the "office" of the householder) and toward the peristyle (10) (a colonnaded courtyard, typically with space for gardens).[12] The experience of the ancient viewer, however, was more complex. Many houses in Pompeii include an entrance vestibule with two sets of doors, the first between the street and the vestibule, and second between the vestibule and the house. Householders could use these two sets of doors strategically, by opening the doors to the street and closing those that led directly into the house.[13] Even when the doors were open, and viewers could appreciate the axial view from the street, once inside they would become aware of rooms that they could not access, or discover that they could not follow a direct path through the house.[14] Partitions within the house, such as doors, screens, and curtains, further obstructed both access and visibility, and made viewers aware of what they could see and what they could not.[15]

For visitors who entered the house, domestic art also shaped their perceptions of the space of the *domus* and of those who lived in it. In the early

Empire, wall painting was becoming increasingly available to different social classes: on the Bay of Naples, we find it not just in grand houses but also in smaller dwellings and even in shops.[16] Ensembles of mythological and landscape panels, often interpreted as allusions to *pinacothecae* or public art galleries, are common throughout Pompeii. Similar decorative schemes, such as the combination of real gardens with paintings of gardens, appear in town houses like the House of the Ceii (I.6.15) and in luxury villas like Villa A at Oplontis.[17] Images of the *scaenae frons* (as I will discuss below) have been found in both Pompeian houses and on the Palatine hill. Lauren Hackworth Petersen argues that decorative motifs were similar across social contexts because "membership in Roman society is arguably what mattered most . . . and may go some way toward explaining why, excepting for scale, so many Roman houses and villas largely shared a common visual and cultural language."[18] Wall painting was one tool that householders could use both to assert their exceptional individual status and to claim membership in a wider group.[19]

Yet if citizens of Pompeii and the elite of the Empire used similar forms of domestic imagery to impress their guests, their guests were not necessarily impressed for the same reasons. In his study of visual culture in the Roman Empire, Emanuel Mayer cautions that "standardization [of imagery] could still provide opportunities for art to have a multiplicity of meanings" depending on the context in which it appeared, and depending on the owners who chose it and the viewers who encountered it.[20] Mythological wall painting in modest houses may point to the dedication of the *paterfamilias* to literary culture and learning—but it may also reflect the desire for an aesthetically pleasing atmosphere, where host and guest could enjoy depictions of beautiful scenery and attractive bodies.[21] When a Pompeian artisan selected a painting of a theatrical scene to decorate his house, his interest in asserting his prestige was probably different from that of Nero, who made similar decorative choices in the Domus Aurea. Yet while we must distinguish between these very different environments, we should not abandon considerations of power in our analysis of domestic wall painting in Pompeii. A more capacious understanding of the interpretive possibilities of ancient art in diverse milieus can also lead us to a more nuanced conception of power relations in the Roman world. Domestic art did not serve only to signify an owner's dominance, nor was dominance the only aspect of power that was of interest to a host or to his visitors.

In this section, I examine images of the theater in domestic frescoes, including representations of the *scaenae frons* (the stage building or backdrop) and dramatic scenes, and I argue that these images point to the authority that viewers enjoy over the viewed. The *scaenae frons* is especially common in paintings from the period of the Second Style, traditionally dated to 80–15 BCE, and the Fourth Style, which flourished from the middle decades of the first century CE until the eruption of Vesuvius in 79 CE.[22] By calling these images "theatrical," my intention is not to limit their range of meanings, but to focus on one key source for them. Theatrical performances were a major component of social life in the ancient city, so the world of the theater would have been one familiar parallel for the architectural forms and mythological stories that are rendered in these frescoes. In her study of Roman wall painting, Eleanor Winsor Leach suggested that the "messages" of images of the *scaenae frons* "concern the distribution of power within varied segments of society ... [and] provide the opportunity for encoding some of those negotiations of power that the real theater represents."[23] Images of stage buildings and dramatic scenes, as I will show, encouraged visitors to reflect on the privilege they enjoyed as viewers, and to associate viewing with special access to and knowledge of the household and their host.

Interest in the role of the viewer and the act of viewing was a distinctive characteristic of Roman domestic art.[24] While Roman paintings of mythological scenes were often inspired by Greek works, Roman painters frequently added supernumerary figures who observed the scene from within the painting and thus modeled or imitated the action of the real audience. The myths of Narcissus and Actaeon, which involve the relationship between viewing and desire and point to the consequences of sight, are common in domestic painting on the Bay of Naples.[25] Like supernumerary figures or myths that revolve around the gaze, theatrical imagery points to an interest in self-conscious spectatorship: theatrical performances promote interaction between the viewer (the spectator) and the viewed (the actor). Theatrical paintings serve in part to situate inhabitants of the household in a context that requires exchange between audience and performer, the viewer and the viewed.

The *scaenae frons* motif typically consists of three doorways, each framed by columns; two smaller doors flank a larger door at the center (figure 5.2).[26] This structure often rests on top of a platform stage and is decorated with dramatic masks, as in the frescoes from rooms 5, 11, and 13 of the (so-called) House of Augustus on the Palatine.²⁷ Similar paintings appear closer to Pompeii, as in rooms 15 and 23 of the luxury Villa A at Oplontis.²⁸ These theatrical frescoes are typical of the allusions to opulent public architecture that characterize Second Style painting.²⁹ In Fourth Style images, the *scaenae frons* is frequently populated with spectators and performers, as in the numerous frescoes in the Esquiline wing of Nero's Domus Aurea.³⁰ The motif of the *scaenae frons*, however, is far from exclusive to palaces and villas: it also appears repeatedly in the houses of Pompeii.³¹ In the modest House of M. Pinarius Cerialis (III.4.4, discussed further below), elaborate versions of the *scanae frons*, complete with actors performing different dramatic scenes, dominate the decor of a small room off the main courtyard: while some of the frescoes are damaged, the *scaenae frons* was likely the central image of the north, east, and west walls of the room. Cameos dis-

Figure 5.2. Scaenae frons (Iphigenia). House of M. Pinarius Cerialis, Pompeii III.4.4. H. Fertik. Su concessione del Ministero per i Beni e le Attività Culturali (MiBAC)-Parco Archeologico di Pompei.

covered in the house suggest that the owner was a gem cutter, and his customers may have visited him in his home, where they could have admired his fine paintings and colonnaded garden.³²

Theatrical frescoes can be explained in part as a reflection of the familiar elite Roman interest in self-promotion. Even for the artisan householder Pinarius, the image of the *scaenae frons* might facilitate his efforts to imagine and assert his local importance. The motifs of public architecture in Roman domestic art bring the city inside the *domus*, and thus they allow the householder to declare his dominance over public space and the life of the community beyond his doors.³³ Yet if the *scaenae frons* images point to the prestige of the master of the house, they also remind his visitors of their essential role as his audience, who recognize him and confirm that he is worthy of esteem. The world of the theater requires spectators who watch the events on the stage and who approve or censure what they observe. Guests similarly enjoy a kind of authority in the house because the householder relies on their acknowledgment, and because they represent the support he commands (or hopes to command) in the wider community.

The idea that the elite householder must assiduously cultivate attention and favor is one theme of the "Election Handbook" attributed to Quintus Cicero. The author offers advice for navigating the demands of politics in Republican Rome:

> Nothing seems more foolish to me than to expect someone you don't know to be devoted to you. You must have an exceptional reputation, status, and great accomplishments if strangers are to grant you honor even when you have no supporters. . . .
>
> Among those who attend your *salutatio* [morning reception], who are of a more common sort and who make many visits, as is the custom nowadays, make this smallest service of theirs seem to be most pleasing to you; if they come to your house, show them that you're taking notice. Point it out to their friends who will report back to them, and express it often to the visitors themselves. (*Comment. pet.* 28, 35)³⁴

This text points to a problem faced by the ruling class in the Roman world, and shows them how to solve it. They need to secure and retain the support of their followers, and they can accomplish this by showing their respect and appreciation for their visitors. For the Roman aristocrat, maintaining his power in society is not automatically guaranteed. He has to operate without "a system of mechanisms" that "[ensures] the reproduction of the established order," which Pierre Bourdieu identifies as a distinguishing feature of capitalist societies: in the absence of such a system, dominant figures must "work directly, daily, personally, to produce and reproduce conditions of domination which are even then never entirely trustworthy."[35] Part of the job of a member of the Roman elite is to personally and continuously claim and demonstrate his position, and his supporters play an essential role in this demonstration.

The patron's obligation to gain his clients' goodwill might well be magnified in communities like Pompeii, where local elections remained important long after the fall of the Roman Republic, and where the potential pool of friends was smaller, and the cost of alienating them greater.[36] Evidence for elections in Pompeii indicates that candidates sought to demonstrate a broad base of support. The *programmata*, graffiti posted on behalf of candidates for office, include the name of the candidate as well as of the *rogator* or endorser, but these notices were not spontaneous displays of enthusiasm. They followed a regular formula and clustered around major thoroughfares, and the endorsers included names of women and slaves, as well as freedmen and members of low-status professions.[37] These notices offer proof that a mass of people was willing to testify to, and thus to produce, a candidate's eminence and prestige. Facades of houses are especially common locations for *programmata*: candidates likely negotiated with householders for the privilege of posting their notices, and these do not seem to have been regularly removed after elections.[38] The facades of Pompeian houses, then, offered an enduring visual record of the need for local elites to develop, and proclaim, widespread support. If theatrical imagery served in part to aid the self-promotion of the *paterfamilias*, it could also remind his visitors of his dependence on them as members of the audience.

Scaenae frons panels, furthermore, invite viewers to actively engage with the imaginary world they represent, and thus to reflect on and recognize the privileges of viewing.[39] Frescoes with theatrical architecture are especially common in corridors in the Domus Aurea, and, as Katharina Lorenz argues, these long, narrow spaces make it difficult for viewers to see the entire composition at once: instead, depending on where they stand in the room, they discover multiple perspectives on these paintings and create multiple ways of seeing them.[40] In the House of M. Pinarius Cerialis, the magnificent architecture of the *scaenae frons* paintings in the small *cubiculum* allow viewers to enter a landscape far removed from the actual room that these paintings decorate; viewers may either embrace the illusion or resist the discrepancy between painted and architectural space. For the viewers of these frescoes, the act of viewing becomes a kind of power in itself—the power to interpret and experience these images, to bring them to life in different ways. This kind of power parallels the power that visitors enjoyed in the *domus*, where their presence and response was essential to confirming and upholding the status of the *paterfamilias*.

Another type of theatrical imagery in Pompeian painting—mythological episodes that evoke scenes on a theater stage—also points to the authority that visitors and viewers enjoyed in the *domus*. Myths are common subjects in Fourth Style frescoes, which are usually dated to the mid–first century CE. These images only rarely represent or correspond to specific literary texts, but dramatic performances of myth offered one possible point of reference for ancient viewers.[41] While the performance contexts of imperial Roman tragedies are much debated (as discussed in chapter 4), the mythic narratives familiar from tragedy were also frequent in pantomime: this was a popular dramatic form in which a single actor used dance, gesture, and masks to portray multiple characters.[42] All of the frescoes I discuss below appear in combination with visual allusions to the world of the theater (such as the *scaenae frons* or dramatic masks), either in the mythological panels themselves or on the walls and floors nearby. Like the *scaenae frons* frescoes, these mythic scenes make a theme of seeing and being seen, this time through painted figures who guide the viewer's gaze and who observe one another.

Studies of mythological and erotic imagery in Pompeian frescoes have demonstrated that these scenes can reflect and reinforce broader power structures in Roman society, especially the subordination of women to men and of enslaved persons to free.[43] In the following images, however, subordinate figures, especially women, play a different role: they guide and direct the viewer's gaze and the gaze of other figures within the painting. I argue that these frescoes associate the position of subordinates and outsiders with a special perspective on the world around them. Viewers familiar with myth, moreover, can recognize these women as decisive figures in their narratives, who possess a privileged knowledge that is unavailable to the other characters.[44] The perspective of subordinate figures in these images is not exactly parallel to the special insight that standpoint theorists (discussed in chapter 2) attribute to marginalized groups—that is, the insight into the artificiality of the established social order. But standpoint theory is again valuable for the interpretation of these images, because it reminds us to consider the perspective of subordinate figures in the painted scenes, and the perspective of members of the *domus* other than the elite male patron.

The *paterfamilias* had a special interest in domestic art that expressed his dominance (although he also benefited, as I have argued above, from showing his appreciation to his audience). Yet while the householder's preferences and objectives played a guiding role in the decoration of a given house, ancient domestic art was available to many viewers, who could respond to these images in different ways.[45] The patron did not have absolute control over how viewers assessed the domestic art in his house: viewers' interpretations of these images depended on the order in which they saw them, the length of time they spent, their posture and movement, and their mythological knowledge.[46] The social standing of each viewer and the occasion on which he or she encountered these images also influenced the way in which audiences made sense of them (an occasional visitor, for example, would likely have a different experience of a given image than a frequent guest or than a household slave).[47] Different householders also had different perspectives: as the ownership of houses changed hands, new owners inherited the decorative choices of their predecessors. The current householder might well interpret a fresco differently than the owner of the same house in a previous generation; he might make changes to the architecture of the house or add new frescoes that affected how viewers perceived the old ones. The experience of domestic art in the Roman world was defined by a diversity of viewers and ways of viewing: to interpret these images today, we must be mindful of their range of possible meanings, rather than seeking to determine a single interpretation.[48]

Few women from ancient myth are more associated with sight and knowledge than Cassandra, who appears as a prophetess in five images from Pompeii.[49] The best-preserved of these panels is from the House of the Menander (I.10.4), in a room near the atrium (room 4) that is decorated with panel paintings of Trojan War scenes.[50] The Trojan frescoes in this house are exceptional both for the combination of episodes from a single narrative and for their focus on the human figures, especially Cassandra, Helen, and Priam, rather than on the landscape of Troy.[51] Images of dramatic masks and a portrait of the comic poet Menander decorate the atrium and peristyle, and thus create a theatrical setting for the Trojan War frescoes.[52] The image on the east wall depicts Cassandra's encounter with the Trojan Horse (figure 5.3). She stands facing the viewer, on the right side of the image; behind her, a mass of fellow Trojans all look towards Cassandra.

Interdependence and Intimacy 115

Figure 5.3. Cassandra and the Trojan Horse. House of the Menander, Pompeii I.10.4. © Jackie and Bob Dunn, www.pompeiiinpictures.com. Su concessione del MiBAC-Parco Archeologico di Pompei.

In contrast to the dark forms of the men behind her and of the horse ahead, Cassandra's bright figure stands out and attracts the viewer's attention. The gaze of the other figures in the crowd, all fixed on Cassandra, similarly guide the viewer to look towards her. For viewers who recognize the narrative, Cassandra's confrontation with the Trojan Horse is simultaneously a moment of privileged awareness and of vulnerability. Only Cassandra understands the ruin that is about to befall Troy; one of her countrymen, uninterested in Cassandra's concerns, grips her as if to lead her away.

A panel on the north wall of the same room represents the end of the Trojan War, the aftermath of Cassandra's unheeded prediction (figure 5.4). Cassandra appears again in the moment before she will be removed from our view: she kneels and clings to the Palladium, while the Greek conqueror Ajax looms above her, already pulling her away. Cassandra's nakedness and vulnerability in the Palladium fresco, as Ann Olga Koloski-Ostrow

Figure 5.4. Fall of Troy. House of the Menander, Pompeii I.10.4. © Jackie and Bob Dunn, www.pompeiiinpictures.com. Su concessione del MiBAC-Parco Archeologico di Pompei.

argues, invite the viewer to take pleasure in her domination: she suggests that the patron who commissioned such images "created a painted script with subtle, and not so subtle, messages of control easily legible to visitors and members of their own households."[53] Yet the expression of dominance (as I have argued above) was not necessarily the only consideration for the *paterfamilias*, and while these images may point to the pleasures of exercising power, this interpretation was not the only one available to ancient viewers. The brightness of Cassandra's flesh calls the viewer's attention to her, and away from the darker forms of the Greek conquerors nearby. She crouches in the right foreground and faces the viewer, exposing her body but also inviting the viewer to focus on her point of view. Her orientation in the frame presents a striking contrast to Helen's, who stands with her back turned, surrounded by Greek soldiers (including her husband, Menelaus). Both women are soon-to-be conquests of the Greeks, but only Cassandra's face is visible. The image of Cassandra and the Trojan Horse in the same room could inspire viewers to notice Cassandra's perspective and to follow her guidance in this fresco as well.

In the House of the Tragic Poet (VI.8.3–5, figure 5.1 above), the room just beyond the atrium—often called the *tablinum*—is also decorated with theatrical motifs.[54] An unusual mosaic *emblema* decorates the floor: this mosaic features a crowd of actors and musicians in costume, preparing to perform a satyr play.[55] The eastern wall of the room was decorated with an image of the myth of Alcestis and her husband Admetus (figure 5.5). A messenger has come to the couple's house to inform them that Admetus will die unless someone else takes his place; Alcestis sacrifices herself to save her husband (although she is ultimately restored to life). Some viewers might have interpreted this image as a scene from Euripides' tragedy, which enjoyed longstanding popularity in Italy.[56] Alcestis exemplifies wifely devotion, and while she presents an appropriate model for female behavior in Roman society, she is also the most prominent figure in the fresco.[57] She occupies the center of the image, seated in a contemplative pose, her left elbow bent and hand tucked under her chin. She faces the viewer, but most of the other characters in the scene face her: the messenger and Admetus, who are seated around her, and Admetus' father and the god Apollo, both occupying the porch in the background. Two women, also on the porch behind Alcestis, watch Apollo. The viewer follows different characters' points of view that all lead to the same object: Alcestis herself. The drama of the moment turns upon the decision that the rest of the characters, and viewers in the know, watch her make. The Alcestis painting, like the image of Cassandra, presents a moment in which a figure who is traditionally subordinate to others enjoys superior understanding of the events at hand. Here it is Alcestis, not her husband or father-in-law, who determines the course of events to come.

Alcestis' perspective is especially remarkable in comparison with the mythological women depicted in other frescoes in the house. In her masterful study of the House of the Tragic Poet, Bettina Bergmann observed that many of the atrium panels depict "women in transition": Hera, about to become the bride of Zeus; Briseis, taken away from Achilles; Helen, boarding the ship to Troy. Similarities in physical stance, hairstyle, and dress encourage the viewer to associate these three characters with one another. These superficial resemblances, however, also "invite consideration of the very different situations of the three women"—the goddess, the captive, and the adulterous wife.[58] A viewer who stood before the Alcestis panel in

Figure 5.5. Alcestis. House of the Tragic Poet, Pompeii VI.8.3–5, Inv. 9026, Naples National Archaeological Museum. Su concessione del Ministero per i Beni e le Attività Culturali–Museo Archeological Nazionale di Napoli.

the *tablinum*, as Bergmann suggests, would compare her with the women visible in other frescoes in the house. Alcestis shares certain visual and narrative characteristics with the other women: she is veiled, like Hera and Briseis, and she is about to leave her husband, just as Helen will do. In the peristyle, also visible from the *tablinum*, was an image of the sacrifice of

Iphigenia: she will be rescued from death, just as Alcestis will be rescued from Hades.[59] The resonances and dissonances between the Alcestis painting and the other panels on the eastern wall of the house encourage the viewer to reflect on the different kinds of power and knowledge available to these women.[60] Briseis and Iphigenia, for example, appear entirely at the mercy of others, and perhaps ignorant of what awaits them. The image of Helen depicts the moment when it is most difficult to determine her responsibility for her actions and to assess her awareness of the devastation to follow. In the context of these women, Alcestis is exceptional for her special comprehension of the events to come (that she will sacrifice herself for her husband) and for her active role in shaping those events: she is at once the dutiful and submissive wife and the essential player in the scene.

A woman also directs the action in the Iphigenia fresco on the north wall of room (a) in the House of M. Pinarius Cerialis (III.4.4).[61] The figures stand against a *scaenae frons* (figure 5.2 above), which indicates that this painting represents a scene from a dramatic production.[62] Theatrical performances are also depicted in the frescoes on the east and west walls: one is too badly damaged to identify, but the other portrays an episode from the myth of Attis, the consort of the goddess Cybele.[63] Images of theatrical masks decorate the walls of the *triclinium*, a room used for dining directly across from room (a). Iphigenia appears on stage at the center of the image on the north wall, accompanied by two female attendants (figure 5.6). Four male figures occupy the area beneath them, on the left and right sides of the fresco: king Thoas (seated) and his servant on the left, and the captives Orestes and Pylades, standing on the right. Iphigenia, the king's priestess, and Orestes and Pylades, his prisoners, face the viewer, but the remaining figures turn toward Iphigenia, inviting viewers to follow their gaze.[64] This panel plays with viewer's expectations about who ought to be the dominant figure in the scene: the king is relegated to the edge of the frame, while Iphigenia demands the viewer's attention. Even for viewers in the main courtyard of the house, outside room (a), Iphigenia is a prominent part of the decor: a window in the south wall of room (a) makes the Iphigenia wall visible from the main courtyard and creates a striking frame around the fresco. As in the Alcestis fresco, viewers familiar with the narrative can appreciate Iphigenia's special position in the scene before them: unlike the ignorant king she serves, Iphigenia will learn the truth of her relationship to Orestes far before the king does, and it will fall to her to save his life. In this painting it is the woman, not the king, the conventionally

Figure 5.6. Iphigenia detail. House of M. Pinarius Cerialis, Pompeii III.4.4. © Jackie and Bob Dunn, www.pompeiiinpictures.com. Su concessione del MiBAC-Parco Archeologico di Pompei.

weaker figure rather than the established superior, who makes the best guide for the story that unfolds.

In an analysis of images in the House of the Vettii in Pompeii, Beth Severy-Hoven has argued that we should "reconsider deploying gender, or rather gender alone, to analyze the power dynamics encoded in Pompeian wall-painting."[65] The frescoes in the House of the Vettii show male and female bodies subject to violence and torture: as Severy-Hoven persuasively argues, images of both men and women can represent the experience of subordination. Similarly, the images of Iphigenia, Alcestis, and Cassandra not only speak to gender relations but reflect broader concerns about the relations of dominant and subordinate, ruler and ruled. Because they are women, Iphigenia, Alcestis, and Cassandra are typically subordinate figures; nevertheless, the frescoes discussed above reveal them in moments when they exercise a kind of power. These women are depicted so as to command the viewers' attention (e.g., because of where they are placed in the space of the fresco), and they are also depicted in moments when they command attention from other figures in the image. Furthermore, their special comprehension of the action in which they take part grants them a kind of authority over the figures they are usually expected to obey. Ancient visitors to these houses shared two important characteristics with the women depicted in the paintings. First, both were outsiders and inferiors—the women always, the visitors at least during the time they spent in a household that they did not control. Second, the visitors and the women can share a special perspective on the episodes represented in the frescoes.[66] Viewers may anticipate Cassandra's warnings to the Trojans, or share Iphigenia's comprehension of the difficulties presented by Orestes' arrival, or recognize Alcestis' decisive role in the story. These paintings, then, unsettle the subordinate position of the women in the myths and of the outsider in the house.

This is not to say that the decor in Pompeian houses primarily served to inspire guests with feelings of self-importance. In some cases, however, the opportunity to see a fresco signaled that the viewer enjoyed privileged access to the space of the *domus*.[67] In the House of M. Pinarius Cerialis, viewers in the main courtyard could look through a window to the Iphigenia panel in room (a), but the doorway to room (a) was not aligned with the front door of the house: it was only visible to those proceeding further back into the courtyard. Viewers might be attracted to the image of Iphigenia, but they could only get a closer look at the painting, and appreciate its connections to the decorative ensemble of room (a), if they were permitted to go inside. The Cassandra panels in the House of the Menander belong to a room that opens onto the atrium, but which (as the jambs at the entrance suggest) could be partitioned by a curtain or screen, and so access to the room and its frescoes could be restricted.[68] The Trojan War paintings, furthermore, might entice visitors standing in the atrium, but they are too small for viewers to examine and to enjoy unless they are allowed to enter the room. In the House of the Tragic Poet, as visitors crossed from the atrium to the *tablinum*, the satyr-mosaic *emblema* would signal that they had arrived in a new space in the house, distinct from the main courtyard.[69] The painting of Alcestis in the *tablinum* was not aligned with the entrance to the room, and was thus not easily accessible to visitors in the atrium: it was best visible from the *tablinum* itself or from a small room facing the Alcestis panel that opened onto the *tablinum*.[70] Visitors who were able to approach and enjoy the paintings of Iphigenia, Cassandra, and Alcestis also enjoyed a special level of admission to and knowledge of the *domus* in which they stood.

Visitors in a household are outsiders who, like the women in the tragic paintings, occupy an inferior position in the hierarchy of which they are a part. When viewing these paintings, however, the visitor encounters characters who possess exceptional knowledge of their circumstances despite their inferior status, and whose understanding of the situations they have found themselves in surpasses that of their superiors. If frescoes with the *scaenae frons* made it easier for the householder to put himself on display, the tragic images drew attention to the consequences of self-display, of revealing oneself to one's subordinates and thus to the public eye: just as these mythological women possessed a special perspective in the world of the frescoes, visitors could gain a special perspective on their host and his house. As I discuss in the next section, this perspective comes with insight into the life of the *domus* that complicates the householder's orchestration of self-promotion.

Insiders, Outsiders, and Multifunctional Space

The most famous passage on domestic space in Roman literature is from the sixth book of Vitruvius' *On Architecture*, a text usually dated to the early first century CE, in which Vitruvius puts forth his vision of the ideal forms and functions of domestic space. He explains,

> Now we have to consider how one should construct spaces in private buildings that are meant for the heads of households personally, and how one should construct those spaces that are meant to be shared with outsiders. For the personal spaces are those which cannot be entered without an invitation, such as *cubicula, triclinia,* baths, and other such places which take these same functions into account. But the common spaces are those where any of the people are permitted to go without invitation, such as vestibules, courts, peristyles, and others which can serve the same function. Therefore persons of ordinary rank do not need grand vestibules or offices or atria, because they manage their affairs by going to see others, and they are not visited by others. (Vitr. 6.5.1)[71]

Vitruvius distinguishes spaces within the house by function and by access. Some spaces serve activities central to the daily life of the *paterfamilias* and perhaps (although these are not mentioned here) other members of the household, such as sleeping, dining, and bathing, and are thus only open to others by invitation; other spaces, which serve first and foremost to facilitate receptions and gatherings, can accommodate larger crowds, and are open to the public. Vitruvius' account of the ideal house, as Wallace-Hadrill emphasized, is attuned to divisions of social and economic position. What a house does, or what a house is for, according to Vitruvius, depends on who one is within a wider society, and different people require different kinds of domestic spaces.[72]

Literary texts mark out the atrium, the front courtyard of the house, as the most public space of the *domus*, in that it is most devoted to asserting the social status of the householder and his family.[73] One distinctive activity that took place in the atrium, at least in aristocratic houses in the city of Rome, was the *salutatio*, a daily morning ceremony in which the elite householder received large numbers of clients.[74] The *cubiculum*, by contrast, often translated as "bedroom," was associated with rest and sex, but also with receiving privileged guests.[75] I use the terms *atrium* and *cubiculum* for convenience, but some archaeologists, especially Penelope Allison and Lisa Nevett, have warned that these names may prejudice our interpretations of ancient domestic space.[76] The evidence for the Pompeian house reveals that rooms were multifunctional: social and economic activity, self-display, and the mundane tasks of daily life occurred side-by-side. The use of a given room might change according to the season or even the time of day. Pompeii also illustrates the variety of house plans and types of dwellings in the Roman world. While atrium houses and houses built around the complex of atrium and peristyle were widespread, we also find houses with no atrium and houses with multiple courtyards.[77] Many larger "houses," moreover, were not necessarily occupied by the owner and his family, but could be divided into rental units of different sizes and with different amenities. Multiple families, who belonged to different social and economic groups, might occupy the same structure—clearly a different situation than Vitruvius imagines.[78]

The multifunctionality of domestic space in Pompeii challenges us to look beyond the elite householder's concerns with performance and display, and studies of Roman domestic life have increasingly turned to the perspectives and experiences of different types of inhabitants.[79] Yet we must also consider how the complex life of the *domus* informed the self-presentation of the householder and the relations between the householder and those who visited him. I argue that the multifunctionality of different spaces in the *domus* served to include guests in the daily life of the household and thus to blur the line between permanent and temporary inhabitants of the house.[80] Power relations in the *domus*, then, involve not only the display of dominance by the *paterfamilias* but intimacy between host and guest. The visitor left his household of origin and became (if only temporarily) integrated into the household of his host.

One space in which residents and guests routinely encountered one another was the atrium. The atrium's position at the front of the house meant that visitors had to pass through this space. Some Pompeian atria were clearly designed to impress, and they were fitted out with frescoes, fine marble tables, statuary, and water features that were decorative rather than simply functional.[81] Household shrines are sometimes found in atria, although no evidence for *imagines,* the ancestor masks that Roman aristocrats displayed in their atria, has been found in Pompeii.[82] The owner of the House of L. Caecilius Iucundus (V.1.26), who was likely a freedman, placed herm portraits dedicated to his former owner at the threshold between his atrium and his *tablinum*.[83] Yet the atrium also facilitated the mundane activities of the household. In a study of thirty houses in Pompeii, Allison identified loom weights, wooden chests, and storage vessels as the most frequent finds in the atrium: in contrast with the literary record, which primarily associates the atrium with the *salutatio* and religious life, these finds suggest that "the atrium had a fairly utilitarian function, acting as a service court around which the mundane household activities revolved."[84] All of the houses in Allison's sample include at least one front hall or courtyard, and all are relatively large structures compared to other houses in Pompeii: they belong to the top two quartiles of Wallace-Hadrill's typology, which distributes Pompeian houses into four tiers based on ground area.[85] While Allison finds some evidence in the atria of luxury goods and of furniture designed for display, these are far less common than furniture that kept items for everyday use.[86] Pompeii was devastated by an earthquake in 62 CE, and although construction and repairs were ongoing in 79, these factors do not fully account for the omnipresence of utilitarian furnishings in Pompeian atria: Allison finds these basic items in decorated and undecorated atria, and even in especially grand houses, such as the House of the Silver Wedding (V.2.1).[87] The frequent occurrence of loom weights and other weaving equipment in the atrium indicate that it was also a center of domestic cloth production.[88] Braziers and other objects associated with cooking have been discovered in and near atria, even in larger houses, and F. Mira Green has argued that slaves involved in preparing food and disposing waste needed to pass through the atrium, where they would encounter guests as well as other inhabitants of the house.[89] The material finds demonstrate that the atrium supported a range of persons and activities beyond the householder and his reception of clients and guests.[90]

When we recognize the multifunctionality of the atrium, we must consider *how* these different functions—reception and production, sustenance and display—affected one another. One consideration is that the atrium could be used primarily for different activities at different times. Portable items (like storage vessels) could be moved; visitors might see looms set up in the atrium without witnessing anyone actually weaving. Furthermore, the different functions of the atrium were in many ways compatible and mutually supporting: the tasks of daily life could complement the business of social engagement and display, rather than distracting from it.[91] Storage vessels and weaving equipment testified to the prosperity of the household, especially in combination with the shops, horticultural areas, and workshops that are common elements of the larger houses of Pompeii.[92] Similarly, weaving equipment might be evidence of a well-ordered domestic life. Spinning wool was associated closely with the virtuous Roman *matrona*, and Augustus took care to make it known that the women of his family produced his clothing.[93] The atrium, then, represents an opportunity for the householder to offer a carefully orchestrated performance of social prestige and power, of his distinction from and dominance over all other inhabitants of his household. Yet it also represents opportunities for staging a more intimate relationship. When the visitor arrived in the house, he encountered a space that supported everyday activities and included many inhabitants other than the *paterfamilias*. The *paterfamilias* might not always succeed in capturing his visitors' attention: the multifunctionality of the atrium meant that host and visitor could meet one another in the midst of the household's more mundane pursuits. Other members of the household might cross through the atrium and appear at inopportune times, or the noise or smells of daily work could interrupt the patron's reception of guests and clients.[94] In the atrium, visitors learned more about the household and about their host than they would if ceremonial and practical activities were kept strictly separate in the *domus*.

The presence of everyday activities in the space of the atrium did more than aid the *paterfamilias'* project of self-display: they also gave the visitor intimate access to the mundane mechanics on which the world of the *domus*, and the *paterfamilias* himself, depended. To elaborate on the experience of the guest in the house, it is helpful to consider the *cubiculum*, another multifunctional space. Anna Anguissola, in her study of the *cubiculum* in Pompeii, defines this space as a small room that included an alcove for a bed (a pattern of mosaic tiles indicates the placement of the bed, which usually does not survive *in situ*).[95] Activities in the *cubiculum* ranged from sleeping and sex to business dealings and the reception of small numbers of guests. Uses of the *cubiculum* probably varied depending on their location within the house: some were more isolated, and thus less suitable for social life, than others.[96] *Cubicula* often formed three-part suites with a *triclinium* (dining space) and *exedra* (a semicircular seating area), even in more modest houses.[97] Guests who entered the *cubiculum* in some sense were included as part of the household itself, in that they were given access to the space that facilitated so many of the inhabitants' needs and desires. The *cubiculum* promotes intimacy between the host and guest not only because of its size, but because it brings the outsider in the house closest to the diverse activities that make up the everyday life of the host and his house.

We might expect the intimacy between host and visitor to be most pronounced in the smallest houses, since they offered limited options for where to perform different activities. Cicero's accounts of Republican aristocratic households, however, suggest that negotiating the intimacy of the *cubiculum* could be a challenge even in grand establishments. In a letter to his brother Quintus, Cicero praises him for welcoming the common people of his province into his *cubiculum* when they needed assistance or advice (*Q.Fr.* 1.1.25).[98] Yet when Cicero attacks Verres, the corrupt governor of Sicily, he repeatedly berates him for carrying out judicial and political business in the *cubiculum*.[99] In a particularly memorable episode, Verres hears complaints about a woman tax collector "in his *cubiculum* . . . actually in his bed . . . when [the complainants] could see fresh traces of that woman tax collector in his bed, by which they understood that he was aroused to carry out this business" (*in cubiculo . . . atque in lecto suo . . . cum in lecto decumanae mulieris uestigia uiderent recentia, quibus illum inflammari ad perseuerandum intellegebant, Verr.* 2.3.34.79).[100] Verres' *cubiculum* is a multifunctional space in an extreme sense, as it facilitates very different kinds of activities (sexual intercourse and tax disputes) almost at the same time. Guests who enter this space have no choice but to acquire some special knowledge of Verres, some privileged insight into the kind of life that goes on in Verres' *domus*. Quintus opens his *cubiculum* in order to perform his special devotion to his office, to show that he values the needs of the community over the unfettered use of his own room; the interests of his clients take precedence over his immediate desires. By contrast, Verres exposes the full range of his daily life in his *cubiculum*, and insists that the Sicilians see it and participate in it.

When Quintus' clients enter the room, they will be most impressed if they remember what he is *not* doing: he is *not* indulging his personal desires, as he might do in this same space on other occasions. The multiple potential uses of the *cubiculum* likewise inform Verres' meetings with his visitors, although he wants them to witness what Quintus aims to hide. These two encounters, however, have more in common than it might initially appear: in both cases, visitors receive special access to the *paterfamilias* and his *domus*. These are high-stakes and challenging encounters for Quintus and Verres. When Cicero praises his brother for making himself accessible, he emphasizes the upheaval and unrest that met Quintus when he arrived as governor, from riots (*seditiones*) to highway robbery (*latrocinia*) (*Q.Fr.* 1.1.25), which suggests that Quintus' visitors were not simply a passive audience for their host's performance of authority. While Verres may have tried to shock the Sicilians into submission, they later sought retribution for his abuses. Quintus and Verres, seeking to display their power in their houses and beyond, invite their visitors to see them at close quarters, but these intimate encounters require the host to expose himself and his house to an audience he might not be able to control.

Conclusion

Much discussion of the *domus* focuses on the resources available to the *paterfamilias* to perform his dominance. The archaeological record, however, reveals the dynamism of the environment in which this performance took place, and the challenges of executing it successfully: the *paterfamilias* was only one of the people in the house, and his objectives of self-promotion and self-display were only a part of the activities that took place there. To the extent that he claimed the central place in his household, and used his house to demonstrate his wider authority, this success was a result of continuous effort and negotiation. The *paterfamilias*' power as well as his need for recognition, the techniques of self-display as well as the mundane habits of daily life, were made palpable in the material world of the *domus*.

In contrast with any other *paterfamilias*, the emperor had greater resources available for performing his dominance in his *domus* and outside it. The stakes of this performance were higher too: without significant competition from his peers, he could claim to be as central a figure outside of his house as he was inside of it.[101] Yet precisely because the role of the *paterfamilias* informed Roman conceptions of the role of the emperor, to understand these conceptions we must also account for the intimacy and interdependence that informed the hierarchy of the *domus*. Domestic archaeology from Pompeii, even though it derives from a different social context than elite literary texts, reveals characteristics of power relations that literature also represents and attempts to explain. Powerful leaders in Lucan's *Bellum civile* perform their concern for their followers and receive acknowledgment from them in turn. Tacitus' account of Nero's reign treats the imperial house as a space of continuous negotiation, where the emperor's power is always subject to challenge. Seneca's philosophy and tragedy show that rulers secure their power through self-display, that they depend on acknowledgment and recognition from those subordinate to them. The Pompeian household is not simply equivalent to the world represented in literary texts, but both draw our attention to the fragility of the position of the powerful in Roman political thought—even as those in power work hard to overcome that fragility, or to distract attention from it. The tension between the performance of dominance and the revelation of fragility is my concern in the next chapter, when I examine bodily functions in the daily life of the ruler's house.

CHAPTER SIX

Bathing, Dining, and Digesting with the Ruler

Of the many strange moments in Suetonius' life of the emperor Claudius, one of the strangest is the report that Claudius "considered an edict to pardon the stomach for breaking wind and rumbling during a banquet, when he discovered that a certain person, because of embarrassment, had been in danger from holding it in" (*meditatus edictum quo ueniam daret flatum crepitumque uentris in couiuio emittendi, cum periclitatum quendam prae pudore ex continentia repperisset*, Suet. *Claud.* 32). Here Claudius imagines or asserts that his power as emperor extends to the interior sounds and movements of his subjects' bodies.[1] Yet his edict also points to a kind of equality between the ruler and the ruled. The emperor recognizes that any human body will put itself at risk by "holding it in"; he thus demands that all bodies should be permitted to find relief. All participants in the banquet, furthermore, are to be intimately exposed to one another: they must endure one another's noises and learn (whether they want to or not) about the workings of one another's bodies.

In this chapter, I focus on bodily functions and how they both facilitate and challenge the performance of dominance in the houses of the powerful. Bodily functions were not exclusively associated with domestic space in the Roman world, as many Romans could satisfy their needs to eat, bathe, and relieve themselves in public. Most dwellings on the Bay of Naples had limited space to host guests for meals, but there were numerous local bars that offered spaces to eat, drink, and gather.[2] By the time of the early Empire, public latrines were a common amenity in Roman Italy.[3] Public bath buildings, widespread throughout the empire, provided space for social interaction and athletic and cultural activity as well as for washing up.[4] Domestic kitchens, baths, and toilets, then, served not only to fulfill the needs of the body but also to communicate the privileges of the bodies that enjoyed them. When the elite householder hosted a banquet, he could show off the resources at his disposal, including the slaves who prepared and served elaborate meals for the master and his guests.[5] Wealthy Romans were frequent visitors to public baths, but they also had access to bathing facilities at their houses and villas or those of their peers that were not open to the general public.[6] While different classes mingled together at the public baths, elite bathers arrived with slaves to carry their equipment and help them cleanse their bodies.[7] Public toilets, as archaeologist Ann Olga Koloski-Ostrow's work shows, were often unpleasant environments, built not as a public amenity but to protect the urban landscape from the urine and feces of the masses.[8] Basic latrines are common in Pompeian houses, but not everyone could rely on slaves to handle their refuse and thus to protect them and their houses from the unsavory consequences of ingestion and digestion.[9] The extent to which the house offered a space to care for the body was one index of the power of the householder in the wider community.

In this chapter, I examine literary representations of the powerful at the table, in their cups, in the bath, or on the chamber pot. I focus on two texts in which banquets structure the interactions of the ruler and the ruled: Petronius' *Satyricon* and Seneca's *De ira*.[10] Trimalchio, the fabulously wealthy freedman in the *Satyricon*, dominates his fellow freedmen with his extraordinary wealth, his imperial pretensions, and his tyrannical tendencies. At Trimalchio's banquet, the bodily functions of the ruler establish his exceptional dominance over the rest, but his insistence on sharing his practices of eating and drinking, of washing and relieving himself, also creates intimate bonds between all members of his community. Seneca's *De ira* is replete with anecdotes of tyrants, emperors, and kings who dine with their subjects, and their banquets demonstrate both their shared humanity and the tremendous and terrible differences in power between them. The *De ira* is usually dated to the reign of Claudius in the 40s CE, while Petronius likely composed the *Satyricon* two decades later, at Nero's court, but in both texts the banquet serves as a space for interrogating the system of one-man rule. While these works represent widely divergent genres and literary styles, I examine their shared concerns about the bodies of rulers and the meaning of those bodies for the community as a whole. In this approach to Petronius and Seneca, I follow Christopher Star's *The Empire of the Self*, in which he frames these very different writers as equal participants in key debates of Julio-Claudian culture.[11]

The *Satyricon* and the *De ira*, a work of fantastical narrative fiction and a treatise on Stoic philosophy, both treat bodily habits as an expression of the ruler's dominance and of the essential sameness between ruler and ruled. Trimalchio's position as at once a slave master and a former slave makes him a particularly important character to consider in light of Stoic philosophy: slaves and freedmen appear frequently in Seneca's philosophical writings, where they serve as figures for the servitude of the mind to the body, the possibility of gaining true freedom through philosophy, and the fickleness of fortune.[12] In the *Satyricon* and the *De ira*, the basic functions of the human body (especially eating and drinking) are points of contest between the ruler and the ruled—at once indicators of the ruler's unique role in the polity and of his all-too-human nature.[13] To dine, bathe, or use the toilet at the ruler's house is both to submit to his dominance and to recognize the equality of ruler and ruled as bodies, with the same bodily desires and the same bodily needs.

Trimalchio's Body

Trimalchio's banquet offers a testing ground for the forces that informed the relationship between ruler and ruled in the political imagination of the first century CE.[14] Trimalchio is not the emperor, but he presents himself that way: he is the writer of the script, the director of the show, and the arbiter of freedom and slavery, and life and death, for those under his rule.[15] Yet while Trimalchio claims to be the absolute ruler of his *domus*, he is also a freedman, for whom many privileges and honors in public life are beyond reach.[16]

What, then, is the basis of Trimalchio's power? His wealth, from his vast estates to his collection of rare luxury objects, plays an important role in impressing his guests and thus confirming his position. His fellow freedmen, who like him have little formal education, may marvel not only at Trimalchio's material possessions but also at his muddled mythological references.[17] His showmanship and the constant appearance of dishes and entertainments (and entertaining dishes) are clearly intended to awe and to overwhelm his guests.[18] I will argue, however, that Trimalchio's position as the ruler of his empire is rooted as much in his intimacy with the members of his *domus* as in their fear of him: by revealing his bodily functions to his guests and to his slaves, and compelling them to participate in them, he both marks out his special position in his community and expresses his shared humanity with those he rules.

Only fragments of the *Satyricon* survive, but the narrative appears to have been modeled on the epic wanderings of Aeneas and Odysseus: Encolpius, the protagonist and narrator, is cursed with impotence by the god Priapus, and endures a torturous voyage in Southern Italy.[19] Unlike his heroic counterparts, Encolpius travels through marketplaces, boarding houses, and brothels, in the company of freedmen, con artists, and prostitutes. Encolpius' own cultural and social background is (at least for modern readers) indeterminate, which makes his perspective as narrator difficult to pin down.[20] His tendency to frame the events of his life in the language of myth, tragedy, and epic compromises his reliability as an interpreter of his own story.[21] Yet while Encolpius is a student of rhetoric and of classical literature, he is also devoted to bodily pleasures: his superior education has not rendered him insensitive to the food, wine, and baths that are on offer at Trimalchio's house. Encolpius sneers at Trimalchio and the other freedmen at the *cena*, but he and his companions are hardly models of refined judgment and good taste.[22] Yet because Trimalchio and Encolpius both function as objects of entertainment and contempt, the hierarchy of the characters in the narrative is never firmly established. We cannot consider the guest or the host, the (supposed) intellectual or the freedman, the narrator or the target of his complaints, to be a certain voice of authority.

Trimalchio and his fellow freedmen face immovable obstacles to participation or recognition in civic life. They are aware of the arrogance of Encolpius and his companions, and the disdain that the unfamiliar guests show for the freedmen and their concerns. Yet the freedmen also seize the opportunity to respond and defend themselves: compared to the rest of the *Satyricon*, Encolpius' voice as narrator is relatively absent during Trimalchio's banquet, an episode known as the *Cena Trimalchionis*.[23] The majority of this section of the novel is devoted to speeches from Trimalchio and his fellow freedmen. When Ascyltos, Encolpius' friend and another guest at the dinner, laughs at Trimalchio, Hermeros, one of the freedmen, replies with indignation: "What do you have to laugh at? . . . You're a Roman knight: and I am the son of a king. . . . I sold myself into slavery, and I preferred to be a Roman citizen rather than a payer of tribute. And now I hope I may live so that I am no one's joke" (*quid habet quod rideat? . . . eques Romanus es: et ego regis filius . . . ipse me dedi in seruitutem et malui ciuis Romanus esse quam tributarius. et nunc spero me sic uiuere, ut nemini iocus sim*, 57.4–5).[24] Hermeros' speech is not only a defense of his host and fellow freedman, but also a reminder of the tenuousness of social status: the king's son can become a slave, and the slave can become a citizen. Even during his years of servitude, Hermeros claims, "no one knew whether I was slave or free" (*nemo tamen sciit utrum seruus essem an liber*, 57.9). The freedman may be funny, but funny is not all he is. In Seneca's writing, as Catharine Edwards has argued, the aristocratic Roman reader is encouraged "to emulate a slave's aspiration to be free. Seneca regularly highlights the possibility that a slave (or a freedman) may be morally superior to his master—more truly 'free.'"[25] When Seneca compels his readers to imagine themselves as slaves, he undermines the notion that master and slave are essentially distinct, or that the division between them can be securely maintained.[26] Similarly, even if Petronius' elite audience is meant to laugh at Hermeros in this scene, Hermeros' presence and voice demonstrate that the hierarchy of ruler and ruled is far from stable, and that it is always subject to negotiation and to chance.

Trimalchio is the ultimate embodiment of the volatility of *fortuna*, as his incredible material success sets him above the other freedmen. Trimalchio's house embraces the extent of the Roman world: the vastness of his lands, his multitude of slaves, and the diversity of food at his disposal allows him to claim dominance over the Roman Empire. Trimalchio describes the size of his holdings in the grandest terms: he announces, "I want to join Sicily to my little estate, so that when I want to go to Africa, I can travel within my own borders" (*coniungere agellis Siciliam uolo, ut cum Africam libuerit ire, per meos fines nauigem*, 48.3).[27] Trimalchio's slaves, too, represent peoples and practices from territories far away from the Bay of Naples. His retinue includes slaves from Ethiopia (34.4) and Egypt (35.6), and those who are specifically marked as "Alexandrian" (31.3, 68.3). When we first meet Trimalchio, he is attended by eunuchs (27.3): he may be reproducing the court practices of Eastern kings (as the Romans imagined them) or imitating Maecenas, one of Augustus' closest associates, who kept two eunuchs as his companions when he walked around in public (Sen. *Ep.* 114.6).[28] Trimalchio's penchant for the exotic points both to his regal pretensions and to the scope of the world contained within his house.

In addition to his diverse assembly of slaves, Trimalchio makes use of and displays luxury goods from all over the world. One of the guests at the dinner informs Encolpius that Trimalchio imported rams from Tarentum to breed with his own flock (38.2). He also acquired Athenian bees to produce Attic honey, and mushroom spores from India (38.4). Trimalchio's tremendous wealth seems to make him uniquely independent from the outside world: Encolpius' conversation partner tells him "there's nothing here which you should think that he bought. Everything is produced at home" (*nec est quod putes illum quicquam emere. omnia domi nascuntur*, 38.1). This passage is just one of the many indications in the *Cena* that point to "Trimalchio's desire to build a self-sufficient kingdom which neither he nor any member of his *familia* will ever need to leave."[29] Producing exotic luxury items for himself also allows Trimalchio to advertise his dominance over the regions from which they normally must be purchased.

Trimalchio has also adopted elements of public life and political institutions that mark his house as a state unto itself. One of Trimalchio's slaves reports that his master has "a water clock in the dining room and a trumpeter ready to go, so that he knows how much life he's spent" (*horologium in triclinio et bucinatorem habet subornatum, ut subinde sciat quantum de uita perdiderit*, 26.9). While obsession with death is a distinctive feature of Trimalchio's character, the water clock and trumpeter serve an additional purpose: they are characteristic of public life, and indicate that Trimalchio's estate operates as an independent polity.[30] During the banquet, part of the varied entertainment provided to the guests is a reading of the transactions of the estate, which Trimalchio's secretary "recited as though they were the *acta* of a city" (*tamquam urbis acta recitauit*, 53.1). Trimalchio is also especially concerned to portray himself as a high public official. He wears a bib adorned with the *latus clauus*, the purple stripe distinguishing senators and other occupants of high office (*laticlauiam . . . mappam*, 32.2), and boasts that he owns both a Greek and a Latin library, like the collections familiar from Augustus' complex on the Palatine (48.4).[31] Before the banquet begins, the great man is escorted to his house in a triumphal procession: he rides in a litter, clothed in red, accompanied by runners and a musician who whispers in his ear (28.5).[32] The characterization of Trimalchio and his house speaks in part to the indecorous self-regard of the freedman who has made good. Trimalchio, in this reading, "tends to claim all types of power, indeed almost to the ultimate extent of styling himself an emperor."[33] Yet Trimalchio's *domus* is also a self-contained model kingdom that, without the distractions of outside influences, keeps our focus on the central position of the ruler and his relationship to those he rules.

Along with his ostentatious wealth and devotion to luxury, Trimalchio is distinguished by his attention to his body and its most basic needs. His revelation of his bodily functions, of processes or habits associated with the inner workings of his body, is key to his performance of absolute power. Trimalchio is not simply too gauche to respect norms about bodily functions, or so dominant that he can violate those norms with impunity: his majesty and his obscenity are mutually reinforcing.[34] When Trimalchio first appears in the narrative, he is playing a ball game at a public bathhouse, where two eunuchs attend him; one of them carries a silver chamber pot (*quorum alter matellam tenebat argenteam*, 27.3).[35] At Trimalchio's signal, "the eunuch held the chamber pot beneath him while he played. Once he had relieved his bladder, he asked for water for his hands, and after just sprinkling his fingers he rubbed them on the boy's head" (*matellam spado ludenti subiecit. exonerata ille uesica aquam poposcit ad manus, digitosque paululum adspersos in capite pueri tersit*, 27.5–6).[36] I will return later to the significance of Trimalchio's interaction with the slave; for now, it is notable that urinating and washing are part of Trimalchio's self-presentation. Encolpius and his companions, watching Trimalchio, are told that "this is the man you're dining with, and now you see the beginning of the banquet" (*hic est . . . apud quem cubitum ponitis, et quidem iam principium cenae uidetis*, 27.5). Trimalchio's tending to his bodily functions is not distinct from the main event of the evening, but central to establishing his position of dominance over others.

From Trimalchio's point of view, the workings of the body—what it does and what it requires to function—are the most important and most interesting aspects of human experience. Trimalchio claims that medicine is among the most challenging professions (*difficillimum artificium*, 56.1), since the doctor "knows what mere men have inside their guts and when fever is coming" (*scit quid homunciones intra praecordia sua habeant et quando febris ueniat*, 56.2); he praises cows and sheep as "the most hardworking dumb beasts" (*mutae bestiae laboriosissimae*, 56.4) since they provide food and clothing for human beings, and calls bees, who "vomit honey" (*mel uomunt*, 56.6), divine. The workings of his own body, however, are the most interesting and important of all.[37] Early in the course of the meal, Trimalchio leaves the table to relieve himself (41.9), but lest we think that he wants to spare his guests the intimate knowledge of their host's bowels, he explains exactly what he was doing—and why—upon his return:

> "Pardon me, friends," he said, "but for many days now my stomach has not cooperated. Nor have the doctors figured it out. Still, pomegranate rind and pinewood boiled in vinegar have helped me. I hope that now my stomach retains some of its old shame. Otherwise there's such booming in my gut, you'd think it was a bull." (47.1–3)[38]

If dinner at Trimalchio's is a kind of tour of the Mediterranean world, then here Trimalchio offers a tour of his body, of the processes that it has carried out or failed to complete, of what he has put inside of it, and of what it might (or might not) excrete.[39] When Trimalchio shares this information with his guests, it is a sign that he knows his audience: health and sickness, and the benefits and uselessness of doctors and of medicine, are frequent topics in the freedmen's conversation.[40] Yet Trimalchio does not allow others to similarly hold forth on their biological processes. In describing and explaining his digestion, he asserts that their attention ought to be directed first and foremost to his body. When Trimalchio confers with an astrologer, he is most impressed that this *consiliator deorum* (divine counselor, 76.10) claimed expertise in Trimalchio's bodily functions: "He knew my intestines: the only thing he couldn't tell me was what I had for dinner on the day before. You would have thought that he had always lived with me" (*intestinas meas nouerat; tantum quod mihi non dixerat quid pridie cenaueram. putasses illum semper mecum habitasse*, 76.11). Trimalchio even compels his guests to witness his medical care: when an acrobat falls on the *dominus* in the middle of a performance, doctors are ready to come to his aid (54.2). The care and keeping of Trimalchio is the best part of the show.[41] While the other freedmen are obsessed with the details of the deaths of their neighbors and friends, Trimalchio does them one better: at the end of the banquet, he pretends to be dead and stages a mock funeral for himself.[42] When Trimalchio spreads himself out on a couch, calls in flute players, and tells the assembled company, "pretend that I am dead . . . say something nice" (*fingite me . . . mortuum esse. dicite aliquid belli*, 78.5) he demands that they witness his experience of the most crucial bodily process of all.

Even compared to his fellow freedmen, then, Trimalchio is especially absorbed by the workings of his own body and by professing his understanding of them before an audience. Trimalchio's interests are not limited to putting his body on display: he compels others to participate in his body's basic functions. All those present in Trimalchio's *domus* must model their own bodily needs and desires, and their approach to satisfying them, on Trimalchio's. When he returns from his toilet recess, after explaining the ins and outs of his own intestines, Trimalchio demands that his guests follow his example. He declares:

> If any of you wishes to take care of his own business, there's nothing to be ashamed of. None of us is born solid. I think that no torture is as great as holding it in. Not even Jupiter can forbid this one thing. . . . Nevertheless, I don't forbid anyone to do what he likes at the table, and the doctors forbid us to hold it in. Or if something bigger is coming on, everything is ready outside: water, chamber pots, and other little things. (47.4–6)[43]

Here Trimalchio presents himself as an *exemplum* of proper bodily upkeep, and as an expert on the physical form of the human body. When he claims that "none of us is born solid," he suggests that his companions are fundamentally just like him; his attention to and knowledge of his own body thus gives him privileged knowledge of their bodies.[44] Trimalchio expects his guests to recognize his power by bearing witness to his bodily functions, but this kind of attention is not enough: they must also commit to treating their bodies just as he treats his (and he has provided the accoutrements for doing so).[45] Trimalchio uses chamber pots, not multiseat latrines, and he is assisted by slaves rather than dealing with his own messes. When Trimalchio requires his guests to imitate the bodily regimen that he observes at his own house, he uses his bodily functions to perform and secure his power.

Trimalchio's efforts to compel his guests to model their bodies on his, and thus to participate in his bodily functions, extends to his habits of eating and drinking. Encolpius describes Trimalchio as "burdened with the foulest drunkenness" at the end of the night (*ebrietate turpissima grauis*, 78.5), but the host is unlikely to be alone in his inebriated state. When Trimalchio invited his guests to help themselves to the toilet facilities, Encolpius reported that "we checked our laughter with frequent nips of wine" (*castigamus crebris potiunculis risum*, 47.8). Trimalchio repeatedly calls for more wine for his guests (34.1, 34.7), and even demands that wine be served to the slaves (64.13). The feast that Trimalchio offers is nothing if not generous and extravagant, but his guests' pleasure is not his foremost concern.[46]

Encolpius finds certain dishes repulsive, or perhaps he is simply too stuffed to enjoy them.[47] He describes "delicacies which it hurts to remember: individual hens, fattened up for the table, were carried about, and goose eggs with caps, which Trimalchio sought most solicitously for us to eat" (*insecutae sunt matteae, quarum etiam recordatio me ... offendit. singulae enim gallinae altiles ... circumlatae sunt et oua anserina pilleata, quae ut comessemus, ambitiosissime <a> nobis Trimlachio petiit*, 65.1–2); there are also "quinces pierced with spikes, which would have been bearable, if the course had not been so absurdly long that we would have preferred to die of hunger" (*Cydonia etiam mala spinis confixa ... haec quidem tolerabilia erant, si non fer[i]culum longe monstrosius effecisset ut uel fame perire mallemus*, 69.7–8). Our narrator is famously unreliable, and it is far from certain that the rest of the company is as disgusted as he is, but the feast is served primarily for Trimalchio: in his *domus*, everyone eats what the ruler eats. He even attempts to extend his domain, and thus the union of his bodily habits with those of his guests, beyond the confines of his estate or the length of the banquet. One dish is an enormous pig, surrounded by "little piglets made from pastry, as if they were nursing ... and these were take-home gifts" (*minores porcelli ex coptoplacentis facti, quasi uberibus imminerent ... et hi quidem apophoreti fuerunt*, 40.4). Should they be able to leave Trimalchio's feast, his guests will continue to ingest it. When Trimalchio gives orders for the sculptural reliefs he wants to decorate his tomb, he asks for "*triclinia*, and the whole people having a good time" (*triclinia ... et totum populum sibi suauiter facientem*, 71.11). Trimalchio's tomb seems like one more attempt to control the eating and drinking habits of those subordinate to him, and to ensure that their bodily functions conform to his example.[48]

Trimalchio uses ingestion, digestion, and elimination as opportunities for self-revelation, intimacy, and control; bodily functions are central to the framework of his miniature empire, so the inner workings of his own body are inevitably of consequence to everyone in his domain, as an object of their attention and as a model for their own behavior. His grooming and washing practices too are both totally exposed and necessarily imposed on his guests. While bathing in public was standard throughout the Roman world, including among the elite, Trimalchio is among the lucky few who may bathe without venturing beyond their own homes. Trimalchio draws attention to the privilege of the domestic bath when he boasts that "nothing is better than to bathe without a crowd" (*nihil melius esse ... quam sine turba lauari*, 73.2). Yet Trimalchio is in fact bathing with a crowd, although a smaller and more select one than he would encounter in the public baths: his desire is not for seclusion and peace in the tub, but to show off his exceptional resources, and to compel his guests to study and imitate his personal habits. When Encolpius and his companions first enter the baths, Trimalchio "was standing upright . . . then as he settled and relaxed, invited by the sound of the bath he opened his drunken mouth to the room and began to mangle the song of Menecrates (as those who could understand him reported)" (*rectus stabat . . . deinde ut lassatus consedit, inuitatus balnei sono diduxit usque ad cameram os ebrium et coepit Menecratis cantica lacerare, sicut illi dicebant qui linguam eius intellegebant*, 73.2–3). Encolpius is apparently put off by Trimalchio's behavior, but the other guests, as boisterous as their host, "resounded with loud voices" (*ingenti clamore exsonabant*, 73.4). To bathe at Trimalchio's house is not only to watch him care for his body, but to bathe just as he does. Later, Encolpius observes that the hot water tub "was tempered for Trimalchio" (*Trimalchioni <tem>perabatur*, 73.5).[49] In Trimalchio's house, bathing is an occasion for the subordinate to copy the behavior of the dominant, and for the ruled to become ever more intimate with the ruler.

Trimalchio's efforts to regulate the hygiene of his guests extend beyond the walls of the bath. Earlier in the narrative, Encolpius expresses his horror at how the household slaves groom the dinner guests. As the guests recline, the Alexandrian slaves pour water on the guests' hands and feet and "trim [the guests'] toenail abscesses with remarkable dexterity; and lest they be silent during this noxious service, they sang all the while" (*paronychia cum ingenti subtilitate tollentibus. ac ne in hoc quidem tam molesto tacebant officio, sed obiter cantabant*, 31.3–4). He is again embarrassed when slaves anoint the guests' feet with oils and bind their legs and ankles with garlands, "an unheard of custom" (*inaudito . . . more*, 70.8). Encolpius' discomfort clearly indicates that these treatments are somehow unexpected, perhaps because of their unabashed luxuriousness and wastefulness.[50] Yet whatever their strangeness, they seem to be mundane at Trimlchio's estate. These practices too establish a particular intimacy between Trimalchio and the gathered company, between the dominant and subordinate members of the house, as they learn about the unusual way Trimalchio tends to his body and are compelled to have their own tended similarly.[51] Despite Encolpius' disdain, he makes no move to reject the slaves' efforts to clean and comfort his body.

These grooming rituals, furthermore, foster an intimacy not only between Trimalchio and his visitors but also between the free and slave members of the company. Ancient audiences would have expected slaves to be present at the banquet and to tend to the bodily needs of the diners, but the *Satyricon* is remarkably sensitive to the complex concerns evoked by bodily contact between dominant and subordinate, slave and free.[52] At Trimalchio's first appearance in the novel, as noted above, he urinates into a chamber pot that a slave holds for him, and after washing his hands, wipes them on the slave's hair (27.5–6). This action serves as a performance of Trimalchio's dominance: the slave's body is a tool of the master's, without the capacity for agency or self-direction. The slaves who tend to Trimalchio and his guests during the dinner hold a slightly different place, as they oversee and carry out the bathing rituals without any apparent input from those they bathe. In this case too, however, the bodily needs of the diners (that is, their needs as Trimalchio defines them) surpass and utterly displace the bodily needs of the slaves.[53] Yet while the slaves may be reduced to instruments at the disposal of their masters, the freedmen recognize the essential humanity of the enslaved.[54] When the freedman Hermeros bristles at the mockery of Encolpius and his learned friends, he points to the human body as proof of the commonalities that unite master and slave. Hermeros announces that, after he became free, "I bought my wife, so that no one would wipe his hands on her hair" (*contubernalem meam redemi, ne quis in <capillis> illius manus tergeret*, 57.6).[55] The freedman knows, just as he knew when he was a slave, that a human body is not simply a tool for bathing others, even when it is used that way.[56] Awareness of one's own humanity and dignity, moreover, is especially compelling at the moment that they are compromised. Being used to service the basic bodily needs of another human being is emblematic of the slave's condition: the experience at once evokes the total subjection of the slave to the master and the absurdity of the distinction between them, as the free and the enslaved have the same bodily processes and needs. The social status of Hermeros' wife, and thus the ways that others may respond to and treat her body, is ultimately a matter of chance, and is always subject to change. The slave's body is an expression of inferior social status, but also of the fictiveness of all social hierarchies. When the enslaved wash the free, their bodily closeness and contact points to the debasement of the subordinate party before the dominant one and to the fundamental equality of both.

Although slaves in Trimalchio's house must serve the bodies of others, their own bodies also become a medium for undermining the distinctions between the ruler and the ruled.[57] Near the end of the banquet, Trimalchio invites his guests to eat and drink until dawn because one of his slaves shaved his beard for the first time that day (73.6). Here Trimalchio demonstrates his awareness of his slaves' bodies and an egalitarian attitude toward the bodily development of members of his household. Enslaved bodies mature just as free ones do, and in Trimalchio's *domus* all bodies deserve (and must endure) the recognition of the *dominus*. Trimalchio also orders wine for his slaves during the banquet (64.13), and later invites them to recline at the table: Encolpius complains that "we were almost kicked off the couch, since the household slaves had occupied the whole *triclinium*. I certainly took notice of the cook positioned above me . . . who stank of brine and spices" (*paene de lectis deiecti sumus, adeo totum triclinium familia occupauerat. certe ego notaui super me positum cocum . . . muria condimentisque fetentem*, 70.11–12).[58] When Trimalchio shares wine with his slaves and seats them with his guests, the free and enslaved attendants at the banquet are invited to experience the same bodily functions. Trimalchio explicitly insists on the common humanity of slave and free: he declares, "Slaves are human beings too, and they also once drank milk like everyone else, even if a bad fate has oppressed them. Yet when I have passed on, they shall soon drink the water of freedom" (*et serui homines sunt et aeque unum lactem biberunt, etiam si illos malus fatus oppresserit. tamen me saluo cito aquam liberam gustabunt*, 71.1). Here Trimalchio seems to distinguish the basic and unchanging bodily processes uniting all human beings from the random events that order them into temporary hierarchies of power.

Trimalchio's proclamation that "slaves are human beings," and his willingness to dine in company with his slaves, evokes Seneca's assessment of the appropriate relationship between master and slave (Sen. *Ep.* 47).[59] Seneca congratulates his friend Lucilius for "living on familiar terms" with his slaves (*familiariter te cum seruis tuis uiuere*, *Ep.* 47.1), and admonishes those who refuse to dine with their slaves or who aim to obstruct the normal functioning of their slaves' bodies. Seneca objects to the master who forbids his slaves to make a sound or even to move their lips while he dines, and who beats them for coughing, sneezing, or hiccupping (47.3).[60] Seneca's assertion of the dignity of slaves is rooted in part in the Stoic conception of *oikeiosis*, "affinity" or (in Alex Dressler's rendering) "ownness," the faculty that causes human beings to recognize and pursue their own interests and to identify with the interests of others.[61] Chrysippus asserted that human beings possess a "natural orientation toward our own bodies" as well as a "natural orientation toward other human beings"; for the Stoics, as Margaret Graver puts it, "progress in ethical understanding is in large part a matter of increasing awareness" of our obligations to other human beings.[62] Trimalchio, obviously, is not a Stoic wise man, but by recognizing and providing for the needs of his slave's bodies, Trimalchio seems to evince the Stoic's commitment to regarding the concerns of all human beings as his own concern.[63]

While Seneca argues for an underlying equality between slaves and masters, Trimalchio pronounces slaves and masters as equally capable of enjoying the pleasures of the banquet.[64] For Seneca, all human beings are slaves to fortune: "'They are slaves.' 'Rather they are fellow-slaves, if you consider that Fortune has the same amount of license over slave and free'" (*Serui sunt. immo conserui, si cogitaueris tantundem in utrosque licere fortunae*, Sen. *Ep.* 47.1). For Trimalchio, all human beings are subject to the natural processes of life and death: when his slaves bring out a silver skeleton to decorate the table, he declares, "Thus we will all be, after Orcus takes us away. So let's live while we can be well" (*sic erimus cuncti, postquam nos auferet Orcus. ergo uiuamus, dum licet esse bene*, *Sat*. 35.1). Nevertheless, Trimalchio's philosophizing, his recognition of the common humanity of slave and free, ultimately reinforces the established hierarchy in the kingdom of his *domus*.[65] As Trimalchio calls for wine for his slaves, he announces, "if anyone refuses, drench his head with it! Discipline in the daytime, now it's time for cheer" (*si quis . . . noluerit accipere, caput illi perfunde. interdiu seuera, nunc hilaria*, 64.13). Just as Trimalchio set himself up as the arbiter of his guests' bodies (what their needs and desires were and how they ought to be fulfilled), he is also the master of his slaves' bodily functions: his interest is not in whether they wish to drink, but in bringing their bodies into harmony with his. When he invites the slaves to join the guests on the dining couches, Encolpius is acutely aware of the unpleasant smells that the enslaved bring with them; the proximity of slave and free emphasizes the distinctions between their bodies (i.e., the different ways they smell) and thus between their roles in the community. Trimalchio, who knows that both the free and the enslaved began their lives by drinking milk, will liberate his slaves to "drink the water of freedom," but only after his death. By insisting that free and slave, ruler and ruled, are equal in terms of the needs and functions of their bodies, Trimalchio cannot avoid drawing attention to (and thus reinforcing) the differences of status that divide them, however temporarily.

The course of Trimalchio's life is a stunning enactment of the equality of ruler and ruled, as he proves that the same man can occupy both roles. His experience, furthermore, makes him familiar with his slaves' bodies and even with their own experiences of their bodies. Because Trimalchio, as the *dominus*, controls the bodies of his slaves, he claims a unique understanding of how their bodies work. He knows what his slaves drank as babies, what they will drink after he has died, when it is time for them to drink wine, and when it is time for them to shave their beards. Trimalchio's physical and erotic contact with his slaves also allows him to assert his special knowledge of their bodies. When Croesus, his boy favorite, arrives on the scene, Trimalchio kisses him and demands that the boy climb on his back. Croesus promptly complies: "without delay he took advantage of the 'horse' and beat his flanks with his hands and feet" (*non moratus ille usus <est> equo manuque plana scapulas eius subinde uerberauit*, 64.12). Trimalchio's temporary submission to the body of his slave (Croesus is literally on top of his master in this moment) is a sign of the access Trimalchio enjoys to the bodies of others: he learns about Croesus' body both by touching it and by performing its typical posture of subordination. The bodily experience of subordination is already familiar to Trimalchio, who as a young slave was the favorite of the master and mistress of his household: "what the master commands isn't shameful, and I surely satisfied the woman herself" (*nec turpe est quod dominus iubet. ego tamen et ipsimae [dominae] satis faciebam*, 75.11).[66] While Trimalchio's close bodily contact with his slaves serves to reflect and secure his position as ruler of his household, he can also take up the slave's perspective on physical relations of free and enslaved bodies. The bodily degradation that Trimalchio's slaves might experience is ultimately an enactment of what they share in common with Trimalchio, and thus a performance of the intimacy between ruler and ruled. Near the beginning of the evening, one of the regular guests tells Encolpius that Trimalchio has so many slaves, "a tenth of them wouldn't recognize their master" (*decumam partem esse quam dominum suum nouerit*, 37.9). The events of the banquet, however, call this claim into question: during the course of the evening, master and slave acknowledge one another's bodies, and they use their bodies to perform both their shared humanity and their different positions within the hierarchy of the *domus*.[67]

To dine with Trimalchio is to become intimately familiar with his body. Trimalchio is wealthy and powerful enough to be able to produce and consume food and drink, and to relieve and bathe himself, in the comfort of home: these activities belong to his *domus*, where he determines how to satisfy the needs of his body, rather than to public spaces, where his own body must accommodate or adapt to the needs and desires of others. Yet Trimlachio does not attempt to conceal the inner workings of his body, but shares them with all the inhabitants of his house and demands that they bear witness to, and even participate in, his habits of bathing, ingestion, and digestion. More than the center of attention, Trimalchio's body is an avenue for intimacy and a kind of equality between ruler and ruled. Trimalchio makes his own body, his conception of its needs and desires, his attitude toward its treatment and care, into the model for all other bodies, and thus he insists on the common humanity of all members of his little community: his body is at once singularly worthy of consideration and essentially the same as all others. Trimalchio's key tools for performing his dominance and control—eating and drinking, bathing, excreting—also reveal the artificiality of the distinction between the ruler and the ruled. In the next section, I focus on the ruler's body at the banquet in Seneca's *De ira*. In this text, as in the *Satyricon*, when the ruler and the ruled eat together, they enact their shared bodily needs and thus recognize their common humanity. The banquet in the *De ira*, however, is also characterized by the violence of rulers against their subjects: it is precisely the equality of all bodies as consumers of food, and the perception and performance of this equality at the banquet, that provokes the ruler to reassert his dominance over the bodies of those he claims to rule.

At the King's Table

In one of the most remarkable episodes in Trimalchio's banquet, a cook claims that he has forgotten to gut a pig that has already been placed on the table (49.1–10). Trimalchio is outraged and demands that the slave be stripped and beaten, but the guests plead for mercy on his behalf. Trimalchio relents. When he orders the cook to gut the pig in front of the guests, the cook reveals the ruse: he cuts open the pig, and sausages tumble out for the diners to eat. Trimalchio and the cook, with the cooperation (witting or unwitting) of the guests, have transformed the banquet into a choreographed display of power, anger, and restraint. The banquet is punctuated by moments in which Trimalchio alternates between wrath and mercy, and when the *dominus* asserts his absolute authority over his *domus* and all who inhabit it, temporarily or permanently.[68]

Seneca's *De ira* also treats the banquet as a key context for negotiating the relationships between ruler and ruled and for investigating the effects of anger on those relationships. The third book of the *De ira* includes a number of anecdotes set in the houses of rulers, where the ruler and his subjects eat and drink together.[69] Like Trimalchio's dinner, the banquet in the *De ira* is in part an occasion for the ruler to demonstrate his dominance and authority, and his ability to compel his subjects to act in accordance with his desires.[70] The basic bodily functions associated with the king's table—eating and drinking—are central to the conception of one-man rule in the *De ira*. In this text, when the ruler eats and drinks, he can either form bonds with other human beings or pervert those bonds, and thus he can sustain the community he rules or devastate it from within. While these two options may always be available to the ruler, the banquet puts them in especially stark relief, as it is during the banquet that ruler and ruled share in the same bodily desires and needs. If Trimalchio's bodily functions allowed him simultaneously to set himself apart from his fellows and to assert his shared humanity with them, dining in the *De ira* demonstrates how threatening this recognition of shared humanity can be for both the ruler and the ruled.

The first book of *De ira* dwells at length on the bodily experience of anger, both for the person becoming angry and for those who observe his anger.[71] Anyone who wants to know whether angry people are healthy (*sanos*) need only observe the condition (*habitum*) of their bodies: in addition to their sorrowful expressions and savage appearance, their quickened steps and restless hands, "their color is changed, their breath is frequent and heaving . . . their eyes blaze and glimmer, redness is all over their faces . . . their lips shake, their teeth are clenched, their hair bristles and stands straight up . . . they groan and moan and interrupt their speech with indistinct cries" (*color uersus, crebra et uehementius acta suspiria . . . flagrant ac micant oculi, multus ore toto rubor . . . labra quatiuntur, dentes comprimuntur, horrent ac surriguntur capilli . . . gemitus mugitusque et parum explanatis uocibus sermo praeruptus*, *Ira* 1.1.3–4).[72] The image of the enraged body is part of Seneca's strategy to persuade his audience to avoid anger and its dangerous effects on themselves and on those around them.[73] The potential of anger to transform our bodies can be thwarted: Seneca insists that "nothing is so difficult and arduous that the human mind cannot overcome it . . . whatever the mind orders itself, it obtains" (*nihil est tam difficile et arduum quod non humana mens uincat . . . quodcumque sibi imperauit animus optinuit*, 2.12.3–4). The power of the mind to rule the body, to keep it from laughing or to forbid it to drink wine or have sex or to sleep, is total (2.12.4). This is not to say, however, that the body does not matter for

Seneca: in fact, he argues that the perceptions, functions, and experiences of our bodies are crucial to determining who we are and how we behave.[74] Our bodily sensations influence the way that others respond to us, and thus shape our engagement with the broader community.

Seneca argues that individual physical experiences (for example, what we touch, eat, and see) play a critical role in how we come to regard others. When Seneca explains how to bring up children so that they are less prone to anger, he draws special attention to the physical stimuli that children might encounter, especially the physical pleasures that come with wealth, luxury, and comfort. Children "should have their parents' wealth to look at, not to use" (*diuitias parentium in conspectu habeat, non in usu*, 2.21.8), and "above all, [the child's] diet should be modest, his clothing inexpensive and his ornaments similar to his peers': he will not be angry for anyone to be compared to him if you've made him equal to many from the beginning" (*tenuis ante omnia uictus <sit> et non pretiosa uestis et similis cultus cum aequalibus: non irascetur aliquem sibi comparari quem ab initio multis parem feceris*, 2.21.11). The things the child eats and wears affect the way he regards his own body and the way he understands the relationship between his body and the bodies of others. If he is accustomed to bodily comfort and pleasure that set him apart, he will refuse to tolerate physical conditions similar to those that others endure.

Nor is the connection between susceptibility to anger and the experiences and comportment of the body exclusive to children. Seneca insists that pleasures and luxury encourage anger, as we grow accustomed to satisfaction and take offense if anything disturbs us (2.25.3–4). Bodily suffering and privation, such as exhaustion and illness, hunger and thirst, are also conducive to anger, and thus to taking offense and engaging in disputes with others: "Those who are weary from illness or from age are quicker to anger. Hunger and thirst must be avoided for the same reason . . . an aggrieved mind is offended by the smallest things, so that a greeting, a letter, a speech, or a question drive some people into a lawsuit" (*iracundiores sunt ualetudine aut aetate fessi. fames quoque et sitis ex isdem causis uitanda est . . . animus adfectus minimis offenditur, adeo ut quosdam salutatio et epistula et oratio et interrogatio in litem euocent*, 3.9.4–5). Any disruption in the steady and moderate functioning of the body may transform the way we perceive ourselves and thus the way we interact with those around us. Seneca also imagines the inculcation and cultivation of virtue and vice as a kind of bodily process whereby we take on these characteristics from those we associate with most closely. Seneca suggests that "we take up the habits of those whose company we keep, and just as certain vices pass through bodily contact, thus the mind passes its failings to those who are nearby" (*sumuntur a conuersantibus mores et ut quaedam in contactos corporis uitia transiliunt, ita animus mala sua proximis tradit*, 3.8.1). For Trimalchio, revealing his own bodily functions and controlling the bodies of others was key to establishing his dominance; for Seneca too, the body is the medium through which members of a community guide and regulate one another's behavior.

The body's sensations and experiences (of hunger and satiety, simplicity and luxury, sickness and health) inform our understanding of our position in the world and our relations to others. Reflecting on what it means to be a body, its different parts and their different needs, is also key to articulating how the community operates as a whole.[75] Seneca asks, "What if the hands wanted to harm the feet, or the eyes wanted to harm the hands? Just as all body parts are in accord among themselves, since it benefits the whole for each part to be protected, so human beings will show consideration to each other, since they are born for fellowship, and indeed society cannot be secure without the guardianship and love of its parts" (*quid si nocere uelint manus pedibus, manibus oculi? ut omnia inter se membra consentiunt quia singula seruari totius interest, ita homines singulis parcent quia ad coetum geniti sunt, salua autem esse societas nisi custodia et amore partium non potest,* 2.31.7). Seneca's turn to the bodily habits of rulers in *De ira*, then, is no incidental move: the body informs our relations with others and thus our role in the broader community of which we are a part, so the bodily functions of rulers become central to understanding the relationship between ruler and ruled.

In the *De ira*, Seneca is interested in both the constructive and destructive capacity of the ruler's body when he drinks and eats. The royal banquet (which he depicts in a variety of cultural and historical contexts) functions as a performance both of the ruler's power and of his equality, on the level of the body, with those he rules. This double effect of the banquet, as an enactment of both profound differences in status between ruler and ruled and the basic shared nature of human beings, is a key element in a story about the emperor Caligula and the *eques* Pastor. The conflict between Caligula and Pastor has a mundane beginning: Caligula took Pastor's son into custody because he was "offended by his elegances and his exceptionally refined hairstyle" (*munditiis eius et cultioribus capillis offensus,* 2.33.3). Caligula's retaliation against Pastor's son has nothing in particular to do with this position as emperor, but instead highlights his proneness to jealousy of others' physical beauty, a failing that anyone might suffer. After Caligula condemns the young man to death, "so that he would not seem to be acting without humanity toward the father, he invited him to dinner on that very day" (*ne tamen omnia inhumane faceret aduersum patrem, ad cenam illum eo die inuitauit*, 2.33.3). If an invitation to dinner is ordinarily an indicator of humane behavior, this party turns out to be an opportunity for Caligula to perform the extent of his power.[76] The emperor uses the activities of the banquet, especially drinking wine, to demonstrate his control over the bodies of his subjects.

Like Trimalchio, who insisted that his guests comport their bodies at the banquet according to his model and his instructions, Caligula serves wine to the suffering Pastor, and insists that he anoint himself with oil and deck himself in garlands.[77] Seneca laments that "on the day when he had buried his son, rather when he had not yet buried him, the old man, beset with gout, lay there among the hundred dinner guests and drained drinks that were hardly appropriate for his children's birthdays. . . . [Caligula] wore the old man out with frequent toasts, urging him to let go of his cares" (*eo die quo filium extulerat, immo quo non extulerat, iacebat conuiua centesimus et potiones uix honestas natalibus liberorum podagricus senex hauriebat . . . propinationibus senem crebris, ut cura leniretur admonens, lacessebat*, 2.33.4–6). The emperor's treatment of the grieving father is torture in the guise of solicitousness and celebration, and it is especially terrible because Pastor must act like all of his companions at the table. He and the other banqueters, including the emperor, the murderer of his son, are responding (at least ostensibly) to the same bodily desires, and they are thus carrying out the same bodily processes. The banquet demonstrates the emperor's exceptional control over those subordinate to him and thus establishes his unique role in his community, but insofar as they are bodies that drink and eat, ruler and ruled are interchangeable. When the emperor forces Pastor to drink, he reveals the nature of the bond between ruler and ruled: the ruler wields power over his subjects' bodies, but ruler and ruled also share key bodily experiences and bodily actions. The commonalities between the bodies of ruler and ruled are a key element of the suffering that Pastor undergoes, as he must accept that he and his torturer are ultimately bodies that take in (and expel) liquid.

The human need or desire to drink, regardless of the social station of the drinker, also informs the relationship between King Cambyses and his unfortunate friend Praexaspes. Cambyses (according to Seneca) was "exceptionally devoted to wine" (*nimis deditum uino*) and Praexaspes advises him "to drink less, saying that drunkenness was beneath a king, since everyone's eyes and ears follow him" (*parcius biberet, turpem esse dicens ebrietatem in rege, quem omnium oculi auresque sequerentur*, 3.14.1).[78] Praexaspes assumes that he can advise the king about the needs of his body: since drunkenness is a consequence of excessive consumption of wine, Praexaspes gives the king the same advice—moderation—that he would give to anyone who should avoid drunkenness.[79] Yet Praexespes also treats the king's drunkenness as an exceptional case. We can imagine other drunks retreating to indulge themselves in peace, but the king cannot escape public view.[80]

Cambyses rejects his courtier's advice, telling him "so that you'll know that I'll never cut back, I'll show that my eyes and hands are up to their jobs even when I'm drunk" (*ut scias . . . quemadmodum numquam excidam mihi, adprobabo iam et oculos post uinum in officio esse et manus*, 3.14.1).[81] To test himself, Cambyses aims an arrow at the heart of Praexaspes' son. The king passes the test, and the boy dies.[82] The conclusion of the story is supposed to be shocking, but Cambyses' initial response to his courtier is also remarkable. The king rejects the notion that his position within the community should guide the care and comportment of his body. For Praexaspes, Cambyses' devotion to wine undermines his kingliness; in Cambyses' view, on the other hand, his fondness for wine is irrelevant—so long as he can control his actions even when he is drunk.[83] The king can indulge his love of wine just like any drunkard, provided that this indulgence does not interfere with his perception and his movements. When Cambyses rejects his courtier's advice to limit his drinking, he shows that he regards himself as a body like all other bodies: as he consumes wine, Cambyses enacts the fundamental equality between ruler and ruled, in that both are bodies that thirst and drink. By yielding to his urges, then, Cambyses inevitably undermines his exceptional position within his community. He calls his own dominance into question by revealing himself to be no different than any body subject to the desire to drink. Praexaspes assumes that Cambyses ought to set himself apart from the bodies of those he rules by moderating his bodily desires; the king ostentatiously draws attention to his desire to indulge in drinking, a desire that he could share with any of his subjects.

Two other stories from the *De ira* also show the dangerous consequences when rulers and ruled recognize their common experiences and needs as human bodies. When the Persian king becomes angry with his courtier

Harpagus, he invites him to dinner and serves him a meal made from the flesh of Harpagus' own children (3.15.1). In order to establish his own superiority, the king has turned Harpagus' own body against him: ingesting food is a basic human need, and dining in company is a basic social activity, but the king perverts these practices, both in his choice of menu and in his failure to share it (although Seneca does not specify whether the king consumed the children's flesh). Alexander the Great similarly took advantage of the human need for food, and of the custom of fulfilling this need in common with others, by murdering his friend Clitus in the middle of a banquet (3.17.1). Yet drinking and eating, even in moments that exemplify the ruler's potential for cruelty, underscore the fact that the ruler participates in bodily processes common to all human beings.

In a sense, the banquet is the place where the subordinate is most equal to the dominant, in that both are consumers of food; thus it is the place where the king's authority, his superiority to those he rules, is most fragile and subject to challenge. Like other human beings, the king has to eat, and yet the king may also insist, and force others to accept, that his bodily needs and desires are somehow different. He achieves this by making the satisfaction of basic bodily functions into an opportunity to demonstrate his capacity for retaliation and domination, and to assert his control of his subjects' bodies. When the king presents the heads of Harpagus' children to him during the dinner, Harpagus responds that "Every banquet is pleasing at the king's house" (*apud regem . . . omnis cena iucunda est*, 3.15.1). Seneca observes, "restraining grief is necessary for those who have obtained this lot in life, who are summoned to the king's table" (*necessaria ista est doloris refrenatio, utique hoc sortitis uitae genus et ad regiam adhibitis mensam*, 3.15.3).[84] While this episode represents an instance of exceptional kingly cruelty, Seneca implies that dining with the king is always potentially an exercise in acknowledging and submitting to the king's authority. No matter what he serves or how he behaves, the ruler, not his fellow diners, sets the rules about what makes a meal "pleasing" or not.

These episodes suggest that mundane bodily functions provide an excuse for the ruler to devastate those he rules and to undermine the political community; or better, that they tempt the ruler to violently perform his unique place in the community. Some of Seneca's accounts of rulers at the table, however, posit that the recognition of common humanity between dominant and subordinate can be constructive and mutually beneficial. Seneca describes a banquet at the house of Peisistratus, tyrant of Athens, when a drunken guest accused his host of cruelty; rather than taking vengeance, Peisistratus "bore it with a peaceful mind and responded to those who were egging him on, that he was no more incensed with him than if someone who was blindfolded ran into him" (*placido animo tulisse et hoc inritantibus respondisse, non magis illi se suscensere quam si quis obligatis oculis in se incucurrisset*, 3.11.4). Here Peisistratus recognizes drunkenness and its effects as a common event, especially in the context of the banquet, and perhaps as one that he himself might have experienced. The weaknesses and foibles of the human body serve to remind the king of what he shares with those around him rather than of the special status that sets him apart.

By far the most famous account of a ruler's forbearance in the *De ira* is the story of Augustus attending a banquet at the house of Vedius Pollio. This story offers two competing examples for how bodily functions might inform the relationship between ruler and ruled, one constructive and one destructive. Pollio becomes enraged when one of his slaves breaks a cup: he orders the slave to be thrown to the eels in his pond, where he will be devoured. The slave begs for mercy from Augustus, "so that he would not become fish food" (*ne esca fieret*, 3.40.3). In response, Augustus pardons the slave, has all of Pollio's crystal cups broken, and orders the pond to be filled in.[85] Both Pollio and Augustus play the role of the ruler in this account. The banquet takes place in Pollio's household, where he is (at least notionally) master of all that takes place. He clearly regards the slave as less than human: his life is cheaper than a crystal cup. The slave is a body to be eaten rather than a body that will eat at the banquet. Yet Pollio must also be aware that the slave, like all human beings, will be terrified of his fate and will resist his punishment: the death sentence, and the mode of death, is so devastating precisely because the slave is *not* simply fish food, but is instead a human being like Pollio and all his guests.

Augustus shares some of Pollio's premises, but he comes to a very different conclusion. The emperor also believes that the slave is human: he asks Pollio, "Do you order human beings to be seized from the banquet and torn to pieces in a new kind of punishment?" (*e conuiuio rapi homines imperas et noui generis poenis lancinari*, 3.40.4). He insists that the slave belongs with his fellow *homines* (human beings), the diners at the banquet, rather than with the watery creatures that they will dine upon. (As Robert Kaster suggests, by tossing the slave into the pond, Pollio was potentially feeding the slave to his guests, who would eventually consume the eels.)[86] Yet even Augustus' act of mercy toward the slave is a performance of his power over other human beings: as the emperor he can decide who will eat and who will be eaten. The banquet, for Augustus and for Pollio as for Trimalchio, compels all participants to reflect on their bodies and on the relationship between their bodies and the bodies of others. In the context of the banquet, as the ruler admits to or indulges in the bodily practices that he shares with his companions, the intimacy and common humanity between ruler and ruled, and the fragility of the hierarchy that orders their community, is most apparent.

Conclusion

At the ruler's table, the relationship of ruler and ruled and the hierarchy of the community to which they belong is enacted and asserted, but also called into question. Through the practices of eating and drinking, bathing and elimination, Trimalchio sets himself above the rest and performs the very acts that ultimately make him equal to his fellows. The royal banquets in Seneca's *De ira* provoke ruler and ruled to recognize and confront what they share as bodies (whether they want to or not). In both texts, attending to the needs of the body threatens to expose the fragility of the ruler's claims to power over the ruled.

Yet while encounters with the ruler's body reveal the contingency of his dominance, this revelation need not prompt resistance or revolution. Encolpius indulges in the pleasures of imitating Trimalchio's bodily functions despite his uneasiness about the events of the evening. If Seneca recounts the miseries inflicted on "those who are summoned to the king's table" (*ad regiam adhibitis mensam*), he surely knows how many would consider the royal table to be worth the risk. Recall, too, the ostentatious generosity of Trimalchio and Augustus to slaves at the table: when they admit to or celebrate their own basic humanity, they make space for others to endure their dominance. Who better to turn to, and who better to identify with, than the all-too-human ruler? For both Petronius and Seneca, the banquet is an opportunity to bear witness to the equality of ruler and ruled, but those who dine with the ruler can also learn to live with him.

Conclusion

The Roman house was a space for elite display of power, but it was also a space for interrogating and contesting power. In this book, I have examined the significance of these contests for ancient conceptions of one-man rule, both during the emergence of dynastic monarchy in Julio-Claudian Rome and for later assessments of this period. If the members of the ruler's household and the architectural space he inhabited expressed his dominance in the polity, they also revealed his dependence on others to recognize, acknowledge, and confirm his power. For Tacitus, the emperor's house becomes a site of competition between the emperor and his family (chapter 2). Seneca emphasizes the subjection of the sole ruler to the public eye (chapter 4). In the *Satyricon* and the *De ira*, the powerful and the powerless confront their equality as bodies that eat and drink, a confrontation that undermines the distinction between ruler and ruled (chapter 6). The house was a space that made the fragility of power visible. Yet while the Romans I have discussed in these pages are attuned to the contestability and contingency of claims to rule, they can also see the appeal of submission or cooperation. Lucan imagines the attractions of loving the ruler and of receiving the ruler's love (chapter 1). Visitors to Nero's park in the Domus Aurea partake of the emperor's private luxuries (chapter 3). In the houses of

Roman Pompeii, domestic art communicates the interdependence of the householder and his visitors (chapter 5). Trimalchio's house allows the master, his guests, and his slaves to share the same bodily pleasures (chapter 6).

I conclude by returning to Tacitus, who is keenly aware of elite efforts and failures to contest imperial power, and also of elite anxieties about the benefits and costs of those contestations. In Tacitus' account, the private life of the household is one potential area for conflict between the emperor and the rest. This book has focused on Roman thinkers' attention to the public significance of the ruler's house and the ruler's exposure to public view. Yet the early principate, as Tacitus describes it, was also a period when emperors sought information about the private lives of their fellow-elites and when the ruling class scrutinized one another. In the *Annals*, the emperor's entanglement in the life of the community prompts invasions into the private lives of his subjects: loss of privacy develops simultaneously as a problem for the ruler and the ruled.

In Tacitus' narrative of Julio-Claudian Rome, the emperor achieves dominance as much through the acquiescence of his aristocratic competitors as through his continuous repression of them. Tacitus suggests that elite Romans in the early Empire have become accustomed to the new order: "with the condition of the state transformed, nothing was left of their old and sound character: everyone, now that equality was gone, looked to the orders of the *princeps*, with no fear at present, while Augustus was strong and sustained himself and his house and peace" (*igitur uerso ciuitatis statu nihil usquam prisci et integri moris: omnes exuta aequalitate iussa principis aspectare, nulla in praesens formidine, dum Augustus aetate ualidus seque et domum et pacem sustentauit, Ann.* 1.4). The empire was secure at home and abroad, and the traditional titles of political offices (if not their functions) had been preserved (1.3). Most Romans were born after Octavian's victory at Actium, or in between the civil wars that devastated the Roman world: "how few were left who had seen the Republic?" (*quotus quisque reliquus qui rem publicam uidisset*, 1.3). Even after the *princeps* became old and frail, and change (*spes nouae*) was anticipated, nevertheless, "few spoke in vain about the advantages of liberty, many feared war, others desired it. By far the majority gossiped about their next rulers" (*pauci bona libertatis in cassum disserere, plures bellum pauescere, alii cupere. pars multo maxima inminentis dominos uariis rumoribus differebant*, 1.4). Most of Rome's former ruling class values peace and prosperity more than the exercise of power, stability and security more than public glory, and they accept that the regime Augustus began will continue.

Tacitus condemns the leading men of the polity for their zealous accommodation to the rule of the *princeps*. He complains that "senators competed to propose more and more vile measures. It is even reported that Tiberius, whenever he left the Curia, used to say in Greek: 'O these men, so ready for slavery!' Apparently even a man who refused to allow public liberty grew weary of such abject and servile submission" (*senatores certatim exsurgerent foedaque et nimia censerent. memoriae proditur Tiberium, quoties curia egrederetur, Graecis uerbis in hunc modum eloqui solitum 'o homines ad seruitutem paratos!' scilicet etiam illum qui libertatem publicam nollet tam proiectae seruientium patientiae taedebat*, 3.65.) Yet Tacitus' own account of Roman political violence suggests that the diffidence of these elites toward public life is not simply a matter of laziness: the experience and fear of war and upheaval is genuine. Periods of prolonged violence and civil conflict awaited the Roman Empire after the fall of the Julio-Claudians, as Tacitus knew well. Tacitus' readers in his own day, moreover, might see themselves in Tiberius' Senate, accustomed to the authority of the *princeps* and unable to imagine a way out.[1] It was not simply that Roman elites no longer had the same opportunities for participating in public life, but that their assessment of the value of those opportunities had changed, and their desire for them (at least in comparison with their desire to avoid civil unrest) had abated.

Seneca evoked the association between peace, order, and one-man rule when he observed that "Caesar has so entangled himself with the state that one is unable to separate from the other without peril for both, for the former needs strength and the latter needs a head" (*ita se induit rei publicae Caesar ut seduci alterum non posset sine utriusque pernicie; nam et illi uiribus opus est et huic capite*, *Clem.* 1.4.3). Seneca's concern that the republic "needs a head" certainly served his own interests as Nero's advisor, but it also pointed to the anxieties that informed the compliance of the Roman aristocracy. The notion of the emperor as the guarantor of collective security was a key trope of early imperial literature, as Michèle Lowrie has recently discussed.[2] Tacitus' version of the Senate meeting after the death of Augustus, when the senators discuss what the role of the new *princeps* is to be, echoes Seneca's arguments. Tiberius initially insists that he cannot assume the powers that his adoptive father once held.[3] He claims that "he had learned from experience how difficult, how subject to fortune the burden of ruling everything was . . . more men would more easily carry out the duties of the republic if they worked together" (*experiendo didicisse quam arduum, quam subiectum fortunae regendi cuncta onus . . . plures facilius munia rei publicae sociatis laboribus exsecuturos*, 1.11). No one believes that Augustus' successor truly wishes to yield his powers—Tacitus observes that "there was more in his speech to honor than to trust" (*plus in oratione tali dignitatis quam fidei erat*)—but no one sees this moment as a chance to restore the Republic. When Asinius Gallus asks what part of the republic Tiberius would like to be entrusted to him (*quam partem rei publicae mandari tibi uelis*), Tiberius insists that he would prefer to give up the whole thing (*in uniuersum excusari mallet*, 1.12). Concerned that he has offended Tiberius, Gallus responds that "the body of the republic is one, and it must be ruled by the mind of one man" (*unum esse rei publicae corpus atque unius animo regendum*, 1.12). Although Gallus' response is motivated by his fear of Tiberius' retaliation, it is also interesting for how he orients the debate toward division and unity in the body politic: the rule of the *princeps*, he suggests, counters the specter of civil strife.

Establishing a new system of government or even installing a new ruler entailed turmoil as much as liberation. Seneca and the senators who address Tiberius equate the emperor's welfare with the continued existence of the Roman polity. They treat the safety of the emperor and the stability of his position as a security problem, which political scientist Ole Waever defines as "something that can undercut the political order within a state. . . . Those issues with this undercutting potential must therefore be addressed prior to all others because, if they are not, the state will cease to exist as a sovereign unit and all other questions will become irrelevant."[4] Claims of security typically involve "security for an established order against whatever seems to threaten, disturb or endanger it from without or within."[5] Seneca and Tacitus both give voice to the view that security is the result of "an ongoing concession to authority," and that order and stability can be worth the cost of the emperor's domination.[6]

One way that Julio-Claudian rulers sought to assert their dominance, ostensibly in the pursuit of communal stability, was by intruding into the private lives of others, especially their fellow members of the elite. Tacitus pays special attention to the activity of the *delatores* (the "informers" or "accusers"), whom he presents as a distinguishing feature—and failing—of the Julio-Claudian era.[7] The *delatores* are sometimes adduced as evidence of a kind of police state in the first century CE: in the *Annals*, the *delator* is typically a "low-born opportunist who seeks power and position . . .

gains a foothold in the *princeps'* inner circle, and works with the emperor against the interests of the senate and the privileged elite."[8] The *delatores* are often responsible for supplying information about speech and actions that disrespect the emperor and thus seem to challenge his authority: they especially target the houses and household activities of the Roman upper classes. The first and "archetypal *delator*," Caepio Crispinus, is an assistant to the governor of Bithynia, whom he accuses of spreading unpleasant stories about the emperor and of doing damage to images of Augustus and Tiberius (1.74, discussed further below).[9] The needy and unknown Caepio communicates his findings to the *princeps* and worms his way into his confidence.[10] In another case, Firmius Catus, a senator, encourages one of his fellow senators, Libo Drusus, to consult astrologers and dream interpreters and to consider himself a rival of the emperor, since "the Caesars were his relatives, his house was also full of the images of distinguished ancestors" (*consobrinos Caesares, plenam imaginibus domum*, 2.27). Catus relays Libo's doings to Tiberius himself, but the emperor is already aware of them, thanks to an informant (an *eques*, rather than a senator) who has become close to the *princeps* (2.28). Tacitus' hostility to the *delatores* is overt, and his depiction of their role in imperial Rome deserves skepticism.[11] I want to suggest, however, that Tacitus' negative representation of the *delatores* functions as a compelling critique of the problem that they purport to address: the security of the emperor and thus the stability of the community as a whole.

Tacitus identifies the reign of Tiberius as the real origin of the dangers that the *delatores* posed, particularly in trials dealing with charges of treason, or *maiestas*.[12] Charges for *maiestas* once applied to those who diminished the "greatness" (historian Clifford Ando's translation of *maiestas*) of the Roman people through the mismanagement of public affairs (1.72).[13] In the old days, Tacitus claims, "deeds were blamed, speech had impunity" (*facta arguebantur, dicta inpune erant*, 1.72); by contrast, "Augustus for the first time conducted an investigation about infamous pamphlets under the pretense of that law, since he was upset by the wantonness of Cassius Severus, which he used to disgrace notable men and women with his shameless writings" (*primus Augustus cognitionem de famosis libellis specie legis eius tractauit, commotus Cassii Seueri libidine, qua uiros feminasque inlustris procacibus scriptis diffamauerat*, 1.72). For Augustus, then, the law offers a tool to preserve the standing and dignity of the Roman nobility.[14] Tiberius, however, ultimately employs it to protect his own reputation, after "he had been irked by poems, whose authors were unknown, that gossiped about his cruelty and arrogance and his conflict with his mother" (*hunc quoque asperauere carmina incertis auctoribus uulgata in saeuitiam superbiamque eius et discordem cum matre animum*, 1.72). Charges for insult to the emperor are clearly easy vehicles for abuses of power. The outcome of the *maiestas* trials under Tiberius, however, is not a foregone conclusion: one reason these proceedings are so emblematic of tyranny is that is impossible to predict whether the emperor will be merciful or severe.[15]

Some of the most unnerving events in the early period of Tiberius' rule involve charges against individuals for actions in their private lives, in their own homes: these accusations make it necessary to "scrutinize the significance of individuals' acts, to determine whether they are meaningful symbolic gestures against the state, or meaningless in relation to the public affairs of Rome."[16] In a sense, the *delatores* carry out the function that Dionysius of Halicarnassus attributed to the censors: they are overseers for domestic life, to ensure that nothing is done "contrary to what was fitting and advantageous to the state" (Dion. Hal. 20.13.3). The *delatores*, however, define public advantage in a very narrow way, as what is amenable or at least unobjectionable to the *princeps*. Trials for *maiestas* take place in the Senate, where the senators participate in assessing evidence and assigning penalties for threats against the emperor.[17]

Tacitus' account of the *maiestas* proceedings raises two important questions: what constitutes a threat to the security of the emperor, and does that threat compromise the security of the polity? The *maiestas* proceedings fall under the rubric of what Waever calls "securitization":

> [We] can regard 'security' as a *speech act* . . . security is not of interest as a sign that refers to something more real; the utterance *itself* is the act. By saying it, something is done. . . . By uttering 'security,' a state-representative moves a particular development into a specific area, and thereby claims a special right to use whatever means are necessary to block it.[18]

In the *Annals*, invocations of the emperor's reputation and well-being are speech acts that drive securitization. To make an accusation of offense against the emperor is to make an argument (not always successful) that certain actions or events should be regarded as potential problems for the security of the community.

My attention to the intersections of privacy and security in Tacitus, like Tacitus' own account of the *delatores*, is not unmotivated. Many readers have sought to determine Tacitus' sympathies and aims in his historical context; they examine his assessment of monarchy and how he made sense of Republican ideals and practices in light of the imperial regime.[19] Beyond the circumstances that Tacitus had to navigate, his narratives of the *maiestas* proceedings offer us a window into the assumptions and values that informed political judgments under one-man rule.[20] Dean Hammer emphasizes that "to political theorists steeped in reason and abstraction, the Roman map seems almost embarrassingly affective and tangible: it is filled with recollections of laws and institutions, names and places, and events and traditions. To read the Romans is to immediately enter this world."[21] Tacitus shows us *what it is like* to hold certain conceptions of security and stability, and then allows us to observe how these conceptions inform and constrict political life. We can read Tacitus, I suggest, to find resources for confronting our own ways of thinking about privacy and security and the consequences of these attitudes for our politics.[22]

At this point, it is important to raise the following question: granting that Tacitus' account belongs to a patriarchal society characterized by gross inequities in power, and that elite Roman conceptions of freedom are inextricably bound up with the violence of slavery and conquest, to what extent should we (or can we) look to the *Annals* to make sense of and rethink political life today?[23] I believe that Tacitus' accounts of the treason charges that appear most frivolous—those for offenses against the image and reputation of the emperor—make the most useful narratives. These episodes show how difficult it is to escape the language of security or to reject arguments about what counts as a security concern, even for those who may be at risk from similar arguments in the future.

The first cases of *maiestas* under Tiberius involve two *equites*, Falanius and Rubrius (1.73). Falanius is accused of including a mime in his household worship of Augustus and of selling a statue of Augustus as part of a larger sale of his property. Rubrius is charged with using the name of Augustus to swear a false oath. Soon thereafter, M. Granius Marcellus, governor of the province of Bithnyia, is accused of gossiping about Tiberius (the stories he tells, Tacitus insists, are offensive but truthful). Marcellus is also charged with offenses against the images of emperors, which he likely kept at home: he sets an image of himself in a higher place (*altius*) than images of the Caesars and removes the head of a statue of Augustus, replacing it with a head of Tiberius (1.74).[24] Falanius, Rubrius, and Marcellus show a less than reverent attitude toward Augustus and thus, perhaps, toward the very system of rule that he established. Marcellus' casual substitution of Tiberius' head for Augustus,' moreover, makes a kind of mockery of the tense negotiations in the Senate that transferred rule of the body of the Republic (*rei publicae corpus*) from the first *princeps* to his heir (1.11–12). These episodes reveal some of the criteria that Tiberius' contemporaries use to establish what counts as a challenge to the emperor and his authority, or some of their approaches to arguing that such a challenge has taken place. Disrespect toward imperial images or toward the emperor himself, these proceedings suggest, could be interpreted as a more fundamental challenge to the Roman polity.[25]

Arguments of this kind do not always succeed. In the case of Falanius, Tiberius tells the consuls that "his father had not been assigned to the heavens for this reason, that the honor might be turned to the ruin of citizens" (*non ideo decretum patri suo caelum, ut in perniciem ciuium is honor uerteretur*, 1.73). For Rubrius, he leaves it up to the gods to defend crimes against them (*deorum iniurias dis curae*, 1.73). Later, he shows similar leniency to Lucius Ennius, charged with melting down a silver image of Tiberius, which he probably kept in his own home (3.70).[26] Near the end of his reign, Tiberius even intervenes on behalf of Cotta Messalinus, who made disdainful comments about the sexuality of the young Gaius Caesar, joked about the deceased Livia, and seemed to mock the *princeps* himself, calling him "my dear little Tiberius" (*Tiberiolus meus*, 6.5). Tiberius urges the Senate "not to adduce the candor of banquet conversation for a criminal charge" (*neu conuiualium fabularum simplicitas in crimen duceretur*, 6.5).[27] In his letter, Tiberius emphasizes his longstanding friendship with Cotta, but his generous response is also remarkable because it is so similar to his forbearance in the previous episodes. These cases show that the emperor's pardons do not put an end to claims that domestic activities, from table talk to the handling of household statues, could be cause for public concern.

Nevertheless, Tiberius is not always so forgiving, and it is not only Tiberius but also the senators who attend to the public ramifications of insult to the emperor. Regardless of whether the senators fear the emperor's retaliation or seek to exploit the *maiestas* proceedings for personal gain, they participate in affirming the public importance of the emperor and of offenses against him. The *princeps* is incensed (*exarsit*) by Marcellus' insults to his reputation and his images, although he is ultimately embarrassed into acquitting him: when the emperor calls for the Senate to vote on the charge, one of the senators, Cornelius Piso, observes that if Tiberius does not cast his vote first, he will be afraid of dissenting unwittingly (*inprudens*) from the emperor's own judgment (1.74). Piso comes close to a direct critique of the outsized influence of the emperor's own judgment about what counts as a security problem. In deferring to Tiberius' decision, however, he inevitably reaffirms the view that Tiberius is the mind (*animus*) of the Roman state (as Asinius Gallus called the *princeps*). The senators sometimes argue for the public significance of private activities even when the emperor himself rejects these concerns. When Libo Drusus is accused of plotting rebellion (*moliri res nouas*, 2.27), some of the most damning evidence produced against him is a document that contains "terrible and secret marks," evidently deemed to be threats of violence, that were "affixed to the names of Caesars or senators" (*nominibus Caesarum aut senatorum additas atrocis uel occultas notas*, 2.30).[28] Libo's slaves attest (under torture) that he wrote the list himself. Libo's accusers clearly want this document to be interpreted as an attack on the security of the Roman polity, and Libo, who evidently suspects that this interpretation will persuade his peers, commits suicide. The Senate continues with the hearings against him, although Tiberius claims that he would have pardoned Libo (2.31). When Tiberius is willing to overlook the offense of the *eques* who melted his image for the silver, Ateius Capito demands harshness on the grounds that "the power of deciding should not be taken from the Senate, and such a crime should not be considered with impunity; [Tiberius] might be reserved in the case of his own vexation, but he should not be lax about violence to the commonwealth" (*non enim debere eripi patribus uim statuendi neque tantum maleficium impune habendum. sane lentus in suo dolore esset: rei publicae iniurias ne largiretur*, 3.70). Tacitus implies that Capito's devotion to senatorial prerogatives is less than sincere (*palam aspernante Ateio Capitone quasi per libertatem*, 3.70), but the way he frames his objection is nonetheless significant.[29] Capito insists that the fate of Tiberius' statue is (or may be interpreted as) a threat to the security of the political community, and he makes the same association between the images of the emperor and communal security that emerged in the earlier cases.

The *delatores* and *maiestas* trials, then, not only represent tyrannical attacks on the privacy of the elite, but also promote a certain vision of how to create security and order, and the emperor plays a central role in this vision. If a treason charge is a tool for establishing who and what constitutes a threat to the wider community, then those who make these charges assert that they understand the true significance, the true motivation, of a suspicious act—that an insult against the emperor is, if not the equivalent of violence, then at least an adequate predictor of it. Identifying and responding to danger requires us to make predictions about the future: when we define a person as "dangerous," we assert not only "a quality immanent to the subject (he or she is dangerous)" but also "a mere probability, a quantum of uncertainty, given that the proof of danger can only be provided after the fact."[30] Even Tiberius questions the value of making such predictions, or of imagining that it is possible to achieve perfect knowledge in the pursuit of perfect security. When a senator proposes that those who are known to be of bad character should be barred from governing provinces, Tiberius objects. He notes that people often conduct themselves in ways that counter expectations, and that "the *princeps* cannot embrace everything through his own inquiry . . . for this reason laws were established for events, since the future is uncertain . . . *principes* have enough burdens, and enough power" (*neque posse principem sua scientia cuncta complecti . . . ideo leges in facta constitui quia futura in incerto sint . . . satis onerum principibus, satis etiam potentiae*, 3.69).[31] Tiberius suggests here that uncertainty, and thus the potential for insecurity, is simply a problem that we all live with; to give the *princeps* greater reach is only to increase his responsibilities, not his knowledge of who or what constitutes a threat. Tacitus claims that the senator's proposal is simply an attempt to flatter the emperor (*adulatio*), and Tiberius' reluctance to take on greater authority should not be taken at face value. Nevertheless, the emperor's response functions as a warning about the limits of security, and of efforts to ensure it. Because the actions and choices of others are uncertain, we must accept a certain amount of risk when we choose to live together: even the emperor cannot predict the future, or prevent it from coming to pass.[32]

While in this instance Tiberius recognizes limitations on his power to control the world around him, his restraint is far from consistent. Tiberius' reign is distinctive for the prevalence of spying, accusations, and mutual suspicion among the Roman elite, who participate in monitoring and seeking to control one another:

> This was the most destructive outcome of those times, when the leaders of the Senate made the basest denunciations, some openly, many in secret; nor could you distinguish foreigners from relatives, friends from strangers, what was just

beginning or what was longstanding and had become hidden: whether in the forum or in the banquet, whatever they were talking about they were blamed, so that everyone hurried to be first to point out the accused, some for their own defense, more infected as if by sickness or touch.[33] (*Ann.* 6.7)[34]

The changing evaluation of privacy is a clear concern in Tacitus' narrative: while Rome's ruling class used to seek public attention, they now live in fear of the scrutiny of one another, in public and in private life.[35] The early *maiestas* proceedings, however, also point to a debate about another kind of privacy: the ability to act without public consequence. The public significance of the emperor provokes a reassessment of the definition of "private life" for his subjects, of where to draw the boundaries between individual and communal concerns. What kinds of actions (e.g., a scurrilous poem, the casual handling of an image) count as offenses against the emperor, and to what extent do those actions threaten the security and stability of the polity? How should we respond to these threats, or can we prevent them from arising in the first place? In other words, what sorts of actions constitute a risk to the community, and to what extent can or should we mitigate these risks?

Tacitus explores these questions through a narrative that involves a relatively restricted group in Roman society: the emperor and the ruling elite.[36] These problems, however, are familiar from recent debates over privacy and security that involve and affect a much larger population. The development of digital technology in the late twentieth and early twenty-first centuries has facilitated the monitoring and collection of personal data on a massive scale. When we browse the Internet, advertising companies, online retailers, and search engines record our shopping habits or political preferences.[37] In the United States, credit agencies collect and sell detailed information on individuals' financial histories.[38] Privacy advocates who seek to restrict surveillance face an enormous range of obstacles, but the key problem for the present discussion is the tension between individual rights and the welfare of the community.[39] The individual right to privacy is usually associated with freedom and autonomy: if we are subject to constant scrutiny, or if we fear retaliation, we will avoid speaking and acting in ways "that might be unpopular, unusual, or unconventional."[40] This kind of self-censorship stunts the intellectual, moral, and creative development of individuals.[41] Privacy is also essential to forming different kinds of relationships of different degrees of intimacy: we share different information about ourselves with close friends than we do with casual acquaintances, and choosing what we share, or with whom we share it, is part of how we create these distinct social bonds.[42] The benefits that the individual derives from privacy, however, cannot always be reconciled with the interests of the wider community. Critics of the right to privacy note that "if the individual does have something to hide, the question is whether it should remain private or whether others need to know about it."[43] The state has a clear interest in discovering if I have committed murder or robbed a bank, even if I would prefer to keep that information to myself.

More difficult cases arise when we consider the costs and benefits of monitoring individuals and collecting information about them in order to predict or to influence their future behavior. If law-enforcement agencies had unlimited access to the email of private citizens, for example, perhaps they could use this information to prevent acts of violence and protect innocent people. This kind of argument, however, "could be used to justify virtually *any* invasion of privacy—or the sacrifice of any number of other public values."[44] Some critics, notably Priscilla Regan, address the conflict between privacy and the public interest by arguing that "privacy serves not just individual interests but also common, public, and collective purposes."[45] For societies that value freedom of expression, tolerance, and pluralism, privacy is essential to protecting and advancing those values.[46] The right to privacy serves "as a restraint on the government or on the use of power," and thus privacy protections have a broader social impact beyond the particular case of each individual.[47] To conceive of privacy as a public good, however, is not to argue that there are no conflicts between individual privacy and the public interest, or that privacy protections will never pose a legitimate risk to public safety. Surveillance, too, has its attractions: as James B. Rule observes, "if knowledge is good, and informed action preferable to the alternative, why shouldn't we expect institutions of all kinds to maximize their grip on the lives of those they deal with?" His response is striking: "if we're serious about privacy, we can't *afford* to have institutions keep such a tight grip on human affairs ... the only meaningful strategy for privacy protection is to bear the significant costs of knowing less about people's lives."[48] Protecting privacy requires that we sacrifice certain advantages of convenience or security, that we rethink the way that we prioritize privacy and security, or that we re-assess our faith in security itself.[49]

Conclusion 165

In Tacitus' account, talking about security can serve the dominance of the emperor and sustain one-man rule in Rome. Members of the Senate, as we have seen, expressly associate public well-being with the person, reputation, and image of the emperor. While the *delatores* often appear to serve the vendettas or personal interests of the emperor and other members of the aristocracy, they must argue that they have evidence of a danger to the welfare of the community, or at least evidence that such a danger could arise in the future.[50] Sometimes informers do have such evidence, as in the case of the Pisonian conspiracy in 65 CE, a plot to assassinate Nero and replace him with C. Calpurnius Piso, a popular aristocrat from a distinguished Republican family. In contrast to the *maiestas* trials under Tiberius, this conspiracy is remarkable for the number of people and social classes involved, from senators and *equites* to soldiers, freedmen, and freedwomen.[51] The conspirators complain about "the crimes of the emperor, that the end of the empire was approaching and somebody must be chosen to rescue the troubled state of affairs" (*scelera principis et finem adesse imperio diligendumque qui fessis rebus succurreret*, 15.50), but they are unable to resolve on a plan. One of the conspirators, the freedwoman Epicharis, attempts to enlist Volusius Proculus, captain of the fleet at Misenum.[52] He reveals the plot to Nero, and although he is unable to provide the names of the conspirators, they are forced to act: they decide to murder Nero at his villa in Baiae, but they are exposed by Milichus, a freedman of one of the senatorial dissidents.

Tacitus implies that the informers in this episode are social climbers, anxious for imperial favor: Proculus had assisted Nero in the murder of Agrippina (he complained that he was not appropriately compensated, 15.51), and Nero rewards Milichus for his help (15.71). Whether or not they were Nero's partisans, these men likely recognized the dangers of joining such a conspiracy, or even of concealing their knowledge of the plot.[53] The emperor's response to the conspirators is severe: he tortures them, puts them to death or forces them to commit suicide, and sends a lucky few into exile. He also uses the plot as an excuse to attack his enemies, regardless of whether they were actually involved (15.68–69). Yet while Tacitus dwells on Nero's bloodthirstiness, he does not doubt the veracity of the threat to the emperor, although he has the opportunity to do so. He repeatedly comments on the difficulty of describing events that were necessarily carried out in secret.[54] He concludes the narrative by admitting that some believed that Nero had invented the conspiracy himself:

[Nero] was even constantly slandered by popular rumor that he had put innocent men to death because of his own ill-will or fear. But those who then cared to know the truth did not doubt that a conspiracy was begun and matured and then repressed, and those who returned to the city after Nero's death report it. (15.73)[55]

Tacitus could have depicted the conspiracy, and thus the danger to Nero, as a figment of the emperor's imagination, as a cynical plot to root out his opponents or as a product of his paranoia. Instead, he reports the conspiracy as a meaningful attempt on Nero's life, even as he details the violence and ferocity of the emperor's retaliation. Nero's response may have been vicious and sensible at the same time: in the early books of the *Annals*, Rome's elite emphasized the need for security and stability, and thus for accepting the entrenchment of one-man rule. Even the Pisonian conspirators seem to imagine that they will find a better ruler to replace Nero (*diligendumque qui fessis rebus succurreret,* 15.50), not that they will return to Republican *libertas*; they are evidently uninterested in pursuing more fundamental political change, or in facing the doubts and risks that such a change could involve.

Like the *maiestas* prosecutions under Tiberius, the Pisonian conspiracy reveals not just the terrors of despotism but also the costs of choosing security as the most important value in political life. The political philosopher Roberto Esposito warns against the "autoimmunitary regime," in which societies focus so obsessively on their own security that "risk is artificially created in order to control it."[56] In these regimes, identifying, assessing, and responding to problems of security is the exclusive preoccupation of politics. Tacitus represents a world in which the scope of the political imagination is severely limited. When the senatorial elite accepts autocratic rule as the price of stability and peace, they are both the victims and perpetrators of "political fear": their chosen object of fear—the social unrest of the late Republic and its potential persistence in their own day—"dominates the political agenda, crowding out other possible objects of fear and concern."[57] Overcoming this fear is impossible without recognizing the limits of controlling the future and the inevitable risks of living with others.[58] Tacitus' characters cannot envision such a fundamental change in their mind-set: they aim above all for "protection from the unknown," and if we question their desire for the security of "a domesticated life," we can also empathize with them.[59]

Respect for privacy requires a degree of vulnerability and trust between citizens: we need to refrain from knowing things about our neighbors, even if we might potentially benefit from access to that knowledge. Roman reflections on one-man rule compel us to consider the costs and the temptations of rejecting trust in political life. In the Julio-Claudian political imagination, fear *for* the ruler can compete with, or even outweigh, fear *of* the ruler and of being ruled. For Tacitus' Romans, the status quo, however terrible, may still be preferable to what comes after it—and it is impossible to know ahead of time. Despite the serious threats presented by the ruler's violence and vengefulness, it is his association with stability and order, and thus with security, that may most undermine the vibrancy of public life. The Romans show us how focusing on security can create obstacles to talking about the kind of community we have, and the kind we want to live in.[60]

NOTES

Introduction

1. See Arendt 1958, 38 and Habermas 1989, 46–49 on intimacy and family life. Ando (2012, 220–21) discusses the very different ideas of "public space" in Habermas' theory and in the work of ancient historians and archaeologists; see also Ando and Rüpke 2015, 4.

2. On the association of women with domestic life in Roman culture, see Milnor 2005 and Russell 2016b. Wallace-Hadrill 1994 is a seminal work on the house as a space for elite self-promotion. See also Drerup 1959; Clarke 1991; Leach 2004.

3. Bartsch 1994 and 2006, discussed further below, are key studies of aristocratic anxieties in the face of the emperor's gaze. On the "retreat of politics behind closed doors" in imperial Rome, see Wallace-Hadrill 1996, 285.

4. On elite self-concealment and withdrawal in Julio-Claudian Rome, see Rudich 1993, xxii–xxxiv. On theatricality in Roman culture, see DuPont 1985; Bartsch 1994; Koloski-Ostrow 1997; in the reign of Nero, Griffin 1984; Edwards 1994; Woodman 1993; Champlin 2003; Keitel 2009. See André 1962; Roller 2001; Bartsch 2006; Acton 2011 on evolving aristocratic valuations of public life in the early Empire.

5. Milnor 2005, 20–21, with reference to Tac. *Agric.* 39.2, Pliny *Ep.* 2.1.2, 5.3.5. See also Russell 2016a, 191–92. Winterling (2009, 71–73) discusses the emergence of a new distinction, *princeps/privatus*, by the time of Seneca (although the emperor was expected to act as a *privatus*).

6. Arendt 1958, 59.

7. Russell (2016a, 1–12) also frames public and private as contested concepts in the Roman world.

8. Russell 2016a, 26–27; see also *D.* 50.16.15. On the terminology of public and private in the ancient world, see Casevitz 1998; Milnor 2005, 16–27; Russell 2016a, 25–42. Winterling (2009, 58–76) discusses the problems that arise from different modern approaches to these concepts in German and Anglophone scholarship on the classical world.

9. See the entry for *res communes omnium* in Berger 1953.

10. On public and private as spheres of interest in the Roman world, see Cooper 2007, 21, 25–26.

11. Van Andringa 2015, 100; see also Begemann 2015, 76–77.

12. Riggsby 2010, 195. When homicide came under the purview of the *iudicia publica* rather than the *iudicia privata* in the late Republic and early Empire, this development

occurred in the context of developing monarchy in the Roman world, and thus of a broader trend toward centralization of power: see Riggsby 2016, 316–17.

13. Suet. *Aug.* 40.5. On political life in the Forum Romanum, see Russell 2016a, 43–45.

14. Arendt 1958, 38. On Arendt's approach to and investment in Greek and Roman antiquity, see most recently Leonard 2018, the preface to a special issue of *Classical Philology* on "Hannah Arendt and the Ancients." For Arendt's engagement with Roman thought in particular, see Hammer 2002 and Connolly 2018.

15. Arendt 1958, 64–65.

16. Arendt 1958, 52.

17. Arendt 1958, 58.

18. Arendt 1958, 58; see also 50–52.

19. Leonard 2018, 3. Arendt (1958, 28–37) treats the distinction between household and *polis*. See Honig 1995 on Arendt and feminist thought.

20. Arendt 1958, 32.

21. Arendt 1958, 64; see also 29–30, 61.

22. Arendt 1958, 65.

23. Arendt 1958, 59.

24. Unless otherwise noted, all translations are my own.

25. On Dionysius' use of Roman sources, see Gabba 1991, 93–147.

26. τῶν δὲ κατ' οἰκίαν γενομένων οὔτε πρόνοιαν οὔτε φυλακὴν ἐποιοῦντο, τὴν αὔλειον θύραν ἑκάστου ὅρον εἶναι τῆς ἐλευθερίας τοῦ βίου νομίζοντες. Ῥωμαῖοι δὲ πᾶσαν ἀναπετάσαντες οἰκίαν καὶ μέχρι τοῦ δωματίου τὴν ἀρχὴν τῶν τιμητῶν προαγαγόντες ἁπάντων ἐποίησαν ἐπίσκοπον καὶ φύλακα τῶν ἐν αὐταῖς γινομένων, οὔτε δεσπότην οἰόμενοι δεῖν ὠμὸν εἶναι περὶ τὰς τιμωρίας οἰκετῶν οὔτε πατέρα πικρὸν ἢ μαλθακὸν πέρα τοῦ μετρίου περὶ τέκνων ἀγωγὰς οὔτε ἄνδρα περὶ κοινωνίαν γαμετῆς γυναικὸς ἄδικον οὔτε παῖδας γηραιῶν ἀπειθεῖς πατέρων οὔτε ἀδελφοὺς γνησίους τὸ πλεῖον ἀντὶ τοῦ ἴσου διώκοντας, οὐ συμπόσια καὶ μέθας παννυχίους, οὐκ ἀσελγείας καὶ φθορὰς ἡλικιωτῶν νέων, οὐχ ἱερῶν ἢ ταφῶν προγονικὰς τιμὰς ἐκλιπούσας, οὐκ ἄλλο τῶν παρὰ τὸ καθῆκον ἢ συμφέρον τῇ πόλει πραττομένων οὐδέν.

27. On Dionysius' treatment of Greek and Roman regulations of family life, see Gabba 1991, 148–51.

28. *cum aedificaret domum in Palatio in eo loco, ubi est quae quondam Ciceronis, mox Censorini fuit, nunc Statilii Sisennae est, promitteretque ei architectus, ita se eam aedificaturum, ut liber a conspectu immunisque ab omnibus arbitris esset neque quisquam in eam despicere posset, "tu vero," inquit, "si quid in te artis est, ita compone domum meam, ut, quidquid agam, ab omnibus perspici possit."*

29. Milnor 2005, 65–66.

30. Barton 2001, 58–61; Fredrick 2002a, 1–4; Barton 2002; Bartsch 2006, 117–64.

31. Parker 1999, 167–68; Cooper 2007, 9–17. Russell (2016a, 34–95) argues that Republican elites endeavored to extend the control they exercised over their private property into public space.

32. On opportunities for seclusion in domestic architecture in Roman Pompeii, see Grahame 1997; Lauritsen 2012; Proudfoot 2013; Berry 2016.

33. Rössler 2004, 7–8.

34. I am grateful to Michèle Lowrie for bringing these passages to my attention.

35. *queri libet quod in secreta nostra non inquirant principes nisi quos odimus. nam si eadem cura bonis ac malis esset, quam ubique admirationem tui, quod gaudium exultationemque deprenderes, quos omnium cum coniugibus ac liberis, quos etiam cum domesticis aris focisque sermones! . . . et alioqui, cum sint odium amorque contraria, hoc perquam simile habent, quod ibi intemperantius amamus bonos principes, ubi liberius malos odimus.*

36. See Connolly 2009a, 271–72 on Pliny's argument for visibility as the grounds for the emperor's legitimate exercise of power.

37. Compare Bartsch 2006, 137–38: "One of the most salient aspects of the transition to empire was . . . the breakdown of these rewards [for visibility] and the breakdown, too, of the reciprocity of the gaze. Along with this went a breakdown in the distinction between safe and unsafe forms of visibility" for aristocratic Romans other than the emperor.

38. Shotter (2005) gives a useful overview of the late Republic, emphasizing the continuities between the end of the Republic and the early Empire. Syme (2002, 313–30) describes Augustus' rise as an unprecedented power grab.

39. Discussed in Shotter 2005, 62–65. See Horace *Ode* 2.1.

40. Gardner 2015, 57–60.

41. Ando (2011b, 101) observes that "no one before had held so many such offices at the same time, nor had anyone else exploited to nearly the same extent the possibility . . . for the powers of a magistracy to be granted by legislative act separate from election into it."

42. Eck 2016, 99–100; see also Ando 2011b, 100–103.

43. On Augustus' efforts to emphasize his commitment to Republican norms, see, e.g., *RG* 34 and Vell. Pat. 2.89.3–4. On how Republican institutions helped to sustain social hierarchies under the principate, see Winterling 2009, 9–33.

44. On continuities between elite Republican households and the imperial household, see Rilinger 2007. Potter (2011) discusses the Republican precedents for the emperor's access to support and financial resources across the Empire, and for his privileged relationship with the gods.

45. See Paterson 2007, 129–30 on the novelty of the principate in the view of contemporaries. See Winterling 2009, 59–60 on the conceptual differences between the emperor's position and the offices of Republican magistrates.

46. See Pandey 2018, 6–11 on the numerous cocreators of Augustus' image in antiquity. Meister (2012, 276) also describes the early principate in terms of experiments to define the emperor's role; he suggests that the upheavals of the first century CE delayed the institutionalization of monarchy in Rome. Ando (2011a, 58) identifies the accession of Vespasian, since he was not a Julio-Claudian, as a turning point for the naturalization of "the constitutional innovations by which the Romans described the principate to themselves and to others."

47. For the range of approaches to representing the emperor and his family in antiquity, see Rowe 2002; Severy 2003; Meister 2012; Hekster 2015. For how local elites used emperor worship to establish and maintain power in their own communities, see Noreña 2011.

48. See Roller 2001, 213–87 for how Latin literature of the early Empire presents different models (*exempla*) for the emperor to follow (e.g., the father) or to avoid (e.g., the slave master). On models and exemplarity in Roman thought, see also Lowrie and Lüdemann 2015; Roller 2016.

49. The key study of Augustan domesticity is Milnor 2005.

50. Pandey 2018; Milnor 2005, 80–93, 303–4.
51. Ginsberg 2017, 1–2, 61–114.
52. *pleraque eorum quae rettuli quaeque referam parua forsitan et leuia memoratu uideri non nescius sum: sed nemo annalis nostros cum scriptura eorum contenderit qui ueteres populi Romani res composuere. ingentia illi bella, expugnationes urbium, fusos captosque reges, . . . discordias consulum aduersum tribunos, agrarias frumentariasque leges, plebis et optimatium certamina libero egressu memorabant: nobis in arto et inglorius labor . . . sic conuerso statu neque alia re Romana quam si unus imperitet, haec conquiri tradique in rem fuerit, quia . . . plures aliorum euentis docentur.*
53. Ginsberg (2017, 25–60) frames the Julio-Claudian period as a kind of playing field in Roman literature for debating imperial rule. See Winterling 2011, 6–8 on ancient imperial biographies as key participants in aristocratic discourse about larger political and social structures.
54. Milnor 2005, especially 27–34, 53–64.
55. Compare Paterson 2007, 122: "Whereas problems about the legal powers of the Roman emperor have absorbed the attention of generations of modern scholars . . . contemporaries of the emperors tended to take the emperor's all-encompassing power as a given." For an assessment of historians' models of Roman imperial administration, see Ando 2015.
56. From Max Weber's definition of domination, included in Lukes 1986, 33.
57. See Wartenberg 1990, 3–31, 71–161. For critiques of defining power in terms of the ruler's command and the obedience of the ruled, see Dreyfus, Rabinow, and Foucault 1983, 216–26 and Foucault, 1990a, 81–102.
58. Many thanks to R. Scott Smith for suggesting this passage.
59. Sen. *Ep.* 90.6: *opus esse legibus coepit, quas et ipsas inter initia tulere sapientes.*
60. Arendt 1970, 39.
61. Pandey (2018, 2–6, 26–29) compares the role of the audience in producing poetic and political authority in the Augustan age.
62. On the exclusion of women, slaves, and foreigners from the *populus Romanus* and thus from politics in Republican Rome, see Russell 2016a, 46–47; on the role of women and slaves in Julio-Claudian political thought, see especially chapters 2, 4, and 6 below.
63. E.g., Seneca's ostensibly sympathetic account of enslavement, discussed in Edwards 2009 (and further in chapter 6 below); see also Dressler 2016, 255.
64. Connolly 2009b, 714.
65. I discuss the dating of these works in the chapters that follow. See Vout 2013, 74 on Tiberius' unique position as the first successor, the first to perform Augustus' "script" for the role of emperor.
66. Roller 2001, 64–126; 264–86.
67. Bartsch 2006, 115–281; on the self in Roman philosophy, see also Dressler 2016. Foucault 1990b is a seminal text on the development of notions of the self in antiquity.
68. Star 2012, 1–113. See also Edwards 1997 on the self in Seneca's letters, and the essays in Bartsch and Wray 2009, especially Ker 2009a on self-examination in Seneca's *De ira*.
69. Recent studies of Roman political thought include Connolly 2007 and 2014; Hammer 2008 and 2014; Kapust 2011; Lowrie 2014, 2015, and 2016.
70. On imagery of Julio-Claudian emperors, see Griffin 1984; Champlin 2003; Osgood 2011; Levick 2015; and chapter 2. Vout (2007) and Pandey (2018) both consider the broader implication of imperial imagery for Roman political culture and political thought.

71. Millar 1984, 43. See also Noreña 2011, 5 on the emperor as a uniquely unifying symbol in an empire otherwise characterized by "diversity and fragmentation. . . . If nothing else, every inhabitant of the Roman Empire shared a single ruler."

72. Russell 2016a, 41; see also 34–40.

73. Russell 2016a, 192; see also 193–94 on the "change in the nature of public space" as "primarily an elite phenomenon."

74. Connolly 2014, 1–2; see also 9–20.

75. See Connolly 2014, 2 on treating Latin "texts as prompts that make ideas available for our active use. Being neither for nor of our time, they grant a sense of the past's difference, and in doing so they grant us a perspective of difference and help us see ourselves and our world anew."

76. See, e.g., Rule 2007 and 2015; Neocleous 2008. President Barack Obama took a more optimistic approach to security and privacy in an "Address to the People of Europe" in Hannover on April 25, 2016, in which he asserted that "security and privacy don't have to be a contradiction. We can protect both. And we have to . . . As free peoples, we cannot allow . . . fears about security or economic anxieties . . . to undermine our commitment to the universal values that are the source of our strength." Even as Obama claims that we can avoid the contradiction of security and privacy, he admits that they are in tension, and that fear can easily overwhelm the values that his audience wants to preserve.

Chapter 1 · *Playing House: New Families and New Rulers in Lucan's* **Bellum Civile**

1. Masters 1992, 17–18. On Lucan's engagement with Vergil, see also Ahl 1976, 64–67; Hardie 1993; Casali 2011. On Lucan and Caesar, Joseph 2017, 298–303.

2. See especially Leigh 1997, 206–10; Roller 2001, 20–54. Discussions of nihilism and destruction (and self-destruction) in Lucan include Henderson 1987; Johnson 1987; Masters 1992; Sklenář 2003. Bartsch (1997, 143) concludes her provocative treatment of violence in Lucan by arguing that the poet's "storytelling sets up the possibility for new beginnings." See also Connolly 2016 on violence as a unifying force in Lucan's account of Rome.

3. For the disruption of family units as a key trope in Lucan and in ancient historical narratives of civil war, see Roller 2001, 44–45.

4. The Latin text of Lucan is from Housman 1927.

5. For Roman attention to immediate family bonds, see Dixon 1992, 11; Severy 2003, 8–9; Hekster 2015, 27; for an opposing view, see Bradley 1987. On *pietas*, see Saller 1994, 105–14.

6. Reydams-Schils (2005, 97) discusses Cicero's distinctive focus on the family in contrast to Stoic conceptions of the growth of social bonds, which begin with the individual rather than the family.

7. Saller 1994, 121–23; Gardner 1998, 211–26. On two occasions, Augustus issued decrees in favor of children whose parents had disinherited them: see Gardner 1998, 225–26. Vuolanto (2016) treats the increasing legal expectations for parental care of children under the Empire.

8. Saller 1994, 110–14.

9. Discussed in Saller 1994, 107–8.

10. Discussed in Saller 1994, 113.

11. For the traits of the ideal commander in Caesar's *Bellum civile*, see Ash 1999, 5–10. See Levene 2010, 167–72, 186–214 on different types of the *dux* in Roman historiography.

12. Roller (2001, 37–38) describes Caesar as a "prototype" for future Julio-Claudian rulers. See Hardie 2010, 20–24 on how Lucan blurs the distinction between military and civilian crowds in their interactions with Caesar in *BC* 1.

13. Hardie (1993, 30) also points out parallels between Caesar and Cato: both are "the one man," *unus*, in "the dialectic of *unus/omnes*" (one man / all men) that is central to Lucan's poem and to epic more generally.

14. See Fantham 1992 *ad loc.* on the shift between public and private life in this passage. On the role of women and the family in Roman burial rites, see Lindsay 2000.

15. Keith 2008, 235.

16. See Narducci 1973, 317–19 on the sack of Troy in *Aeneid* 2 as a model for Lucan's mourning *matronae*; for further examples, see Keith 2008, 243.

17. Lucan's narrative is likely based on the mutiny that took place in Placentia (today's Piacenza, in northern Italy) in 49 BCE. See Fantham 1985 for the contrast between the epic and the historical narratives in Appian and Dio. Caesar omits this mutiny from his own narrative of the civil war.

18. See Berthold 1975; Borgo 1976; Johnson 1987, 112–17; Gall 2005; Hardie 2010.

19. See O'Gorman 2000, 27–33 on how mutineers in Tacitus' *Annales* represent themselves as an "indiscriminate mass" in opposition to commanders' attention to "distinction and rank" (quotation on 27).

20. On the evidence for mass graves in Rome, see Hope 2000, 111. D'Alessandro Behr (2007, 40–41) argues that *BC* 7.630–46 undermines the significance of the death of an individual and of the positive value of recognition for that death: she claims that mourning for an individual loses its meaning in comparison with the devastation of the battle of Pharsalus. Yet even after the battle, funeral rites and the failure to perform them remain a concern in the poem for both Pompeians and Caesarians: Lucan's attention to the death and funeral of Pompey in book 8 and of the Pharsalian dead in book 9 (both discussed below) weighs against the claim that, because of the suffering brought by civil war, a single death no longer deserves to be grieved.

21. Naiden (2006, 32) identifies Caesar as one of the most frequent recipients of supplication in ancient literature (the other is Alexander); in this role he foreshadows the Roman emperor, who becomes "the most powerful and desirable" object for suppliants (110).

22. Coffee 2011, 424.

23. For examples of veterans demanding recompense from Caesar and Augustus, see Roller 2001, 207–8.

24. Asso (2010 *ad loc.*) interprets *quo iaceat . . . loco* as a reference to burial; the soldiers' happiness, then, would correspond to other characters' anxieties about who will receive appropriate funeral rites.

25. *felix qui potuit mundi nutante ruina*
    quo iaceat iam scire loco. non proelia fessos
    ulla uocant, certos non rumpunt classica somnos.
    iam coniunx natique rudes et sordida tecta
    et non deductos recipit sua terra colonos.
    hoc quoque securis oneris fortuna remisit,
    sollicitus menti quod abest fauor: ille salutis
    est auctor, dux ille fuit. sic proelia soli
    felices nullo spectant ciuilia uoto.

26. Morford (1967) sees book 9 as the crucial transition from the cause of Pompey to the cause of *libertas*.
27. *nos, Cato, da ueniam, Pompei duxit in arma*
    non belli ciuilis amor, partesque fauore
    fecimus. ille iacet quem paci praetulit orbis
    causaque nostra perit: patrios permitte penates
    desertamque domum dulcesque reuisere natos.
    nam quis erit finis si nec Pharsalia pugna
    nec Pompeius erit? perierunt tempora uitae,
    mors eat in tutum; iustas sibi nostra senectus
    prospiciat flammas: bellum ciuile sepulchra
    uix ducibus praestare potest.
28. On *amor* as a term for political relations, see Hellegouarc'h 1972, 146–47.
29. *inspicit et gladios, qui toti sanguine manent,*
    qui niteant primo tantum mucrone cruenti,
    quae presso tremat ense manus, quis languida tela,
    quis contenta ferat, quis praestet bella iubenti,
    quem pugnare iuuet, quis uultum ciue perempto
    mutet.
30. See Gagliardi (1975 *ad loc.*) for how Caesar's actions are consistent with his role as the *dux par excellence*. In the *Annales*, Germanicus performs similar actions toward his soldiers: after a military defeat, he visits the wounded (*circumire saucios*), looks at their wounds (*uulnera intuens*), and offers encouragement (1.71.3, cited in Pelling 2012, 295). Germanicus does not live up to his predecessor's example: Caesar makes the rounds in the middle of battle, not after it, and his efforts to heal his men with his own hands make Germanicus' medical attention seem merely cursory.
31. Leigh 1997, 104–5.
32. See Hölscher 2008 on the importance of role playing in Roman society.
33. Translation of *esse nihil recuso* from Dilke 1978 *ad loc.*
34. *non mihi res agitur, sed, uos ut libera sitis*
    turba, precor, gentes ut ius habeatis in omnes.
    ipse ego priuatae cupidus me reddere uitae
    plebeiaque toga modicum componere ciuem,
    omnia dum uobis liceant, nihil esse recuso.
    inuidia regnate mea.
35. Hardie (1993, 55) proposes that Caesar "uses the rhetoric (or plays the role, claims the costume) of being just one among many rather than the one leader." I argue rather that Caesar claims the role of leader by insisting that his devotion to his men surpasses his investment in the pursuit of power.
36. On self-sufficiency as a trope of one-man rule, see chapter 6.
37. Leigh (1997, 216–17) compares this passage to historical accounts of Caesar's treatment of his enemies during the civil war.
38. Roller 2001, 43; see also 39–41 for the Caesarian Laelius' vow to kill his family if Caesar demands it.

39. Roller 2001, 59–63. For the loyalty oaths, see Harris 1982 and Sherk 1988, 15.

40. For how Lucan's poetry embodies the conflict and disruption caused by civil war, see e.g., Henderson 1987; Masters 1992 9–10, 251–59; Leigh 1997, 299; Roller 2001, 62–63; Sklenář 2003, 2.

41. On Cato as Stoic hero, see Brisset 1964; Ahl 1976; Narducci 2002; and D'Alessandro Behr 2007. Skeptics include Johnson 1987; Bartsch 1997; and Leigh 1997. Seo (2013) argues that Lucan's Cato is an *exemplum* of *virtus* whom other characters (like Vulteius) endeavor to emulate; their failures suggest how easily Cato is transformed into the stuff of parody rather than of moral education. Roller (2001, 53–54) suggests that Cato offers the only possibility of reconciliation between the competing ethical systems explored in the epic. Our understanding of Lucan's Cato is further complicated by the fact that he appears only in books 2 and 9, with no account of his famous suicide in Africa, although some scholars speculate that the poem was meant to conclude with Cato's death.

42. See Seo 2013, 70–71 for Cato's grief as anti-Stoic. Reydams-Schils (2005, 121–23) argues that the Stoic sage was expected to experience grief at the loss of a child, but that he was also supposed to control it.

43. *ceu morte parentem*

   natorum orbatum longum producere funus
   ad tumulos iubet ipse dolor, iuuat ignibus atris
   inseruisse manus constructoque aggere busti
   ipsum atras tenuisse faces, non ante reuellar
   exanimem quam te conplectar, Roma; tuumque
   nomen, Libertas, et inanem persequar umbram.

44. On the titles *parens patriae* and *pater patriae*, see Alföldi 1971, 80–101.

45. On Cato's outburst as "righteous anger" see Wick 2004 *ad loc.*

46. On the contrast between Cato and Marcia's marriage and traditional Roman marriage ceremonies, see Fantham 1992 *ad loc.* On how this marriage ceremony reflects on Cato, see Johnson 1987, 43–44. Bartsch (1997, 125) discusses this passage as a key example of Lucan's peculiar use of the negative: he describes the ceremony in terms of what is missing rather than what is present.

47. Wick 2004 *ad loc.*

48. See Leigh 1997, 259–64 and Seo 2013, 75–79 on Vulteius making a spectacle of himself. In book 6, Scaeva also explicitly courts the most gruesome death for the Caesarian cause: he too wishes that Caesar could witness his sacrifice, although unlike Vulteius he does not speak of his *amor* for Caesar (6.158–60). Seo (2013, 79–82) offers discussion and bibliography.

49. Later in the poem the narrator insists that future generations will admire and support Pompey's valiant opposition to Caesar (7.207–13). Bartsch (1997) sees the tension between Pompey's two roles—as potential future monarch and as hero of a lost cause—as central to the enactment of political engagement in the epic (73–100); see 85–90 for an overview of the different scholarly assessments of Lucan's Pompey.

50. Brennan (1969) argues that the name Cordus is an allusion to Aulus Cremutius Cordus, a historian who committed suicide during the reign of Tiberius: see *Tac. Ann.* 4.34–35.

51. See Mebane 2016, 199–212 on the relationship between the beheading of Pompey, Pompey's failure as head of the body politic, and the destructive consequences of civil war in Lucan's epic.

52. See Mayer 1981 *ad loc.* on the motif of tears (and other bodily fluids) shed over corpses in Latin literature.

53. Some sources (Dio Cass. 56.42.4, Dion. Halic. 8.59.4, Prop. 3.16.24) indicate that kinsmen were supposed to keep watch over the body: see Mayer 1981 *ad loc.* Lindsay 2000, 152–54 argues that funeral rites were confined to the household in order to protect the rest of the community from ritual pollution.

54. Keith 2008, 248; see also 245–53.

55. On Lucan's sources for the characterization of Cornelia (Livy, Vergil, and Ovid), see Bruère 1951.

56. *"ergo indigna fui," dixit "Fortuna, marito*
accendisse rogum gelidosque effusa per artus
incubuisse uiro, laceros exurere crines
membraque dispersi pelago conponere Magni,
uolneribus cunctis largos infundere fletus . . .
numquam dare iusta licebit
coniugibus? numquam plenas plangemus ad urnas?"

57. On these parallels, see Wick 2004 *ad loc.*

58. Augoustakis (2011, 193–94) sees this second funeral as an effort "to bring closure after Pompey's death" and clear the way for Cato's leadership.

59. Keith (2008, 248–53) elaborates on the inspirational force of Cornelia's laments: in addition to being a model mourner, she persuades her sons to follow Cato after their father's death, and so directs the conclusion of the epic (*BC* 9.84–87).

60. Discussed in the conclusion to this book.

61. *uidisse maestos ciuium uultus, audire secretas querimonias, quod tantum itineris aditurus esset, cuius ne modicos quidem egressus tolerarent, sueti aduersum fortuita adspectu principis refoueri. ergo ut in priuatis necessitudinibus proxima pignora praeualerent, ita populum Romanum uim plurimam habere parendumque retinenti.*

62. Champlin (2003, 187) suggests that Tacitus is paraphrasing Nero's official edict. Tacitus casts doubt on Nero's interpretation of the people's grief: the people were only concerned about losing Nero's company because of their desire for entertainments and grain.

Chapter 2 · *Contest and Control in the Emperor's House*

1. *RG* 35.1; Suet. *Aug.* 58. On the title *pater patriae*, see Alföldi 1971; Strothmann 2000; Stevenson 2015.

2. Text and translation from Dixon 2016, 464.

3. On Ovid's account of the *domus Augusta*, see Millar 1993; see Flory 1996 on statue groups that attest to the official use of the term *domus Augusta* in the last years of Augustus' reign. On the Tiberian inscriptions, see Potter and Damon 1999; Severy 2000; Rowe 2002. All these inscriptions relate to the death of Germanicus, Tiberius' nephew and adopted son. The Tabula Hebana and the Tabula Siarensis preserve parts of senatorial decrees for funeral honors for Germanicus; the *Senatus consultum de Pisone patre* reports the Senate's judgment against Piso, a rival of Germanicus who was accused of his murder and committed suicide.

4. On the wide range of meanings of *familia* and *domus*, see Saller 1994, 74–88.

5. On the preference for the term *domus* in the principate, see Saller 1984, 345–47 and Severy 2003, 68.

6. Corbier 1995; Hurlet 1997, 416–19; Severy 2003, 62–72.

7. See especially Rowe 2002; Hekster 2015; McIntyre 2016. Meister (2012, 19, 192–218) makes a related point in his analysis of images of the emperor's body: representations of the emperor as a god (most common in the Greek East) may not reflect his official status as accepted by the senatorial elite, but they are equally valuable as guides to what the emperor meant. See also Noreña 2011, 271: local honors for the emperors "became an important means for provincial communities . . . to represent the emperor to themselves."

8. See Kleiner 1978, 772–76, on the unprecedented images of women and children on the Ara Pacis Augustae. Kampen (1991, 218–19) notes that images of women (with the exception of goddesses and personifications) are relatively rare in Roman historical reliefs.

9. On the public role of the women in Augustus' household, see Severy 2003, 86–95, 104–10, 131–38, 180–84, and Milnor 2005, 56–65, 85–93.

10. On the identification of the boy, see Ramsby and Severy-Hoven 2007, 53–55. They argue that he is a Gallic prince, but the child's proximity to Agrippa, and the importance of Augustus' grandsons Gaius and Lucius in other Julio-Claudian imagery, suggest that Augustan audiences could also have identified him with heirs of the *princeps*.

11. Severy 2003, 110.

12. On Aphrodisias' longstanding loyalty to Rome and to the Julian family, see Smith 2013, 4. See Price 1985 for the standard discussion of the relationship between the imperial cult and self-promotion in the Greek East. For a more recent treatment, focusing on the Latin West, see McIntyre 2016.

13. For an overview of the imagery of Julio-Claudian women, see Wood 1999. Ginsburg (2006) focuses specifically on images of Agrippina the Younger.

14. For the two possible identifications of the togate figure, see Smith 2013, 135–36. In Rome, the *Genius Senatus*, not the Roman people, would be represented in a toga, but in Aphrodisias a toga was suitable in either case, to mark the Roman identity of the figure.

15. Rose 1997, 44; Ginsburg 2006, 87.

16. Ramsby and Severy-Hoven (2007, 46–49) discuss the parallels between the Sebasteion and the fragments of the interior reliefs of the Ara Pacis, which also use female figures to represent peoples defeated by Rome.

17. Smith 2013, 78.

18. Surveys of images of the emperor and the imperial family include Rose 1997; Hurlet 1997; Wood 1999; Dahmen 2001; Severy 2003; Hekster 2015.

19. See especially Rowe 2002; Hekster 2015; McIntyre 2016.

20. Rowe 2002, 106–23.

21. Rowe 2002, 114–15.

22. Translation of the decrees from Rowe 2002, 114.

23. McIntyre (2016, 31) points out that while Augustus was burdened with responsibility for the entire world, "Gaius . . . could be co-opted by individual communities as their own savior." See also Hurlet 1997, 482 for how the decree emphasizes the hereditary basis for Gaius' claims to prominence.

24. On coins of Livia in Tiberius' reign, see Hekster 2015, 119–20. On the circulation of imperial coinage, see Noreña 2011, 191–200. Purcell (1996a) discusses the exceptional honors that Livia received in her life and after her death, especially as a priestess and as a *diva*.

On Livia the patron, see Flory 1984; Severy 2003, 131–38; Milnor 2005, 56–64. Hemelrijk (2007) argues that imperial women like Livia, who served as priestesses for deified emperors, offered a model for priestesses of the imperial cult elsewhere in the Empire.

25. Rose 1997, 10.

26. Rose 1997, 10, 21; Wood 1999, 30. For the inscriptions with Julia's name, see Rose 1997, catalog nos. 70, 76, 82, 87, 91, 112, 122. Hekster (2015, 117) observes that women were not typically included in dynastic statue groups in Italy.

27. Rose 1997, 37: the inscription from Mytilene is included in Smallwood 1967, 128b. See Hekster 2015, 125–26 on the special connections between Mytilene and the children of Germanicus.

28. On Caligula's restoration of Agrippina the Elder, see Varner 2001, 62; on Caligula's program of dynastic imagery more generally, see Hekster 2015, 122–27.

29. Hekster 2015, 126.

30. Compare Noreña 2011, 271 on monuments erected to honor the emperor: the "main audience ... was not external but internal—not imperial ... but local." See McIntyre 2016, 41–62 on the lack of centralized control over the imperial cult, including the question of who should receive worship.

31. Hekster 2015, 131.

32. Hekster 2015, 132.

33. Ginsburg 2006, 55–57, 72–74.

34. Wood 1999, 302; see also 302–3 on the colossal portrait bust of Agrippina discovered in Trajan's Forum.

35. Hekster 2015, 135.

36. Bean 1956, 215–16; Rose 1997, 48 and cat. 98.

37. See McIntyre 2016, 47 on promoting dynastic continuity as a key principle of Julio-Claudian monuments.

38. Latin text of Suetonius from Kaster 2016.

39. Gardner 1995, 377.

40. Osgood (2013) shows that the problem of succession was a signal aspect of the ancient reception of Augustus' legacy, at least by the time of Suetonius.

41. Corbier 1995, 182–3. Hekster (2015, 5–6) reviews Augustus' strategic use of marriage and official honors to distinguish members of household. Rowe (2002) offers a rich discussion of the developing role of the heirs of the *princeps* in the institutions of the early Empire; see also Hurlet 1997, 421–84 and Severy 2003, 68–86.

42. On the Augustan marriage legislation, see Treggiari 1991, 60–80; Edwards 1993, 41–42; Severy 2003, 55–56. Milnor (2007) treats these laws as representative and constitutive of broader ideas about the relation of house and society in Augustan culture.

43. See Severy 2003, 180–84 on Julia's adultery as an act of treason.

44. Suet. *Tib.* 53; Tac. *Ann.* 6.25; Dio Cass. 58.22.4–5. See also Levick 1999, 169–70; Varner 2001, 61–62; Seager 2013, 47–48.

45. See Ginsberg 2017, 2 on the association between concord in the imperial house and peace in the Republic in Julio-Claudian literature and imagery.

46. Caligula's sisters were the first living women to be depicted and named on imperial coinage: Wood 1999, 289; Hekster 2015, 122–23.

47. Latin text of the *Annals* from Fisher 1906. Following modern orthographical conventions, I have changed consonantal "v" in Fisher's text to "u."

48. See Millar 1977, 69–78 on imperial freedmen in the Julio-Claudian period.

49. Santoro L'Hoir (2006, 237) discusses Tacitus' allusions to mime in the Silius narrative (cuckoldry was a staple of the genre).

50. Winterling (2009, 71) notes that "no emperor would have been able to pursue this program" of *discreta domus et res publica*.

51. See Fischler 1994, 116, 120–30. On this attitude in Tacitus' treatment of the Julio-Claudian dynasty, see Rutland 1978; Santoro L'Hoir 1994 and 2006, 111–57; Milnor 2012, 467–73. On women's political influence in crisis periods in ancient Rome, especially in the transition from Republic to Empire, see Dettenhofer 1994.

52. On the Roman imperial court, see Wallace-Hadrill 1996 and 2011; Winterling 1999 and 2009; Paterson 2007; Acton 2011; Potter 2011; Sumi 2011. The foundational twentieth-century study of the structure of the royal court is Elias 1983; for an assessment of Elias' missteps and of his enduring insights, see Duindam 2004.

53. Purcell (1996a, 97) comments on scholarly tendencies to reproduce ancient biases against women's power.

54. On Tacitus' Nero in contrast to his predecessors, see Keitel 2009, 137–38. O'Gorman (2000, 146) argues that Tacitus' Nero is trapped by the "monotonous repetition" of his Julio-Claudian heritage; see also Milnor 2005, 286 on "Nero as both the culmination and the nadir of the first *domus Caesarum*."

55. Milnor 2012, 473. On critiques of Julio-Claudian women in the ancient historians, see Rutland 1978; Späth 2000; Ginsburg 2006; Santoro L'Hoir 1994 and 2006; Gillespie 2014; Benoist 2015; for the Severan period, see Langford 2013.

56. Harding 2004, 7. Harding and other standpoint theorists insist that the "standpoint" is not the inevitable result of occupying a particular position in society, but rather "an achievement, something for which oppressed groups must struggle" (8). On the problems of "essentialism and universalism" in standpoint theory, see Hirschmann 2004.

57. On this lost work, see Lewis 1993, 652–57; Tacitus identifies Agrippina the Younger's own writing as a source for his narrative of Agrippina the Elder (Tac. *Ann.* 4.53).

58. Hirschmann 2004, 323. See also Harding 2009, 194: "what one does both enables and limits what one can know. In hierarchically organized societies, the daily activities and experiences of oppressed groups enable insights about how the society functions that are not available—or at least not easily available—from the perspective of dominant-group activity."

59. For a related approach to reading Julio-Claudian women, see Ginsberg 2017, 14–59: she argues that the female characters of the *Octavia* counter official Julio-Claudian claims of establishing peace and harmony.

60. See Rutland 1978, 23 on Tacitus' contrasting presentation of Messalina's and Agrippina's sexuality.

61. Pliny *NH* 22.46.92; Suet. *Claud.* 44–45; Tac. *Ann.* 12.66–68.

62. *uocabatur interim senatus uotaque pro incolumitate principis consules et sacerdotes nuncupabant, cum iam exanimis uestibus et fomentis obtegeretur, dum quae res forent firmando Neronis imperio componuntur. iam primum Agrippina, uelut dolore uicta et solacia conquirens, tenere amplexu Britannicum, ueram paterni oris effigiem appellare ac uariis artibus demorari ne cubiculo egrederetur. Antoniam quoque et Octauiam sorores eius attinuit, et cunctos aditus custodiis clauserat, crebroque uulgabat ire in melius ualetudinem principis.*

63. Gillespie (2014, 279) calls Agrippina an "insightful 'reader'" of the imperial past but ultimately argues that she "misreads" her actual role in public life (289).

64. On Agrippina, Livia, and Tanaquil, see also Rutland 1978, 28. On Agrippina's use of her predecessors as models, see Gillespie 2014, 279–84.

65. O'Gorman (2000, 122) argues that imperial women serve as "sites of recollection and anticipation, as monuments or embodied texts of dynastic history" in Tacitus' account; see 126–38 on how Tacitus' portrayals of Livia and Agrippina the Younger inform each other. Foubert (2010a) discusses "parallel lives" of women as a rhetorical technique in the *Annals*, especially in the context of Tacitus' critiques of female power.

66. Claudius pardons the prisoners, and they show their gratitude to both the emperor and his wife.

67. Santoro L'Hoir (2006, 132) points out that Agrippina's cloak is a garment for actors as well as triumphal generals.

68. Hillard (1992, 42) suggests that this arrangement was expedient for Agrippina; Barrett (1996, 150–52) sees it as a sign of her prestige.

69. Ginsburg (2006, 39) notes that "Agrippina and her encroachment on public affairs" is the central theme of the passage, not the official activities of the Senate.

70. Tacitus uses *occurrere* for intentional contact rather than an accidental meeting: Betensky 1978, 420, 423–24.

71. Gillespie (2014, 285–7) describes Agrippina's appearance before the Armenian embassy as a failed attempt to repeat her successful self-presentation during Claudius' rule.

72. Dio Cass. 54.10.5, as discussed in Sumi 2011, 81–83.

73. Agrippina had even threatened to back Britannicus' claims to the throne (*Ann.* 13.14).

74. See Hallett 1984, 56 on the ability of elite women (including Agrippina the Younger) to trade on the legacy of their fathers. See also Hallett 1989, 62–63 for Agrippina the Elder's use of tactics typically identified as "male," e.g., vaunting her ancestry.

75. On the ruler's need for recognition as a key concern in Roman political culture, see chapters 4 and 5 below.

76. Milnor (2005, 292) observes that numerous rivals to Nero trace their claims to rule through female members of the Julian *gens*; see also Rogers 1955.

77. See Milnor 2012, 473 on how "imperial women were often most powerful when they were performing their most domestic of functions—when they were occupying their positions as sisters, mothers, and wives of imperial men."

78. Conquest 1990, 73. On whether Nero's reign can meaningfully be compared to the rule of twentieth-century dictators, see Gallia 2009, 200–202.

79. Compare Ginsburg 2017, 59: imperial women in the *Octavia* "recognize the futility of their struggle" but also "demand that their voices be heard."

Chapter 3 · *Where to See the Emperor: Augustus and Nero in Rome*

1. *non eadem uulgusque decent et lumina rerum:*
   est quod praecipuum debeat ista domus.
   imposuit te alto Fortuna locumque tueri
   iussit honoratum: Liuia, perfer onus.
   ad te oculos auresque trahis, tua facta notamus,
   nec uox missa potest principis ore tegi.
   alta mane supraque tuos exurge dolores
   infragilemque animum, quod potes, usque tene.

2. Bodel 1997, 7–11.

3. On different ancient accounts of this event, see Bodel 1997, 10.

4. See Newlands 1997, 36–37 and Miller 2009, 212–14 for Vergil and Suetonius on Augustus' humble home, and Ovid's critique of these claims; see also Milnor 2005 and Pandey 2018, discussed below.

5. Royo (1999, 70–117) discusses elite residents of the Palatine prior to Augustus.

6. Quenemoen (2001, 9–23) offers a useful survey of literary and epigraphic evidence for the development of the complex; see also Meyboom 2005, 221–24.

7. Suet. *Aug.* 72.1.

8. Iacopi and Tedone (2005–06) revised the influential proposals of Carettoni 1983 and Zanker 1990, 51–53; see also Tomei 2000; Meyboom 2005; Quenemoen 2006; Wiseman 2009; Foubert 2010a, 72–74; Pandey 2018, 83–86.

9. Tomei 2000, 31–33; Meyboom 2005, 255–58.

10. Tomei 2000, 8; Meyboom 2005, 254–55. See also *LTUR II*, s.v. "Domus: Augustus (Palatium)."

11. Carettoni 1983, 52–60. For these motifs in wall painting on the Bay of Naples, see chapter 5 below.

12. Iacopi and Tedone 2005–06, 370–71; see also Foubert 2010a, 74.

13. Suet. *Aug.* 29.3 and Dio Cass. 53.1.3; Miller 2009, 185–89.

14. For the Temple of Vesta, see *LTUR V*, s.v. "Vesta, Ara, Signum, Aedes (in Palatio)" and Meyboom 2005, 245n77.

15. On the portico and the Temple, see Suet. *Aug.* 29.3 and Dio Cass. 53.1.3; Prop. 2.31.3–4 and Ov. *Tr.* 3.1.61–62 describe the statues of the Danaids. See Quenemoen 2006 for a recent reconstruction of the Portico of the Danaids on the terrace of the Temple of Apollo, and Pandey 2018, 94–96 on the herms.

16. For divergent but provocative interpretations of the complex, see Milnor 2005, 51–53, 64–65 and Pandey 2018, 94–96.

17. On recreational walking in monumental porticos in Rome, see Macaulay-Lewis 2011, 276–79. Prop. 2.32.7 and Ov. *Am.* 2.2.3–4 associate the portico-temple complex on the Palatine with strolling: see Pandey 2018, 102, 115.

18. Huskey (2006) maps the sites passed on a journey up to Augustus' Palatine complex, based on Ov. *Tr.* 3.1.

19. Miller 2009, 328, 370. See also Ov. *Tr.* 3.1.38–42. On Ovid's account of the Augustan Palatine, see Newlands 1997 and Miller 2009, 212–20.

20. On the connections between Augustus' house and Rome's divine protectors and mythological founders, see Meyboom 2005. See Stambaugh 1978, 586–87 on the multifunctionality of the Temple of Apollo; Pliny *NH* 36.32 mentions the statue of Diana. Egelhaaf-Geiser (2007, 211, 214–18) discusses traffic at the temple.

21. See Dix and Houston 2006, 680–88 on Augustus' library; on uses and users of the public libraries in Rome, see 709–10. For the Senate meetings, see Thompson 1981 and Suet. *Aug.* 29.3.

22. One important local model for Augustus' Palatine complex was Pompey's theater complex in the Campus Martius, which also included a meeting space for the Senate and Pompey's house: see Russell 2016a, 153–86 and Davies 2017, 229–36. Nielsen (1994, 164–80) discusses Hellenistic palaces as key models for the imperial complexes on the Palatine, as well as for late Republican elite constructions.

23. Russell 2016a, especially 75–95; see also Miller 2009, 186.
24. Pandey 2018, 8–11; 83–141.
25. *RG* 34; see also Milnor 2005, 25–27 and Pandey 2018, 9.
26. On the inscription, see *RG* 35 and Starr 2010: it was also placed in the Senate house and in Augustus' Forum.
27. Milnor 2005, 87; see also 80–93.
28. Foubert (2010a, 73–76) reviews the evidence for the preservation and veneration of houses associated with Augustus and later emperors. Suetonius does not say whether he actually visited Augustus' house: see Milnor 2005, 81n69.
29. On the importance of clothing for communicating status among Roman aristocrats, see Meister 2012, 106–31; he argues that this system of communication began to break down during the late Republic, when traditional garb could not correspond to the extraordinary powers of Rome's most important leaders.
30. I am grateful to Chris Gregg for bringing this evidence to my attention.
31. Vell. Pat. 2.81.3; Dio Cass. 49.15.5; discussed in Wiseman 2009, 528–29.
32. Wiseman 2009, 533. See also Suet. *Gram.* 17.2; Suet. *Calig.* 18.3.
33. Miller 2009, 214; see also 212–18, and Newlands 1997, 67.
34. Suetonius describes Augustus doing public business while on vacation (*Aug.* 72.2–3).
35. Champlin (2003, 178–91) assesses the evidence that Nero started the Great Fire of 64 CE and comes down on the side of Nero's accusers. For a recent overview of the scholarship on the Domus Aurea, discussed further below, see Meyboom and Moormann 2013, 14–25.
36. See Zarmakoupi 2014, 157–77 on villa pools. Marzano (2007, 38) identifies pools (for fish breeding and display) as a standard feature of coastal villas.
37. Archaeologists have applied the term *villa* to a broad range of sites in the Mediterranean: see Terrenato 2001, 5–6; Marzano 2007, 1–8.
38. For pre-Neronian remains in the Colosseum valley, see Panella 1990, 59–61 and *LTUR II*, 53. Morford (1968, 159–63) treats the literary evidence for buildings in this area.
39. Morford 1968, 160–61, 163.
40. Tac. *Ann.* 15.42, Suet. *Nero* 31, and Mart. *Spect.* 2 are the most detailed ancient accounts of the Domus Aurea, although they date to a generation after its construction. See also *LTUR II*, s.v. "Domus Aurea: Il palazzo sull'Esquilino"; "Domus Aurea: Area dello Stagnum"; "Domus Aurea: Vestibulum." Nero's building on the Palatine is also sometimes included in discussions of the Domus Aurea: see *LTUR II*, s.v. "Domus Aurea: Complesso del Palatino." Meyboom and Moormann (2013) offer a comprehensive guide to the stuccoes and frescoes in the Esquiline building.
41. Panella 1996, 168.
42. *LTUR* II, s.v. "Domus Aurea: Area dello Stagnum," 54; see also Panella 1996, figs. 156 and 162.
43. Albertson 2001, 110–11. See Dio Cass. 65.15.1 on the dedication of the Colossus during the reign of Vespasian.
44. Panella 1996, 172; *LTUR II*, 51.
45. For the lake and porticos, see Panella 1990, 67–73; Panella 1996, 181–88.
46. *LTUR II*, 53; Carandini 2010, 251; Longfellow 2011, 28–30.
47. Davies 2000, 38 and Zarmakoupi 2014, 151.

48. On the Domus Aurea and the Fourth Style, see Moormann and Meyboom 2013, 84–99; Lorenz (2013) discusses the theatrical imagery.

49. Meyboom and Moormann 2013. Exactly what construction properly counted as the Domus Aurea in Nero's day is a matter of debate. Champlin (2003, 205) notes that the literary sources speak of the Domus Aurea as a single structure: Suetonius indicates that the Domus Aurea replaced the Domus Transitoria, which occupied the area between the Palatine and the Esquiline, and so (according to Champlin) the name *Domus Aurea* should apply only to the construction in this valley. But Meyboom and Moormann (2013, 3) point out that late antique authors identify the Domus Aurea with the Esquiline palace.

50. Marzano 2007, 22. For images of colonnaded pools at villas in Pompeian frescoes, see Panella 1996, figs. 163–64.

51. Champlin 2003, 208; Carandini 2010, 156–60.

52. Marzano 2007, 72–75.

53. On the implication of the villa in elite self-representation, see especially Purcell 1995; Wallace-Hadrill 1998; Zanker 1998, 16–20; Spencer 2010, 62; Marzano 2007, 13–33.

54. Spencer (2010, 46) explains that "from the first century BCE onwards, expansive villas were increasingly zoned *intellectually* as landscapes of cultured *otium* and self-display" (emphasis in the original). For the conceptual contrasts between Rome and the villa, see also Hales 2003, 34–35 and Spencer 2010, 118–19, 126–27.

55. See Newlands 2012, 137–38 on Campania as a site of leisure and withdrawal in elite Roman texts.

56. For Seneca's conception of Campania as a space of elite withdrawal, see Newlands 2012, 149–50.

57. On Pliny's solitude at his villas, see George 1997a, 317–18.

58. On Nero's evocation of *rus in urbe* (countryside in the city), see Boëthius 1960, 94–128 and Purcell 1996b, 127–8.

59. Griffin 1984, 139–41 (quotation on 140); see also Champlin 2003, 205–6. On the Temple of Fortuna, Pliny *NH* 36.163.

60. Davies 2000, 41.

61. Hemsoll 1990, 14–16; Davies 2000, 40–42; Champlin 2003, 206–9. See also Champlin 2003, 156–60 for Nero's efforts to recreate Baiae in Rome.

62. D'Arms 1998, 37; Coarelli 1983, 215–17.

63. On public gatherings at Pompey's complex, see D'Arms 1998, 34–35; Russell 2016a, 166–67; Davies 2017, 234–36.

64. Val. Max. 9.15.1, following the interpretation of D'Arms 1998, 40–42. D'Arms also cites an inscription assigned to the *fasti* of 45, albeit in need of heavy restoration, as evidence for the event.

65. Panella 1990, 73.

66. Champlin (2003, 208–9) also suggests that aristocratic *horti* in Rome offered a model for the Domus Aurea, but he interprets the Domus Aurea as a public park and thus as an innovative fusion of the private *hortus* and the public *domus*. I think it is more likely that public access to the Domus Aurea took place under the same limited conditions as the public feasting in the *horti*. Unlike the leaders of the late Republic, however, Nero had little need to compete for attention. Hemsoll (1990, 16) notes the possibility of controlled public access to the grounds of the palace.

67. Tacitus reports that the Senate trooped over to Antium when Nero's daughter was born (*Ann.* 15.23).

68. Tacitus claims that Nero was accused of singing an epic poem on the sack of Troy during the Great Fire (*Ann.* 15.39); Suetonius has a similar story (*Nero* 38.2).

69. See Morford 1968, 165 for how Nero's immediate successors handled the Domus Aurea; see also Davies 2000, 40.

70. Suet. *Nero* 57; Tac. *Hist.* 1.4. See also Champlin 1998; Van Overmeire 2012, 480–81.

71. On the Domus Aurea as the palace of the sun, see L'Orange 1973 (originally published in 1942); his thesis was revived by Hemsoll (1990) and Champlin (2003, 209), who argues that the Domus Aurea was presented simultaneously as a god's house and the house of the Roman people.

72. Robert 1968; his interpretation aligns with other evidence for mythological play-acting in the arena, where criminals were costumed and executed to evoke famous crimes and punishments from mythology: see Coleman 1990, 60–61. Griffin (1984, 146–47; 273n31) argues that the epigram predates the Domus Aurea.

73. See Zaccaria Ruggiu 1990, 77–78 on the legal authority of the *dominus* over everything on and within his property. See Russell 2016a, 167 on Pompey's methods for regulating the movements and activities of visitors to his *horti* (e.g., gatekeepers, architectural barriers).

74. On emperors doing business at their villas, see Millar 1977, 24–28.

75. Champlin (2008, 418–19) discusses the ancient historians' handling and mishandling of their sources for Tiberius. Feldherr (2009, 184) suggests that "history and rumor . . . grow together" in Tacitus' account of the reign of Tiberius.

76. Vout 2009a, 33.

77. Maiuri 1957, 32–43; Krause 1998, 230. For a detailed reconstruction, see Krause 2003, 63–78.

78. Maiuri 1957, 36–38; Krause 1988, 359; Krause 2003, 76–78.

79. Maiuri 1957, 39–42; Krause 1988, 361–63.

80. Maiuri 1957, 42–43.

81. Krause 1988, 363; Krause 2003, 75.

82. Krause 1998, 237.

83. See Booms 2012 on large gatherings at the villas of Domitian, Trajan, and Hadrian.

84. Houston 1985, 187–91; Booms 2010.

85. Houston 1985, 183–84; Dio Cass. 58.3.8, Suet. *Calig.* 10, Suet. *Vit.* 3.2, Tac. *Ann.* 6.20.

86. Champlin (2008, 422–23) discusses these instances of Tiberius' return; see also Dio Cass. 58.24.1 and 58.25.2.

87. *Campaniam praelegebat, ambiguus an urbem intraret, seu, quia contra destinauerat, speciem uenturi simulans. et saepe in propinqua degressus, aditis iuxta Tiberim hortis, saxa rursum et solitudinem maris repetiit pudore scelerum et libidinum, quibus adeo indomitis exarserat ut more regio pubem ingenuam stupris pollueret.*

Chapter 4 · *Exposing the Ruler: Seneca on Visibility and Complicity*

1. On the glamour and disgrace associated with theatrical performers, see Edwards 1994. On Nero's penchant for theatrical performance, see Bartsch 1994, 36–62.

2. Key discussions include Edwards 1997; Roller 2001, 64–126; Bartsch 2006; Bartsch and Wray 2009; Star 2012.

3. For the emperor's role in the economy of honor, see Lendon 1997.

4. On the danger of the emperor's gaze, see Bartsch 1994, 1–35. On withdrawal, see Rudich 1993, 171–76 and Acton 2011. On the dynamics of viewing and being viewed among the Roman elite, see Barton 2002; Bartsch 2006; Cooper 2007; and the discussion in the introduction.

5. On the dating of the work, see Braund 2009, 16–17.

6. See Volk 2006, 197 on the Thyestes story as a familiar "testing-ground for assessing the relationship of potentially tyrannical rulers and their subjects" in Rome.

7. On Julius Caesar's reputation for *clementia* as a sign of tyranny, see Dowling 2006, 17–24; Konstan (2005), however, argues that the Roman aristocracy understood *clementia* as a positive virtue, not a tyrannical one.

8. Latin text from Braund 2009. For the development of the concept of *clementia*, see Mortureux 1989, 1658–64; Dowling 2006, especially 18–28 (late Republic) and 194–212 (under Nero); Braund 2009, 30–44.

9. On the genres that inform this text, see Braund 2009, 17–30. Adam (1970, 12–20) discusses Seneca's use of Hellenistic "mirror for princes" treatises; see also Fears 1975 on Seneca's use of Hellenistic kingship literature and Griffin 2002 on Seneca's theory of educating the ruler. Seneca's definition of *clementia* as a characteristic of the *sapiens* may represent a genuine innovation in the Stoic ethical system: see Griffin 1976, 154–70.

10. Leach (1989, 227) suggests that Seneca wrote the *De clementia* to demonstrate his own influence and authority over Nero.

11. See Bartsch 2006, 185–86 on Seneca's combination of two traditions about mirrors in Roman literature: the mirror as a source of vanity and as a goad to self-improvement.

12. Star (2012, 118–120) discusses the mutual judgment of ruler and ruled in the *De clementia*.

13. Translation adapted from Braund 2009, 103.

14. Translation adapted from Braund 2009, 109. The phrase *contra te lux est* has caused some concern for commentators: see Braund 2009, 252 for a discussion of a fragment from Ecphantus of Syracuse, who (like Seneca) portrays the king as both equivalent to the sun and facing the sun.

15. Grimal (1971, 214) traces Seneca's use of solar imagery to Egyptian sources. On the sun in ancient ruler cult more generally, see Braund 2009, 250–52.

16. Roller 2001, 84. Bartsch (2006, 196) argues that, for Seneca, the community can be "the source of negative models"; the *sapiens* must learn to judge himself rather than rely upon the judgment of his peers.

17. On the ruler's subjects as his judges in the *De clementia*, see Star 2012, 121–25.

18. On the title, date, and author of this work, see Eden 1984, 1–8. On literary genres in the *Apocolocyntosis*, see Damon 2010 and Freudenburg 2015. Osgood (2011, 252–56) details the correspondences between the *Apocolocyntosis* and Nero's first speech to the Senate (which Seneca was believed to have written) as reported in Tacitus; see also Leach 1989 on the *Apocolocyntosis* as part of Seneca's self-positioning on Nero's rise to power.

19. Braund and James (1998, 298) argue that Claudius' misshapen body "evokes the distortion of civic life" during his rule. For a similar argument applied to Claudius' voice in the *Apocolocyntosis*, see Osgood 2007.

20. Star 2012, 156.
21. Robinson (2005, 252–54) argues that the panegyric is also satirical.
22. Seneca is not alone among Roman authors for his interest in the political life of bees: Seneca cites Vergil, *G.* 4.212–13 to show the suffering the hive experiences if the king is lost; as Braund and other commentators have observed, he cites the same verse at *Apocol.* 3.2. Lowrie (2015) discusses the Vergilian passage as a window into other key tropes in Roman political thought; see also Lowrie 2016, 74–79.
23. Xenophon's *Hiero* employs similar tropes regarding the vulnerability of the tyrant, although there it is the tyrant, and not his advisor, who worries about the limitations he faces.
24. Translation adapted from Braund 2009, 129.
25. *Non est hic sine ratione populis urbibusque consensus sic protegendi amandique reges et se suaque iactandi, quocumque desiderauit imperantis salus. . . . quemadmodum totum corpus animo deseruit et, cum hoc tanto maius tantoque speciosius sit, ille in occulto maneat tenuis et in qua sede latitet incertus, tamen manus, pedes, oculi negotium illi gerunt, illum haec cutis munit . . . sic haec immensa multitudo unius animae circumdata illius spiritu regitur, illius ratione flectitur pressura se ac fractura uiribus suis, nisi consilio sustineretur.*
26. E.g., Livy 2.32.9–12; Tac. *Ann.* 1.12 (discussed in the conclusion to this book). On the transformation of this trope in the late Republic and early Empire, see Mebane 2017, 173–212. See also Star 2012, 142–44 on how the emperor functions as the "soul of the empire" in the *De clementia* and the *Apocolocyntosis*.
27. Star (2012, 136–7) and Mebane (2017, 179–82) also emphasize the threats of upheaval and unrest that inform Seneca's political argument.
28. Mortureux (1989, 1679) argues that Seneca has reduced the Roman Empire to two elements, the ruler and the ruled, and it is *clementia* that unites these two parties and ensures their cohesion. See also Manuwald (2002, 112) on the dependence of the commonwealth on the ruler's character and decisions.
29. Mebane 2017, 182.
30. There is a rich literature on how Seneca's tragedies reflect and critique Stoic thought. Examples include Lefèvre 1981 and Boyle 1983 on the different visions of the human-divine relationship in Senecan tragedy and Stoic philosophy; Rosenmeyer 1989 and Volk 2006 on Stoic cosmology in Seneca drama; Nussbaum 1994, 439–83 and Bartsch 2006, 256–81, on Seneca's *Medea* as a challenge to Stoic conceptions of the good and of the self; Schiesaro 2003, 228–51, for whom Senecan tragedy undermines Stoic approaches to reading poetry.
31. Tarrant (1978) contrasts Senecan tragedy with classical Greek drama. For his own *Thyestes*, Seneca may have drawn on Varius' tragedy of the same name, a celebrated work in antiquity that was performed at the games in honor of Octavian's victory at Actium; only six words of that play are extant, however, and any links between Varius' work and Seneca's must remain speculative. On Varius' *Thyestes* and the surviving fragment (quoted in Quintilian *Inst. Or.* 3.8.45), see Leigh 1996. On Republican tragedies on the Thyestes myth and their influence on Seneca, see La Penna 1979, 127–41.
32. See Henry and Henry 1985, 68 and Tarrant 2006, 14–15 on the prevalence of autocrats in Seneca's tragedies. For Picone (1984, 131–32), *regnum* (rule) is the protagonist of Seneca's *Thyestes*.
33. On the history of the performance debate, see Boyle 2011, xl–xliii, who supports the argument that the tragedies were suitable for full-scale performance on the stage. Calder

(1975) suggests performance by a household troupe of actors (slaves). Hollingsworth (2001) argues that *recitatio* would not be a suitable mode for Senecan tragedy. Sutton (1986) and Kohn (2013) discuss possible approaches to performing of Senecan tragedy on the Roman stage. See also Boyle 2011, xxxiii–xl on the Roman imperial theater. Although we have no direct reports of the performance of Senecan tragedy in antiquity, one graffito from Pompeii records a line of Cassandra's from Seneca's *Agamemnon*: "I see the groves of Ida" (*Idaea cerno nemora, Ag.* 730). For the grafitto, see Lebek 1985 and Kohn 2013, 13. Quintilian asserts that Seneca was the only author whom the young men of his (Quintilian's) day cared to read, and he includes speeches, poems, letters, and dialogues among his works (*Inst. Or.* 10.1.126, 129).

34. Harrison 2000, 138; Schiesaro 2003, 224; Littlewood 2004, 172.

35. The House of Atreus is one prominent exception to Seneca's interest in the family as a site of moral education: see Gloyn 2017, 142–50, on the Julio-Claudian house as an "anti-*exemplum*" of the family in Seneca's prose works.

36. Latin text of the tragedies from Zwierlein 1986.

37. *Satelles. Fama te populi nihil*
    aduersa terret? At. Maximum hoc regni bonum est,
    quod facta domini cogitur populus sui
    tam ferre quam laudare. Sat. Quos cogit metus
    laudare, eosdem reddit inimicos metus.
    at qui fauoris gloriam ueri petit,
    animo magis quam uoce laudari uolet.
    At. Laus uera et humili saepe contingit uiro,
    non nisi potenti falsa. quod nolunt uelint.

38. Mader 1998, 41. See Schiesaro 2003, 154–163 on Atreus as a representative of *Realpolitik*.

39. See also Sen. *Phaedra* 140–57, where the Nurse cautions Phaedra against thinking she could conceal an affair with her stepson Hippolytus.

40. *non uertice alti montis impositam domum*
    et imminentem ciuitas humilis tremit
    nec fulget altis splendidum tectis ebur . . .
    nulla culminibus meis
    imposita nutat silua . . .
    sed non timemur, tuta sine telo est domus
    rebusque paruis magna praestatur quies.

41. See Rose 1986 on Thyestes' and Atreus' contrasting attitudes toward power.

42. On the identity of the chorus in the *Thyestes*, see Davis 1993, 58.

43. A recurring trope in ancient drama: see, e.g., Aeschylus *Ag.* 773–891; Sophocles *OT* 873–82. Later in the play, Atreus makes a similar point when he tells Thyestes that "having power is a matter of chance" (*habere regnum casus est*, 529), and invites him to accept a share in ruling their city. Of course, while Atreus nods to fortune, he has set a careful trap to gain power over Thyestes and get his revenge against him.

44. Zwierlein (1966, 113–17) regarded these passages as extraneous displays of rhetorical skill; more recent studies have rejected this view.

45. Faber (2007) discusses numerous correspondences between this speech and other passages in the *Thyestes*.

46. Smolenaars (1998) discusses the Vergilian intertexts for this passage (the palace of King Latinus, the temple of Apollo at Cumae, Aeneas' path to the underworld). See Picone 1984, 94–95 on similarities between the messenger's speech and Thyestes' critique of royal life (*Thy.* 455–69, discussed above). Aygon (2004, 229–31) treats the shifts in perspective in this passage (high to low, exterior into interior). For Schiesaro (2003, 85–89), the grove represents the unconscious.

47. *in arce summa Pelopiae pars est domus*
   conuersa ad Austros, cuius extremum latus
   aequale monti crescit atque urbem permit
   et contumacem regibus populum suis
   habet sub ictu; fulget hic turbae capax
   immane tectum, cuius auratas trabes
   uariis columnae nobiles maculis ferunt.
   post ista uulgo nota, quae populi colunt,
   in multa diues spatia discedit domus.
   arcana in imo regio secessu iacet,
   alta uetustum ualle compescens nemus, penetrale regni.

In translating this passage, I draw on Tarrant 1985.

48. See Davis 1993, 58–62 and Allendorf 2013, 134–38 on the ignorance and lack of authority of the chorus in the *Thyestes*.

49. Littlewood (2004, 226) suggests that the messenger shares Atreus' pleasure in the crime committed.

50. On the chorus' failure to connect their knowledge of Atreus' crime to the cosmic disruption they witness, see Tarrant 1985, 204, Volk 2006, 187–95, and Allendorf 2013, 136–38.

51. See Tarrant 1985, 95–97 on textual parallels between the Fury's instructions and Atreus' activities later in the play.

52. Schiesaro 2003, 46. On varieties of spectatorship in Senecan tragedy, see also Littlewood 2004, 172–258.

53. Tarrant (1976, *ad loc.*) notes the unsavory significance of the Atreid banquet hall, given the history of dining in this royal house.

54. Seneca's tragic characters are often conscious of their own literary and mythological history: see Littlewood, 2004, 181 on Medea and Atreus, and Seo 2013, 9 on Oedipus.

55. Littlewood (2004, 227–28) regards Tantalus as the "author" of Atreus' crime.

56. Schiesaro 2003, 26; see also 45–49.

57. In a similar vein, Schiesaro (2003, 45) argues that the audience must "deliberate whether they can enjoy the aesthetic emotions offered by Seneca's poetry without colluding" in its unspeakable crimes.

58. See Schiesaro 2003, 60 on Atreus' love of seeing and being seen.

59. See Kohn 2013, 16, 129 on the machinery available for staging this scene in the Roman theater.

60. *turba famularis, fores*
   templi relaxa, festa patefiat domus . . .
   miserum uidere nolo, sed dum fit miser.
   aperta multa tecta conlucent face.

resupinus ipse purpurae atque auro incubat,
uino grauatum fulciens laeua caput.
eructat. o me caelitum excelsissimum,
regumque regem!

61. Littlewood (2004, 181–83) discusses the desire of Senecan protagonists (especially Atreus and Medea) to compel both their victims and a wider audience to recognize the act of vengeance.

62. Star (2012, 182) points out that Seneca's *Thyestes* and *Medea* both end with the victim of vengeance recognizing the avenger: compare Thyestes' "I recognize my brother" with Medea's question to Jason, "do you recognize your wife?" (*coniugem agnoscis tuam*, *Medea* 1021).

63. Calder (1976, 32) sees Cassandra as the central character of Seneca's play. Benton (2002) argues that the Trojan women (as in Seneca's *Troades*) were particularly compelling to the Roman elite as they confronted their own vulnerability and loss of standing in the early Empire.

64. Schiesaro 2014, section 36: "present and future have fused" in Seneca's play.

65. Littlewood 2004, 225.

66. Tarrant (1976, 343) notes the allusions to gladiatorial competition in the death scene.

67. Schiesaro (2014, section 33) suggests that women's ambivalence toward victory is a key feature of the choral odes in Seneca's *Agamemnon* (this play includes two choruses of women, one Trojan and one Argive); see also Schiesaro 2014, section 5 on the divergence between Clytemnestra's and Cassandra's interpretations of the death of Agamemnon.

68. On the possibilities for staging the rite, see Boyle 2011, 186–87; Kohn 2013, 37–38.

69. Allendorf (2013, 125–29) emphasizes the unusual elusiveness of the signs in this scene, for the characters and for the audience.

70. On Senecan tragedy as a commentary on his contemporary politics, see Volk 2006, 196–200; Star 2016, 53.

71. Ker (2009b, 42–49) argues persuasively that Seneca's suicide in Tacitus' *Annals* shows how Nero's victims (especially Seneca) were complicit in Nero's violence and autocracy.

Chapter 5 · Interdependence and Intimacy: Power at Home in Roman Pompeii

1. Roller 2001, 129–264; see also Stevenson 2015, 196–97.

2. See Cooper 2007, 7–11 on the demands for "symmetrical recognition" between the *paterfamilias* and members of his household, including women, slaves, and guests; she is especially interested in the threat that Christianity (with women and slaves among its early adherents) posed to the dominance of the *paterfamilias*.

3. For the legal authority of the *paterfamilias*, see Gardner 1993, 52–56.

4. On the different settlements and foundations of Pompeii, and on the development of its urban landscape in comparison to other cities in the Roman Empire, see Zanker 1998, 27–133; Laurence 2007, 20–38; Hales 2003, 97–101; Guzzo 2007, 3–5. On the different phases of the forum, from the archaic period to 79 CE, see Ball and Dobbins 2013, 468–91. Hingley (2005, 79–81) describes Rome's promotion of urbanism, especially the architectural development of urban centers, as a part of a "strategy of unification" of the empire,

which also supported "the authority of the local elite within their own communities." Compare the discussion in Purcell 2005 of Roman communities outside of Italy, e.g. in the Greek East, where "rules and customs of the elite Roman society were made available for others to observe and imitate" (98). Dench (1995, 144–53) argues for the survival of local social and political practices in the communities of Roman Italy into the early Empire: for example, elite accumulation and display of wealth were less pervasive among the Samnites through the early first century BCE, which prevented them from entering the Senate in significant numbers until the first to second centuries CE.

5. Grahame (2000, 94–97) argues against counting Pompeian archaeology as evidence for Roman culture or identity, but this may presume too fixed a conception of what may counts as "Roman." See e.g. Lomas 1995, 110–15 on how inhabitants of the Bay of Naples promoted their Greek cultural background to attract patronage from Roman aristocrats; she describes Hellenism and Romanization as "mutually compatible" processes (117). On Greek culture as a critical element in the construction of Roman identity, see Wallace-Hadrill 2008 and Newby 2016, 10–19. See also Versluys 2015, 153 on Rome's use of *others* (e.g., Greece and Egypt) in forming its own identity.

6. Hales 2003, 100; she argues that Pompeians used their houses to perform and thus to claim Roman identity. Wallace-Hadrill (2015, 184) suggests that "what marks a Roman house as Roman is the perceived necessity of providing a suitable framework not only for private but also for public life."

7. See Woolf 2005, 122–24; Hingley 2005, 72–90; Ando 2010, 40–43; Ando 2012, 223; Versluys 2015, 143. See also Whitmarsh 2010, who observes that imperial Roman culture does not obviate local and regional distinctiveness: to the contrary, awareness of what is specifically local emerges in opposition to the imperial and the global. Laurence and Trifilò (2015, 114–16) compare baths in Campanian villas to bath buildings for auxiliary troops (noncitizens) in Britain in the Flavian period. Lavan (2016) argues that elite integration was far less developed in the early Empire than in succeeding generations, but Italy is a special case in his discussion: the legal privileges of Italian communities, and the dominance of Italians in imperial administration, set it apart from the provinces (156–58).

8. D'Arms 1970 is the seminal treatment of Roman aristocratic villas in the Bay of Naples. For a more recent overview of villas in the region, see Gazda 2016. For ties between local communities and the senatorial elite in Rome, see Tacoma 2015, 132. See also Newby 2016, 16 on contact between Rome and Campania.

9. On the evidence for the two Poppaei families and the links between them, see Koloski-Ostrow 1997, 252–54; Gazda 2016, 34; Gazda and Clarke 2016, 188.

10. On the imperial cult in Pompeii, see Laurence 2007, 27–32. See chapter 2 on the imperial family in urban life across the Empire.

11. Berry (2016, 126–27) discusses the textual evidence for open doors. On the house as a space for display, see also Wallace-Hadrill 1994, Hales 2003. Hartnett (2008, 101–2; 2011, 155–58) argues that benches and raised sidewalks served to draw viewers' attention to particular houses.

12. See Drerup 1959, 155–59 on the atrium-*tablinum*-peristyle axis of the Roman *domus*, which guides the view of the visitor; for an overview of this attitude in later scholarship, see Proudfoot 2013, 91–92.

13. Proudfoot 2013, 97–107; see also Berry 2016, 130–33 on doors and strategies for display.

14. Hales 2003, 107–12. See also Wallace-Hadrill 1994, 47. Leach (2004, 25) points out that the atrium might often have been too crowded for visitors to appreciate the axial view.

15. Lauritsen (2012, 105–6) has shown that *cubicula* near the peristyle, in the rear of the house, were less likely to have evidence of barriers (doors, partitions, or curtains) than those near the atrium: boundaries were less important for regulating spaces that were more remote. On barriers inside the house, see also George 1997a, 305–6 and Berry 2016, 130–41. See Grahame 1997 and 2000 on morphic mapping, a method used to reconstruct paths of movement through a house, and thus to determine the relative accessibility of different parts of the house.

16. Wallace-Hadrill 1994, 149–74; Stewart 2008, 47–51; Mayer 2012, 166–78.

17. Petersen 2006, 136–62; see 144–62 on the combination of painted and real nature as a key aspect of Roman aesthetics (and thus a key component of claiming Roman identity).

18. Petersen 2006, 183.

19. On luxury items, social distinction, and group identity, see Wallace-Hadrill 1994, 145–47; Zanker 1998, 19–24; Wallace-Hadrill 2008, 354–55. On the Pompeian house as an expression of identity, see also Hales 2003.

20. Mayer 2012, 168.

21. Mayer 2012, 199–212. Lorenz (2008, 437) observes that viewers might simply enjoy the story depicted in a fresco.

22. On the development of the *scaenae frons* motif in the different styles, see Leach 2004, 93–100; on the Fourth Style specifically, see Picard 1982; Moormann 1983; Perrin 2002; Lorenz 2013. Vitr. 7.5.2 discusses the motif of the *scaenae frons* in wall painting.

23. Leach 2004, 100.

24. Elsner 2007, 100–109, 175.

25. On supernumerary figures as a Roman innovation, see Michel 1982. See Platt 2002 on Actaeon and Artemis and Elsner 2007, 132–76 on Narcissus. Lorenz (2008, 248–49) argues that female figures are represented as observers in mythological painting far more frequently than male figures, and that female viewers are one of the few examples of dominant women in wall painting. Green (2015, 144–49) examines depictions of slaves as witnesses of sexual encounters in erotic wall painting.

26. We lack architectural evidence for this structure in antiquity. Stone theaters in Rome and elsewhere in the Mediterranean include stage buildings with columnar structures similar to those depicted in wall paintings, but most Roman theaters (especially during the Republic) were wooden and temporary, and thus have not survived. On the evidence for Roman stages, see Beacham 1991, 56–85.

27. This structure is discussed in chapter 3. For images of the frescoes, see Carettoni 1983. Eristov 1994, 10–13 warns that the combination of tripartite doorway and columns need not represent a stage building but could allude more generally to public architecture; I focus on frescoes that include actors, dramatic masks, or other indicators of the world of the theater.

28. For images of the frescoes in Villa A, see De Franciscis 1975 and Gazda and Clarke 2016. The King's Visualization Lab website provides stunning digital renderings of theater buildings based on these frescoes.

29. See Wallace-Hadrill 1994, 28–29 on the "feeling of rich luxury" produced by representations of grand architectural forms in small spaces, and how this grandeur facilitates the self-presentation of the elite.

30. Lorenz 2013, 374–77. For a comprehensive survey of the frescoes in the Domus Aurea, see Meyboom and Moormann 2013.

31. See Little 1971; Picard 1982; Moormann 1983; Beacham 1991; Leach 2004; Lorenz 2013.

32. Leach 2004, 117–19; Mayer 2012, 54–55.

33. These images also allude to the role of the elite householder as a sponsor of building projects, festivals, and games: Leach 2004, 104. For discussion of allusions to public architecture in Roman domestic art, see especially Wallace-Hadrill 1994, 17–37 and Leach 2004, 93–155.

34. *mihi quidem nihil stultius uidetur quam existimare esse eum studiosum tui quem non noris. eximiam quandam gloriam et dignitatem ac rerum gestarum magnitudinem esse oportet in eo quem homines ignoti nullis suffragantibus honore adficiant . . . in salutatoribus, qui magis uulgares sunt et hac consuetudine quae nunc est ad pluris ueniunt, hoc efficiendum est ut hoc ipsum minimum officium eorum tibi gratissimum esse uideatur; qui domum tuam uenient, iis significato te animaduertere (eorum amicis qui illis renuntient ostendito, saepe ipsis dicito).*

35. Bourdieu 1977, 190; see also 187–94.

36. Dyson (1992, 159–61) notes that local elections, and the negotiations between mass and elite that accompanied them, remained vibrant in Pompeii and other municipalities in Roman Italy long after they had declined in Rome. For an overview of the political institutions of Pompeii, see Mouritsen 1988, 28–29. On the pluralism of patronage in the Republic, see Wallace-Hadrill 1989, 78–81.

37. See Mouritsen 1988, 31–69; Mouritsen 1990, 148–49.

38. See Viitanen and Nissin 2017, 124–29 on house facades as prime locations for posting *programmata*; they argue, contra Mouritsen, that these facades were not a "free for all" but under the control of the householder. On the survival of *programmata* long after the conclusion of elections, see Viitanen and Nissin 2017, 128 and Mouritsen 1988, 33–4.

39. Lorenz (2013, 365–79) argues that the interplay of real and fictive space is the defining characteristic of Neronian wall painting; see also Perrin 2002 and Bergmann 2002.

40. Lorenz 2013, 375.

41. Koloski-Ostrow 1997, 245–46. On the numbers of mythological images in Pompeii, see Fredrick 1995, 271–72.

42. Beacham 1992, 142–50; Hall 2008, 2–8; Boyle 2011, xxxiii–xxxvi.

43. Koloski-Ostrow 1997; Clarke 1998, 4; Fredrick 1995, 2002b, and 2003; Severy-Hoven 2012; Green 2015.

44. Lorenz (2008, 250) argues that increasing frequency of mythological painting in Pompeii reflects the increase of visual literacy in Roman society; see also Newby 2016.

45. Gazda (2010, xiv–xviii), Joshel and Petersen (2014, 5), and Newby (2016, 21–28) advocate for considering diverse viewers and ways of viewing in the Roman world.

46. For examples of this approach, see especially Bergmann 1994, 1996, and 2002; Lorenz 2014.

47. Petersen (2006, 163–83) and Severy-Hoven (2012) analyze domestic decor from the perspective of freedmen owners in the House of L. Caecilius Iucundus (Petersen) and the

House of the Vettii (Severy-Hoven). On how domestic decor served to choreograph the movements of slaves through the house, and on evidence for slaves' contributions to art in the *domus*, see Joshel and Petersen 2014, 24–86. It is also important to consider how householders' attitudes towards domestic art might vary based on their social and economic positions. Clarke (2003, 221–68) discusses the ways that "everyday" citizens of the Bay of Naples used domestic art to communicate their identities and social status. Mayer (2012, 100–212) argues for a distinctive aesthetics of the "ancient middle classes" as opposed to the imperial elite.

48. See Gazda 2010, xvi: domestic art should be seen as "a backdrop for, and participant in, spectacle and performance, chance encounters, movement through space—all of which animate the circumstances of viewing art and destabilize the apprehension of its meaning." See also Newby 2016, 193–94.

49. See Lorenz 2008, 238 on the different image types for Cassandra.

50. Ling (1997, 142–43) discusses the evidence for a connection between the *gens Poppaea*, to which Nero's wife belonged, and the House of the Menander.

51. Baldassare and Carratelli 1990–2003, vol. 2, 276–81; Ling and Ling 2005, 72–77; Lorenz 2014, 191–205.

52. On the theatrical imagery, see Koloski-Ostrow 1997, 246–47 and Ling and Ling 2005, 104–5.

53. Koloski-Ostrow 1997, 257.

54. Baldassare and Carratelli 1990–2003, vol. 4, 546–47.

55. Bergmann 1994, 254. Euripides' *Alcestis* was first performed in place of a satyr play (the fourth of the plays presented by the tragedians in Athenian festivals); the assembly of mosaic and painting may have reminded educated viewers of this historical circumstance.

56. For Alcestis images in Southern Italian vase painting and in other Pompeian houses, see Bergmann 1994, 234. Accius wrote an Alcestis tragedy (second century BCE): see Beacham 1991, 123.

57. See Newby 2016, 200 on gender roles in the decorative program of the House of the Tragic Poet.

58. Bergmann 1994, 245.

59. Bergmann 1994, 249; on the Iphigenia painting, see 234–35. This Iphigenia is very different from the scene represented in the House of M. Pinarius Cerialis: here she appears nude and restrained by two men while Agamemnon stands to the side and covers his face.

60. See Bergmann 1996 and 2002 on an ensemble of images from the House of Jason that features myths of knowledgeable wives (Helen, Medea, Phaedra) and their ignorant (and endangered) husbands.

61. Baldassare and Carratelli 1990–2003, vol. 3, 460–73.

62. Lorenz (2008, 238–41) discusses other Pompeian images of Iphigenia.

63. On the Attis frescoes, see Moormann 1983, 79–84.

64. Lorenz (2013, 369–70) suggests that the distribution of the figures across the wall and their position at eye level encourages viewers to engage with each one individually.

65. Severy-Hoven 2012, 572.

66. Bergmann (1996, 208) makes a related observation about the paintings of tragic wives from the House of Jason: "The viewer has a privileged position by seeing what the husbands cannot see and foreseeing what will happen to them."

67. On the relationship between a visitor's status and his access to the space of the house, see Wallace-Hadrill 1994, 58; Dickmann 1999, 103; Anguissola 2011, 45.

68. See Ling 1997, 49 on evidence for the partitioning of the room. Allison (2006, 400–404) argues that the House of the Menander had been undergoing years of upheaval, construction, and renovation before 79 CE, and so was probably not functioning normally at the time of the eruption.

69. See Berry 2016, 135–36 on how thresholds and mosaics signaled to viewers that they were crossing boundaries inside the house.

70. Bergmann 1994, 249–50.

71. *tunc etiam animaduertendum est, quibus rationibus priuatis aedificiis propria loca patribus familiarum et quemadmodum communia cum extraneis aedificari debeant. namque ex his quae propria sunt, in ea non est potestas omnibus intro eundi nisi inuitatis, quemadmodum sunt cubicula, triclinia, balneae ceteraque, quae easdem habent usus rationes. communia autem sunt, quibus etiam inuocati suo iure de populo possunt uenire, id est uestibula, caua aedium, peristylia, quaeque eundem habere possunt usum. igitur is, qui communi sunt fortuna, non necessaria magnifica uestibula nec tabulina neque atria, quod in aliis officia praestant ambiundo neque ab aliis ambiuntur.*

72. Wallace-Hadrill 1994, 10–12.

73. Leach 2004, 21–34; Dwyer 2010.

74. Most hosts of the *salutatio* were of senatorial rank; the most prominent exceptions are praetorian prefects, like Sejanus, and emperors' wives. Governors in the provinces may also have held *salutationes*. See Speksnijder 2015, 88–91.

75. Riggsby (1997) treats the range of activities associated with the *cubiculum* in Latin literature. For an archaeological approach to the *cubiculum*, see Anguissola 2011, especially 7–35 and 69–182 (discussed further below).

76. See especially Allison 1993, 2004 and Nevett 2010.

77. On the regularity and ubiquity of the atrium house in Pompeii, see Dickmann 1999, 103 and Hales 2003, 99. On various Pompeian house plans, see Grahame 2000, 56–73.

78. On what constitutes a "house" in the archaeological record, see Wallace-Hadrill 1994, 72–74: he defines a "house" as a unit that can only be accessed from the street, but cautions that "habitation" and "ownership" are different categories. On the rental market in Pompeii, especially for structures divided into multiple commercial and living spaces, see Laurence 2007, 134–53 and Mayer 2010, 22–60.

79. George 1997a and 1997b are pioneering examples; for more recent studies, see Nevett 2010, 89–118, Joshel and Petersen 2014, Green 2014, 135–252. On this movement in scholarship on Roman domestic art, see above.

80. On the visitor as a "temporary inhabitant," see Grahame 1997, 142.

81. Dickmann 1999, 114–16, 299–308; Longfellow 2010, 27–28.

82. On the *imagines*, and their absence in Pompeii, see Leach 2004, 26. On the symbolic marriage couch as a fixture of the atrium, see Richardson 1988, 388–89 (most evidence is literary). See Allison 2004, 67–69 on material evidence for *lararia* in Pompeian houses.

83. When he annexed a neighboring house and expanded the size of his property, he seems to have relegated service activities to the new space and dedicated the old core of the house (including the atrium) to entertaining and self-display: see Petersen 2006, 170–82.

84. Allison 1993, 4–6.

85. See Allison 2004, 29; Wallace-Hadrill 1994, 80–82.

86. Allison 2004, 69.

87. Allison 2004, 70.
88. Allison 2004, 146–48.
89. Green 2014, 216–60; see also chapter 6 below.
90. See Nevett 2010, 89–118.
91. Nevett 2010, 110–13.
92. On the prevalence of these production spaces in houses of the upper two quartiles in Pompeii, see Wallace-Hadrill 1994, 137–40; he argues that "the important distinction is not between houses with a reception function and those with an economic one but between houses with an economic function and those with an economic *and* a reception function" (139–40). Purcell (1995) argues for economic success as an important component of elite self-presentation; his discussion focuses on agricultural production at the villa, but the same values might be at work here; see also Allison 2004, 122. Flohr (2012) discusses the types of workshops most frequently associated with atrium houses: he distinguishes between those that apparently were not considered to conflict with the social and display functions of the house, and those that householders made an effort to conceal.
93. On the symbolic resonance of weaving, see Milnor 2005, 29–32, 83–85.
94. See Joshel and Petersen 2014, 37–40, 59–73 on the disruptions that slaves could cause in the elite householder's performance of power at the banquet.
95. See Anguissola 2011, 7–9 and 71–115 on the development of the cubiculum according to the chronology of the canonical four styles. Allison (2004, 134–35) argues that bedding and furnishings are necessary to establish that a room was suitable for sleeping; she finds no consistent pattern for the distribution of sleeping spaces in her sample of Pompeian houses.
96. Anguissola 2011, 8; she also includes the size of the entrance to the *cubiculum* as a factor in its usefulness as a reception space (240).
97. Anguissola 2011, 209–13. On connections between dining and sleeping spaces, see also Wallace-Hadrill 1994, 57–58, Leach 2004, 49, and Karivieri 2014, 94–99.
98. Discussed in Leach 2004, 49.
99. Cic. *Verr.* 2.2.53.133; 2.3.23.56; 2.5.11.27–28. On Verres' *cubiculum*, see Riggsby 1997, 41.
100. On the *domus* as a standard environment for judicial proceedings, see Bablitz 2015.
101. Russell 2016a, 191–92.

Chapter 6 · *Bathing, Dining, and Digesting with the Ruler*

1. Star (2012, 146) describes Claudius' edict as "an example of imperial micromanaging . . . that baffles the imagination." Claudius was famous for his tenuous control over his own body, a problem that is central to Seneca's critique of the emperor in the *Apocolocyntosis*: see chapter 4.
2. DeFelice 2007; Mayer 2012, 29–30. On Nero's predilection for visiting *popinae*, or public eateries, and elite hostility toward this practice, see Goddard 1994, 74.
3. Koloski-Ostrow (2015, 3–26) discusses the prevalence of public toilets in Pompeii, Herculaneum, Rome, and Ostia ca. 200 BCE–100 CE.
4. On the history and architecture of the baths, and on their significance for Roman society and culture, see Nielsen 1990, Fagan 1999, and Yegül 2010.

5. On the performance of social status and power relations at the *convivium*, see D'Arms 1990 and 1999, Bradley 1998, Roller 2006.

6. Rimell (2015, 158–223) discusses elite anxieties about bathing (in public and in private).

7. See Fagan 1999, 192–210 and Yegül 2010, 35–39 on social mixing at the baths; the emperors Titus, Hadrian, and Alexander Severus are reported to have visited public baths and bathed among the other attendants. Fagan (1999, 215) points out the opportunities for elite status display at the baths. See Nielsen 1990, 124 for cases of wealthy citizens (or even the emperor) providing free access to public baths and 132 on slaves attending wealthy bathers.

8. Koloski-Ostrow 2015, 95.

9. Koloski-Ostrow (2015, 30–31; 84–98) argues that the darkness and foul smell of most ancient latrines makes them poor candidates for extended social interaction, and she doubts that those with the means to avoid public toilets would have made use of them; she also suggests that Roman clothing would have afforded some privacy for those using multiseat toilets. See Beard 2008, 93 on the frequency of basic latrines (essentially benches placed over cesspits) in small houses in Pompeii. On waste disposal as an element of elite self-display, see Green 2014, 241–55, discussed in chapter 5 (above).

10. Star (2012, 4–5) reviews the scholarly debates over the relationship between Petronius and Seneca.

11. See especially Star 2012, 1–19.

12. Fitzgerald 2000, 35–36; Asmis 2009, 120, 124; Edwards 2009. For Griffin (1976, 257), Trimalchio's pronouncements on slavery point to the widespread but superficial influence of Stoic precepts on elite culture of the first century CE.

13. Meister (2012) treats the emperor's body as a site for expressing or denying the distinction between the emperor and the senatorial elite. Kantorowicz 1997 is the seminal treatment of the ruler's body in European political thought, beginning with medieval theology and law.

14. Many have seen Trimalchio as a parody of Nero. On potential allusions to Nero and Neronian Rome in the *Cena*, see Crum 1952a and 1952b; Sullivan 1968, 22–26; Slater 1994; Byrne 2007. See Courtney 2001, 7–9 and Schmeling 2011, xiii–xvii for summaries of the arguments and evidence for dating the text to the Neronian period; more recently, Laird (2007) has proposed dating the novel to the second century CE. Vout (2009b, 109) suggests that "the *Cena* is not a text about Nero's Rome so much as a text which alerts us to the artifice or ingredients involved in representing Roman imperial culture, especially perhaps Neronian culture."

15. On Trimalchio the stage director, see Conte 1996, 123, and Rosati 1999. For Trimalchio as an author, see Rimell 2002, 39.

16. For a standard discussion of Trimalchio's banquet as evidence for freedmen in Rome, see Veyne 1961 and the assessment by Andreau 2009. Petersen (2011, 6–10) argues that the compelling portrait of Trimalchio and his fellow freedmen has compromised the assessment of other kinds of evidence for freedmen in the Roman world.

17. Rimell (2002, 47) insists that Trimalchio is not simply mixing up his myths, but showing how everyone (even mythological characters) can switch roles. Perkins (2009, 134–36) argues that Trimalchio is questioning the knowledge of fiction (and thus elite learning more broadly) as the basis for allocating status and power.

18. On Roman banquets as spectacles, see D'Arms 1999.

19. On the different texts and genres that influence the *Satyricon*, and the problem of classifying the text as belonging to a specific genre, see Walsh 1970, 7–31; Panayotakis 1995; Courtney 2001, 12–33; Schmeling 2011, xxx–xxxviii. See Rimell 2002 on consuming different forms of literature (and being consumed by it) as a central motif in the *Satyricon*.

20. Courtney (2001, 40–42) discusses the contradictory remarks about the identity of Encolpius and his friends in the novel.

21. On Encolpius as a "mythomaniac narrator," see Conte 1996.

22. For Conte (1996, 123–25), Encolpius and his friends are the freedmen's victims, but the reader is meant to find Encolpius' suffering amusing.

23. Laird 1999, 228, 252–55.

24. Latin text from Müller 2009.

25. Edwards 2009, 141.

26. Edwards 2009, 152. See also Fitzgerald 2000, 88–93 on the instability of freedom and slavery in Seneca and other Roman texts.

27. Schmeling (2011, *ad loc.*) interprets this boast as a parody of Seneca's attacks against extravagant estates in a number of his letters (e.g., Sen. *Ep.* 89.20).

28. On Roman associations between Eastern kings and eunuchs, see Smith 1975, 55. On Seneca's treatment of Maecenas, see Star 2012, 173–79. Trimalchio later identifies himself as a freedman of a Maecenas (71.12).

29. Slater 1990, 56. On domestic productivity and elite self-display, see chapter 5 (above).

30. Schmeling (2011, *ad loc.*) observes that "clocks of this sort were used in law-courts and by physicians when measuring heart-beats," neatly tying Trimalchio's self-aggrandizement to his interest in death. On Trimalchio's obsession with controlling the passage of time, see Toohey 1997.

31. Starr 1987; see also chapter 3.

32. Schmeling 2011, *ad loc.*

33. Rosati 1999, 103. See also Walsh 1970, 128.

34. Here I am inspired by political theorist Achille Mbembe's (2001, 107) suggestive discussion of the body as "the principal locale of the idioms and fantasies used in depicting power" in postcolonial Cameroon. Obscenity is not simply "the province of ordinary people," but rather central to how the state represents itself and "makes manifest its majesty" (103–4). For readings of Latin literature that draw on Mbembe, see Fertik 2017 on obscenity in Cicero's *Philippics* and Connolly 2016 on violence in Lucan.

35. Schmeling (2011, *ad loc.*) notes that these vessels are usually earthenware.

36. Clarke (1992) argues that Trimalchio's behavior toward his slave is inspired by Roman ideas of Jewish table manners. Epictetus (*Discourses* 1.2.8–10) suggests that holding a chamber pot is a standard (and acceptable) activity for a slave. Seneca (*Ep.* 77.14) describes a Spartan soldier, captured and enslaved, who was ordered to fetch a chamber pot for his master and committed suicide by knocking his head against a wall.

37. See Star 2012, 160–64 on Trimalchio's combination of Stoic and medical discourses; see also Perkins 2009, 132–33 on Trimalchio's body as a challenge to Stoicism and other schools of philosophy. Toohey (1997, 52–54) associates Trimalchio's intestinal problems with his anxieties about time and death.

38. *"ignoscite mihi," inquit, "amici, multis iam diebus uenter non respondit. nec medici se inueniunt. profuit mihi tamen malicorium et taeda ex aceto. spero tamen, in ueterem pudorem sibi imponit. alioquin circa stomachum mihi sonat, putes taurum."*

39. Braund (1996, 46–47) compares Trimalchio's exhibition of his bodily functions to Pliny's account of Domitian in the *Panegyricus*. Schmeling (2011, *ad loc.*) observes that Trimalchio's recounting of his gastrointestinal problems alludes to well-known characters from mime. Star (2012, 110) calls Trimalchio's attention to his gut a bodily "supplement" to Senecan ideals of self-control. See Rimell 2002, 42–43 on Trimalchio's "privileged knowledge of interiors."

40. See for example 41.10–12, 42.1–6. Rimell (2002, 189–90) argues that freedmen have a special understanding both of freedom and of man's inevitable subjugation to his body.

41. Encolpius even suspects that the whole event might have been staged (54.3).

42. See 42.6–7; 43.1–2; 65.9–10. Bodel (1994) links the motif of death in the *Cena* to the social status of freedmen, who are "dead" in that they are cut off from full membership in their communities; see also Bodel 1999 for comparisons between Trimalchio's mock funeral and imperial funeral processions. Schmeling (2011, *ad loc.*) identifies the mock funeral as a topos of Stoic philosophy and elegiac poetry.

43. *itaque si quis uestrum uoluerit sua re causa facere, non est quod illum pudeatur. nemo nostrum solide natus est. ego nullum puto tam magnum tormentum esse quam continere. hoc solum uetare ne Iouis potest... nec tamen in triclinio ullum uetuo facere quod se iuuet, et medici uetant continere. uel si quid plus uenit, omnia foras parata sunt: aqua, lasani et cetera minutalia.*

44. Rimell (2002, 44) observes that Trimalchio "doesn't seem to be any more in control of his insides than the victimized guests."

45. See Koloski-Ostrow 2015, 87–88 on sponge sticks as part of Roman toilet habits.

46. Star (2012, 105–8) traces the relationship in the *Satyricon* between imperial power and the power to force others to eat and drink.

47. Edwards (1993, 136–37) discusses Roman moralizing critiques of excessive eating.

48. See Star 2012, 107–8 on the sealed and broken wine jars represented on Trimalchio's tomb, an "attempt to control what goes in and what comes out of those around him."

49. Schmeling (2011, *ad loc.*) prefers *seruabatur*, which suggests that Encolpius has entered a tub reserved especially for Trimalchio. Yegül (2010, 18) notes that individual bathers had discretion (at least at the public baths) over the order in which they visited the different parts of the baths, the length of time they spent there, etc.

50. On parallels for this "unheard of custom," especially in the Gospels, see Clarke 1992, 262–63.

51. Bradley (1994, 26) observes that slaves were intimately involved in the daily routines of their masters (even children). Seneca (*Ep.* 47.8) expects that slaves will know their masters' personal tastes and habits.

52. See Canali 1987, 47–48 on the unusual symbiosis between masters and slaves throughout the *Satyricon*.

53. Roller (2006, 22) points out that slaves were instruments for the pleasure of the privileged diners. Joshel and Petersen (2014, 40–68) reconstruct the movement of slaves during the banquet.

54. On the textual considerations in the following passage, see Clarke 1992, 257.

55. If (following Mueller) we supply *capillis*, then the freedman describes exactly the same action that Trimalchio performs preceding the banquet, when he used the chamber pot, rinsed his hands, and wiped them on the eunuch's hair. Other editors suggest *sinu* instead of *capillis*, but in any case the speaker marks the experience as undesirable and degrading for his *contubernalis*.

56. See Armstrong 2012 on conceptual and metaphorical links between the slave and the tool, beginning with Aristotle's treatment of the slave as a "thinking tool" in the *Politics*.

57. On the material conditions of slaves' daily lives, see Bradley 1994, 81–102 and Joshel and Petersen 2014.

58. See Roller 2006 for a comprehensive study of the cultural significance of physical posture at the *convivium*. When Trimalchio calls for the slaves to recline at the table, he orders one to "tell your *contubernalis* to recline" (70.10). He thus recognizes a kinship bond between slaves that had no legal standing: see Bradley 1994, 27.

59. Star 2012, 201. See Griffin 1976, 257–66 for how Stoicism informs Seneca's account of appropriate behavior towards slaves; she is careful, however, to point out the limits of philosophy's impact on "ordinary social prejudice" in the Roman world (266). See Harris 2004, 329–30 on the laws that were enacted in Seneca's time to regulate the treatment of slaves.

60. See Edwards 2009, 155–57 on how Seneca's treatment of slavery may provoke his readers to empathize with real slaves without challenging the institution itself.

61. Dressler 2016, 4, 46–48; he argues that "ownness" is foundational to Roman philosophy, not limited to a particular school. Reydams-Schils (2006) focuses on the development of *oikeiosis* in the Roman philosophical tradition.

62. Graver 2007, 175–76. Dressler (2016, 48–55; 98–108) shows how each account of *oikeiosis* (personal and social) includes and produces the other.

63. The *cena*, furthermore, may offer an ideal environment for practicing virtue. See Graver 2007, 186, on Stoic texts that identify the virtue of the wise man as "convivial" and "erotic": the wise man must have knowledge of "what is appropriate at a dinner party, how to conduct the party and how one ought to drink with others" and even how to "chase after young persons of good nature."

64. Star (2012, 201–8) compares Trimalchio's sentiments and Seneca's ideas of slavery.

65. See Habinek 1998, 137–50 and Roller 2001, 264–86 on how Seneca's philosophy may also serve to strengthen the social order that favors the traditional elite.

66. Schmeling (2011, *ad loc.*) describes Trimalchio's sexual relations with his slaves as a reenactment of his own experiences as a slave.

67. On Seneca's treatment of the *domus* as the *res publica* for the enslaved, see Griffin 1976, 265; Fitzgerald (2000, 4–5) discusses affective bonds between free and enslaved members of the *familia* in Latin literature.

68. E.g., *Sat.* 54.1–5 (Encolpius suspects another set-up); 74.9–75.7.

69. Kaster (2010) discusses Seneca's sources for these stories. See Roller 2001, 3–4 on how Seneca's stories of foreign kings function to model the role of the Roman emperor and the appropriate and inappropriate relations between emperor and aristocrats; see also Roller 2015 on Seneca's reworking of traditional Roman approaches to *exempla*.

70. See Goddard 1994 and Braund 1996 on negative and positive examples of rulers at the banquet in early imperial Latin literature.

71. Star (2012, 189) describes the opening of *De ira* as a "phenomenology of anger."

72. Latin text from Reynolds 1977.

73. See Nussbaum 1994, 410–13 on Seneca's arguments against anger.

74. On the importance of perception for Stoic ethics, and Stoic views of the mixing of body and psyche, see Graver 2007, 17–26. Nussbaum (1994, 419–22) argues that, for Seneca, anger is alien to human nature but produced by our encounters with the (unjust) circumstances of life.

75. On this trope, especially in Seneca's *De clementia*, see chapter 4 (with further bibliography).

76. See Braund 1996, 37–40 on eating together as a key element of civilization in Greek and Roman literature.

77. The unwritten coda to this story, as Roller (2001, 164) observes, is that Caligula was eventually killed: "the ruler who conducts his exchange relations in this way exposes himself first to aristocratic censure, and eventually to assassination."

78. In Herodotus' version (3.34), Praexaspes is considerably less direct: when Cambyses asks Praexaspes what the Persians think of him, the courtier responds that the Persians say that he is too fond of wine.

79. When Seneca suggests that we must rely on our friends to prevent us from behaving in inappropriate ways, he uses the example of those who are prone to drunkenness: "they fear that they will be rash and careless when they are drunk, and trust their friends to take them away from the banquet" (*ebrietatis suae temeritatem ac petulantiam metuunt, mandant suis ut e conuiuio auferantur*, 3.13.5).

80. On the unique publicity of the emperor, see chapters 3 and 4.

81. Translation adapted from Kaster and Nussbaum 2010.

82. See Nussbaum (1994, 432–438) for Seneca's ideas of appropriate responses to the most extreme injustice, such as the murder of one's children: one option that he advises is suicide.

83. See Habinek 1998, 142 on anger as a threat to social position, and on how Seneca's argument against anger thus "reasserts [aristocrats'] claims to privileged treatment." See Kaster 2005, 13–27 on elite Roman ideals of behavior appropriate to one's social position.

84. See Roller 2001, 116 on Harpagus' response in the context of Seneca's larger concern about the desirability of flattering autocrats.

85. On Augustus' intervention as a model for interactions between emperor and aristocrats, see Roller 2001, 171.

86. Kaster and Nussbaum 2010, *ad loc*. The confusion of the categories of "eater" and "eaten" occurs throughout Trimalchio's banquet: see Rimell 2002.

Conclusion

1. See Syme 1986, 439–54 for a withering analysis of aristocratic defenses of the principate. On the "loss of politics" as a central problem in Roman political thought, see Hammer 2008.

2. Lowrie 2016. I am grateful to her for bibliographical suggestions that were fundamental to developing this discussion.

3. For how emperors reject the model set by their predecessors, see Gotter 2015.

4. Waever 1995, 52–53.

5. Gorz 1983, 1; see also Enzensberger 1976, 63 on how internal and external threats collapse into one another.

6. Neocleous 2008, 4; see also Aradau 2004 and Peoples 2011.

7. But see Bartsch 1994, 123–24 on the continuing influence of the *delatores* under Vespasian and Nerva as the "subtext" of Tacitus' *Dialogus*. Rutledge (2001) and Rivière (2002) examine the social, political, and legal history of delation.

8. Rutledge 2007, 113–14. Rudich (1993, 135) admits that there is no evidence for a secret police in the Roman Empire, although he insists that "intuition and common sense . . . point to the inevitability, under tyrannical rule, of some kind of a special repressive and investigative machinery." Rivière (2002, 3) contrasts the role of delation in the ancient world and in modern totalitarian societies.

9. Strunk 2016, 84.

10. *egens, ignotus, inquies . . . occultis libellis saeuitiae principis adrepit* (1.74); see Strunk 2016, 84–85.

11. See Rutledge 2001, especially 9–16. For Tacitus' attitude toward the *delatores*, see also Strunk 2016, 79–131.

12. *Ann.* 1.73; 2.28. Rutledge (2001, 152) observes that the *delatores* are absent from Tacitus' account of the year 59 (after the death of Agrippina the Younger) until 62 CE: "their disappearance is ominous, and indicates that the legal niceties that had been a part of court life were now abandoned." On the laws of *maiestas*, see Bauman 1974.

13. See Ando 2011b, 103–7 on the transformation of *maiestas* from a quality of the Roman people in its relations with foreign powers to an attribute of the emperor in domestic contexts, and on the significance of *maiestas* for the "social and conceptual revolution" that attended Roman monarchy (i.e., the identification of the emperor with the Roman people). Levick 1999, 184 emphasizes the flexibility of the concept of *maiestas*, depending on who was in power and who accusers thought should be in power.

14. See Bauman 1974, 32–35 on Augustus' extension of the laws of *maiestas* to include defamation.

15. Roller 2001, 167–68 and O'Gorman 2000, 85–86.

16. O'Gorman 2000, 84–85.

17. Levick 1999, 184–88.

18. Waever 1995, 55; Aradau (2011, 395–96) explains that those who invoke "security" are successful because they claim institutional authority or specific knowledge and expertise. See Agamben 2005, 29–30 on states of emergency or necessity as subjective judgments.

19. See Kapust 2011, 111–71 and Strunk 2016, especially 7–22 for an overview of these debates in scholarship.

20. On the ways that Roman texts model the experience of political life, such as making judgments, see Connolly 2014, 18–20.

21. Hammer 2008, 7.

22. On reading Roman texts as resources for modern political thought, see Connolly 2014, 1–2.

23. Dressler (2016) confronts this question in his study of Roman philosophy.

24. Ando (2000, 236) also infers that Marcellus had these statues in his house; compare to the case of Lucius Ennius (3.70), discussed below.

25. See Ando 2000, 236–37 on *maiestas* charges for the handling of imperial images, rooted not in law but in the "presumed identity between the interests of the *res publica* and those of one man."

26. Woodman and Martin 1996, *ad loc.*

27. Tiberius' inscrutable alternations between mercy and harshness prompt Tacitus to observe that "it was considered all the more remarkable that, although he knew better and knew what reputation comes with clemency, he preferred a gloomier course" (*quo magis mirum habebatur gnarum meliorum et quae fama clementiam sequeretur tristiora malle*, 4.31) The emperor's efforts to protect himself, Tacitus suggest, are a dubious enterprise: even if Tiberius perceives insults as genuine threats, he should not risk the ill-will that his aggression will produce.

28. Libo is a nephew of Scribonia, Augustus' first wife. On the mysterious notes in Libo's list, see Goodyear 1981 *ad loc.*: some commenters interpret them as a magical or astrological, but Goodyear thinks they were "a private code" of Libo's. Rutledge (2001, 159–61) argues that Libo was probably guilty of conspiracy, as multiple *delatores* seem to have acted independently against him (rather than on the initiative of Tiberius).

29. Woodman and Martin (1996, *ad loc.*) offer two possible explanations of *quasi per libertatem*: either Capito is offering Tiberius the opportunity to reaffirm his clemency, or he is speaking as if his speech is free (even though it is not).

30. Castel 1991, 283.

31. The virtue of *providentia* was attributed to Tiberius in official media (and perhaps used in imperial coinage for the first time under Tiberius): see Woodman and Martin 1996, 468–69.

32. Beck (1992, 21–80) and Giddens (1999, 7–10) offer helpful discussions of the relationship between awareness of risk and the desire to control the world we live in, although both are specifically concerned with risks produced in the industrialized world (especially the impact of technology on the environment). I do not use "risk" in the technical sense of Castel 1991, 287–89, who distinguishes between "dangerousness," which involves the concrete experience of individuals or groups, and "risk," which emerges from the statistical assessment of populations. On the relationship between the statistical study of populations and security, see also Foucault 2007, 65–79.

33. See Hammer 2008, 162–70 on Tacitus' treatment of the *delatores* as an ailment of the body politic.

34. *quod maxime exitiabile tulere illa tempora, cum primores senatus infimas etiam delationes exercerent, alii propalam, multi per occultum; neque discerneres alienos a coniunctis, amicos ab ignotis, quid repens aut uetustate obscurum: perinde in foro, in conuiuio, quaqua de re locuti incusabantur, ut quis praeuenire et reum destinare properat, pars ad subsidium sui, plures infecti quasi ualetudine et contactu.*

35. Gallia (2009, 200–202) argues that, in the *Dialogus*, the *delatores* constitute a threat to freedom of expression apart from (and even in addition to) any restrictions that the emperor himself may impose.

36. The *delatores* appear to be a kind of inefficient and *ad hoc* surveillance system, but their chief targets (the ruling elite) represent a much narrower group than a "surveillance society" encompasses. In his famous discussion of surveillance, Foucault (1977, 216–17) distinguishes the society of spectacle, which he identifies with Greco-Roman antiquity,

from the modern society of surveillance: the spectacle society makes a limited number of objects visible to a multitude of observers, while the surveillance society makes the multitude visible to a limited number of observers.

37. Nissenbaum 2010, 27–31.
38. Rule 2007, 13–22.
39. On the metaphor of "balance" between liberty and security, see Waldron 2003. One key problem for the idea of balance is that loss of liberty typically affects only minority groups within a broader community, and thus we are not all equally implicated (or vulnerable) in the project of striking a balance between ostensibly competing values: see Dworkin 2002 and Aradau 2004, 398–402.
40. Nissenbaum 2010, 75; see also Rule 2007 6, 10–13.
41. See Schoeman 1984, 413–16; Nissenbaum 2010, 76–77, 81–84.
42. Rachels 1975; Schoeman 1984, 404–9; Nissenbaum 2010, 84–85.
43. Regan 1995, 215.
44. Rule 2007, 167.
45. Regan 1995, 221. Regan (2015) assesses and reaffirms her previous argument in light of social, political, and technological developments.
46. Regan 1995, 220–31.
47. Regan 1995, 225.
48. Rule 2007, 192. See also Rule 2015, 29–31.
49. For a provocative rejection of the political value of security, see Neocleous 2008, 1–10.
50. Rutledge (2001, 174) argues that the *delatores* prevented civil strife even when they protected bad emperors; he defends the practical necessity of the *delatores* for the functioning of the Empire.
51. Griffin 1984, 166–69; crucially, the emperor's own freedmen did not participate (imperial freedmen had joined the successful assassination of Caligula in 41 CE).
52. Epicharis refuses to give up the conspiracy, even under torture: see Pagán 2004, 78–83 on Ephicharis as an *exemplum* of courage.
53. Rudich (1993, 103) takes Milichus as evidence that the culture of secrecy and spying, inevitable under the rule of a despot, even affected the lower classes; Rutledge (2001, 169) points out the dangers that Milichus and all of his former master's household might have suffered if their knowledge of the conspiracy was discovered.
54. On the challenges for historians of conspiracies, who must "produce narratives" that "resist retelling," see Pagán 2004, 89; on Tacitus' approach to these challenges, 74–78.
55. *etenim crebro uulgi rumore lacerabatur, tamquam uiros et insontes ob inuidiam aut metum extinxisset. ceterum coeptam adultamque et reuictam coniurationem neque tunc dubitauere, quibus uerum noscendi cura erat, et fatentur qui post interitum Neronis in urbem regressi sunt.*
56. Esposito 2013, 62–64; see also Esposito 2011, 15–16.
57. Robin 2004, 16. In a 2017 opinion piece, two staff members from the Obama administration discussed the dominant role of terrorism in the political discourse of the post-9/11 United States. In their experience in Washington, "policy arguments couched in the language of counterterrorism carried inordinate weight. . . . Claiming to have found the better way to fight terrorism became the surest way to win the debate." This played out, they note, "in an administration that came to office concerned about the overemphasis on

terrorism." See Jon Finer and Robert Malley, "How Our Strategy against Terrorism Gave Us Trump," *The New York Times*, March 4, 2017. Accessed March 4, 2019. https://www.nytimes.com/2017/03/04/opinion/sunday/how-our-strategy-against-terrorism-gave-us-trump.html.

58. Hamilton (2013, 28) associates the longing for security with "a vain hope in the perfect efficacy of our calculations" about the future. On the necessary and worthwhile risks of "human solidarity, friendship, and partnerships," see Bauman 2003, 71–74.

59. Der Derian 1995, 33–34.

60. On the political necessity of open-ended and critical dialogue, see Bauman 2003, 152–54; Aradau 2004, 392–93; Butler 2004, xix–xxi; 1–18.

Acton, Karen. 2011. "Vespasian and the Social World of the Roman Court." *American Journal of Philology* 132: 103–24.

Adam, Traute. 1970. *Clementia Principis: Der Einfluss hellenistischer Fürstenspiegel auf den Versuch einer rechtlichen Fundierung des Principats durch Seneca*. Stuttgart: Ernst Klett Verlag.

Agamben, Giorgio. 2005. *State of Exception*. Chicago: University of Chicago Press.

Ahl, Frederick. 1976. *Lucan: An Introduction*. Ithaca, N.Y.: Cornell University Press.

Albertson, Fred C. 2001. "Zenodorus's 'Colossus of Nero.'" *Memoirs of the American Academy in Rome* 46: 95–118.

Alföldi, Andreas. 1971. *Der Vater des Vaterlandes im römischen Denken*. Darmstadt: Wissenschaftliche Buchgesellschaft.

Allendorf, T. S. 2013. "The Poetics of Uncertainty in Senecan Drama." *Materiali e discussioni per l'analisi dei testi classici* 71: 103–44.

Allison, Penelope. 1993. "How Do We Identify the Use of Space in Roman Housing?" In *Functional and Spatial Analysis of Wall Painting: Proceedings of the Fifth International Congress on Ancient Wall Painting*, edited by Eric M. Moorman. Leiden: Stichting Babesch.

———. 2004. *Pompeian Households: An Analysis of Material Culture*. Los Angeles: Cotsen Institute of Archaeology, University of California, Los Angeles.

———. 2006. *The Insula of the Menander at Pompeii: Volume 3, The Finds; A Contextual Study*. Oxford: Oxford University Press.

Ando, Clifford. 2000. *Imperial Ideology and Provincial Loyalty in the Roman Empire*. Berkeley: University of California Press.

———. 2010. "Imperial Identities." In *Local Knowledge and Microidentities in the Imperial Greek World*, edited by Tim Whitmarsh, 17–45. Cambridge: Cambridge University Press.

———. 2011a. "From Republic to Empire." In *The Oxford Handbook of Social Relations in the Roman World*, edited by Michael Peachin, 37–66. Oxford: Oxford University Press.

———. 2011b. *Law, Language, and Empire in the Roman Tradition*. Philadelphia: University of Pennsylvania Press.

———. 2012. "Empire, State, and Communicative Action." In *Politische Kommunikation und öffentliche Meinung in der antiken Welt*, edited by Christina T. Kuhn, 219–30. Stuttgart: Franz Steiner.

———. 2015. "Petition and Response, Order and Obey: Contemporary Models of Roman Government." Accessed March 4, 2019: https://www.academia.edu/11785231/Petition_and_response_order_and_obey_contemporary_models_of_Roman_government.

Ando, Clifford, and Jörg Rüpke, eds. 2015. *Public and Private in Ancient Mediterranean Law and Religion*. Boston: De Gruyter.

André, J.-M. 1962. "Otium et vie contemplative dans les lettres à Lucilius." *Revue des études latines* 40: 125–28.

Andreau, J. 2009. "Freedmen in the *Satyrica*." In *Petronius: A Handbook*, edited by J. R. W. Prag and Ian Repath, 114–24. Chichester, West Sussex, U.K.: Wiley-Blackwell.

Anguissola, Anna. 2011. *Intimità a Pompei: riservatezza, condivisione e prestigio negli ambienti ad alcova di Pompei*. New York: De Gruyter.

Aradau, Claudia. 2004. "Security and the Democratic Scene: Descuritization and Emancipation." *Journal of International Relations and Development* 7, no. 4: 388–413.

Arendt, Hannah. 1958. *The Human Condition*. Chicago: University of Chicago Press.

———. 1970. *On Violence*. New York: Harcourt.

Armstrong, Tim. 2012. *The Logic of Slavery: Debt, Technology, and Pain in American Literature*. Cambridge: Cambridge University Press.

Ash, Rhiannon. 1999. *Ordering Anarchy: Armies and Leaders in Tacitus' Histories*. Ann Arbor: University of Michigan Press.

Asmis, Elizabeth. 2009. "Seneca on Fortune and the Kingdom of God." In *Seneca and the Self*, edited by Shadi Bartsch and David Wray, 115–38. Cambridge: Cambridge University Press.

Asso, Paolo. 2010. *A Commentary on Lucan, De bello civili IV: Introduction, Edition, and Translation*. Berlin: De Gruyter.

Augoustakis, Antony. 2011. "Burning Pyres in Lucan and Silius Italicus' *Punica*." In *Brill's Companion to Lucan*, edited by Paolo Asso, 185–98. Leiden: Brill.

Aygon, J. P. 2004. *Pictor in fabula: L'ecphrasis-descriptio dans les tragédies de Sénèque*. Brussels: Éditions Latomus.

Bablitz, Leanne. 2015. "Bringing the Law Home: The Roman House as Courtroom." In *Public and Private in the Roman House and Society*, edited by Kaius Tuori and Laura Nissin, *Journal of Roman Archaeology Supplementary Series* 102: 63–76.

Baldassare, Ida, and Giovanni Pugliese Carratelli. 1990–2003. *Pompei: Pitture e mosaici*. 11 vols. Rome: Istituto della enciclopedia italiana.

Ball, Larry F., and John J. Dobbins. 2013. "Pompeii Forum Project: Current Thinking on the Pompeii Forum." *American Journal of Archaeology* 117, no. 3: 461–92.

Barrett, Anthony. 1996. *Agrippina: Sex, Power, and Politics in the Early Empire*. New Haven, Conn.: Yale University Press.

Barton, Carlin A. 2001. *Roman Honor: The Fire in the Bones*. Berkeley: University of California Press.

———. 2002. "Being in the Eyes: Shame and Sight in Ancient Rome." In *The Roman Gaze: Vision, Power, and the Body*, edited by David Fredrick, 216–35. Baltimore: Johns Hopkins University Press.

Bartsch, Shadi. 1994. *Actors in the Audience: Theatricality and Doublespeak from Nero to Hadrian*. Cambridge, Mass.: Harvard University Press.

———. 1997. *Ideology in Cold Blood: A Reading of Lucan's Civil War*. Cambridge, Mass.: Harvard University Press.

———. 2006. *The Mirror of the Self: Sexuality, Self-Knowledge, and the Gaze in the Early Roman Empire*. Chicago: University of Chicago Press.

Bartsch, Shadi, and David Wray. 2009. *Seneca and the Self*. Cambridge: Cambridge University Press.

Bauman, Richard A. 1974. *Impietas in Principem: A Study of Treason against the Roman Emperor with Special Reference to the First Century AD*. Munich: Beck.

Bauman, Zygmunt. 2003. *Liquid Love: On the Frailty of Human Bonds*. Malden, Mass.: Polity Press.

Beacham, Richard C. 1991. *The Roman Theatre and Its Audience*. London: Routledge.

Bean, G. E. 1956. "An Inscription from Amisus." *Belleten Türk Tarih Kurumu* 20: 215–16.

Beard, Mary. 2008. *The Fires of Vesuvius: Pompeii Lost and Found*. Cambridge, Mass.: Belknap.

Beck, Ulrich. 1992. *Risk Society: Toward a New Modernity*. Translated by Mark Ritter. London: SAGE Publications.

Begemann, Elisabeth. 2015. "*Ista tua pulchra libertas*: The Construction of a Private Cult of Liberty on the Palatine." In *Public and Private in Ancient Mediterranean Law and Religion*, edited by Clifford Ando and Jörg Rüpke, 75–98. Boston: De Gruyter.

Benoist, Stéphane. 2015. "Women and *Imperium* in Rome: Imperial Perspectives." In *Women and War in Antiquity*, edited by Jacqueline Fabre-Serris and Keith Alison, 266–88. Baltimore: Johns Hopkins University Press.

Benton, Cindy. 2002. "Split Vision: The Politics of the Gaze in Seneca's *Troades*." In *The Roman Gaze: Vision, Power, and the Body*, edited by David Fredrick, 31–56. Baltimore: Johns Hopkins University Press.

Berger, Adolf. 1953. *Encyclopedic Dictionary of Roman Law*. Philadelphia: American Philosophical Society.

Bergmann, Bettina. 1994. "The Roman House as Memory Theater: The House of the Tragic Poet in Pompeii." *Art Bulletin* 76, no. 2: 225–56.

———. 1996. "The Pregnant Moment: Tragic Wives in the Roman Interior." In *Sexuality in Ancient Art*, edited by Natalie Boyle Kampen et al, 199–218. Cambridge: Cambridge University Press.

———. 2002. "Playing with Boundaries: Painted Architecture in Roman Interiors." In *The Built Surface, Vol. 1: Architecture and Pictorial Arts from Antiquity to the Enlightenment*, edited by C. Anderson, 15–46. Farnham, U.K.: Ashgate.

Berry, Joanne. 2016. "Boundaries and Control in the Roman House." *Journal of Roman Archaeology* 29, no. 1: 125–41.

Berthold, H. 1975. "Die Rolle der Massen in Lucan." In *Die Rolle der Volksmassen in der Geschichte der vorkapitalistischen Gesellschaftsformationen: Zum XIV. Internationalen Historiker-Kongress*, edited by J. Hermann and I. Sellnow, 293–300. East Berlin.

Betensky, A. 1978. "Neronian Style, Tacitean Content: Ambiguous Confrontations in the Annals." *Latomus* 37: 419–35.

Bodel, J. 1994. "Trimalchio's Underworld." In *The Search for the Ancient Novel*, edited by J. Tatum, 237–59. Baltimore: Johns Hopkins University Press.

———. 1997. "Monumental Villas and Villa Monuments." *Journal of Roman Archaeology* 10: 5–35.

———. 1999. "Death on Display: Looking at Roman Funerals." In *The Art of Ancient Spectacle*, edited by Christine Kondoleon and Bettina Ann Bergmann, 259–81. Washington: National Gallery of Art.
Boëthius, Axel. 1960. *The Golden House of Nero: Some Aspects of Roman Architecture*. Ann Arbor: University of Michigan Press.
Booms, D. 2012. "Problematizing Privacy at the Imperial Villas." In *Making Roman Places, Past and Present: Papers Presented at the First Critical Roman Archaeology Conference Held at Stanford University in March 2008*. Journal of Roman Archaeology Supplementary Series 89: 91–102.
Borgo, A. 1976. "Aspetti della psicologia di massa in Lucano ed in Tacito." *Vichiana* 5: 243–57.
Bourdieu, Pierre. 1977. *Outline of a Theory of Practice*. Translated by Richard Nice. Cambridge: Cambridge University Press.
Boyle, A. J. 1983. "*Hic epulis locus*: The Tragic Worlds of Seneca's *Agamemnon* and *Thyestes*." In *Seneca Tragicus: Ramus Essays on Senecan Drama*, edited by A. J. Boyle, 199–228. Victoria, Australia: Aureal Publications.
———. 2008. *Octavia: Attributed to Seneca*. Oxford: Oxford University Press.
———. 2011. *Seneca: Oedipus*. Oxford: Oxford University Press.
Bradley, K. R. 1994. *Slavery and Society at Rome*. Cambridge: Cambridge University Press.
———. 1998. "The Roman Family at Dinner." In *Meals in a Social Context*, edited by I. Nielsen and H. Nielsen, 36–55. Aarhus, Denmark: Aarhus University Press.
Bradley, Keith R. 1987. "Dislocation in the Roman Family." *Historical Reflections* 14: 33–62.
Braund, S., and S. James. 1998. "'Quasi Homo': Distortion and Contortion in Seneca's *Apocolocyntosis*." *Arethusa* 31: 285–311.
Braund, Susanna. 1996. "The Solitary Feast: A Contradiction in Terms?" *BICS* 41: 37–52.
———. 2009. *Seneca: De clementia*. Oxford: Oxford University Press.
Brennan, D. B. 1969. "Cordus and the Burial of Pompey." *Classical Philology* 64, no. 2: 103–4.
Brisset, J. 1964. *Les idées politiques de Lucain*. Paris: Les Belles Lettres.
Bruère, Richard T. 1951. "Lucan's Cornelia." *Classical Philology* 46, no. 4: 221–36.
Butler, Judith. 2004. *Precarious Life: The Powers of Mourning and Violence*. New York: Verso.
Byrne, Shannon N. 2007. "Maecenas and Petronius' Trimalchio Maecenatianus." *Ancient Narrative* 6: 31–49.
Carettoni, Gianfilippo. 1983. *Das Haus des Augustus auf dem Palatin*. Mainz am Rhein, Germany: P. von Zabern.
Calder, William M., III. 1975. "The Size of the Chorus in Seneca's *Agamemnon*." *Classical Philology* 70, no. 1: 32–35.
———. 1976. "Seneca's *Agamemnon*." *Classical Philology* 71, no. 1: 27–36.
Canali, Luca. 1987. *Vita, sesso, morte nella letteratura latina*. Milan: Il Saggiatore.
Carandini, Andrea. 2010. *Le case del potere nell'antica Roma*. Rome: Laterza.
Casali, Sergio. "The *Bellum Civile* as Anti-*Aeneid*." In *Brill's Companion to Lucan*, edited by Paolo Asso, 81–109. Leiden: Brill.
Casevitz, M. 1998. "Note sur le vocabulaire du privé et du publique" *Ktema* 3: 39–46.

Castel, R. 1991. "From Dangerousness to Risk." In *The Foucault Effect: Studies in Governmentality*, edited by Graham Burchell, Colin Gordon, and Peter Miller, 281–98. Chicago: University of Chicago Press.

Champlin, Edward. 1998. "Nero Reconsidered." *New England Review* 19, no. 2: 97–108.

———. 2003. *Nero*. Cambridge, Mass.: Harvard University Press.

———. 2008. "Tiberius the Wise." *Historia* 57, no. 4, 408–25.

Clarke, John R. 1991.*The Houses of Roman Italy, 100 BC–AD 250: Ritual, Space, and Decoration*. Berkeley: University of California Press.

———. 1998. *Looking at Lovemaking: Constructions of Sexuality in Roman Art, 100 BC–AD 250*. Berkeley: University of California Press.

———. 2003. *Art in the Lives of Ordinary Romans: Visual Representation and Non-Elite Viewers in Italy, 100 BC–AD 315*. Berkeley: University of California Press.

Clarke, William M. 1992. "Jewish Table Manners in the *Cena Trimalchionis*." *Classical Journal* 87, no. 3: 257–63.

Coarelli, F. 1983. "Architettura sacra e architettura privata nella tarda repubblica." *CEFR* 66: 191–217.

Coffee, Neil. 2011. "Social Relations in Lucan's *Bellum Civile*." In *Brill's Companion to Lucan*, edited by Paolo Asso, 417–32. Leiden: Brill.

Coleman, K. M. 1990. "Fatal Charades: Roman Executions Staged as Mythological Enactments." *Journal of Roman Studies* 80: 44–73.

Connolly, Joy. 2007. *The State of Speech: Rhetoric and Political Thought in Ancient Rome*. Princeton, N.J.: Princeton University Press.

———. 2009a. "Fear and Freedom: A New Interpretation of Pliny's *Panegyricus*." In *Ordine e sovversione nel mondo greco e romano*, edited by Gianpaolo Urso, 247–266. Pisa: ETS.

———. 2009b. "Political Theory." In *The Oxford Handbook of Roman Studies*, edited by A. Barchiesi and W. Scheidel, 713–27. Oxford: Oxford University Press.

———. 2014. *The Life of Roman Republicanism*. Princeton, N.J.: Princeton University Press.

———. 2016. "A Theory of Violence in Lucan's *Bellum Ciuile*." In *Wordplay and Powerplay in Latin Poetry*, edited by Phillip Mitsis and Ioannis Ziogas, 273–97. Berlin: De Gruyter.

———. 2018. "The Promise of the Classical Canon: Hannah Arendt and the Romans." *Classical Philology* 113, no. 1: 6–19.

Conquest, Robert. 1990. *The Great Terror: A Reassessment*. New York: Oxford University Press.

Conte, Gian Biagio. 1996. *The Hidden Author: An Interpretation of Petronius' "Satyricon."* Berkeley: University of California Press.

Cooper, Kate. 2007. "Closely Watched Households: Visibility, Exposure, and Private Power in the Roman *Domus*." *Past and Present* 197: 3–33.

Corbier, M. 1995. "Male Power and Legitimacy through Women: The *Domus Augusta* under the Julio-Claudians." In *Women in Antiquity: New Assessments*, edited by Richard Hawley and Barbara Levick, 178–93. London: Routledge.

Courtney, E. 2001. *A Companion to Petronius*. Oxford: Oxford University Press.

Crum, Richard H. 1952a. "Petronius and the Emperors, I: Allusions in the *Satyricon*." *The Classical Weekly* 45, no. 11: 161–68.

———. 1952b. "Petronius and the Emperors, II: Pax, Palamedes!" *The Classical Weekly* 45, no. 13: 197–201.

Dahmen, Karsten. 2001. *Untersuchungen zu Form und Funktion kleinformatiger Porträts der römischen Kaiserzeit*. Munster: Scriptorium.

D'Alessandro Behr, Francesca. 2007. *Feeling History: Lucan, Stoicism, and the Poetics of Passion*. Columbus: Ohio State University Press.

D'Arms, J. H. 1970. *Romans on the Bay of Naples: A Social and Cultural Study of the Villas and Their Owners from 150 BC to AD 400*. Cambridge, Mass.: Harvard University Press.

———. 1990. "The Roman *Convivium* and the Idea of Equality." In *Sympotica: A Symposium on the Symposion*, edited by Oswyn Murray, 308–19. Oxford: Clarendon Press.

———. 1998. "Between Public and Private: The *Epulum Publicum* and Caesar's *Horti trans Tiberim*." In *Horti Romani: Atti del convegno internazionale: Roma, 4–6 Maggio 1995*, edited by Maddalena Cima and Eugenio La Rocca, 33–43. Rome: L'Erma di Bretschneider.

———. 1999. "Performing Culture: Roman Spectacle and the Banquets of the Powerful." In *The Art of Ancient Spectacle*, edited by Christine Kondoleon and Bettina Ann Bergmann, 301–19. Washington: National Gallery of Art.

Damon, Cynthia. 2010. "Too Close?: Historian and Poet in the *Apocolocyntosis*." In *Latin Historiography and Poetry in the Early Empire: Generic Interactions*, edited by J. F. Miller and A. J. Woodman, 49–70. Leiden: Brill.

Davies, P. 2000. "'What Worse than Nero, What Better than His Baths?': '*Damnatio Memoriae*' and Roman Architecture." In *From Caligula to Constantine: Tyranny and Transformation in Roman Portraiture*, edited by E. Varner, 27–44. Atlanta: Michael C. Carlos Museum.

———. 2017. *Architecture and Politics in Republican Rome*. Cambridge: Cambridge University Press.

Davis, P. J. 1993. *Shifting Song: The Chorus in Seneca's Tragedies*. Hildesheim, Germany: Olms-Weidmann.

DeFelice, John. 2007. "Inns and Taverns." In *The World of Pompeii*, edited by John J. Dobbins and Pedar W. Foss, 474–86. New York: Routledge.

Dench, Emma. 1995. *From Barbarians to New Men: Greek, Roman, and Modern Perceptions of Peoples of the Central Apennines*. Oxford: Oxford University Press.

Der Derian, J. 1995. "The Value of Security: Hobbes, Marx, Nietzsche, and Baudrillard." In *On Security*, edited by Ronnie D. Lipschutz, 24–45. New York: Columbia University Press.

Dettenhofer, Maria H. 1994. "Frauen in politischen Krisen: zwischen Republik und Prinzipat." In *Reine Männersache? Frauen in Männerdomänen der antiken Welt*, edited by Maria H. Dettenhofer, 133–57. Cologne: Böhlau.

Dickmann, Jens-Arne. 1999. *Domus frequentata: anspruchsvolles Wohnen im pompejanischen Stadthaus*. Munich: Verlag Dr. F. Pfeil.

Dilke, Oswald Ashton Wentworth. 1978. *De bello civili, VII*. Bristol, U.K.: Bristol Classical Press.

Dix, Keith T., and George W. Houston. 2006. "Public Libraries in the City of Rome: From the Augustan Age to the Time of Diocletian." *Mélanges de l'École Française de Rome: Antiquité* 118: 671–717.

Dixon, Suzanne. 1992. *The Roman Family*. Baltimore: Johns Hopkins University Press.

———. 2016. "Family." In *The Oxford Handbook of Roman Law and Society*, edited by Paul J. du Plessis, Clifford Ando, and Kaius Tuori, 461–72. Oxford: Oxford University Press.

Dowling, Melissa Barden. 2006. *Clemency and Cruelty in the Roman World.* Ann Arbor: University of Michigan Press.

Drerup, Heinrich. 1959. "Bildraum und Realraum in der römischen Architektur."*Römische Mitteilungen* 66: 147–74.

Dressler, Alex. 2016. *Personification and the Feminine in Roman Philosophy.* Cambridge: Cambridge University Press.

Dreyfus, Hubert L., Paul Rabinow, and Michel Foucault. 1983. *Michel Foucault: Beyond Structuralism and Hermeneutics.* Chicago: University of Chicago Press.

Duindam, Jeroen F. J. 2004. "Norbert Elias and the History of the Court: Old Questions, New Perspectives." In *Hof und Theorie: Annäherungen an ein historisches Phänomen*, edited by Reinhardt Butz, Jan Hirschbiegel, and Dietmar Willoweit, 91–104. Cologne: Böhlau.

Dupont, Florence. 1985. *L'acteur roi, ou le théâtre dans la Rome antique.* Paris: Belles Lettres.

Dworkin, R. 2002. "The Threat to Patriotism." *The New York Review of Books*, Feb. 28, 2002.

Dwyer, Eugene. 2010. "The Pompeian Atrium House in Theory and Practice." In *Roman Art in the Private Sphere: New Perspectives on the Architecture and Decor of the Domus, Villa, and Insula*, edited by Elaine K. Gazda and Anne E. Haeckl, 25–48. Ann Arbor: University of Michigan Press.

Dyson, Stephen L. 1992. *Community and Society in Roman Italy.* Baltimore: Johns Hopkins University Press.

Eck, Werner. 2016. "The Emperor, the Law, and Imperial Administration." In *The Oxford Handbook of Roman Law and Society*, edited by Paul J. du Plessis, Clifford Ando, and Kaius Tuori, 98–110. Oxford: Oxford University Press.

Eden, P. T. 1984. *Seneca, Apocolocyntosis.* Cambridge: Cambridge University Press.

Edwards, Catharine. 1993. *The Politics of Immorality in Ancient Rome.* Cambridge: Cambridge University Press.

———. 1994. "Beware of Imitations: Theatre and the Subversion of Imperial Identity." In *Reflections of Nero: Culture, History, and Representation*, edited by Jaś Elsner and Jamie Masters, 83–97. Chapel Hill: University of North Carolina Press.

———. 1997. "Self-Scrutiny and Self-Transformation in Seneca's Letters." *Greece and Rome* 44, no. 1: 23–38.

———. 2009. "Free Yourself! Slavery, Freedom, and the Self in Seneca's Letters." In *Seneca and the Self*, edited by Shadi Bartsch and David Wray, 139–59. Cambridge: Cambridge University Press.

Egelhaaf-Geiser, U. 2007. "Roman Cult Sites: A Pragmatic Approach." In *A Companion to Roman Religion*, edited by Jörg Rüpke, 205–21. Malden, Mass.: Blackwell.

Elias, Norbert. 1983. *The Court Society.* Translated by Edmund Jephcott. Oxford: Blackwell.

Elsner, Jaś. 2007. *Roman Eyes: Visuality and Subjectivity in Art and Text.* Cambridge: Cambridge University Press.

Elsner, Jaś, and Jamie Masters. 1994. *Reflections of Nero: Culture, History, and Representation.* Chapel Hill: University of North Carolina Press.

Enzensberger, H. M. 1976. *Raids and Reconstructions: Essays on Politics, Crime, and Culture.* London: Pluto Press.

Eristov, H. 1994. *Les éléments architecturaux dans la peinture Campanienne du IVe style.* Collection de l'École Française de Rome 187. Rome.

Esposito, R. 2011. *Immunitas*. Translated by Zakiya Hanafi. Cambridge, U.K.: Polity.

———. 2013. *Terms of the Political: Community, Immunity, Biopolitics*. Translated by Rhiannon Noel Welch. New York: Fordham University Press.

Faber, Riemer A. 2007. "The Description of the Palace in Seneca *Thyestes* 641–82 and the Literary Unity of the Play." *Mnemosyne* 60: 427–42.

Fagan, Garrett G. 1999. *Bathing in Public in the Roman World*. Ann Arbor: University of Michigan Press.

Fantham, Elaine. 1985. "Caesar and the Mutiny: Lucan's Reshaping of the Historical Tradition in *De Bello Civili* 5.237–373." *Classical Philology* 80, no. 2: 119–31.

———. 1992. *De bello civili II*. Cambridge: Cambridge University Press.

Fears, J. Rufus. 1975. "Nero as the Viceregent of the Gods in Seneca's *De Clementia*." *Hermes* 103, no. 4: 486–96.

Fertik, Harriet. 2017. "Sex, Love, and Leadership in Cicero's *Philippics* 1 and 2." *Arethusa* 50, no. 1: 65–88.

Feldherr, Andrew. 2009. "The Poisoned Chalice: Rumor and Historiography in Tacitus' Account of the Death of Drusus." *Materiali e discussioni per l'analisi dei testi classici* 61: 175–89.

Fischler, Susan. 1994. "Social Stereotypes and Historical Analysis: The Case of the Imperial Women at Rome." In *Women in Ancient Societies: An Illusion of the Night*, edited by Léonie J. Archer, Susan Fischler, and Maria Wyke, 115–33. New York: Routledge.

Fisher, C.D., ed. 1906. *Cornelii Taciti annalium ab excessu divi Augusti libri*. Oxford: Clarendon.

Fitzgerald, William. 2000. *Slavery and the Roman Literary Imagination*. Cambridge: Cambridge University Press.

Flohr, Miko. 2012. "Working and Living under One Roof: Workshops in Pompeian Atrium Houses." In *Privata Luxuria: Towards an Archaeology of Intimacy, Pompeii and Beyond. International Workshop, Center for Advanced Studies, Ludwig-Maximilians-Universität München (24–25 March 2011)*, edited by Anna Anguissola, 51–72. Munich: H. Utz.

Flory, M. B. 1984. "*Sic Exempla Parantur*: Livia's Shrine to Concordia and the Porticus Liviae." *Historia* 33, no. 3: 309–30.

———. 1996. "Dynastic Ideology, the *Domus Augusta*, and Imperial Women: A Lost Statuary Group in the Circus Flaminius." *TAPA* 126.

Foubert, L. L. 2010a. "Literary Constructions of Female Identities: The Parallel Lives of Julio-Claudian Women in Tacitus' *Annals*." In *Studies in Latin Literature and Roman History*, edited by Carl Deroux, 344–65. Collection Latomus 323. Brussels: Latomus.

———. 2010b. "The Palatine Dwelling of the *Mater Familias*: Houses as Symbolic Space in the Julio-Claudian Period." *Klio* 92, vol. 1: 65–82.

Foucault, Michel. 1977. *Discipline and Punish: The Birth of the Prison*. Translated by Alan Sheridan. New York: Pantheon.

———. 1990a. *The History of Sexuality: An Introduction*. Translated by Robert Hurley. New York: Vintage.

———. 1990b. *The History of Sexuality: The Care of the Self*. Translated by Robert Hurley. New York: Vintage.

Foucault, Michel, Michel Senellart, François Ewald, and Alessandro Fontana. 2007. *Security, Territory, Population: Lectures at the Collège de France, 1977–78*. New York: Palgrave Macmillan.

Fredrick, David. 1995. "Beyond the Atrium to Ariadne: Erotic Painting and Visual Pleasure in the Roman House." *Classical Antiquity* 14: 266–87.

———. 2002a. "Introduction: Invisible Rome." In *The Roman Gaze: Vision, Power, and the Body*, edited by David Fredrick, 1–30. Baltimore: Johns Hopkins University Press.

———. 2002b. "Mapping Penetrability in Late Republican and Early Imperial Rome." In *The Roman Gaze: Vision, Power, and the Body*, edited by David Fredrick, 236–64. Baltimore: Johns Hopkins University Press.

———. 2003. "Grasping the Pangolin: Sensuous Ambiguity in Roman Dining." *Arethusa* 36, no. 3: 309–43.

Freudenburg, Kirk. 2015. "Seneca's *Apocolocyntosis*: Censors in the Afterworld." In *The Cambridge Companion to Seneca*, edited by Shadi Bartsch and Alessandro Schiesaro, 93–105. Cambridge: Cambridge University Press.

Gabba, Emilio. 1991. *Dionysius and the History of Archaic Rome*. Berkeley: University of California Press.

Gagliardi, Donato. 1975. *M. Annaei Lucani, belli civilis liber septimus*. Florence: La Nuova Italia.

Gall, Dorothee. 2005. "Masse, Heere und Feldherren in Lucans Pharsalia." In *Lucan im 21. Jahrhundert*, edited by Christine Walde, 89–110. Munich: Saur.

Gallia, Andrew. 2009. "*Potentes* and *Potentia* in Tacitus's *Dialogus de Oratoribus*." *Transactions of the American Philological Association* 139: 169–206.

Gardner, J. 1993. *Being a Roman Citizen*. London: Routledge.

———. 1995. "Gender-Role Assumptions in Roman Law." *Échos du monde classique/Classical Views* 39, no. 14: 377–400.

———. 1998. *Family and Familia in Roman Law and Life*. Oxford: Oxford University Press.

———. 2015. "The Dictator." In *A Companion to Julius Caesar*, edited by Miriam Griffin, 57–71. Malden, Mass.: Wiley-Blackwell.

Gazda, Elaine K. 2010. "Domestic Art and the Instability of Cultural Meaning: Roman Art in the Private Sphere Revisited." In *Roman Art in the Private Sphere: New Perspectives on the Architecture and Decor of the Domus, Villa, and Insula*, 2d ed., edited by Elaine K. Gazda with assistance from Anne E. Haeckl, xi–xxxvii. Ann Arbor: University of Michigan Press.

———. 2016. "Villa on the Bay of Naples: The Ancient Setting of Oplontis." In *Leisure and Luxury in the Age of Nero: The Villas of Oplontis near Pompeii*, edited by Elaine K. Gazda and John R. Clarke, 30–45. Ann Arbor, Mich.: Kelsey Museum of Archaeology.

Gazda, Elaine K., and John R. Clarke, eds. 2016. *Leisure and Luxury in the Age of Nero: The Villas of Oplontis near Pompeii*. Ann Arbor, Mich.: Kelsey Museum of Archaeology.

George, Michele. 1997a. "Repopulating the Roman House." In *The Roman Family in Italy: Status, Sentiment, Space*, edited by Beryl Rawson and P. R. C. Weaver, 299–320. Oxford: Oxford University Press.

———. 1997b. "*Servus* and *Domus*: The Slave in the Roman House." In *Domestic Space in the Roman World: Pompeii and Beyond*, edited by Ray Laurence and Andrew Wallace-Hadrill, Journal of Roman Archaeology Supplementary Series 22, 15–24.

Giddens, A. 1999. "Risk and Responsibility." *The Modern Law Review* 62: 1–10.

Gillespie, Caitlin C. 2014. "Agrippina the Younger: Tacitus' *Unicum Exemplum*." In *Valuing the Past in the Greco-Roman World: Proceedings from the Penn-Leiden Colloquia on

Ancient Values VII, Mnemosyne Supplements 359, edited by Christoph Pieper, 269–93. Leiden: Brill.

Ginsberg, Lauren. 2017. *Staging Empire, Staging Strife: Empire and Civil War in the "Octavia."* Oxford: Oxford University Press.

Ginsburg, Judith. 2006. *Representing Agrippina: Constructions of Female Power in the Early Roman Empire.* Oxford: Oxford University Press.

Gloyn, Liz. 2017. *The Ethics of the Family in Seneca.* Cambridge: Cambridge University Press.

Goddard, J. 1994. "The Tyrant at Table." In *Reflections of Nero: Culture, History, and Representation*, edited by Jaś Elsner and Jamie Masters, 67–82. Chapel Hill: University of North Carolina Press.

Goodyear, Francis Richard David. 1981. *The Annals of Tacitus, Vol. 2: Annals 1.55–81 and Annals 2.* Cambridge: Cambridge University Press.

Gorz, A. 1983. "Security: Against What? For What? With What?" *Telos: Critical Theory of the Contemporary* 58: 158–68.

Gotter, Ulrich. 2015. "Penelope's Web, or: How to Become a Bad Emperor Post Mortem." In *Antimonarchic Discourse in Antiquity*, edited by Henning Börm and Wolfgang Havener, 215–33. Stuttgart: Franz Steiner Verlag.

Grahame, Mark. 1997. "Public and Private in the Roman House: Investigating the Social Order of the Casa del Fauno." *Domestic Space in the Roman World: Pompeii and Beyond*, Journal of Roman Archaeology Supplementary Series 22: 137–64.

———. 2000. *Reading Space: Social Interaction and Identity in the Houses of Roman Pompeii, a Syntactical Approach to the Analysis and Interpretation of Built Space.* Oxford: Archaeopress.

Graver, Margaret. 2007. *Stoicism and Emotion.* Chicago: University of Chicago Press.

Green, F. Mira. 2014. "In and Out: Food, the Body, and Social Hierarchy in Roman Households." PhD diss., University of Washington.

———. 2015. "Witnesses and Participants in the Shadows: The Sexual Lives of Enslaved Women and Boys." *Helios* 42, no. 1: 143–62.

Griffin, Miriam T. 1976. *Seneca: A Philosopher in Politics.* Oxford: Oxford University Press.

———. 1984. *Nero: The End of a Dynasty.* London: Routledge.

———. 2002. "Political Thought in the Age of Nero." In *Neronia VI: Rome à l'époque Néronienne*, edited by J.-M. Croisille and Y. Perrin, 325–37. Brussels: Éditions Latomus.

Grimal, Pierre. 1971. "Le De Clementia et le royauté solaire de Néron." *Revue des études latines* 49: 205–17.

Guzzo, Pier Giovanni. 2007. "City and Country: An Introduction." In *The World of Pompeii*, edited by John J. Dobbins and Pedar W. Foss, 3–8. New York: Routledge.

Habermas, Jürgen. 1989. *The Structural Transformation of the Public Sphere: An Inquiry into a Category of Bourgeois Society.* Translated by Thomas Burger with the assistance of Frederick Lawrence. Cambridge, Mass.: MIT Press.

Habinek, Thomas N. 1998. *The Politics of Latin Literature: Writing, Identity, and Empire in Ancient Rome.* Princeton, N.J.: Princeton University Press.

Hales, Shelley. 2003. *The Roman House and Social Identity.* Cambridge: Cambridge University Press.

Hall, Edith. 2008. "Introduction: Pantomime, a Lost Chord of Ancient Culture." In *New Directions in Ancient Pantomime*, edited by Edith Hall and Rosie Wyles, 1–40. Oxford: Oxford University Press.

Hallett, Judith P. 1984. *Fathers and Daughters in Roman Society: Women and the Elite Family*. Princeton, N.J.: Princeton University Press.

———. 1989. "Women as Same and Other in the Classical Roman Elite." *Helios* 16: 59–78.

Hamilton, John T. 2013. *Security: Politics, Humanity, and the Philology of Care*. Princeton, N.J.: Princeton University Press.

Hammer, Dean. 2002. "Hannah Arendt and Roman Political Thought: The Practice of Theory." *Political Theory* 30, no. 1: 124–49.

———. 2008. *Roman Political Thought and the Modern Theoretical Imagination*. Norman: University of Oklahoma Press.

———. 2014. *Roman Political Thought: From Cicero to Augustine*. Cambridge: Cambridge University Press.

Hardie, Philip R. 1993. *The Epic Successors of Virgil: A Study in the Dynamics of a Tradition*. Cambridge: Cambridge University Press.

———. 2010. "Crowds and Leaders in Imperial Historiography and Epic." In *Latin Historiography and Poetry in the Early Empire: Generic Interactions*, edited by J. F. Miller and A. J. Woodman, 9–28. Leiden: Brill.

Harding, Sandra G. 2004. "Introduction: Standpoint Theory as a Site of Political, Philosophic, and Scientific Debate." In *The Feminist Standpoint Theory Reader: Intellectual and Political Controversies*, edited by Sandra G. Harding, 1–15. New York: Routledge.

———. 2009. "Standpoint Theories: Productively Controversial." *Hypatia* 24, no. 4: 192–200.

Harris, B. F. 1982. "Oaths of Allegiance to Caesar." *Prudentia* 14, no. 2: 109–22.

Harris, William V. 2001. *Restraining Rage: The Ideology of Anger Control in Classical Antiquity*. Cambridge, Mass.: Harvard University Press.

Harrison, George William Mallory. 2000. "*Semper ego auditor tantum?*: Performance and Physical Setting of Seneca's Plays." In *Seneca in Performance*, edited by George William Mallory Harrison, 137–49. London: Duckworth.

Hartnett, Jeremy. 2008. "*Si quis hic sederit*: Streetside Benches and Urban Society in Pompeii." *American Journal of Archaeology* 112, no. 1: 91–119.

———. 2011. "The Power of Nuisances on the Roman Street." In *Rome, Ostia, Pompeii: Movement and Space*, edited by Ray Laurence and David J. Newsome, 135–59. Oxford: Oxford University Press.

Hekster, Olivier. 2015. *Emperors and Ancestors: Roman Rulers and the Constraints of Tradition*. Oxford: Oxford University Press.

Hellegouarc'h, Joseph. 1972. *Le vocabulaire latin des relations et des partis politiques sous la république*. Paris: Les Belles Lettres.

Hemelrijk, Emily. 2007. "Local Empresses: Priestesses of the Imperial Cult in the Cities of the Latin West." *Phoenix* 61, nos. 3–4: 318–49.

Hemsoll, D. 1990. "The Architecture of Nero's Golden House." In *Architecture and Architectural Sculpture in the Roman Empire*, edited by Martin Henig, 10–38. Oxford: Oxford University Committee for Archaeology.

Henderson, John. 1987. "Lucan / The Word at War." *Ramus* 16, nos. 1–2: 122–64.

Henry, Denis, and Elisabeth Henry. 1985. *The Mask of Power: Seneca's Tragedies and Imperial Rome*. Warminster, UK: Aris & Phillips.

Hillard, Tom. 1992. "On the Stage, Behind the Curtain: Images of Politically Active Women in the Late Roman Republic." In *Stereotypes of Women in Power: Historical*

Perspectives and Revisionist Views, edited by Barbara Garlick, Suzanne Dixon, and Pauline Allen, 37–64. New York: Greenwood Press.

Hingley, Richard. 2005. *Globalizing Roman Culture: Unity, Diversity, and Empire*. New York: Routledge.

Hirschmann, Nancy J. 2004. "Feminist Standpoint as a Postmodern Strategy." In *The Feminist Standpoint Theory Reader: Intellectual and Political Controversies*, edited by Sandra G. Harding, 317–32. New York: Routledge.

Hollingsworth, Anthony. 2001. "Recitational Poetry and Senecan Tragedy: Is There a Similarity?" *Classical World* 94, no. 2: 135–44.

Hölscher, Tonio. 2008. "The Concept of Roles and the Malaise of 'Identity': Ancient Rome and the Modern World." In *Role Models in the Roman World: Identity and Assimilation*, edited by Sinclair Bell and Inge Lyse Hansen, 41–56. Ann Arbor: University of Michigan Press.

Honig, Bonnie. 1995. *Feminist Interpretations of Hannah Arendt*. University Park, Pa.: Pennsylvania State University Press.

Hope, Valerie M. 2000. "Contempt and Respect: The Treatment of the Corpse in Ancient Rome." In *Death and Disease in the Ancient City*, edited by Valerie M. Hope and Eireann Marshall, 104–27. London: Routledge.

Housman, A. E., ed. 1927. *M. Annaei Lucani belli civilis libri decem*. Cambridge, Mass.: Harvard University Press. .

Hurlet, F. 1997. *Les collègues du prince sous Auguste et Tibere: de la legalité republicaine à la légitimité dynastique*. Rome.

Huskey, Samuel J. 2006. "Ovid's (Mis)Guided Tour of Rome: Some Purposeful Omissions in *Tr*. 3.1." *Classical Journal* 102, no. 1: 17–39.

Iacopi, Irene, and Giovanna Tedone. 2005–06. "Bibliotheca e Porticus ad Apollinis." *Mitteilungen des Deutschen Archaeologischen Instituts: Roemische Abteilung* 112: 351–78.

Johnson, W. R. 1987. *Momentary Monsters: Lucan and His Heroes*. Ithaca, N.Y.: Cornell University Press.

Joseph, Timothy A. 2017. "Caesar in Vergil and Lucan." In *The Cambridge Companion to the Writings of Julius Caesar*, edited by Luca Grillo and Christopher B. Krebs, 289–303. Cambridge: Cambridge University Press.

Joshel, Sandra R., and Lauren Hackworth Petersen. 2014. *The Material Life of Roman Slaves*. New York: Cambridge University Press.

Kampen, N. B. 1991. "Between Public and Private: Women as Historical Subjects in Roman Art." In *Women's History and Ancient History*, edited by S. B. Pomeroy, 218–48. Chapel Hill: University of North Carolina Press.

Kantorowicz, Ernst H. 1997. *The King's Two Bodies: A Study in Mediaeval Political Theology*. Princeton, N. J.: Princeton University Press.

Kapust, Daniel J. 2011. *Republicanism, Rhetoric, and Roman Political Thought: Sallust, Livy, and Tacitus*. New York: Cambridge University Press.

Karivieri, Arja. 2014. "Mythic, Public and Private Memory: Creation of a Pompeian Identity in the House of Caecilius Iucundus." In *Attitudes towards the Past in Antiquity: Creating Identities; Proceedings of an International Conference Held at Stockholm University, 15–17 May 2009*, edited by Brita Alroth and Charlotte Scheffer, 87–111. Stockholm: Stockholm University Press.

Kaster, Robert A. 2005. *Emotion, Restraint, and Community in Ancient Rome*. Oxford: Oxford University Press.

———, ed. 2016. *C. Suetoni Tranquilli: De vita Caesarum libros VIII et De grammaticis et rhetoribus librum*. Oxford: Oxford University Press.

Kaster, Robert A., and Martha C. Nussbaum, eds. and trans. 2010.*Seneca: Anger, Mercy, Revenge*. Chicago: University of Chicago Press.

Keitel, E. E. 2009. "'Is Dying So Very Terrible?' The Neronian *Annals*." In *The Cambridge Companion to Tacitus*, edited by A. J. Woodman, 127–43. Cambridge: Cambridge University Press.

Keith, Alison. 2008. "Lament in Lucan's *Bellum Civile*." In *Lament: Studies in the Ancient Mediterranean and Beyond*, edited by Ann Suter, 233–57. Oxford: Oxford University Press.

Ker, James. 2009a. "Seneca on Self-Examination: Rereading *On Anger* 3.36." In *Seneca and the Self*, edited by Shadi Bartsch and David Wray, 160–87. Cambridge: Cambridge University Press.

———. 2009b. *The Deaths of Seneca*. Oxford: Oxford University Press.

Kleiner, Diana E. E. 1978. "The Great Friezes of the Ara Pacis Augustae: Greek Sources, Roman Derivatives, and Augustan Social Policy." *Mélanges de l'école française de Rome: Antiquité* 90, no. 2: 753–85.

Kohn, Thomas D. 2013. *The Dramaturgy of Senecan Tragedy*. Ann Arbor: University of Michigan Press.

Koloski-Ostrow, Ann Olga. 1997. "Violent Stages in Two Pompeian Houses: Imperial Taste, Aristocratic Response, and Messages of Male Control." In *Naked Truths: Women, Sexuality, and Gender in Classical Art and Archaeology*, edited by Ann Olga Koloski-Ostrow and Claire L. Lyons, 243–66. London: Routledge.

———. 2015. *The Archaeology of Sanitation in Roman Italy: Toilets, Sewers, and Water Systems*. Chapel Hill: University of North Carolina Press.

Konstan, David. 2005. "Clemency as a Virtue." *Classical Philology* 100, no. 4: 337–46.

Krause, Clemens. 1988. "Das Hauptgeschoss der Villa Iovis auf Capri." In *Kanon: Festschrift Ernst Berger zum 60. Geburstag am 26. Februar 1988 gewidmet*, Vol. 1, edited by Margot Schmidt, 356–65. Basel: Vereinigung der Freunde antiker Kunst c/o Archäologisches Seminar der Universität.

———. 1998. "L'edificio residenziale di Villa Iovis." In *Capri antica : Dalla preistoria alla fine dell'età romana*, edited by Eduardo Federico and Elena Miranda, 225–40. Capri: La Conchiglia.

———. 2003. *Villa Iovis: Die Residenz des Tiberius auf Capri*. Mainz: Zabern.

L'Orange, H. P. 1973. "Domus Aurea—Der Sonnenpalast." In *Likeness and Icon: Selected Studies in Classical and Early Medieval Art*, 292–312. Odense, Denmark: Odense University Press.

La Penna, Antonio. 1979. *Fra teatro, poesia, e politica romana*. Turin: G. Einaudi.

Laird, Andrew. 1999. *Powers of Expression, Expressions of Power: Speech Presentation and Latin Literature*. Oxford: Oxford University Press.

———. 2007. "The True Nature of the *Satyricon*?" In *The Greek and the Roman Novel: Parallel Readings*, edited by Michael Paschalis, 151–68. Groningen, The Netherlands: Barkhuis & Groningen University Library.

Langford, Julie. 2013. *Maternal Megalomania: Julia Domna and the Imperial Politics of Motherhood*. Baltimore: Johns Hopkins University Press.

Laurence, Ray. 2007. *Roman Pompeii: Space and Society*. London: Routledge.

Laurence, Ray, and Francesco Trifilò. 2015. "The Global and the Local in the Roman Empire: Connectivity and Mobility from an Urban Perspective." In *Globalisation and the Roman World: World History, Connectivity, and Material Culture*, edited by Martin Pitts and M. J. Versluys, 99–122. New York: Cambridge University Press.

Lauritsen, M. Taylor. 2012. "The Form and Function of Boundaries in the Campanian House." In *Privata Luxuria: Towards an Archaeology of Intimacy, Pompeii and Beyond. International Workshop, Center for Advanced Studies, Ludwig-Maximilian-Universität München (24–25 March 2011)*, edited by Anna Anguissola, 95–114. Munich: H. Utz.

Lavan, Myles. 2016. "'Father of the Whole Human Race:' Ecumenical Language and the Limits of Elite Integration in the Early Roman Empire." In *Cosmopolitanism and Empire: Universal Rulers, Local Elites, and Cultural Integration in the Ancient Near East and Mediterranean*, edited by Myles Lavan, Richard E. Payne, and John Weisweiler, 153–68. New York: Oxford University Press.

Leach, Eleanor Winsor. 1989. "The Implied Reader and the Political Argument in Seneca's *Apocolocyntosis* and *De Clementia*." *Arethusa* 22: 197–231.

———. 2004. *The Social Life of Painting in Ancient Rome and on the Bay of Naples*. Cambridge: Cambridge University Press.

Lebek, W. D. 1985. "Senecas Agamemnon in Pompeji (CIL IV 6698)." *ZPE* 59: 1–6.

Lefèvre, Eckard. 1981. "A Cult without God, or the Unfreedom of Freedom in Seneca Tragicus." *Classical Journal* 77, no. 1: 32–36.

Leigh, Matthew. 1996. "Varius Rufus, Thyestes, and the Appetites of Antony." *Proceedings of the Cambridge Philological Society* 42: 171–97.

———. 1997. *Lucan: Spectacle and Engagement*. Oxford: Oxford University Press.

Lendon, Jon. 1997. *Empire of Honour: The Art of Government in the Roman World*. Oxford: Oxford University Press.

Leonard, Miriam. 2018. "Hannah Arendt and the Ancients: Preface." *Classical Philology* 113.1: 1–5.

Levene, D. S. 2010. *Livy on the Hannibalic War*. Oxford: Oxford University Press.

Levick, Barbara. 1999. *Tiberius the Politician*. London: Routledge.

———. 2015. *Claudius*. London: Routledge.

Lewis, R. G. 1993. "Imperial Autobiography, Augustus to Hadrian." In *ANRW*, II.34.1:629–706.

Lindsay, Hugh. 2000. "Death-Pollution and Funerals in the City of Rome." In *Death and Disease in the Ancient City*, edited by Valerie M. Hope and Eireann Marshall, 152–72. London: Routledge.

Ling, Roger. 1991. *Roman Painting*. Cambridge: Cambridge University Press.

———. 1997. *The Insula of the Menander at Pompeii, Vol. 1*. Oxford: Oxford University Press.

Ling, Roger, and Lesley Ling. 2005. *The Insula of the Menander at Pompeii: Vol. 2, the Decorations*. Oxford: Oxford University Press.

Little, Alan MacNaughton Gordon. 1971. *Roman Perspective Painting and the Ancient Stage*. Wheaton, Md.: Star Press.

Littlewood, C. A. J. 2004. *Self-Representation and Illusion in Senecan Tragedy*. Oxford: Oxford University Press.

Lomas, Kathryn. 1995. "Urban Elites and Cultural Definition: Romanization in Southern Italy." In *Urban Society in Roman Italy*, edited by T. J. Cornell and K. Lomas, 113–26. New York: Routledge.

Longfellow, Brenda. 2011. *Roman Imperialism and Civic Patronage: Form, Meaning, and Ideology in Monumental Fountain Complexes*. Cambridge: Cambridge University Press.

Lorenz, Katharina. 2008. *Bilder machen Räume: Mythenbilder in pompeianischen Häusern*. New York: De Gruyter.

———. 2013. "Neronian Wall-Painting: A Matter of Perspective." In *A Companion to the Neronian Age*, edited by Emma Buckley and Martin T. Dinter, 363–81. London: Blackwell.

———. 2014. "The Casa del Menandro in Pompeii: Rhetoric and the Topology of Roman Wall Painting." In *Art and Rhetoric in Roman Culture*, edited by Jas Elsner, 183–210. Cambridge: Cambridge University Press.

Lowrie, Michèle. 2014. "Politics by Other Means in Horace's *Ars Poetica*." *MD* 72: 121–42.

———. 2015. "*Rege Incolumi*: Orientalism, Civil War, and Security at *Georgics* 4.212." In *Virgilian Studies: A Miscellany Dedicated to the Memory of Mario Geymonat (26.1.1941–17.2.2012)*, edited by Hans Christian Günther and Paolo Fedeli. *Studia Classica et Mediaevalia*, vol. 10. Nordhausen, Germany: Verlag Traugott Bautz.

———. 2016. "Le salut, la sécurité et le corps du chef: transformations dans la sphère publique à l'époque d'Horace." In *La poésie lyrique dans la cité antique: Les odes d'Horace au miroir de la lyrique grecque archaïque*, edited by B. Delignon, N. Le Meur, and O. Thévenaz, 71–86. Paris: Diffusion Librairie de Boccard.

Lowrie, Michèle, and Susanne Ludemann, eds. 2015. *Exemplarity and Singularity: Thinking through Particulars in Philosophy, Literature, and Law*. New York: Routledge.

Lukes, Steven, ed. 1986. *Power*. New York: New York University Press.

Macaulay-Lewis, Elizabeth. 2011. "The City in Motion." In *Rome, Ostia, Pompeii: Movement and Space*, edited by Ray Laurence and David J. Newsome, 262–89. Oxford: Oxford University Press.

Mader, Gottfried. 1998. "*Quod nolunt velint*: Deference and Doublespeak at Seneca, *Thyestes* 334–35." *Classical Journal* 94, no. 1: 31–47.

Maiuri, Amedeo. 1957. *Capri: storia e monumenti*. Roma: Istituto Poligrafico dello Stato.

Manuwald, G. 2002. "Der 'Fürstenspiegel' in Senecas *De Clementia* und in der *Octavia*." *MH* 59: 107–26.

Marzano, Annalisa. 2007. *Roman Villas in Central Italy: A Social and Economic History*. Leiden: Brill.

Masters, Jamie. 1992. *Poetry and Civil War in Lucan's "Bellum civile."* Cambridge: Cambridge University Press.

———. 1994. "Deceiving the Reader: The Political Mission of Lucan BC 7." In *Reflections of Nero: Culture, History, & Representation*, edited by Jaś Elsner and Jamie Masters, 151–77. Chapel Hill: University of North Carolina Press.

Mayer, Emanuel. 2012. *The Ancient Middle Classes: Urban Life and Aesthetics in the Roman Empire, 100 BCE–250 CE*. Cambridge, Mass.: Harvard University Press.

Mayer, Roland. 1981. *Lucan, Civil War VIII*. Warminster, UK: Aris & Phillips.
Mbembe, Achille. 2001. *On the Postcolony*. Berkeley: University of California Press.
McIntyre, Gwynaeth. 2016. *A Family of Gods: The Worship of the Imperial Family in the Latin West*. Ann Arbor: University of Michigan Press.
Mebane, Julia. 2016. "Pompey's Head and the Body Politic in Lucan's *De bello civili*." *Transactions of the American Philological Association* 146, no. 1: 191–215.
———. 2017. "The Body Politic and Roman Political Languages." PhD diss., University of Chicago.
Meister, Jan Bernhard. 2012. *Der Körper des Princeps: Zur Problematik eines monarchischen Körpers ohne Monarchie*. Stuttgart: Steiner.
Meyboom, P. G. P. 2005. "The Creation of an Imperial Tradition: Ideological Aspects of the House of Augustus." In *The Manipulative Mode: Political Propaganda in Antiquity: A Collection of Case Studies*, edited by K. A. E. Enenkel and Ilja Leonard Pfeijffer, 219–63. Leiden: Brill.
Meyboom, P. G. P., and Eric M. Moormann. 2013. *Le decorazioni dipinte e marmoree della Domus Aurea di Nerone a Roma*. Leuven, Belgium: Peeters.
Michel, D. 1982. "Bemerkungen über Zuschauerfiguren in sogennanten pompejanischen Tafelbildern." In *La regione sotterrata dal Vesuvio: studi e prospettive: atti del convegno internzaionale, 11–15 Novembre 1969*, 537–98.
Millar, Fergus. 1977. *The Emperor in the Roman World (31 BC–AD 337)*. Ithaca, N.Y.: Cornell University Press.
———. 1984. "State and Subject: The Impact of Monarchy." In *Caesar Augustus: Seven Aspects*, edited by Fergus Millar and E. Segal, 37–60. Oxford: Clarendon Press.
———. 1993. "Ovid and the *Domus Augusta*: Rome Seen from Tomoi." *Journal of Roman Studies* 83: 1–17.
Miller, John F. 2009. *Apollo, Augustus, and the Poets*. Cambridge: Cambridge University Press.
Milnor, Kristina. 2005. *Gender, Domesticity, and the Age of Augustus: Inventing Private Life*. Oxford: Oxford University Press.
———. 2007. "Augustus, History, and the Landscape of the Law." *Arethusa* 40, no. 1: 7–23.
———. 2012. "Women and Domesticity." In *A Companion to Tacitus*, edited by Victoria Emma Pagán, 458–75. Malden, Mass.: Wiley-Blackwell.
Morford, M. P. O. 1967. "The Purpose of Lucan's Ninth Book." *Latomus* 26: 123–29.
———. 1968. "The Distortion of the Domus Aurea Tradition." *Eranos* 66: 158–79.
Mortureux, B. 1989. "Les idéaux stoiciens et les premières responsabilités politiques: Le 'De clementia'" In *ANRW* II.36.3:1639–85.
Moormann, E. M. 1983. "Rappresentazioni teatrali su scaenae frontes di quarto stile a Pompei." *Pompeii, Herculaneum, Stabiae* 1: 73–117.
Mouritsen, Henrik. 1988. *Elections, Magistrates, and Municipal Élite: Studies in Pompeian Epigraphy*. Analecta Romana Instituti Danici 15. Rome: L'Erma di Bretschneider.
———. 1990. "A Note on Pompeian Epigraphy and Social Structure." *Classica et Mediaevalia* 41: 131–49.
Müller, Konrad. 2009. *Petronii Arbitri Satyricon Reliquiae*. Berlin: De Gruyter.
Naiden, F. S. 2006. *Ancient Supplication*. Oxford: Oxford University Press.
Narducci, E. 1973. "Il tronco di Pompeo (Troia e Roma nella Pharsalia)." *Maia* 25: 317–25.

———. 2002. *Lucano: Un'epica contro l'impero: interpretazione della "Pharsalia."* Rome: GLF Editori Laterza.
Neocleous, Mark. 2008. *Critique of Security*. Edinburgh: Edinburgh University Press.
Nevett, Lisa C. 2010. *Domestic Space in Classical Antiquity*. Cambridge: Cambridge University Press.
Newby, Zahra. 2016. *Greek Myths in Roman Art and Culture: Imagery, Values, and Identity in Italy, 50 BC–AD 250*. Cambridge: Cambridge University Press.
Newlands, Carole. 1997. "The Role of the Book in *Tristia* 3.1." *Ramus* 26, no. 1: 57–79.
———. 2012. *Statius: Poet between Rome and Naples*. London: Bristol Classical Press.
Nielsen, Inge. 1990. *Thermae et Balnea: The Architecture and Cultural History of Roman Public Baths*. Aarhus, Denmark: Aarhus University Press.
———. 1994. *Hellenistic Palaces: Tradition and Renewal*. Aarhus, Denmark: Aarhus University Press.
Nissenbaum, Helen Fay. 2010. *Privacy in Context: Technology, Policy, and the Integrity of Social Life*. Stanford, Calif.: Stanford Law Books.
Noreña, Carlos F. 2011. *Imperial Ideals in the Roman West: Representation, Circulation, Power*. Cambridge: Cambridge University Press.
Nussbaum, Martha C. 1994. *The Therapy of Desire: Theory and Practice in Hellenistic Ethics*. Princeton, N.J.: Princeton University Press.
O'Gorman, Ellen. 2000. *Irony and Misreading in the Annals of Tacitus*. Cambridge: Cambridge University Press.
Osgood, Josiah. 2007. "The *Vox* and *Verba* of an Emperor: Seneca, Claudius, and Le Prince Ideal." *Classical Journal* 102, no. 4: 329–53.
———. 2011. *Claudius Caesar: Image and Power in the Early Roman Empire*. Cambridge: Cambridge University Press.
———. 2013. "Suetonius and the Succession to Augustus." In *The Julio-Claudian Succession: Reality and Perception of the "Augustan Model,"* edited by A. G. G. Gibson, 19–40. Mnemosyne Supplements 349. Leiden: Brill.
Pagán, Victoria Emma. 2004. *Conspiracy Narratives in Roman History*. Austin: University of Texas Press.
Panayotakis, Costas. 1995. *Theatrum Arbitri: Theatrical Elements in the Satyrica of Petronius*. Leiden: Brill.
Pandey, Nandini. 2018. *The Poetics of Power in Augustan Rome: Latin Poetic Responses to Early Imperial Iconography*. Cambridge: Cambridge University Press.
Panella, C. 1990. "La valle del Colosseo nell'antichità." *Boll. Arch.* 1–2: 34–88.
———, ed. 1996. *Meta Sudans, I*. Rome: Istituto poligrafico e zecca dello stato: Libreria dello Stato.
Parker, Holt N. 1999. "The Observed of All Observers: Spectacle, Applause, and Cultural Poetics in the Roman Theater Audience." In *The Art of Ancient Spectacle*, edited by Christine Kondoleon and Bettina Ann Bergmann, 163–79. Washington: National Gallery of Art.
Paterson, Jeremy. 2007. "Friends in High Places: The Creation of the Court of the Roman Emperor." In *The Court and Court Society in Ancient Monarchies*, edited by A. J. Spawforth, 121–56. Cambridge: Cambridge University Press.
Pelling, Christopher. 2012. "Tacitus and Germanicus." In *Tacitus*, edited by Rhiannon Ash, 281–314. Oxford: Oxford University Press.

Peoples, Columba. 2011. "Security after Emancipation? Critical Theory, Violence, and Resistance." *Review of International Studies* 37: 1113–35.

Perkins, Judith. 2009. *Roman Imperial Identities in the Early Christian Era*. London: Routledge.

Perrin, Yves. 2002. "IVe style, culture, et société à Rome: Propositions pour une lecture historique de la peinture murale d'époque néronienne." In *Neronia VI : Rome à l'époque néronienne : institutions et vie politique, économie et société, vie intellectuelle, artistique et spirituelle : actes du VIe Colloque international de la SIEN (Rome, 19–23 mai 1999)*, edited by Jean-Michel Croisille and Yves Perrin, 384–404. Brussels: Latomus.

Petersen, Lauren Hackworth. 2006. *The Freedman in Roman Art and Art History*. New York: Cambridge University Press.

Picard, G.-C. 1982. "Les peintures théâtrales du IVe style et l'idéologie Néronienne." In *Neronia 1977: actes du 2e colloque de la société internationale d'études Néroniennes, Clermont-Ferrand, 27–28 Mai 1977*, eds. J.-M. Croisille and P.-M. Fauchère, 55–59.

Picone, G. 1984. *La fabula e il regno*. Palermo: Palumbo.

Platte, V. 2002. "Viewing, Desiring, Believing: Confronting the Divine in a Pompeian House." *Art History* 25: 87–112.

Potter, David. 2011. "Holding Court in Republican Rome (105–44)." *American Journal of Philology* 132: 59–80.

Potter, David, and Damon, Cynthia. 1999. "The 'Senatus Consultum de Cn. Pisone Patre.'" *Transactions of the American Philological Association* 120: 13–42.

Price, S. R. F. 1986. *Rituals and Power: The Roman Imperial Cult in Asia Minor*. Cambridge: Cambridge University Press.

Proudfoot, Evan. 2013. "Secondary Doors in Entranceways at Pompeii: Reconsidering Access and the 'View from the Street.'" In *TRAC 2012: Proceedings of the Twenty-Second Annual Theoretical Roman Archaeology Conference, Frankfurt 2012*, edited by A. Bokern, M. Bolder-Boos, S. Krmnicek, D. Maschek, and S. Page, 91–115. Oxford: Oxbow Books.

Purcell, Nicholas. 1995. "The Roman Villa and the Landscape of Production." In *Urban Society in Roman Italy*, edited by T. J. Cornell and K. Lomas, 151–79. New York: Routledge.

———. 1996a. "Livia and the Womanhood of Rome." *Proceedings of the Cambridge Philological Society* 32: 78–105.

———. 1996b. "The Roman Garden as a Domestic Building." In *Roman Domestic Buildings*, ed. I. M. Barton, 121–52. Exeter, Devonshire, U.K.: University of Exeter Press.

———. 2005. "Romans in the Roman World." In *The Cambridge Companion to the Age of Augustus*, edited by Karl Galinsky, 85–105. Cambridge: Cambridge University Press.

Quenemoen, Caroline Kerrigan. 2001. "The Architectural Significance of the House of Augustus." PhD diss., Yale University.

———. 2006. "The Portico of the Danaids: A New Reconstruction." *American Journal of Archaeology* 110, no. 2: 229–50.

Rachels, James. 1975. "Why Privacy Is Important." *Philosophy and Public Affairs* 4: 323–33.

Ramsby, Teresa R., and Beth Severy-Hoven. 2007. "Gender, Sex, and the Domestication of the Empire in Art of the Augustan Age." *Arethusa* 40, no. 1: 43–71.

Regan, Priscilla M. 1995. *Legislating Privacy: Technology, Social Values, and Public Policy.* Chapel Hill: University of North Carolina Press.

———. 2015. "Privacy and the Common Good: Revisited." In *Social Dimensions of Privacy: Interdisciplinary Perspectives*, edited by Beate Rössler, 50–70. New York: Cambridge University Press.

Reynolds, L. D., ed. 1977. *L. Annaei Senecae: dialogorum libri duodecim.* Oxford: Oxford University Press.

Reydams-Schils, Gretchen J. 2005. *The Roman Stoics: Self, Responsibility, and Affection.* Chicago: University of Chicago Press.

Richardson, Lawrence. 1988. *Pompeii: An Architectural History.* Baltimore: Johns Hopkins University Press.

Riggsby, A. M. 1997. "Public and Private in Roman Culture: The Case of the *Cubiculum*." *Journal of Roman Archaeology* 10: 36–56.

———. 2010. *Roman Law and the Legal World of the Romans.* Cambridge: Cambridge University Press.

———. 2016. "Public and Private in Roman Law." In *The Oxford Handbook of Roman Law and Society*, edited by Paul J. du Plessis, Clifford Ando, and Kaius Tuori, 310–21. Oxford: Oxford University Press.

Rilinger, R. 2007. *Ordo und dignitas: Beitrage zur römischen Verfassungs- und Sozialgeschichte.* Stuttgart.

Rimell, Victoria. 2002. *Petronius and the Anatomy of Fiction.* Cambridge: Cambridge University Press.

———. 2015. *The Closure of Space in Roman Poetics: Empire's Inward Turn.* Cambridge: Cambridge University Press.

Rivière, Yann. 2002. *Les délateurs sous l'empire romain.* Rome: École française de Rome.

Robert, Louis. 1968. "Dans l'amphithéâtre et dans les jardins de Néron. Une épigramme de Lucillius." *CRAI* 112.2, 280–88.

Robin, C. 2004. *Fear: The History of a Political Idea.* Oxford: Oxford University Press.

Robinson, Timothy J. 2005. "In the Court of Time: The Reckoning of a Monster in the Apocolocyntosis of Seneca." *Arethusa* 38: 223–57.

Rogers, Robert Samuel. 1955. "Heirs and Rivals to Nero." *Transactions of the American Philological Association* 86: 190–212.

Roller, Matthew B. 2001. *Constructing Autocracy: Aristocrats and Emperors in Julio-Claudian Rome.* Princeton, N.J.: Princeton University Press.

———. 2006. *Dining Posture in Ancient Rome: Bodies, Values, and Status.* Princeton, N.J: Princeton University Press.

———. 2016. "Precept(or) and Example in Seneca." In *Roman Reflections: Studies in Latin Philosophy*, edited by Gareth D. Williams and Katharina Volk, 129–56. Oxford: Oxford University Press.

Rosati, G. 1999. "Trimalchio on Stage." In *Oxford Readings in the Roman Novel*, edited by S. J. Harrison, 85–104. Oxford: Oxford University Press.

Rose, Charles Brian. 1997. *Dynastic Commemoration and Imperial Portraiture in the Julio-Claudian Period.* Cambridge: Cambridge University Press.

Rose, Amy R. 1986. "Power and Powerlessness in Seneca's Thyestes." *Classical Journal* 82, no. 2: 117–28.

Rosenmeyer, Thomas G. 1989. *Senecan Drama and Stoic Cosmology.* Berkeley: University of California Press.

Rössler, Beate. 2004. *The Value of Privacy.* Translated by R. D. V. Glasgow. Cambridge: Polity.

Rowe, Greg. 2002. *Princes and Political Cultures: The New Tiberian Senatorial Decrees.* Ann Arbor: University of Michigan Press.

Royo, M. 1999. *Domus imperatoriae: topographie, formation et imaginaire des palais imperiaux du Palatin, IIe siècle av. J.-C.–Ier siècle ap. J.-C.* Rome: École française de Rome.

Rudich, Vasily. 1993. *Political Dissidence under Nero.* London: Routledge.

Rule, James B. 2007. *Privacy in Peril.* Oxford: Oxford University Press.

———. 2015. "Privacy: The *Longue Durée.*" In *Social Dimensions of Privacy: Interdisciplinary Perspectives,* edited by Beate Rössler, 11–31. New York: Cambridge University Press.

Russell, Amy. 2016a. *The Politics of Public Space in Republican Rome.* Cambridge: Cambridge University Press.

———. 2016b. "On Gender and Spatial Experience in Public: The Case of Ancient Rome." In *TRAC 2015: Proceedings of the Twenty-Fifth Annual Theoretical Roman Archaeology Conference,* edited by M. J. Mandich, T. J. Derrick, S. Gonzalez Sanchez, G. Savani, and E. Zampieri, 164–76. Oxford: Oxbow.

Rutland, L. W. 1978. "Women as Makers of Kings in Tacitus' *Annals.*" *Classical World* 72, no. 1: 15–29.

Rutledge, Steven H. 2001. *Imperial Inquisitions: Prosecutors and Informants from Tiberius to Domitian.* London: Routledge.

———. 2007. "Oratory and Politics in the Empire." In *A Companion to Roman Rhetoric,* edited by William Dominik and Jon Hall, 109–22. Malden, Mass.: Wiley-Blackwell.

Saller, Richard P. 1984. "*Familia, Domus,* and the Roman Conception of the Family." *Phoenix* 38, no. 4: 336–355.

———. 1994. *Patriarchy, Property, and Death in the Roman Family.* Cambridge: Cambridge University Press.

———. 1999. "Pater Familias, Mater Familias, and the Gendered Semantics of the Roman Household." *Classical Philology* 94, no. 2: 182–97.

Santoro L'Hoir, Francesca. 1994. "Tacitus and Women's Usurpation of Power." *Classical World* 88, no. 1: 5–25.

———. 2006. *Tragedy, Rhetoric, and the Historiography of Tacitus' "Annales."* Ann Arbor: University of Michigan Press.

Schiesaro, Alessandro. 2003. *The Passions in Play: Thyestes and the Dynamics of Senecan Drama.* Cambridge: Cambridge University Press.

———. 2014. "Seneca's *Agamemnon*: The Entropy of Tragedy." *Pallas* 95. https://doi.org/10.4000/pallas.1726.

Schmeling, Gareth L. 2011. *A Commentary on the "Satyrica" of Petronius.* Oxford: Oxford University Press.

Schoeman, Ferdinand. 1984. "Privacy and Intimate Information." In *Philosophical Dimensions of Privacy: An Anthology,* edited by Ferdinand Schoeman, 403–18. Cambridge: Cambridge University Press.

Seager, Robin. 2013. "Perceptions of the *Domus Augusta,* AD 4–24." In *The Julio-Claudian Succession: Reality and Perception of the "Augustan Model,"* edited by A. G. G. Gibson, 41–58. Mnemosyne Supplements 349. Leiden: Brill.

Seo, J. Mira. 2013. *Exemplary Traits: Reading Characterization in Roman Poetry.* Oxford: Oxford University Press.

Severy, Beth. 2000. "Family and State in the Early Imperial Monarchy: The *Senatus Consultum de Pisone Patre, Tabula Siarensis*, and *Tabula Hebana.*" *Classical Philology* 95, no. 3: 318–37.

———. 2003. *Augustus and the Family at the Birth of the Roman Empire.* New York: Routledge.

Severy-Hoven, Beth. 2012. "Master Narratives and Wall Painting of the House of the Vettii, Pompeii." *Gender and History* 24: 540–80.

Sherk, Robert K., ed. 1988. *The Roman Empire: Augustus to Hadrian. Translated Documents of Greece and Rome, vol. 6.* Cambridge: Cambridge University Press.

Shotter, David. 2005. *The Fall of the Roman Republic.* London: Routledge.

Sklenář, R. 2003. *The Taste for Nothingness: A Study of* Virtus *and Related Themes in Lucan's "Bellum civile."* Ann Arbor: University of Michigan Press.

Slater, Niall W. 1990. *Reading Petronius.* Baltimore: Johns Hopkins University Press.

———. 1994. "From *Harena* to *Cena*: Trimalchio's *Capis* (Sat. 52.1–3)." *Classical Quarterly* 44, no. 2: 549–51.

Smallwood, E. Mary. 1967. *Documents Illustrating the Principates of Gaius, Claudius, and Nero.* Cambridge: Cambridge University Press.

Smith, R. R. R. 2013. *The Marble Reliefs from the Julio-Claudian Sebasteion.* Darmstadt, Germany: Verlag Philipp von Zabern.

Smolenaars, J. J. 1998. "The Vergilian Background of Seneca's *Thyestes* 641–82." *Vergilius* 44: 51–65.

Späth, Thomas. 2000. "Skrupellose Herrscherin? Das Bild der Agrippina minor bei Tacitus." In *Frauenwelten in der Antike: Geschlechterordnung und weibliche Lebenspraxis: mit 162 Quellentexten und Bildquellen*, edited by Thomas Späth and Beate Wagner-Hasel, 262–80. Stuttgart: Metzler.

Speksnijder, Simon. 2015. "Beyond 'Public' and 'Private:' Accessibility and Visibility during *Salutationes.*" In *Public and Private in the Roman House and Society*, edited by Kaius Tuori and Laura Nissin, *Journal of Roman Archaeology Supplementary Series* 102, 87–100.

Spencer, Diana. 2010. *Roman Landscape: Culture and Identity.* Cambridge: Cambridge University Press.

Stambaugh, J. E. 1978. "The Functions of Roman Temples." In *ANRW* II.16.1: 554–608.

Star, Christopher. 2012. *The Empire of the Self: Self-Command and Political Speech in Seneca and Petronius.* Baltimore: Johns Hopkins University Press.

———. 2016. "Seneca *Tragicus* and Stoicism." In *Brill's Companion to the Reception of Senecan Tragedy: Scholarly, Theatrical and Literary Receptions*, edited by Eric Dodson Robinson, 34–53. Leiden: Brill.

Starr, Raymond J. 1987. "Trimalchio's Libraries." *Hermes* 115, no. 2: 252–53.

———. 2010. "Augustus as '*Pater Patriae*' and Patronage Decrees." *ZPE* 102: 296–98.

Steinby, E. M., ed. 1995. *Lexicon Topigraphicum Urbis Romae.* Rome.

Stevenson, Tom. 2015. "Andreas Alföldi on the Roman Emperor as *Pater Patriae.*" In *Andreas Alföldi in the Twenty-First Century*, edited by James H. Richardson and Federico Santangelo, 187–200. Stuttgart: Franz Steiner Verlag.

Stewart, Peter. 2008. *The Social History of Roman Art.* Cambridge: Cambridge University Press.

Strothmann, Meret. 2000. *Augustus—Vater der Res Publica: Zur Funktion der drei Begriffe Restitutio-Saeculum-Pater Patriae im augusteischen Prinzipat*. Stuttgart: Steiner.

Strunk, Thomas E. 2016. *History after Liberty: Tacitus on Tyrants, Sycophants, and Republicans*. Ann Arbor: University of Michigan Press.

Sullivan, J. P. 1968. *The "Satyricon" of Petronius: A Literary Study*. London: Faber.

Sumi, Geoffrey. 2011. "Ceremony and the Emergence of Court Society in the Augustan Principate." *American Journal of Philology* 132: 81–102.

Sutton, Dana Ferrin. 1986. *Seneca on the Stage*. Leiden: E.J. Brill.

Syme, Ronald. 1986. *The Augustan Aristocracy*. Oxford: Oxford University Press.

———. 2002 (1939). *The Roman Revolution*. Oxford: Oxford University Press.

Tacoma, Laurens E. 2015. "Roman Elite Mobility under the Principate." In *"Aristocracy" in Antiquity: Redefining Greek and Roman Elites*, edited by N. R. E. Fisher and Hans van Wees, 125–45. Swansea: Classical Press of Wales.

Tarrant, R. J. 1976. *Seneca, Agamemnon*. Cambridge: Cambridge University Press.

———. 1978. "Senecan Drama and Its Antecedents." *Harvard Studies in Classical Philology* 82: 213–63.

———, ed. 1985. *Seneca's "Thyestes."* Atlanta: Scholars Press.

———. 2006. "Seeing Seneca Whole?" In *Seeing Seneca Whole: Perspectives on Philosophy, Poetry, and Politics*, edited by Katharina Volk and Gareth D. Williams, 1–18. Leiden: Brill.

Terrenato, Nicola. 2001. "The Auditorium Site in Rome and the Origins of the Villa." *Journal of Roman Archaeology* 14: 5–32.

Thompson, David L. 1981. "The Meetings of the Roman Senate on the Palatine." *American Journal of Archaeology* 85, no. 3: 335–39.

Tomei, M. 2000. "Le case di Augusto sul Palatino." *Mitteilungen des deutschen archaeologischen Instituts, römische Abteilung* 107: 7–36.

Toohey, Peter. 1997. "Trimalchio's Constipation: Periodizing Madness, Eros, and Time." In *Inventing Ancient Culture: Historicism, Periodization, and the Ancient World*, edited by Mark Golden and Peter Toohey, 50–65. London: Routledge.

Treggiari, Susan. 1991. *Roman Marriage: Iusti Coniuges from the Time of Cicero to the Time of Ulpian*. Oxford: Oxford University Press.

Veyne, Paul. 1961. "Vie de Trimalcion." *Annales d'histoire économique et sociale* 2: 213–47.

Van Andringa, William. 2015. "'M. Tullius . . . aedem Fortunae August(ae) solo et peq(unia) sua:' Private Foundation and Public Cult in a Roman Colony." In *Public and Private in Ancient Mediterranean Law and Religion*, edited by Clifford Ando and Jörg Rüpke, 99–114. Boston: De Gruyter.

Van Overmeire, Sam. 2012. "Nero, the Senate and People of Rome: Reactions to an Emperor's Image." In *Studies in Latin Literature and Roman History*, edited by Carl Deroux, 472–91. Collection Latomus 338. Brussels: Latomus.

Varner, Eric R. 2001. "Portraits, Plots, and Politics: 'Damnatio Memoriae' and the Images of Imperial Women." *Memoirs of the American Academy in Rome* 46: 41–93.

Versluys, M. J. 2015. "Roman Visual Material Culture and Globalising *Koine*." In *Globalisation and the Roman World: World History, Connectivity, and Material Culture*, edited by Martin Pitts and M. J. Versluys, 141–74. New York: Cambridge University Press.

Viitanen, Eeva-Maria, and Laura Nissin. 2017. "Campaigning for Votes in Ancient Pompeii: Contextualizing Electoral Programmata." In *Writing Matters: Presenting and Perceiving Monumental Inscriptions in Antiquity and the Middle Ages*, edited by Irene Berti,

Katharina Bolle, Fanny Opdenhoff, and Fabian Stroth, 117–44. Materiale Textkulturen, vol. 14. Berlin: De Gruyter.
Volk, Katharina 2006. "Cosmic Disruption in Seneca's *Thyestes*: Two Ways of Looking at an Eclipse." In *Seeing Seneca Whole: Perspectives on Philosophy, Poetry, and Politics*, edited by Katharina Volk and Gareth Williams, 183–200. Leiden: Brill.
Vout, Caroline. 2007. *Power and Eroticism in Imperial Rome*. Cambridge: Cambridge University Press.
———. 2009a. "Representing the Emperor." In *The Cambridge Companion to the Roman Historians*, edited by Andrew Feldherr, 261–75. Cambridge: Cambridge University Press.
———. 2009b. "The *Satyrica* and Neronian Culture." In *Petronius: A Handbook*, edited by J. R. W Prag and Ian Repath, 101–13. Malden, Mass.: Wiley-Blackwell.
———. 2013. "Tiberius and the Invention of Succession." In *The Julio-Claudian Succession: Reality and Perception of the "Augustan Model,"* edited by A. G. G. Gibson, 59–77. Leiden: Brill.
Vuolanto, Ville. 2016. "Child and Parent in Roman Law." In *The Oxford Handbook of Roman Law and Society*, edited by Paul J. du Plessis, Clifford Ando, and Kaius Tuori, 487–97. Oxford: Oxford University Press.
Wagenvoort, H. Hendrik. 1980. *Pietas: Selected Studies in Roman Religion*. Leiden: Brill.
Waever, Ole. 1995. "Securitization and Desecuritization." In *On Security*, edited by Ronnie D. Lipschutz, 46–86. New York: Columbia University Press.
Waldron, Jeremy. 2003. "Security and Liberty: The Image of Balance." *The Journal of Political Philosophy* 11: 191–210.
Wallace-Hadrill, Andrew. 1982. "*Civilis Princeps*: Between Citizen and King." *Journal of Roman Studies* 72: 32–48.
———. 1989. "Patronage in Roman Society: From Republic to Empire." In *Patronage in Ancient Society*, edited by Andrew Wallace-Hadrill, 63–88. London: Routledge.
———. 1994. *Houses and Society in Pompeii and Herculaneum*. Princeton, N.J.: Princeton University Press.
———. 1996. "The Imperial Court." In *The Cambridge Ancient History, Vol. 10: The Augustan Empire, 43 BC to AD 69*, 283–308. Cambridge: Cambridge University Press.
———. 1998. "The Villa as Cultural Symbol." In *The Roman Villa: Villa Urbana*, edited by A. Frazer, 43–53. Philadelphia: University of Pennsylvania Press.
———. 2008. *Rome's Cultural Revolution*. Cambridge: Cambridge University Press.
———. 2011. "The Roman Imperial Court: Seen and Unseen in the Performance of Power." In *Royal Courts in Dynastic States and Empires: A Global Perspective*, edited by Jeroen Frans, et al., 91–102. Leiden: Brill.
———. 2015. "What Makes a Roman House a 'Roman House'?" In *Public and Private in the Roman House and Society*, edited by Kaius Tuori and Laura Nissin, *Journal of Roman Archaeology Supplementary Series* 102: 177–86.
Walsh, P. G. 1970. *The Roman Novel. The "Satyricon" of Petronius and the "Metamorphoses" of Apuleius*. Cambridge: Cambridge University Press.
Wartenberg, Thomas E., ed. 1992. *Rethinking Power*. Albany: State University of New York Press.
Whitmarsh, Tim, ed. 2010. *Local Knowledge and Microidentities in the Imperial Greek World*. Cambridge: Cambridge University Press.

Wick, Claudia. 2004. *Bellum civile, liber IX*. Munich: K. G. Saur.
Winterling, A. 1999. *Aula Caesaris: Studien zur Institutionalisierung des römischen Kaiserhofes in der Zeit von Augustus bis Commodus (31 v. Chr.–192 n. Chr.)*. Munich: Oldenbourg Verlag.
———. 2009. *Politics and Society in Imperial Rome*. Malden, Mass.: Wiley-Blackwell.
———. 2011. "Zu Theorie und Methode einer neuen Römischen Kaisergeschichte." In *Zwischen Strukturgeschichte und Biographie: Probleme und Perspektiven einer neuen Römischen Kaisergeschichte zur Zeit von Augustus bis Commodus*, edited by Aloys Winterling, 1–12. Berlin: De Gruyter.
Wiseman, T. P. 2009. "The House of Augustus and the Lupercal." *Journal of Roman Archaeology* 22: 527–45.
Wood, Susan. 1999. *Imperial Women: A Study in Public Images, 40 BC–AD 68*. Leiden: Brill.
Woodman, A. J. 1993. "Amateur Dramatics at the Court of Nero (*Annals* 15.48–74)." In *Tacitus and the Tacitean Tradition*, edited by T. James Luce and A. J. Woodman, 104–28. Princeton, N.J.: Princeton University Press.
Woodman, A. J., and Ronald H. Martin. 1996. *The Annals of Tacitus: Book 3*. Cambridge: Cambridge University Press.
Woolf, Greg. 2005. "Provincial Perspectives." In *The Cambridge Companion to the Age of Augustus*, edited by Karl Galinsky, 106–29. Cambridge: Cambridge University Press.
Yegül, Fikret K. 2010. *Bathing in the Roman World*. New York: Cambridge University Press.
Zaccaria Ruggiu, A. 1990. "L'Intervento pubblico nella regolamentazione dello spazio privato." *Rivista di Archeologia* 1: 77–94.
Zanker, Paul. 1990. *The Power of Images in the Age of Augustus*. Ann Arbor: University of Michigan Press.
———. 1998. *Pompeii: Public and Private Life*. Cambridge, Mass.: Harvard University Press.
Zarmakoupi, Mantha. 2014. *Designing for Luxury on the Bay of Naples: Villas and Landscapes (c. 100 BCE–79 CE)*. Oxford: Oxford University Press.
Zwierlein, Otto, ed. 1986. *L. Annaei Senecae: Tragoediae*. Oxford: Oxford University Press.

INDEX LOCORUM

Numbers in *italics* indicate passages in the ancient sources.

Ad Herennium: 2.19, 22
Aeschylus
—*Agamemnon: 773–891*, 188n43; *1099–1129*, 100; *1223–38*, 100; *1333–71*, 100

Cicero, Marcus Tullius
—*De Doma sua: 100*, 63
—*Off.: 1.54*, 22
—*Q.Fr.: 1.1.25*, 126, 127
—*Verr.: 2.2.53.133*, 196n99; *2.3.23.56*, 196n99; *2.3.34.79*, 126–27; *2.5.11.27–28*, 196n99
Cicero, Quintus Tullius
—*Commentariolum Petitionis: 17*, 62; *28*, 111; *35*, 62, 111; *44*, 63
"Consolation to Livia": *347–55*, 60

Digest of Justinian: 1.8.2. pr.1, 3
Dio Cassius
—*Roman History: 49.15.5*, 63, 183n31; *53.1.3*, 182n13, 182n15; *54.10.5*, 181n72; *54.23.6*, 61; *54.27.3*, 63; *55.12.4*, 63; *55.12.5*, 64; *56.42.4*, 177n53; *58.3.8*, 185n85; *58.22.4–5*, 179n44; *58.24.1*, 185n86; *58.25.2*, 185n86
Dionysius of Halicarnassus
—*Roman Antiquities: 8.59.4*, 177n53; *20.13.2–3*, 5; *20.13.3*, 158

Epictetus: *Discourses: 1.2.8–10*, 198n36

Gaius: *Institutes: 1.55*, 39

Livy
—*Ab Urbe Condita: 1.41*, 54; *2.7.6*, 5–6, 61; *2.7.11*, 5, 61; *2.32.9–12*, 187n26
Lucan
—*Bellum civile: 1.119–20*, 22; *1.125–26*, 34; *2.23–28*, 23; *2.25–26*, 29; *2.27*, 35; *2.35–36*, 24; *2.38–42*, 26; *2.297–303*, 32; *2.322–23*, 31; *2.342–43*, 33; *2.350–59*, 33; *2.360–66*, 33; *2.378–80*, 33; *2.388*, 33; *4.393–401*, 25; *4.500–502*, 34; *4.512–14*, 34; *4.572–73*, 34; *4.575–79*, 34; *5.270*, *276*, 28; *5.271*, 25; *5.272*, 25; *5.273*, 25; *5.274–77*, 24; *5.278–82*, 22, 24; *5.280*, 28; *5.281*, 29, 35; *5.281–82*, 35; *5.364–74*, 27; *6.158–60*, 176n48; *6.303–6*, 22; *7.264–69*, 29, 33; *7.287–89*, 28; *7.318–22*, 30; *7.323*, 29; *7.557–68*, 29; *7.560–65*, 28; *7.565*, 29; *7.566–67*, 28, 30; *7.577*, 29; *7.578–80*, 30; *7.739–42*, 36; *7.789–94*, 31; *7.796–99*, 31; *8.67*, 33, 38; *8.727–28*, 35; *8.746–47*, 35; *8.767–70*, 35–36; *9.24–26*, 32; *9.25*, 33, 38; *9.27*, 32; *9.55–59*, 68–69, 36; *9.169–70*, 37; *9.173*, 37; *9.175–78*, 36; *9.178–80*, 37; *9.179*, 36; *9.227–36*, 22, 26; *9.507–10*, 32–33; *9.601*, 32
Lucillius, *AP: 11.184*, 73

Martial: *De Spectaculis 2*, 183n40

Octavia/Oct.: 276–78, 57
Ovid
—*Am.*: 2.2.3–4, 182n17
—*Fasti*: 4.949–50, 65
—*Met.*: 15.865, 65
—*Pont.*: 2.2.74, 40
—*Tristia*: 3.1.34, 66–67; 3.1.38–42, 182n19; 3.1.61–62, 182n15

Petronius
—*Satyricon*: 26.9, 134; 27.3, 133, 135; 27.5, 135; 27.5–6, 135, 140; 28.5, 134; 31.3, 133; 31.3–4, 139; 32.2, 134; 34.1, 137; 34.4, 133; 34.7, 137; 35.1, 142; 35.6, 133; 37.9, 143; 38.1, 134; 38.2, 134; 38.4, 134; 40.4, 138; 41.9, 136; 47.1–3, 136; 47.4–6, 137; 47.8, 137; 48.3, 133; 48.4, 134; 49.1–10, 144; 53.1, 134; 54.2, 136; 56.1, 135; 56.2, 135; 56.4, 135; 56.6, 135; 57.4–5, 133; 57.6, 140; 57.9, 133; 64.12, 143; 64.13, 137, 141, 142; 65.1–2, 138; 68.3, 133; 69.7–8, 138; 70.8, 139; 70.11–12, 141; 71.1, 141; 71.11, 138; 73.2, 138; 73.2–3, 139; 73.4, 139; 73.5, 139; 73.6, 141; 75.11, 143; 76.10, 136; 76.11, 136; 78.5, 136, 137
Pliny the Elder
—*NH*: 7.121, 22; 22.46.92, 180n61; 36.163, 184n59
Pliny the Younger
—*Ep.*: 2.17.2, 71; 2.17.3, 71; 2.17.8, 71; 2.17.9, 71; 2.17.17–19, 71; 2.17.22, 71; 2.17.24, 71; 6.31.2, 74; 6.31.13, 74
—*Pan.*: 68.6–7, 7; 83.1, 8
Plutarch: *Pomp.*: 44.3, 72
Propertius: 2.31.3–4, 182n15; 2.32.7, 182n17; 3.16.24, 177n53

Quintilian: *Inst. Or.*: 10.1.126, 187–88n33; 10.1.129, 187–88n33

Res Gestae Divi Augusti: 34, 171n43; 35.1, 177n1

Seneca
—*Agamemnon*: 6–11, 96; 43, 96; 148, 92; 166, 101; 191, 101; 199, 101; 264, 101; 730, 187–88n33; 867–71, 100; 881–900, 100; 901–3, 100
—*Apocolocyntosis*: 1.2, 84; 4.1.30–32, 85; 4.3, 84; 5.3, 84

—*Consolation to Polybius*: 6.1, 83; 6.2, 83
—*De brev. vit.*: 4.5, 48
—*De clementia*: 1.1.1, 81; 1.1.2, 13; 1.1.6, 11; 1.1.9, 82, 87; 1.3.3, 81, 87; 1.3.4–5, 86; 1.4.1, 87; 1.4.2, 88; 1.4.3, 88, 155; 1.5.3, 82, 87; 1.5.4, 87; 1.8.1, 82–83, 87; 1.8.2, 85–86; 1.8.2–4, 81; 1.8.3, 84, 87; 1.8.4, 82, 87, 88; 1.8.5, 81, 86; 1.8.6, 86; 1.15.1, 87; 1.15.5, 83; 1.19.2, 85; 1.19.3, 85, 87; 1.19.5, 85, 87; 1.19.6, 86, 87; 2.5.1, 81
—*De ira*: 1.1.3–4, 145; 2.12.3–4, 145; 2.12.4, 145; 2.21.8, 146; 2.21.11, 146; 2.25.3–4, 146; 2.31.7, 147; 2.33.3, 147, 148; 2.33.4–6, 148; 3.8.1, 147; 3.9.4–5, 146; 3.11.4, 151; 3.13.5, 201n79; 3.14.1, 149; 3.15.1, 150; 3.15.3, 150; 3.17.1, 150; 3.40.3, 151; 3.40.4, 151
—*Ep.*: 43.2–3, 83; 47, 141; 47.1, 141, 142; 47.3, 141; 55.3, 70, 71; 55.4, 71; 55.5, 71; 55.7, 70; 77.14, 198n36; 90.4, 13; 90.5, 13; 90.6, 13, 172n59; 114.6, 133
—*Medea*: 1021, 190n62
—*Oed.*: 296–97; 301–2, 102; 303–99, 101; 323, 101; 325–27, 102; 354–55, 101–2; 380, 102
—*Q. Nat.*: 7.32.3, 79; 7.32.4, 79
—*Thy.*: 1–2; 4–6, 95; 23–24, 97; 52–53, 97; 54–62, 95–96; 65–66, 97; 83–85, 97; 95, 97; 96–99, 97; 100, 97; 101, 97; 103–4, 97; 105, 97; 191–92, 90; 204–13, 91; 216–17, 91; 218, 91; 334–35, 91; 338, 96; 391–95, 92; 421–90, 96; 455–69, 92, 189n46; 623–788, 93; 641–652, 93; 644, 94; 645, 94; 646–47, 94; 648, 94; 651–664, 93; 652, 94; 652–54, 94; 655–67, 94; 668–70, 94; 782–83, 95; 788, 95; 789–884, 95; 893–95, 99; 901–12, 99; 1005, 99; 1006, 99; 1067–68, 99
Sophocles: *OT*: 873–82, 188n43
Suetonius
—*Aug.*: 29.3, 182n13, 182n15; 40.5, 170n13; 58, 177n1; 65.1, 48; 65.3, 48; 65.4, 48; 69.1, 47; 72.1, 65, 66, 182n7; 72.2, 67; 73, 66
—*Calig.*: 10, 185n85; 18.3, 183n32; 24.1, 49
—*Claud.*: 32, 129; 44–45, 180n61
—*Gram.*: 17.2, 183n32
—*Nero*: 10.1, 11; 29, 68; 31, 183n40; 31.1, 69, 70; 38.2, 185n68; 57, 185n70
—*Otho*: 7, 73
—*Tib.*: 42.1, 75; 53, 179n44; 72.1, 77
—*Vit.*: 3.2, 185n85

Tacitus
—*Ann.*: *1.3*, 154; *1.4*, 154; *1.5*, 54; *1.11*, 155–56; *1.11–12*, 160; *1.12*, 156, 187n26; *1.72*, 157, 158; *1.73*, 159, 160, 202n12; *1.74*, 157, 159, 161; *2.27*, 157, 161; *2.28*, 157, 202n12; *2.30*, 161; *2.31*, 161; *3.4*, 48–49; *3.65*, 155; *3.69*, 162; *3.70*, 160, 161; *4.31*, 203n27; *4.32–3*, 11; *4.53*, 180n57; *4.58*, 76, 77; *4.67*, 75; *6.1*, 77; *6.5*, 160; *6.6*, 77; *6.7*, 162–63; *6.20*, 185n85; *6.25*, 179n44; *6.39*, 77; *11.26–27*, 50; *11.28*, 50; *11.30*, 50; *11.31*, 50; *11.35*, 51; *12.1*, 50; *12.3*, 50; *12.4*, 50; *12.5*, 49, 54; *12.6*, 50; *12.7*, 53; *12.36–7*, 55; *12.37*, 55; *12.56*, 55; *12.66*, 53; *12.66–68*, 180n61; *12.68*, 53; *13.4*, 51; *13.5*, 55–56; *13.18*, 56; *13.19*, 57, 58; *14.7*, 57; *14.59*, 57; *14.61*, 57; *15.36*, 38; *15.37*, 72; *15.39*, 73, 185n68; *15.41*, 67; *15.42*, 69–70, 183n40; *15.50*, 165, 166; *15.51*, 165; *15.68–69*, 165; *15.71*, 165; *15.73*, 166
—*Hist.*: *1.4*, 185n70

Valerius Maximus: *Facta et Dicta Memorabilia*: *5.4–7*, 22
Velleius Paterculus:
—*Roman History*: *2.14.3*, 6; *2.81.3*, 63, 183n31; *2.89.3–4*, 171n43
Vitruvius: *On Architecture*: *6.5.1*, 122

GENERAL INDEX

Actium, battle of, 10
adultery, 39, 48, 49, 50, 117
Aegyptus, King, 64
Aeneas, 22, 132
Aeschylus, *Agamemnon,* 100
Agrippa, Marcus, 41, 47
Agrippa Postumus, 48
Agrippina the Elder, 45, 48–49, 180n57
Agrippina the Younger, 179n46, 180n57, 181n65, 181nn67–69, 181n71; and Augustus, 41, 56; and Caligula, 45; and Claudius, 42, 43, 49–50, 53–55; coins depicting, 45, 46; and Nero, 42, 43, 46, 51, 52, 55–57, 58; power and influence of, 53–56, 57; and Proculus, 165; and Sebasteion, 41–42, 43; and Senate, 55, 56
Alcestis (painting), 117–18, 119, 120, 121, 122
Alexander the Great, 150
Amisus statue group, 46
Antony, Mark, 47
Aphrodisias, 41, 44
Apollo, 65
Apollo, Temple of, 63, 64, 65
Appian Way, 77
Ara Pacis Augustae, 41, 44, 178n8, 178n10
architecture, 16, 61, 64, 65, 105, 110, 111, 112. *See also* Domus Aurea; Palatine hill; Pompeian houses; *scaenae frons*
Arendt, Hannah, 2, 3–4, 13–14
aristocracy, 14, 40, 41, 70, 71, 72, 106; and Claudius, 50; compliance of, 155; and Domitian, 7; and Nero, 51, 73; and one-man rule, 14–15; and public eye, 63;

self-promotion by, 2, 79; and Seneca, 79, 83; and Vitruvius, 123. *See also* elites
Asinius Gallus, 156, 161
Asinius Pollio, Gaius, 9
Ateius Capito, 161
Athenian tragedy, 89
Athens, 4, 5
Atreus, myth of, 89, 90
Augustus, 11, 30; accommodation to rule of, 154–55; and Agrippa Postumus, 48; and Agrippina the Younger, 41, 56; and Aphrodisias, 41; and Apollo, 65; and Caepio Crispinus, 157; and Claudius, 49, 50; death of, 54, 155; and Dionysius of Halicarnassus, 4; and *domus Augusta,* 11, 17–18, 39, 40, 47–48, 58, 59, 125; and Forum Romanum, 3; *imperium* of, 10; and Julia, 39, 45, 48; and Julia the Younger, 48; and Livia, 47, 54; and Lucan, 21; and Lucius and Gaius, 44, 45, 47; and *maiestas,* 157, 159–60; marriages and adoptions arranged by, 47; modesty of, 18, 62, 65–66, 67, 73, 74, 81; and Nero, 45; and one-man rule, 9–11; and Ovid, 65; Palatine hill complex of, 61, 62, 63–67, 68, 75, 76, 77, 134, 182n22; Palatine hill house of, 62, 63, 64–67, 110; as *pater* and *paterfamilias,* 11, 39, 41, 47–48, 59; as *pater patriae,* 39, 65; as *pontifex maximus,* 63–64; as *primus inter pares,* 11; as *princeps,* 10, 39, 59, 154–55; as *proconsul,* 10; and public eye, 6, 18, 62, 66, 67, 75, 77, 81, 82, 83; and public life, 63, 67; rise of, 10; and Rubellius Plautus, 57; and Senate, 10, 56; and Tiberius, 14, 49, 155;

and *tribunicia potestas,* 10; and Vedius Pollio, 61, 151–52; and Velleius Paterculus, 6; and violence against women, 47; and virtue, 11

Baiae, 70, 106
banquets. *See under* Petronius, *Satyricon;* Seneca
bathing, 19, 122, 123, 130, 131, 138–39. *See also* Petronius, *Satyricon*
baths, public, 7, 105, 129–30, 139
Bay of Naples, 64, 69, 70, 71, 104, 108
body/bodily functions, 17, 18–19, 37, 129, 131. *See also under* Petronius, *Satyricon*
Bourdieu, Pierre, 112
Britannicus, 46, 53
Burrus, 56–57

Caepio Crispinus, 157
Caesar, Gaius (Augustus' grandson), 44–45, 47, 160
Caesar, Julius, 9–10, 41, 72, 73; *De bello civili,* 21; mutinous soldiers of, 24–26, 27, 28, 32, 34, 35, 36, 37; and Nero, 38; and Pompey, 21, 22, 34–35; soldiers cared for by, 17, 23, 27–31, 32, 33, 34, 35, 38, 175n30
Caesar, Lucius (Augustus' grandson), 44–45, 47
Caligula, 45, 49, 50, 76, 147–48, 179n46
Calpurnius Piso, C., 165–66
Cambyses, 148–49, 201n78
Campania, 75, 106
Capri, 75, 76, 77
Cassandra (painting), 114–15, 116–17, 120, 121. *See also under* Seneca
Cassius Severus, 157
Cato the Younger, 17, 23, 26, 27–28, 31–33, 176n41
censors, 5, 6, 8, 158
children: and Ara Pacis, 41; and Augustus, 47, 48, 173n7; and Dionysius of Halicarnassus, 5; and fathers, 39; in Lucan, 22, 27; and parents, 22; and Pliny the Younger, 8; in Seneca, 95, 99, 101, 146, 148, 150, 201n82
Chrysippus, 141
Cicero, Marcus Tullius, 61, 62, 71; *De Doma sua,* 63; *On Duties,* 22; *Against Verres,* 126–27

Cicero, Quintus Tullius, 126, 127; *Commentariolum Petitionis* ("Election Handbook"), 62–63, 111
Circus Maximus, 69
civil wars, 63, 154; and Aphrodisias, 41; between Caesar and Pompey, 9; and Cato the Younger, 32; and family, 21, 22; in Lucan, 17, 24, 26, 29, 30, 31, 38, 40; new order after, 31; and Republic, 17
Claudius, 55, 129, 186n19; and Agrippina the Younger, 41–42, 43, 45, 49–50, 53–55; and bodily functions, 129; and Britannicus, 46; and Caligula, 50; and *domus Augusta,* 49–51, 53, 54, 58; and Messalina, 49–51, 58; murder of, 53, 54; naval battle staged by, 55; and Octavia, 52, 57; and Octavian, 50; and Sebasteion, 41–42; and Seneca, 84–85, 130; weakness of, 55
Claudius, Temple of the Deified, 69
clementia (clemency), 80–81, 82, 86, 87, 186n7, 186n9, 187n28
clients, 1, 62, 112, 123, 125, 127. *See also salutatio*
Clitus, 150
coins, 44, 45, 46, 179n46
Colosseum, 68, 69
commanders. *See* soldiers
community, 1, 2, 3, 4, 5, 22; and Augustus, 49, 75; Caesar's devotion to, 31; and emperors, 8, 16, 19, 154; in Lucan, 24; and Marcus Livius Drusus, 7; and Nero, 74; and rulers, 12, 81, 86–88, 89; security of, 9, 18, 163, 165; Seneca on, 86–88, 102; and soldiers, 24–25. *See also* polity, security of
"Consolation to Livia," 60, 74
Cordus, 35–37
Cornelia, 33, 35–37
Cornelius Piso, 161
Cotta Messalinus, 77, 160
Crassus, 9

Danaids, portico of, 64–65
Danaus, King, 64
delatores (accusers, informers), 19, 156–58, 161, 165, 202n12, 203–4n36, 204n50
Diana, image of, by Timotheus, 65
digital age, 19

Dio Cassius, *Roman History*, 61, 63–64
Dionysius of Halicarnassus, *Roman Antiquities*, 4–5, 6, 8–9, 158, 177n53
Domitian, 7
domus Augusta (imperial family), 17–18, 38, 52, 53; and Agrippina the Younger, 45, 46; and Amisus statue group, 46; and Ara Pacis, 41, 44; and Augustus, 11, 18, 39, 40, 47–48, 58, 59; and Caligula, 49; and Claudius, 49–51, 53, 54, 58; definition of, 40; imperial vs. local definitions of, 41–47, 58; and Lucius and Gaius, 44–45; and Nero, 51, 55–59; and people of Rome, 57; and Sebasteion, 41–44; and Tiberius, 48–49; women of, 12, 14, 18, 40, 41, 51–58
Domus Aurea, 18, 61, 62, 67–75, 77, 82, 108, 153, 184n66, 185n71; and coastal villas, 70, 74; definition of, 184n49; frescoes of, 69, 110; guarded access to, 73–74; and public eye, 62, 74; rooms of, 69; as shared with inhabitants of Rome, 72; situation of, 68–69, 71–72, 73; structures and features of, 68, 69–70, 72, 73, 74. *See also* Nero
Domus Transitoria, 68
Drusilla, 49
Drusus (son of Livia), 60
Drusus, Marcus Livius, 6–7, 8

elites, 4, 16, 59, 61, 66, 70, 73, 108, 123, 155; of Amisus, 46; and Augustus's Palatine hill complex, 65; and bodily needs, 18–19; of city of Rome, 106; and clients, 123; and *delatores*, 19, 161; and emperors, 154; and imperial gaze, 15, 80; local, 40, 43, 44–45, 58, 104, 106; and *maiestas* trials, 161; mutual suspicion among, 162–63; and one-man rule, 166; and Pliny the Younger, 8; and political fear, 166–67; private lives of, 154; self-promotion by, 1, 17, 18; Seneca's value system for, 15; and villas and *otium*, 68; and women of imperial household, 14. *See also* aristocracy
emperors, 30, 43, 106, 153; and collective security, 155; and community, 8, 16, 19, 154, 156; contingent claims to power of, 41; control of public space by, 16; court of, 71, 180n52; criticism of through female family members, 52; and *delatores*, 19; and elites, 80, 104, 154; house of, 10, 18, 61; images of, 10, 16, 41–44, 157–58, 159, 160, 178n7; and Palatine hill, 63; and paternal authority, 41; and performance of authority, 58, 128; and privacy, 2, 8, 9, 156; and public eye, 9, 62, 79–80, 81; reputation of, 157–58; security of, 19, 156, 157, 158, 160, 163, 165; self-presentation of, 11; vulnerability of aristocracy to, 15; welfare of, 156; and women, 14, 40. *See also* *domus Augusta* (imperial family)
Ennius, Lucius, 160
Epicharis, 165
Epictetus, *Discourses*, 198n36
Euripides, *Alcestis*, 117, 194n55

Falanius, 159–60
Fall of Troy (painting), 115–16, 120, 121
families, 1, 22, 40; and Ara Pacis, 41; Arendt on, 4; bonds of, 17; and Caesar, 22, 23, 38; and Cato the Younger, 23, 31–33; and civil wars, 21, 22; commanders and soldiers as, 17, 21, 23, 27–28, 35, 36, 37, 128, 175n30; Julio-Claudian, 40; in Lucan, 17, 21–38, 40; and Pompey, 22, 23; ruler and ruled as, 21, 38; of soldiers, 22–23, 24–25. *See also* *domus Augusta* (imperial family); husbands; soldiers; wives
fathers, 5, 22, 39. *See also paterfamilias*
feminism, 4, 52
Firmius Catus, 157
Fortuna, Temple of (Domus Aurea), 71
Fortune, temple to (Pompeii), 106
Forum Romanum, 3, 71
freedmen, 50, 51, 76. *See also under* Petronius, *Satyricon*; Seneca
freedom, 6, 131, 133, 142, 159, 166, 204n39
funeral rites/burials, 5, 24–25, 26, 27, 31, 32, 35–37, 44–45

Gaius, *Institutes*, 39
Gardens of Agrippa, 72
Gardens of Maecenas, 68
Germanicus, 45, 47, 48, 57, 76, 175n30
gods, 22, 24, 41, 84, 87, 178n7
Granius Marcellus, M., 159–61
Great Fire in Rome, 67, 72–73
Greeks, 4, 5, 82, 89, 105, 109
guests/visitors, 7, 121–22, 124, 125–27, 130; and Domus Aurea, 69, 73–74; and

M. Tullius Cicero, 126–27; and Pliny, 71; and theatrical frescoes, 18; to Villa Iovis, 62, 76, 77. *See also under* Petronius, *Satyricon;* Pompeian houses

Hadrian, 69
Halotus, 53
Harpagus, 150
Herodotus, 201n78
Hortensius Hortalus, 63
House of Catulus, 66
House of Hortensius, 66
House of L. Caecilius Iucundus, 124
House of M. Pinarius Cerialis, 110–11, 112–13, 119–20, 121, 194n59
House of the Ceii, 108
House of the Menander, 114–17, 195n68
House of the Silver Wedding, 124
House of the Tragic Poet, 106–7, 117–18, 121–22, 194n59
House of the Vettii, 120
husbands, 5, 25, 36, 37. *See also* families

Iphigenia (painting, House of M. Pinarius Cerialis), 110, 119–21, 194n59
Iphigenia (painting, House of the Tragic Poet), 119, 120–21, 122, 194n59
iudicia publica (public courts), 3

Julia (daughter of Augustus), 39, 40, 45, 47, 48
Julia (daughter of Caesar), 22
Julia Livilla, 45, 179n46
Julia the Younger, 48
Julio-Claudians, 2, 11, 12, 19, 74–75; and Aphrodisias, 41; competing images of, 40; and *domus Augusta,* 58; era of as transformative, 17; and family, 40; houses built by, 61; and Nero, 52; and public eye, 61, 62; and Seneca, 79, 103

kingship treatises, Hellenistic, 81

law, 3, 19, 22, 47, 48, 157–58, 162
Lenin, V. I., 58
lex Iulia de maritandis ordinibus, 48
lex Pappia Poppaea, 48
Libo Drusus, 157, 161, 203n28

libraries, 63, 64, 65, 134
Livia, 41, 45, 47, 54, 60–61, 160, 178–79n24, 181n65
Livy, *Ab Urbe Condita,* 5–6, 9, 54, 61
Lucan: *Bellum civile,* 14, 17, 21–38, 40, 128, 153, 174n17, 174n20, 176n48; commanders and soldiers in, 17, 21, 23, 27–28, 35, 36, 37, 128, 175n30; death in, 24–25, 26, 27, 34, 35–37; families in, 17, 21–38, 40; grief in, 29; mourning in, 23–24, 32, 35–37
Lucillius, *Anthologia Palatina,* 73

Maecenas, 133
magistrates, 3, 9, 10, 53–54
Magna Mater, temple of, 63
maiestas (treason), 157–63, 165, 166, 202nn12–13, 203n25
Marcellus, 47
Marcia, 33
matronae, 23–24, 26, 27, 28, 29, 32, 125
Meniskos, 73
Messalina, 49–51, 58
Milichus, 165, 204n53
mosaics, 117, 121–22
Mount Vesuvius, 106
Munda, battle of, 72
Mytilene, 45

Narcissus (freedman of Claudius), 50–51
Naulochus, battle of, 63
Nero, 53, 54, 68, 88, 108, 184n66; and Agrippina the Younger, 41–42, 43, 45, 46, 51, 52, 55–57, 58; and Amisus statue group, 46; and aristocracy, 51, 73; and Armenian delegation, 55; and Augustus, 11, 45; and Baiae, 106; and Caesar, 38; coinage depicting, 46; colossal statue of, 69, 72, 73; and *domus Augusta,* 51, 55–59; and Domus Aurea, 18, 61, 62, 67–75, 77, 82, 153; fall of, 10; and Great Fire, 67, 72–73; and hospitality, 72–73; and Lucan, 21, 38; and Octavia, 57; and one-man rule, 52; and people of Rome, 38; and Petronius, 131, 197n14; and Pisonian conspiracy, 165–66; and Poppaea, 52, 57; popularity of, 38, 73; populism of, 72; and privacy, 18, 68, 74; and public eye, 18, 68, 74, 75, 77, 81–84; and Sebasteion, 43; and Seneca,

Nero (*cont.*)
11, 13, 80, 81–84, 85, 103, 155, 190n71; and Tacitus, 12, 165–66; and villas, 71, 72, 74; and women, 11, 51–52

Obama, Barack, 173n76
Obama administration, 204–5n57
Octavia (daughter of Claudius), 52, 53, 57–58
Octavia (historical tragedy), 57
Octavia (sister of Augustus), 40
Odysseus, 132
one-man rule, 12–15, 104; and aristocracy, 14–15; and Augustus, 9–11; and Caesar, 31; and Cato the Younger, 32; and *domus Augusta*, 18, 41, 52, 53, 54, 58; and elites, 166; and emperor's security, 165; fragility of, 17, 18, 41, 53, 54, 88, 155; in imperial images and architecture, 16; in Lucan, 21, 26, 27, 37; and Nero, 52; and Pisonian conspiracy, 103, 166; and private vs. public, 2, 16–17; rise of, 2, 9–11; and Seneca, 18, 102, 155; and Tacitus, 12, 58, 159; and Tiberius, 155–56. *See also* rulers
Oplontis, Villa A at, 106, 108, 110
Otho, 73
otium, 70–71
Ovid, 60; *Amores*, 182n17; *Epistulae ex Ponto*, 40; *Fasti*, 65; *Metamorphoses*, 65; *Tristia*, 66–67

paintings: of Admetus, 117; of Ajax, 115; of Alcestis, 117–18, 119, 120, 121, 122; of Apollo, 117; of Attis, 119; of Briseis, 117, 118, 119; of Cassandra, 114–17, 120, 121, 122; in Domus Aurea, 69, 110; of dramatic masks, 110, 113, 114; of Fall of Troy, 115–16, 120, 121; Fourth Style, 69, 109, 110, 113; of Helen, 114, 116, 117, 118, 119; of Hera, 117, 118; of Iphigenia, 110, 119–21, 122, 194n59; of Menander, 114; of Menelaus, 116; mythological, 106, 108, 109, 113–22; of Orestes, 121; of Orestes and Pylades, 119; of Priam, 114; Second Style, 109, 110; theatrical, 18, 106, 108, 109–13, 114, 117, 119, 122; of Thoas, 119; of Trojan War, 114–17
Palatine hill, 6, 61, 63, 68, 71, 108. *See also under* Augustus

panegyric, 8, 81
pantomime, 113
Pastor, 147–48
paterfamilias, 11, 59, 104, 123, 127–28; *patria potestas* of, 47; and Pompeian houses, 105, 106, 108, 112, 113, 114, 116, 124, 125–26
pater patriae, 33, 39, 65
patrons, 112, 114. *See also* clients
Peisistratus, 150–51
Petronius, *Satyricon*, 14, 15, 130–45, 153, 197n14; banquets in, 18, 19, 130, 152; bodily functions in, 18–19, 130, 132, 135–44, 145, 147, 148, 152, 154; common humanity in, 141, 142, 143, 144; freedmen in, 130, 131–33, 136–37, 140; guests in, 131, 132–33, 134, 136–39, 140, 142; slaves in, 132, 133, 134, 135, 139–43, 152, 197n12, 198n36
Pharsalus, battle of, 27, 28, 30–31, 32, 33, 37, 174n20
Philippi, battle of, 63
pietas, 22, 173n5
pinacothecae (public art galleries), 108
Pisae, 44–45
Pisonian conspiracy, 103, 165–66
Placentia, 28
Pliny the Elder, *Natural History*, 22, 180n61, 184n59
Pliny the Younger: *Epistles*, 71, 74; *Panegyricus*, 7–9; and privacy, 7–9, 71; on Trajan, 74; and villa in Laurentum, 71
Plutarch, 72
polity, security of, 156, 158, 160, 161, 162, 163, 166. *See also* community
Pompeian houses, 16, 64, 105, 154; atria of, 106, 114, 117, 121, 122, 123, 124–26; and bodily functions, 130; business dealings in, 126; clients in, 125; and cooking, 125; courtyards of, 107, 110, 119, 121, 122, 123, 124; *cubiculum* in, 112, 123, 126, 192n15, 196n95; domestic art in, 106–22; frescoes in, 70, 107–9, 124; gardens in, 108; and gender, 120–21; hosts and guests in, 105, 106, 107, 108, 109, 111, 113, 114, 121, 122, 123, 124, 125–26; intimate relationships in, 125–28; multifunctional spaces of, 123, 124–26; and performance and display in, 123, 125–26; pools in, 106–7; and *salutatio*, 124; storage vessels and weaving equipment

in, 124, 125; *triclinium* of, 119, 126; viewing of, 106–7; and Vitruvius, 122–23

Pompeii, 16, 190–91n4; bars in, 130; commercial spaces in, 105; and earthquakes, 124; elections in, 112; everyday life in, 18; Italian and Greek culture in, 105; *programmata* graffiti in, 112; public architecture of, 105; and Rome, 105; Samnite, 105; temples in, 105

Pompey, 9, 34, 176n49; allies of, 22, 26–27; assassination of, 35; body of, 35, 36; and bribes, 72; and Caesar, 21, 22, 34–35; and Cornelia, 33; death and funeral of, 35, 174n20; defeat of, 27, 31, 32; and family, 23; gardens of, 72, 73; in Lucan, 21, 22, 23, 26; military costume and equipment of, 36; mourning for, 35–37; soldiers as family to, 17, 27, 35; soldiers of, 23, 25, 31

Poppaea, 46, 52, 57–58, 106

praetorian guard, 56–57

Praexaspes, 148–49, 201n78

Priapus, 132

priests, 41, 53–54

private property, 4

private sphere/privacy, 68, 74, 75; Arendt on, 3–4; and Augustus, 64; definition of, 1–2, 163; and *delatores* and *maiestas* trials, 161; in digital age, 19, 163–64; and emperors, 2, 8, 9, 156; and grief, 60–61; and inaccessibility, 7; and intimacy, 163–64; loss of, 154; and mutual suspicion among elite, 163; and Nero, 18, 68, 74; and one-man rule, 16–17; and Pliny the Younger, 7–9, 71; as public good, 164; public significance of, 161; and public sphere, 1, 2–9; respect for, 167; and security, 159; and Tiberius, 158

privatus (private individual), 2, 3

proconsul, 10

Ptolemaic images, 46

public eye, 1, 8, 61; and aristocracy, 63, 83; and Augustus, 6, 18, 62, 66, 67, 75, 77, 81, 82, 83; and Cicero, 63; and Domus Aurea, 62, 74; and emperors, 9, 62, 79–80, 81; and Julio-Claudians, 61, 62; and Livia, 60–61; and Nero, 18, 62, 68, 74, 75, 77, 81–84; and Pliny the Younger, 8; and Publicola, 6, 61; and rulers, 12, 19, 61; in Seneca, 79; in Seneca's *De clementia*, 18, 80–88; in Seneca's tragedies, 18, 89–103; and Suetonius, 77–78; and Tacitus, 77–78; and Tiberius, 62, 75, 76–78; and Villa Iovis, 62

Publicola, Publius Valerius, 5–6, 8, 61

public sphere, 1, 4, 5, 16, 60–61; Arendt on, 3–4; and Augustus, 62, 64, 65, 67; and one-man rule, 16–17; and private sphere, 1, 2–9; retreat from, 7, 80

publicus, 2–3

Quintilian, 187–88n33

Republic, 3, 9, 10, 14, 16, 17, 22, 31, 32, 38, 79, 89, 154

res communes omnium, 3

res privatae, 3

res publica, 5

res publicae, 3

Roman tragedy, 89

Rome, 41, 44, 61, 67; and *domus Augusta*, 49; imperial, 14; *imperium* in city of, 10; in Lucan, 23–24, 32, 33, 35; and Pompeii, 104, 105; and Tiberius, 75, 76, 77

Rome, people of: and Augustus as *pater patriae*, 39; Augustus's honorary house decorations from, 65; and Claudius, 49, 50; and *domus Augusta*, 57; and Julia, 48; and Marcus Livius Drusus (tribune), 7; and Nero, 38, 73, 74; and Octavia, 57, 58; Seneca on, 88

Rubellius Plautus, 57

Rubrius, 159–60

rulers, 8, 17, 23, 104, 111; and community, 86–88, 89; and gaze of others, 15, 18; as gods, 87; private life of, 2, 7–9, 12; and public eye, 12, 19, 61; self-promotion by, 63; and stability, 16, 18, 19, 49, 58, 81, 88, 91; vulnerability of, 2, 19, 85–86, 87, 88. *See also under* one-man rule; Seneca

rulers and ruled, 2; and bodily functions, 129, 131; and body, 19, 131; and Cato the Younger, 31–32, 33; equality of, 131; as family, 21, 38; interdependence of, 15, 16, 19, 23, 102, 103; love between, 26–27, 34–35, 38, 153; in Lucan, 34; in Petronius, 133, 139, 140–41, 142–43, 144, 145, 152; and Pompeiian houses, 121; positions of as unstable, 14; and subordination, 13–14. *See also under* Seneca

salutatio, 62, 111, 123, 124, 195n74. *See also* clients
Samnites, 105
satyr-mosaic *emblema* (House of the Tragic Poet), 117, 121–22
scaenae frons, 108, 109–11, 112–13, 119, 122
Sebasteion, 41–44
Sejanus, 76
Seleucid images, 46
Senate, 44; and Agrippina the Younger, 55, 56; and Ara Pacis, 41; and Augustus, 10, 39, 56, 65; as Caesar's enemy, 30; and Claudius, 49, 50; and Claudius and Messalina, 50, 58; and Cotta Messalinus, 77, 160; and Livia, 45; and Lucius and Gaius, 44; and *maiestas*, 158, 160–61; mutual suspicion among, 162–63; and Sebasteion, 42; and security of emperor, 165; and Tiberius, 155, 160
senators: and autocratic rule, 166; and emperor's safety and communal security, 19
Seneca, 78, 79–103, 128; and Agrippina the Younger, 55; and Armenian delegation, 55; Atreus in, 90, 91, 92, 93, 94, 95, 98, 99, 100; audience in, 90, 102; audience of, 93, 95, 96–97, 98, 99, 100, 103; Augustus in, 47–48, 151–52; banquets in, 18, 19, 147, 148, 150, 151, 152; on bees, 85, 187n22; body in, 18, 19, 144–52; Caligula and Pastor in, 147–48; Cambyses and Praexaspes in, 148–49; Cassandra in, 100, 101, 102; children in, 146; chorus in, 92, 93, 95, 100; common humanity in, 145, 150–51, 152; community in, 146, 147, 149; *ekphrasis* in, 93–94; exposure in, 93, 98, 99; fortune in, 142; freedmen in, 131; freedom in, 131, 133; humanity in, 152; kings in, 14, 18, 19, 80, 85, 86, 89, 90, 93, 94, 97, 98, 99, 102, 130; Manto in, 101, 102; master and slave in, 141; and Nero, 11, 51, 80, 81–84, 103, 155, 190n71; and one-man rule, 18, 102, 155; on *otium*, 70–71; Peisistratus in, 150–51; as philosopher, 80; and Pisonian conspiracy, 103; revenge in, 99, 101; rulers in, 13, 18, 80, 81–89, 90, 93–96, 97, 98, 99, 100; rulers and ruled in, 13, 80, 81, 82, 86–88, 89, 90–92, 93, 94–95, 98, 99, 100–101;
102, 103, 144–45, 147–52, 187n28; security in, 156; and Servilius Vatia, 70–71; slaves in, 131, 133, 141, 142, 151, 152; and solar imagery, 82, 186n15; subordinates in, 150–51; suicide of, 190n71; Tantalus in, 95–96, 97, 98; Thyestes in, 90, 92, 93, 95, 96, 99, 102; tragedies of, 14, 15, 18, 80, 89–102, 103, 187–88n33, 187n30, 190n61; Vedius Pollio in, 151–52; viewing in, 81–82, 93, 98, 99; virtue and vice in, 146–47; visibility and power in, 99; wine drinking in, 149; WORKS: *Agamemnon*, 18, 80, 89, 90, 92, 93, 96–97, 98, 100–101, 187–88n33, 190n63, 190n67; *Apocolocyntosis*, 84–85, 186n18, 196n1; *Consolation to Polybius*, 83; *De brevitate vitae*, 47–48; *De clementia*, 11, 13, 18, 80–89, 90, 91, 102, 155, 186n10; *De ira*, 18, 19, 130–31, 144–52, 153, 201n79; *Epistles*, 13, 70, 71, 83, 133, 141, 172n59, 198n36; *Medea*, 187n30, 190n62; *Naturales quaestiones*, 79; *Oedipus*, 101–2; *Thyestes*, 18, 80, 89, 90–91, 92, 93–96, 97–100, 187n31, 188n43, 189n46, 190n62; *Troades*, 190n63
Servilius Vatia, villa of, 70–71
slaves, 1, 5, 14, 22, 51, 113, 125, 130, 159, 161; in Petronius, 132, 133, 134, 135, 139–43, 152, 197n12, 198n36; in Seneca, 131, 133, 141, 142, 151, 152; and Tiberius, 76
Smith, Zadie, 17
Social Wars, 105
soldiers: and Cato the Younger, 23, 32–33; and Claudius and Messalina, 50, 58; commanders as family of, 17, 21, 23, 27–28, 35, 36, 37, 128, 175n30; devotion of to Pompey, 35; families of, 22–23, 24–25. *See also under* Julius Caesar; Pompey
Sol/Helios, 69
Sophocles: *Oedipus Tyrannus*, 188n43
Stalin, Joseph, 58
standpoint theory, 52, 113–14, 180n56, 180n58
Stoicism, 81, 131, 141–42, 187n30, 197n12
Suetonius, 170n13, 184n49; on Augustus, 67; on Augustus's daughter and grandchildren, 48; on Augustus's *domus*, 62; on Augustus's house, 65–66; on Augustus's violence against women, 47; on Caligula's relations with sister, 49; on Claudius, 129;

on Domus Aurea, 70; on Nero, 11, 68; on Otho, 73; and public eye, 77–78; on Tiberius, 62, 75, 76–77; WORKS: *De grammaticis*, 183n32; *Divus Augustus*, 3, 47, 48, 65, 66, 67, 170n13, 177n1, 182n7, 182n13, 182n15; *Divus Claudius*, 129, 180n61; *Gaius Caligula*, 49, 183n32, 185n85; *Nero*, 11, 68, 69, 70, 183n40, 185n68, 185n70; *Otho*, 73; *Tiberius*, 75, 77, 179n44; *Vitellius*, 185n85
Sulla, 105

tablinum, 107, 121, 122
Tacitus, 153; on Agrippina the Elder, 48–49; on Agrippina the Younger, 53–57, 181n65; audience of, 51, 54; on Claudius, 49–51, 58; on *delatores*, 156–58, 161, 165; on Domus Aurea, 69–70; on Great Fire, 67; Livia in, 54, 181n65; on Messalina, 49–51; on Nero, 38, 51–52, 57, 72–73, 128, 165–66; on Octavia, 57; and one-man rule, 12, 58, 159; on Poppaea, 57; on principate, 11–12; and public eye, 77–78; security in, 156; on Seneca, 190n71; on Tiberius, 19, 48–49, 62, 75, 76–77, 203n27; women in, 18, 52–53, 54, 55, 56, 59; WORKS: *Annales* (*Annals*), 11–12, 18, 38, 41, 48–49, 50, 51, 52–53, 54, 55, 56, 57, 58, 69–70, 72, 73, 75, 76, 77, 154–63, 165–67, 175n30, 179n44, 180n57, 180n61, 181n65, 183n40, 185n68, 185n85, 187n26, 190n71, 202n12, 203n27; *Historiae*, 185n70
Tanaquil, 54
theater, 7, 69, 79, 93, 96, 111, 113. *See also* under paintings
Thyestes, myth of, 89
Tiberius, 11, 40, 54, 155–56, 203n27; and Agrippina the Elder, 45, 48–49; and Augustus, 14, 47, 49, 160; and Caepio Crispinus, 157; and Claudius, 49; and *delatores*, 157; divorce of first wife by, 47; and *domus Augusta*, 48–49; and Germanicus, 47; and Julia, 47; and limits of security, 162; and Livia, 45, 47; and *maiestas*, 157–63, 165, 166; and one-man rule, 155–56; and private lives, 158; prosecutions for insult to, 19; and public

eye, 62, 75, 76–77; reputation of, 157–58; and Senate, 155; and Servilius Vatia, 70; and tyranny, 158; and Velleius Paterculus, 6; and Villa Iovis, 62, 75–77
Timotheus, 65
tragedy, 89, 113. *See also* under Seneca
Trajan, 7, 8, 74
tribunicia potestas, 10
Trojan War, 22, 72, 100, 101

Valerius Maximus, *Facta et Dicta Memorabilia*, 22
Varius, *Thyestes*, 187n31
Vedius Pollio, 61, 151–52
Velian hill, 5, 61
Velleius Paterculus, *Roman History*, 6–7, 9, 63, 171n43, 183n31
Venus and Roma, Temple of, 69
Vergil, 22, 173n1, 182n4, 187n22, 189n46; *Aeneid*, 21
Verres, 126–27
Vesta, 64, 65
Vesta, Temple of (Forum Romanum), 64
Villa Iovis, 62, 75–77
villas, 70–71, 184n54
Vitellius, 76
Vitellius, Lucius, 49–50
Vitruvius, *On Architecture*, 122–23
Volusius Proculus, 165
Vulteius, 34

Weber, Max, 13
wives, 5, 8, 25, 34, 52, 64; in Lucan, 22, 23, 25, 26, 35, 36, 37. *See also* families
women, 181n77; and Augustan culture, 12; and Augustus, 47, 125; and *domus*, 1; of *domus Augusta*, 12, 14, 18, 40, 41, 51; and family, 24; and House of the Tragic Poet, 117–18; in Livy, 54; in Lucan, 23–24, 26, 36; in martial epic, 24; and misogyny, 4, 52, 180n53; and Nero, 11, 51–52; and Pompeiian houses, 113, 121, 122; as subject to emperor, 14; subordination of, 52, 113; in Tacitus, 18, 52–53, 54, 55, 56, 59

Xenophon, *Hiero*, 187n23